W9-ALN-366

The Environmental Policy Paradox
Fourth Edition

Zachary A. Smith
Northern Arizona University

Prentice
Hall

Upper Saddle River, NJ 07458

Library of Congress Cataloging-in-Publication Data

Smith, Zachary A. (Zachary Alden), (date)
    The environmental policy paradox/Zachary A. Smith—4th ed.
        p. cm.
    Includes bibliographical references and index.
    ISBN 0-13-099308-5 (pbk.)
    1. Environmental policy—United States. 2. Environmental policy. I. Title.

GE180 .S45 2004
363.7′00973—dc21

2002027424

VP/Editorial Director: Charlyce Jones Owen
Senior Acquisitions Editor: Heather Shelstad
Editorial Assistant: Jessica Drew
Editorial/production supervision and interior design: Mary Araneo
Marketing Manager: Claire Bitting
Prepress and Manufacturing Buyer: Tricia Kenny
Cover Art Director: Jayne Conte
Cover Designer: Jayne Kelly
Cover photo: Getty Images/EyeWire, Inc.

This book was set in 10/11 Times by Pine Tree Composition, Inc.,
and was printed and bound by RR Donnelley & Sons. The cover was
printed by Lehigh.

© 2004, 2000, 1995, 1992 by Pearson Education, Inc.
Upper Saddle River, New Jersey 07458

All rights reserved. No part of this book may be
reproduced, in any form or by any means,
without permission in writing from the publisher.

Printed in the United States of America

10 9 8 7 6 5 4 3 2 1

ISBN 0-13-099308-5

Pearson Education LTD., London
Pearson Education Australia PTY, Limited, Sydney
Pearson Education Singapore, Pte. Ltd
Pearson Education North Asia Ltd, Hong Kong
Pearson Education Canada, Ltd., Toronto
Pearson Educación de Mexico, S.A. de C.V.
Pearson Education—Japan, Tokyo
Pearson Education Malaysia, Pte. Ltd
Pearson Education, Upper Saddle River, New Jersey

Contents

PART TWO: ENVIRONMENTAL POLICY

5 Air Pollution   82

6 Water   122

7   Energy   142

8   Toxic and Hazardous Materials and Waste Management   182

9   Land Management Issues   213

10   International Environmental Issues   239

11 International Environmental Management   261

Preface

The policy-making process described in many public policy and American government texts reveals just the tip of the iceberg. This book, designed for courses on environmental policy, environmental studies, and public policy and as supplemental reading in American government, public administration and planning, and other courses, exposes the rest of the iceberg: the workings of government that are rarely visible but necessary for an appreciation of the formation of environmental policy. It examines U.S. environmental policy in air, water, land use, agriculture, energy, waste disposal, and other areas, and, in so doing, provides an introduction to the policy-making process in the United States.

A paradox is an apparently contradictory combination of opposing ideas. The paradox of environmental policy is that we often understand what the best short- and long-term solutions to environmental problems are, yet the task of implementing these solutions is either left undone or is completed too late. Although this is a general characteristic of policy formation in the United States, it is particularly true of environmental policy. The explanation lies in the nature of the policy-making process. A few broad examples will illustrate the nature of the environmental policy paradox.

Problems of farming and food production in the United States include the loss of topsoil due to soil erosion, the loss of soil productivity, and the overuse of pesticides and fertilizers. Although opinions vary, there is strong evidence that a shift to organic farming would increase farm income and reduce soil erosion and nutrient depletion while meeting American food needs and reducing oil imports. Most people who study the matter feel we would be better off in the long run converting to organic farming. However, regardless of the potential benefits of organic farming, the incentives operating on policy makers, which include, for example, the money and influence of the manufacturers of pesticides, make it difficult to make significant changes in U.S. farm policy. That is what we call a paradox of environmental policy.

Energy provides another good example. Although estimates vary as to how long fossil fuels will last, there is widespread agreement that a transition must be made from fossil to renewable fuels. This transition will have a significant impact on our economic, social, cultural, and political lives. The paradox is that today little is being done in the public sector to prepare for this change.

Any examination of environmental policy must begin with a discussion of the setting in which policy is formulated. No simple explanations or definitions can completely convey why or why not a given policy comes into being. Limitations on human comprehension, as well as in the quality and extent of information available, make it difficult to fully understand the cause-and-effect relationships in public policy formation.

This book, nevertheless, provides a basic understanding of why some environmental ideas shape policy while others do not. We describe the formal institutional setting in which environmental policy is developed, the major participants involved, and the political and institutional incentives that motivate those attempting to influence the policy-formation system. Through an understanding of the informal political and institutional incentives that influence policy formation, the reader will be able to see that the system, though complex and uncertain, does respond to appropriate inputs. It is important to know how the system works because only when we understand how the game is played can we affect changes in the system.

ORGANIZATION

The book is divided into two parts. Part One, The Policy-Making Process, provides an overview of how governmental policy is made in the United States. It emphasizes informal and noninstitutional aspects of the process and the incentives in the policy-making process that direct participant behavior. Also, Part One examines the rise of environmentally based litigation in the United States. Specifically we discuss the legal processes that come into play when citizens pursue environmental policy goals in the courts. This in an important consideration because, as we will see, often the courts are the only policy avenue available to groups, like many environmental groups, that lack the resources needed to have influence in other policy-making arenas—like legislative bodies.

Before delving into the policy-making process of environmental policy, however, Chapter 1 introduces ecosystems and the study of ecology, thus setting the stage for the chapters that follow. Good environmental policy is based on an understanding of how the physical environment works. Chapter 1 also provides a general discussion of the interdependence of ecosystems and explains the need to evaluate environmental policy from a multidisciplinary perspective. The complexity of ecosystem interdependence requires, in many cases, an international or global perspective.

Chapter 2 explores the relationship of our dominant social paradigm (those clusters of Western cultural beliefs, values, and ideals that influence our thinking about society, government, and individual responsibility) to environmental policy formation. The chapter also summarizes the history of the environmental movement and public opinion about environmental problems—two important components of the Western industrial dominant social paradigm.

Chapter 3 examines the regulatory environment in the environmental policy area. This discussion includes an examination of the current regulatory framework in the United States, various regulatory alternatives that have been suggested, and some of the assumptions that underlie current thinking about appropriate environmental regulations.

Chapter 4 examines the institutional setting of the policy-making process. The incentives operating on participants in the process and the role of interest groups are discussed along with advantages certain policy-making participants enjoy when attempting to influence environmental policy. These incentives include the short-term incentives available to policymakers for evaluating policy options; incentives or disincentives in dealing with externalities (i.e., those costs or benefits of a course of action not directly involved in the policy); the status quo orientation of the system; the role of sub-governments or "iron triangles" in certain policy areas; and the incremental nature, in most cases, of policy formation in the United States. Chapter 4 also describes more formal means of environmental control, such as the requirement of an environmental impact statement, or EIS, and introduces the administrative agencies most involved in environmental administration in the United States. Finally, the effects of environmental litigation on the system are examined and the environmental laws governing environmental policies are discussed, here and in Part Two of the book.

In Part Two we examine environmental policy in seven chapters that discuss air pollution, energy policy, solid and hazardous waste policy, land management, international environmental problems, and international environmental management. In each area there are current policies that do not effectively address the problems they were meant to deal with. This is true even though experts are often in agreement about what needs to be done. As a result, the paradox of environmental policy is that the system often produces policies that are fundamentally unable to address environmental problems adequately. We will examine these policies.

It is my hope that after reading this book you will have a better understanding of environmental problems, the system that produced these problems, and what you can do to help produce a better future. There is much you can do when you understand how the system works.

ACKNOWLEDGMENTS

Many people provided guidance and support for this project, for the first, second, third, and now fourth editions. Early on I asked for input on the topics to be covered and the treatment afforded each topic. I want to thank Richard C. Allison, Richard N.L. Andrews, Mary Timney Bailey, C. Richard Bath, James S. Bowman, M. Paul Brown, Gary Bryner, Susan J. Buck, John A. Busterud, Lynton K. Caldwell, Jerry W. Calvert, Henry P. Caulfield, Jr., Jeanne Nienaber Clarke, Bruce Clary, Barbara Coe, Hanna J. Cortner, W. Douglas Costain, John Crow, Paul J. Culhane, Kenneth A. Dahlberg, Ralph C. D'Arge, Clarence J. Davies, David Howard Davis, Riley E. Dunlap, Robert E. Eagle, Sheldon M. Edner, Ward E. Elliott, John G. Francis, John C. Freemuth, William Green, Forest Grieves, George M. Guess, Marjorie Randon Hershey, Sandra K. Hinchman, William W. Hogan, John D. Hutcheson, Jr., Susan Hunter, Harold C. Jordahl, Jr., Lauriston R. King, John Kingdon, Michael E. Kraft, Henry Krisch, Berton L. Lamb, Kai N. Lee, James P. Lester, Harvery Lieber, Daniel R. Mandelker, Dean E. Mann, David L. Martin, Albert R. Matheny, Daniel McCool, Stephen P. Mumme, Charles S. Pearson, John Duncan Powell, Barry G. Rabe, James L. Regens, Mark E. Rushefsky, William Russell, Dean Schooler, Ronald G. Shaiko, Gilbert B. Siegel, J. Allen Singleton, Henry B. Sirgo, Nancy Paige Smith, Dennis L. Soden, Marvin S. Soroos, Peter G. Stillman, Lawrence Susskind, Dennis Thompson, Richard Tobin, Evert Vedung, Norman J. Vig, Lettie M. Wenner, and Clifton E. Wilson for their valuable suggestions. Several others, notably government officials, desired anonymity. Since they know who they are, I thank them just the same.

For research and editorial assistance I would like to thank Mary Brentwood, Connie Brooks, Marcie Demillion, Sandra Demoruelle, Kathleen Dorn, Patrick Holman, Lucinda John, and Sharon Ridgeway. Their input was crucial. For research and editorial assistance in producing the fourth edition, I want to particularly thank Jeremy Legg.

Finally, I would like to thank Amy, my wife, for her continued love and support.

I, of course, hold all of the above blameless for the results.

Abbreviations

AEC	Atomic Energy Commission
AQCRs	Air Quality Control Regions
BIA	Bureau of Indian Affairs
BLM	Bureau of Land Management
CAA	Clean Air Act
CEQ	Council on Environmental Quality
CFCs	Chlorofluorocarbons
COET	Crude Oil and Equalization Tax
CWA	Clean Water Act
DOE	Department of Energy
DOI	Department of Interior

DSP	Dominant social paradigm
EA	Environmental Assessment
ECE	United Nations Economic Commission for Europe
EEC	European Economic Community
EIS	Environmental Impact Statement
EPA	Environmental Protection Agency
ERC	Emission Reduction Credit
ERDA	Energy Research and Development Administration
FAO	Food and Agricultural Organization
FEMA	Federal Emergency Management Administration
FERC	Federal Energy Regulatory Commission
FIPS	Federal Implementation Plans
FLPMA	Federal Land Policy and Land Management Act
FONSI	Finding of No Significant Impact
FPC	Federal Power Commission
GAO	General Accounting Agency
IAEA	International Atomic Energy Commission
IGO	International Government Organization
IWC	International Whaling Commission
JCAE	Joint Committee on Atomic Energy
LCEP	Least Cost Energy Planning
LDC	Less Developed Countries
LEAF	Legal Environmental Assistance Foundation
LNG	Liquid Natural Gas

LULU	Locally Unwanted Land Use
LWR	Light water reactor
MOIP	Mandatory Oil Import Program
MU	Multiple use
NAAQS	National Ambient Air Quality Standards
NARUC	National Association of Regulatory Utility Commissioners
NASA	National Aeronautics and Space Administration
NEP	National Energy Plan
NEPA	National Environmental Policy Act
NO_x	Nitrogen oxides
NPDES	National Pollution Discharge Elimination System
NRC	Nuclear Regulatory Commission
NRDC	Natural Resources Defense Council
NSPS	New source performance standards
OPEC	Organization of Petroleum Exporting Countries
OSHA	Occupational Safety and Health Administration
ppm	Parts per million
PURPA	Public Utilities Regulatory Policies Act
PV	Photovoltaic
R & D	Research and development
RARE	Roadless Area Review and Evaluation
RCRA	Resource Conservation and Recovery Act
REA	Rural Electrification Act
SARA	Superfund Acceleration and Recovery Act of 1996

SDWA	Safe Drinking Water Act
SIP	State Implementation Plan
SO_2	Sulfur dioxide
SO_3	Sulfur trioxide
TCE	Trichloroethylene
TMI	Three Mile Island
TVA	Tennessee Valley Authority
UNEP	United Nations Environmental Programme
USDA	United States Department of Agriculture
WMO	World Meteorological Organization

About the Author

Zachary A. Smith is a Regents' Professor of Political Science at Northern Arizona University. He received his B.A. from California State University, Fullerton, and his M.A. and Ph.D. from the University of California, Santa Barbara. He has taught political science and public administration at Northern Arizona University, the Hilo branch of the University of Hawaii, Ohio University, and the University of California at Santa Barbara; he has served as the Wayne Aspinall Visiting Professor of political science, public affairs, and history at Mesa State College in Grand Junction, Colorado. A consultant both nationally and internationally on natural resource and environmental matters, he is the author or editor of seventeen books as well as numerous articles on environmental and natural resource policy topics. He currently teaches environmental and natural resource policy and administration in the public policy Ph.D. program at Northern Arizona University. He invites students interested in pursuing graduate work in environmental or natural resources policy to contact him at zachary.smith@nau.edu to discuss the opportunities available at Northern Arizona University.

Ecosystem Interdependence

No examination of environmental policy can be complete without an understanding of the laws and forces that drive the natural world. In this chapter we explore ecology, the subfield of biology that strives to explain the interrelationships among people, other living things, and their environments. Only through an understanding of how a natural environment works can we understand the impact of policies designed to regulate that environment. We also will examine some of the most pressing issues involved in managing ecosystems.

An ecosystem is any group of plants, animals, or nonliving things interacting within their external environment. Typically, ecologists study individual organisms (the life cycle of the organism, its requirements of its environment, its functioning in the environment); populations of organisms (including questions such as stability, decline, or growth in populations); communities of organisms; or the ecosystem as a whole (including the biogeochemical cycles of carbon, oxygen, hydrogen, soil minerals, and energy).[1]

Ecosystems may seem to be independent units that interact very little with their external environments. Some ecologists describe them as "a watershed in New Hampshire, a Syrian desert, the Arctic icecap, or Lake Michigan."[2] Yet ecosystems are "open," in the sense that they interact with everything else in the environment. In fact, the earth itself is an ecosystem commonly referred to as the ecosphere or biosphere.[3]

Earth, like all ecosystems, receives energy from the sun. Otherwise, there is very little interaction between the earth and the external environment. Consequently, with the exception of energy from the sun, the resources that the planet started with are the same as those that exist today (although constantly changing form). This is why some use the term *spaceship earth* to describe the earth's relationship with the external environment. Like a spaceship, the planet must work with what it has. When certain resources are exhausted or converted into a form in which they are no longer useful to humans, new supplies cannot simply be imported from "somewhere else." The utility that they provided humans is essentially lost forever.

To better understand how an ecosystem functions, let's use the oversimplified example of a freshwater ecological cycle. Fish in a river or a lake produce organic waste that settles to the bottom, nourishing bacteria and creating inorganic products from which algae feed. The fish in turn feed off the algae. This example suggests that the interrelationships within an ecosystem are relatively simple. But, as Edward Kormondy, a leading ecologist, wrote, "The ecologist, in studying natural systems, is confronted by the complexities of almost unlimited variables."[4] Barry Commoner, in his book *The Closing Circle,* identifies four "laws of ecology" that are based on widely accepted norms in the science of ecology. These "laws" are useful in understanding how ecosystems function and the limits to humankind's ability to manipulate them.[5]

The first law of ecology is that everything is connected to everything else. "An ecosystem consists of multiple interconnective parts, which act on one another."[6] The interconnectedness of ecosystems suggests it is difficult, if not impossible, to manipulate one aspect of an ecosystem without impacting, often unintentionally, other aspects of the ecosystem. The first law of ecology "reflects the existence of the elaborate network of interconnections in the ecosphere: among different living organisms, and between populations, species, and individual organisms in their physicochemical surroundings."[7] That is, an ecosystem is a house of cards where each card may directly or indirectly support other cards or even the whole house.

When an ecosystem is disrupted by the introduction of a foreign element, for example, changes occur in the relationship between organisms within the system, as well as between organisms and their physical environment (that is, the biochemical balances within the ecosystem may also be upset). However, they can often adjust and regain their balance. For example, in the case of drought in grassland, lack of food will result in malnutrition of mice, which will eventually lead to their hibernation. During hibernation they are, of course, eating less, allowing the grasses to rejuvenate and protecting their own numbers by being less exposed to predators.[8]

If an imbalance occurs within an ecosystem, that system may not go back into equilibrium in quite the same way. For example, in the case of a freshwater lake, the organic waste that appears in the lake naturally plays an important role in the food chain, affecting the growth of algae. If, however, a foreign source of nutrient is introduced to the lake, it can lead to the rapid growth of algae, resulting in eutrophication. In this example the nutrient might be septic tank sewage. The bacteria from a septic tank stimulate the growth of algae, which consumes available oxygen. The lack of oxygen eventually kills other life forms in the lake.

The second law of ecology is that everything must go somewhere. Commoner uses the example of the mercury in a typical AA dry cell battery to illustrate this point.

> First it is placed in a container of rubbish; this is collected and taken to an incinerator. Here the mercury is heated; this produces mercury vapor, which is emitted by the in-

cinerator stack, and mercury vapor is toxic. Mercury vapor is carried by the wind, eventually brought to earth in rain or snow. Entering a mountain lake, let us say, the mercury condenses and sinks to the bottom. Here it is acted on by bacteria, which convert it to methyl mercury. This is soluble and taken up by fish; since it is not metabolized, the mercury accumulates in the organs and flesh of the fish. The fish is caught and eaten by a man and the mercury becomes deposited in his organs, where it might be harmful. And so on.[9]

This second law of ecology is applicable when thinking of the earth. It is an enclosed unit, like a spaceship. Nothing is just thrown away. When fossil fuels burn, they release the energy needed to push our cars, but they also release sulfur dioxide and nitrogen oxides that must go somewhere. As we have learned, this "somewhere" often may be into our rivers and lakes as acid rain or into the upper atmosphere contributing to the greenhouse effect and, in turn, global warming. As we will see later, some environmental policies, such as those governing solid waste disposal, seem to ignore the second law of ecology.

The third law of ecology is that nature knows best. Throughout most of human history, at least in Western culture, there has been an assumption that humans can, or perhaps should, conquer nature. This third law of ecology suggests that when it comes to manipulating relationships in nature, humankind is at best a poor judge of how their manipulations of the environment will impact nature. Commoner uses the analogy of the watch to explain the third law of ecology.

Suppose you were to open the back of your watch, close your eyes, and poke a pencil into the exposed works. The almost certain result would be to damage the watch. . . . Over the years numerous watchmakers, each taught by a predecessor, have tried out a huge variety of detailed arrangements of how a watch works, have discarded those that are not compatible with the overall operation of the system and retain the better features. . . . Any random change made in the watch is likely to fall into a very large class of inconsistent, or harmful, arrangements, which have been tried out in past watchmaking experience and discarded.[10]

The third law of ecology suggests that humans' tinkering with natural systems, like the random poke of your watch with a pencil, will ultimately prove detrimental to those systems.

To understand the importance of the third law of ecology, we must remember that ecosystems have developed through natural selection over billions of years. The interactions within natural systems sometimes present a very delicate balance, and interfering can disrupt that system. Nature is usually a better judge of what is good for the long-term viability of any given system. Commoner goes on to note, "The artificial introduction of an organic compound that does not occur in nature, but is man-made and is nevertheless active in a living system, is very likely to be harmful."[11] There are many new chemical compounds floating around the biosphere since humanity learned chemical engineering. One can only imagine the effects these "new ecosystem players" have on their natural peers or what cumulative, long-term impacts they may have on humans.

The fourth law of ecology is that there is no such thing as a free lunch. Simply stated, this law provides that any interaction with nature, any extraction, use, or disruption, carries with it some cost. That cost may be in the form of the conversion of resources to a form in which they are no longer of use to humans or the disruption of an ecosystem that renders it unstable. Commoner notes, "Because the global ecosystem is a connected whole, in which nothing can be gained or lost and which is not subject to overall improvement, anything extracted from it by human effort must be replaced. Payment of this price cannot be avoided; it can only be delayed."[12]

While Commoner's four laws of ecology provide a useful orientation for our study of humankind's interaction with its environment, there are two additional components of our relationship with nature that need to be expounded on: the notion of sustainability and a steady state and the common pool nature of natural resources.

THE STEADY STATE

A *steady state* refers to that level of activity within an ecosystem that can be maintained over a long period of time. For example, given the limitations on arable land and water resources, there is some upper limit of human population that the world can sustain. Given the finite nature of the earth's resources, the exhaustion of resources has an impact on earth's ultimate steady state form.

All ecosystems have a point at which they reach a steady state. This is not to suggest that resource utilization cannot be greater than that necessary for sustaining the steady state, but only that those resources used today impact the nature and circumstances of the balance necessary to create a steady state within an ecosystem in the future. The steady state idea—as applied to environmental policy—is problematic in that there is disagreement regarding an ecosystem's upper limit, or carrying capacity.

Closely related to the notion of the steady state is the concept of sustainability. Resource use, either by nonrenewable extraction or by degradation (pollution), must be limited to a point where it does not threaten the regenerative capacity of natural systems. Otherwise, those systems are not being used in a sustainable manner (or managed to maintain a steady state). As we will see throughout the book, the institutions that manage the planet often are not geared toward sustainability.

For example, in many Sunbelt cities in the southern and southwest United States, political, economic, and even the health of social and cultural institutions are predicated upon continued growth and expansion of building and construction. This is nonsustainable in the long run and will ultimately lead to the demise or redefinition of these institutions and the assumptions upon which they are founded. In natural resource management, we cannot cut more trees than we grow, and in pollution and environmental management we cannot introduce more pollutants into a natural system than it can absorb and still provide life-sustaining ecosystem services. These are both examples of nonsustainability.

COMMON POOL RESOURCES

Garrett Hardin, in his influential essay "The Tragedy of the Commons,"[13] drew attention to the problems associated with common pool resources. He uses the analogy of a common green, or the sharing of a common pasture, where the rational individual will seek to maximize his or her returns from that pasture by putting as many additional cattle as he or she can afford onto the commons. This rational individual behavior, however, will result in destruction through overgrazing of the common pasture. No individual in this situation has an incentive to protect the pasture. In fact, the incentives operating on individuals are to increase their return from the pasture, the result being the hastened destruction of the pasture for everyone.

Common pool resource problems are very much a part of environmental policy. The groundwater in an aquifer underlying several farms, for example, may be a common pool resource. Farmers located above the aquifer have no incentive to save the groundwater for future use. In fact, if the groundwater supply lies beneath adjacent farms, landowners may have an incentive to pull as much out of the ground as possible as soon as possible, there being no individual incentive to manage the resource for the long-term beneficial use of all.

Air is also a common pool resource. Individual polluters have no incentive to protect the common pool resource of clean air. In fact, the individual has every incentive to continue polluting. The cost of air pollution is not borne only by the polluter but rather by the community as a whole.

Polluters on a body of water are in a similar situation, as are users of any resource who are not responsible and have no incentive to ensure the use and management of that resource over the long term. The oceans are a classic example of a common pool resource problem. Nations have little or no incentive to restrict their harvesting of fish when they are competing with other nations that are not willing to similarly restrict their fishing activities. The result is the depletion, and possibly the eventual destruction, of common pool fisheries. Fisheries off the coasts of Japan and the northeastern United States are facing severe reductions in fish populations. It is presumed that this depletion is the result of years of commercial overfishing, without paying much regard to the needs of the aquatic ecosystems.

Because there is not a strong international body governing pollution discharges into the ocean, individual nations have little or no incentive to regulate their polluting activities in a way that will provide for a clean ocean environment for all the inhabitants of the earth. Again, what is rational for the individual, in this case the nations that are polluting, could lead to the destruction of the overall resource. As you will see later, common pool resources have proven problematic to environmental policy development and implementation.

SUMMARY

We live in a world of finite resources. Every time we drive our cars there is *less* irreplaceable oil in the world (a resource management problem). There is also *more* carbon dioxide released into the atmosphere (a pollution or environmental problem). This thickens the layer of greenhouse gas that, in turn, artificially heats our planet (everyone's problem). Each time we write on another piece of paper, there may be fewer trees to help cleanse the air. These same trees could provide habitat for a dozen species, in addition to providing flood and erosion protection. For every action there are inputs and outputs; everything must go somewhere. The consequences of our actions may lead to unanticipated, undesirable, and unsustainable outcomes. Nature can be strong and resilient, but only on one side of a fine line.

When this line is crossed, nature's fragility and humans' ecosystem interdependence become known and crucial life support systems fail.

We must know our limits as well as those of our environment. For example, we rely everyday on freshwater to replenish our bodies, irrigate our crops, and provide electricity. Yet we use this natural resource faster than nature can replenish it. We overwork our farmland and pollute it (and our freshwater) with chemicals that reduce the land's agricultural lifespan. The remaining fertile land we turn into roads and new subdivisions to fit our growing population. These activities are not ultimately sustainable. That is, they are not conducive to the all-important steady state to which nature must return. Nature will reach homeostasis even if this means indefinitely shutting down crucial life-sustaining ecosystem services.

Though environmental policy is so important, it is also a paradox. We must force ourselves not to deplete needed natural resources or pollute in a way that suddenly thrusts a pencil into nature's delicate watch. But it is humans who make environmental policy, and they have limited knowledge and time. We must use and pay for resources every day, and we must be responsive to a diverse public (that is, there is politics involved). It is paradoxical because we must protect the very environment that gives us life while at the same time protect the interests of those who exploit it (all of us to some extent).

Understanding ecological relationships, the notion of sustainability and the steady state, and common pool problems provides the background necessary for appreciating the complexities involved in environmental policy formation and implementation. It is just as important, however, to possess an understanding of the values, culture, and politics that drive the policy-making process. That is the subject of the next chapter.

NOTES

1. Thomas C. Emmel, *Ecology & Population Biology* (New York: W W Norton, 1973), pp. 3,13.
2. Jonathan Turk, *Introduction to Environmental Studies,* 2nd ed. (Philadelphia: Saunders, 1985), p. 26.
3. Edward J. Kormondy, *Concepts of Ecology,* 3rd ed. (Upper Saddle River, NJ: Prentice-Hall, 1984), p. 8.
4. Ibid., p. 9.
5. Barry Commoner, *The Closing Circle* (New York: Knopf, 1971).
6. Ibid., p. 33.
7. Ibid.
8. This example was taken from Turk, *Introduction to Environmental Studies,* p. 39.
9. Commoner, *The Closing Circle,* p. 40.
10. Ibid., p. 42.
11. Ibid., p. 43.
12. Ibid., p. 46.
13. Garrett Hardin, "The Tragedy of the Commons," *Science,* 162 (1968), pp. 1243–1248.

Changing Cultural and Social Beliefs: From Conservation to Environmentalism

DOMINANT SOCIAL PARADIGM

Many argue that environmental problems and the policies that have been adopted to deal with them are a direct result of our dominant social paradigm (DSP). The DSP constitutes those clusters of beliefs, values, and ideals that influence our thinking about society, government, and individual responsibility. The DSP can be defined in various ways but includes acceptance of laissez-faire capitalism, individualism, growth, and progress, and a faith in science and technology. Our DSP has influenced the history of environmental policy, public attitudes toward the environment, and environmental regulations. The most important components of the DSP are free market economics, faith in science and technology, the growth orientation common in Western democracies, and a sense of separation from the natural environment.

In the United States, the DSP is rooted in the early history of the country—a period when individualism and growth did not seem to conflict with sound resource management. Political philosophers such as John Locke, Emmerich von Vattel, and Jean-Jacques Rousseau had an important influence on the framers of the U.S. Constitution. These and other philosophers held that humans had certain natural rights, rights we were born with, including the right to life, liberty, and private property. As the Declaration of Independence proclaims, "[W]e hold these truths to be self-evident, that all men are created equal, that they are endowed by their Creator with certain inalienable Rights, that among these are Life, Liberty, and the pursuit of Happiness." The idea of individual freedom and the right to hold and use one's property is and always has been fundamental to our DSP and our understanding of what American Democracy is all about.[1] For most of our history this has meant a freedom to pollute the environment. Today, these freedoms—particularly private property rights—may often be inconsistent with sound environmental management.

The DSP contributes to environmental problems in a variety of ways. Furthermore, individual commitment to the various components of the DSP is linked to lower levels of environmental concern.[2] So let us examine the major components of the DSP.

Economics and Growth

Economic growth to the extent it is dependent on inputs from the environment has obvious limitations. The resources for additional automobiles, washing machines, and toasters cannot continue forever—even with highly efficient recycling.[3] Yet it is an assumption of all industrial societies, regardless of the political system they operate under, that growth based on additional inputs of resources will and should continue. In capitalist countries, the profit motive drives the economy to produce and induce consumption. As William Ophuls wrote, "[A]ll the incentives of producers are toward growth.... [I]t is in the interest of producers to have a high throughput proliferation and promotion, rapid obsolescence, and the like."[4] It is rational, in such a system, to produce goods designed for a short or predictable lifespan. Although planned obsolescence may not be the best way to manage finite resources, it often is a logical and rational tool in business planning.

Economists study the distribution, production, exchange, and consumption of goods and services. Examining supply and demand in markets that consist of mutual voluntary exchanges where both parties hope to gain is, in large part, the study of economics. Economists assume that consumers attempt to maximize utility, or to spend their money in ways that give them as much pleasure as possible. They assume consumers pursuing their own self-interest in the marketplace will seek out those goods and services that provide them the most comfort. Producers, responding to or anticipating consumer demand, provide the goods and services as efficiently as possible, thereby maximizing their profits. All participants in the process, pursuing their own interests, contribute to national income and contribute, it is argued, to the material betterment of society. This is the mechanism of the "invisible hand" that Adam Smith referred to in his early economic theory. Market mechanisms such as self-interest and supply and demand are seen to provide not only the maximum available material benefits for individuals, but also for society as a whole.

Only in the last few decades have economists turned their attention to environmental issues. The field of economics has long recognized there are certain public goods (such as defense) that private markets do not adequately provide for or provide for at all; therefore, economists accept a role for government in the provision of such goods. Only recently, however, have economists addressed themselves to the environmental problems that private markets sometimes ignore. What follows are some criticisms of the assumptions of classic economics as it relates to environmental problems.

Economic transactions do not always incorporate the full range of cost and benefits associated with the production or distribution of goods. For example, when you purchase a set of tires for your car, you anticipate that the cost includes the price of materials, labor, and a reasonable profit for the producer. The cost of those tires may or may not include the cost of cleaning up the pollution that was a by-product of their production. Yet the air pollution coming from the tire manufacturing plant, if unregulated, presents a real cost to society in terms of contributing to respiratory illness or damage to fish and wildlife through acid rain. This additional cost is referred to as an *externality*. There are both positive and negative externalities. Air pollution is a negative externality. An example of a positive externality would be the benefits one receives by building one's home adjacent to a public park. Theoretically, if the cost of negative externality is internalized into the cost of a product, then the product's price will reflect its true cost to society. Unfortunately, oftentimes the environmental costs of goods are not internalized.

Two additional criticisms sometimes leveled at market mechanisms for the distribution of goods and services involve information and participation. A perfect market would operate with participants possessing perfect knowledge of the cost and benefits of their transactions. Oftentimes, however, consumers lack even rudimentary knowledge of those costs and benefits. With respect to benefits, most economists argue that if the consumer perceives the exchanges as beneficial, then for that consumer the exchange is worthwhile. Concerning the true cost of a transaction, often the information, such as the amount of unregulated polluted air that resulted in the manufacturing process, is not available. Under those circumstances, critics argue, even environmentally aware consumers find it difficult, if not impossible, to make environmentally responsible market decisions.

In the author's opinion, perhaps the most fundamental criticism of market mechanisms for distributing goods and services is the failure to consider all the participants affected by market transactions. Assuming that markets maximize the benefits for the individuals who participate in them and even accepting that the sum total of all those transactions contributes to the betterment of society, there are affected parties whose interests are not represented in the marketplace. Interests of nonhuman participants, such as plants and animals or ecosystems, and some human participants, such as future generations, are not reflected in market transactions. For example, my decision to clear-cut the timber from the slopes of my property may maximize my benefits and produce income for both me and the lumber company to which the timber is sold today. But it is my children and grandchildren who will have to live with the cost associated with the soil erosion that may result from the removal of the watershed. Similarly, the rapid development of fossil fuels heavily discounts, if not ignores, the potential benefits those fuels could have for future generations.

Market systems often pay little attention to the future values of natural resources and little if any attention to intrinsic values that are not measurable in monetary terms. An example would be if a developing country has hardwood stocks that are worth $100 million on the open market today, which, if sold, can be put in a bank to earn 10 percent interest a year. As Colin Clark, a professor of Applied Mathematics at the University of British Columbia explained, "If dollars in banks are growing faster than a timber company's forests, it is more profitable (indeed, more economical) to chop down the trees, sell them, and invest the proceeds elsewhere."[5] Under those conditions clear-cutting a forest or harvesting whales to extinction will often make economic sense.

The theory of substitution in economics (that is, that when the price of a good becomes too high consumers will substitute other goods or producers will develop alternative goods) also presents problems for some critics of market economies. Substitution may work quite well in many simple transactions. For example, when the price of a box of cornflakes goes beyond an acceptable threshold set by the consumer, substitution can easily be made to a more economic alternative, such as puffed rice. However, markets are less adept at dealing with absolute scarcity. In a famine situation markets for food collapse.[6] A related problem is that in response to increased prices, consumer preferences do not always lead to substitution. For example, after the 1973 Arab oil embargo, small cars enjoyed a boom in the automobile market but manufacturers soon discovered that even with the increased cost of gas, consumers wanted large cars. Hence, car manufacturers continued to produce them.[7]

Finally, mention should be made of how a society measures economic progress. Traditionally, gross national (or domestic) product (GNP or GDP) has been used as the yardstick we use to measure the economic health of the nation. This may not be the best way to measure our "success" as an economy.

First, this numerical descriptor only captures part of the total economic process. It measures only marginal utility rather than the total utility of goods and services. For example, if trees are cut down to make paper, this may add a few dollars to the GDP. If the trees are left alone, they will produce oxygen, remove carbon dioxide, and provide soil and flood protection. But trees left standing add nothing to GDP. Although not included in the GDP, clearly these services are not worthless, and they may be more valuable to society than paper.

But since we do not buy and sell these services in markets, their value is difficult to quantify. Therefore economists often just ignore these inputs or take them for granted. Our way of measuring economic growth then—the GDP—ignores the value of natural systems or assumes they are "free."

As Paul and Anne Ehrlich[8] have noted, "Just how much genuine economic growth (if any) is actually taking place at present is difficult to ascertain because the depreciation of natural capital (forests, fossil fuels) is not captured in standard economic statistics such as GNP." This does not mean, however, that progress can never be determined or measured in some quantifiable way. Herman Daly, an economist who once worked for the World Bank, states that GNP and GDP ought to be replaced by ISEW, or the Index for Sustainable Economic Welfare. This figure would take into account income distribution and depreciation of natural capital in addition to traditional measures of economic progress.[9]

Finally, economists view their science as "value free." As Richard McKenzie and Gordon Tullock put it, "[T]he approach of economics is amoral. . . . [A]s economists we cannot say what is just or fair."[10] Yet it seems that the commitment to markets or efficiency or the maximization of utility are in themselves values—and they may be values that preclude other values such as equity, beauty, or the preservation of nature for its own sake.

Whatever the flaws of market mechanisms, there is no denying the growth orientation of markets and the DSP that embraces them. If we are to accept ultimate limits to economic growth, at *some point* the growth orientation of market economies and our DSP will have to give way to a sustainable societal orientation. In this sense, capitalism may not be consistent with sound long-term environmental management. Again quoting William Ophuls, "[E]cological scarcity undercuts the basic laissez-faire, individualistic premises of the American political economy, so that current institutions are incapable of meeting the challenges of scarcity; what is needed is a new paradigm of politics."[11] Ophuls may be right. However, as we see in Part Two, other political ideologies, such as communist and socialist systems, have fared no better in protecting the environment.

Science and Technology: Our Views of Nature

Modern science and technology have their roots in Western civilization and have always had, as a major driving force, the purpose of conquering nature for utilitarian ends.[12] Faith in science and technology and the idea that science will provide solutions for our problems with nature is an important component of our social paradigm. (Many contemporary thinkers, such as post-modernists, question the positivist assumption of science. However, as of this writing, the next scientific revolution awaits.) The twentieth century saw a number of developments that could lead the casual observer to conclude little in nature is beyond the capacity of people to manipulate. Our grandparents and great-grandparents lived in a world without the polio vaccine, jet travel, the development of antibiotics, or the computer.

In environmental policy, faith in science and technology, and technological breakthroughs that will make everything okay, can be found everywhere. For example, both the Clean Air and Clean Water acts, as we see later, contain "technology forcing" aspects, in the sense that, when initiated, these acts were based on the assumption that technological breakthroughs would make their requirements possible to implement. In a similar vein, during the nuclear age, many assumed that technological developments would produce ways to neutralize the hazards of radioactive waste. That, of course, has not yet happened.

Faith in science and technology and humankind's ability to manipulate nature also permeates popular and governmental thinking about how to approach environmental problems. For example, as we see later, traditional wastewater treatment involves the removal of solids, floating matter, along with aeration and possibly some level of chemical treatment. Chemicals used in treatment process may have negative impacts on the ecosystem in which wastewater has been discharged. In contrast, water that does not contain toxic waste can largely be recycled producing soil fertilizers, nutrients that may be used in aquaculture, and plant matter that may be used as animal feed. The former method is potentially disruptive of ecosystems whereas the latter, which simulates nature, is designed to work with natural systems.

Our faith in science as a cure for environmental problems and the science-based civilization that has dominated the twentieth century has produced dramatic environmental changes, both in quantity and quality. Modern medical technology has led to the creation of numerous antibiotic medicines that have helped protect humans against many different kinds of disease.[13]

Faith in science has, for many, replaced other values. Many nations have adopted a blind faith in science as a cure-all for our environmental problems. If it is the "scientific" solution to a problem, it is automatically believed to be the best one. Actually, there are no absolute scientific measures too many questions. Science almost never offers a technological quick fix to ecological problems. In fact, in the enthusiastic flush of scientific do-gooding, much environmental harm can and has been done.

Indeed, social commentators often say that Western society is addicted to technology. Like other addicts, Westerners look to science with the expectation of the "technological fix" or "magic bullet"—with no changes in human values or morality. Examples of the negative impacts from these technological fixes abound. Modern medicine offers the cure of antibiotics for many fatal infectious diseases of childhood, but this has also contributed to overpopulation. Pesticides, the technological fix that helps to feed the burgeoning global populations, also cause numerous cancers.

There are a number of problems associated with the use of science in policy making. Some of these are problems from the perspective of the scientist. From the perspective of the policy maker, scientific information is not delivered in neat usable bundles that are readily adaptable to the policy problems at hand. As former Colorado governor Richard Lamm put it, "I find that the scientific community has a tendency to formulate problems narrowly—to have a specialized tunnel vision which does not see or fully appreciate all the public policy factors of a decision."[14] The same could be said of specialist bureaucrats.

Scientific input into the policy-making process often suffers from the hammer and nail syndrome. If all you have is a hammer the whole world looks like nail. Quite naturally, a biologist might first think of ecosystem problems in terms of species populations. In contrast, a chemist might think of the chemical properties of the air or water in the ecosystem. This specificity and specialization required of science may not be conducive to the comprehensiveness and generalizabilty needed in policy formation.

The second problem deals with the currency used in politics and science. Politics is about bargaining, compromise, and the balancing of interests. Science, on the other hand, tries to deal in "truth" or, to the extent possible, absolutes. The scientifically correct answer to a problem may not be politically viable.[15]

There is one final problem between the relationship of science and policy formation that is important to our understanding of the role of science in environmental policy formation. There is often a presumption that in environmental policy making, decisions should not be made without all the available information at hand. Furthermore, it is argued that decisions should not be made about the environment unless the scientific evidence establishes clear causality, without uncertainty, and is direct and provable. Science is not well suited to providing this kind of evidence. The standard of uncertainty and unquestioned causality is, in fact, rarely met in science. Scientific conclusions are often necessarily drawn from the probabilities of a particular outcome. Nonscientific policy makers often seem to not understand this about science and demand "hard scientific fact" before proceeding to policy conclusions. As Wade Robinson has written, "In fact we are never in a position to know, regarding any environmental matter of any moment, that we have all the relevant information. Requiring that we have all relevant information thus sets up an heuristic ideal, powering continual demands for more information, and thus more research."[16]

This need for information may pose a serious problem for environmental policy formation. If we wait for all the data to be collected and all the tests to be conducted, some environmental problems will become much worse before we act on them. Others argue that too much caution places an unnecessary burden on society. As a solution, some environmentalists offer the precautionary principle as a guide.

This hotly debated concept holds that we should err on the side of caution, or preservation, when it comes to the environment. Elements of our environment are irreplaceable as well as necessary for life as we know it—so caution should be the first concern, not waiting for absolute proof of causality.[17]

Policy makers will continue to push for the certainty in science and "fact." And scientists may, under the right conditions, provide the desired certainty. As Paul Feyerbend wrote in a critique of contemporary science

> Unanimity is often the result of a political decision: dissenters are suppressed, or remain silent to preserve the reputation of science as a source of trustworthy almost infallible knowledge. On other occasions, unanimity is the result of shared prejudices: positions are taken without detailed examination of the matter under review and are infused with the same authority, which proceeds from detailed research.[18]

Some, in and out of the policy-making community, are skeptical of science for other, often political, reasons. People who know little about probability are fond of saying, "statistics lie." Policy makers have, when confronted with scientific evidence that is contrary to their political ideals, dismissed scientific contributions out of hand. Research on global warming, for example, has regularly been criticized, when not ignored, by representatives of fossil fuel industry and their supporters in the U.S. Congress.[19]

Finally, some scholars have questioned the assumptions and role of science and scientific research in general. As Brian Martin has written, "The priorities for ostensibly 'pure' research are often influenced by government and corporate priorities. A purulent example is high energy physics, an indirect beneficiary of the priority placed on nuclear weapons and nuclear power."[20] These scholars point out that most research is driven by corporate and government priorities. The defense industry is a prominent example. Much of the work in computing, climate, and materials engineering is funded by the military. In addition, much of the basic research in areas from pharmaceuticals to pesticides is driven by corporate profit priorities. The scientific community would argue, correctly, in my opinion, that scientific research can be carried out objectively regardless of the source of funding. The sources of funding are, however, problematic. Furthermore, there is no question that research priorities lead us down one environmental path as opposed to another. There is, for example, more money spent figuring out how to mitigate the negative effects of existing technological adaptations—such as the internal combustion engine—than is spent on creating completely new and ecologically sustainable technologies.[21]

The Role of Religion

Religion has played a crucial role in the development of our DSP and defining perceptions of the relationship of humans to their physical environment. The primacy of humans in nature—a central tenet in Judeo-Christian thought—has provided a possible moral justification for the development of the environment in ways that pay little heed to, or ignore, ecosystem balance. At its extreme our religious beliefs may dictate an orientation toward a specific type of environmental management. James Watt, President Reagan's first Secretary of the Interior, exemplified this when he testified before Congress in 1981 that long-term management of natural re-

sources was not problematic because he did not "know how many future generations we can count on before the Lord returns."[22]

Although religions differ in their formal theories of the relationship of people
to the natural world, in practice none of the world's major religious belief systems
have motivated their adherents to exercise sound environmental practices.

At societal levels, religion has been used in most cultures to uphold the status
quo with minimal turmoil.[23] Religious beliefs are often a critical element in defining
and upholding a culture. For example, many tribal peoples have enjoyed prosperity
and unity under the auspices of a successful shaman or other such holy personage
who acted as a mediator between the gods and the community.

Historically, religion, in supposedly advanced civilizations, often acted to
sanction the state by authorizing rulers to govern, sharing the wealth and power
amassed through this governance and restraining the masses from objecting when
corruption occurred during these liaisons. Examples of church-state collaborations
abound, and many are unsavory. The Russian Revolution involved the overthrow of
greedy priests along with conspiring nobles; similarly, Martin Luther joined forces
with German princes against the then all-powerful Roman Catholic Church and the
Holy Roman Empire. The Buddhists, after a thousand years of assimilation, have
engaged in a centuries-old struggle for secular control of Japan with the endemic
Shinto religion.

The role of religion in shaping modern industrial societies that value change
is generally less identifiable than in traditional societies. Western civilization in the
past three centuries has experienced and welcomed ongoing changes accompanied
by a decline in the blending of religion and state. Prior to the secularization process
of the Enlightenment, a moral consensus was seen to arise out of Christendom, with
traditional values dominating the populace.[24] During the Age of Enlightenment a
shift occurred from belief in the myth and tradition in Christianity to belief in reason and empiricism. The increase in reliance on human experience as the basis for
judging morality in place of divine decrees led to the acceptance of the utilitarian
ethical dichotomy of "pleasure" as righteous and "pain" as evil. It was a short step
to the sensualist "pleasure principle" that has fostered the craving for materialistic
consumption so prominent in many more developed countries today. Along with the
constant materialistic demand for new, consumable items that proceeded from the
era of the Enlightenment was the concept of the "perfectibility of man," the Victorian ideal of the perpetual improvement of the human race.

This human-centered moral view permeates Western society. Humans, not
God, determine destiny through progressive improvements. Increasing secularism
placed value on material abundance and eschewed poverty. At least since the Industrial Revolution, the only value placed on natural objects, such as trees and rivers,
has been their usefulness to humans, especially in regard to their applications in industry. Economic concerns were paramount without consideration for the environmental costs.

The drive for material possessions is not the sole explanation for the ecological problems in the West. Our brethren in the East have had their own escalating environmental degradation dilemmas. In Japan, a person has customarily been Shinto
simply by virtue of birth. Although the Shinto belief values cleanliness and purity,
abhorring pollutants, Japan has had terrible environmental problems, such as the
mercury poisoning that went on for 20 years at Minamata Bay.[25] Meanwhile, in

Hindu India and Muslim Pakistan, the reverence for life has resulted in burgeoning populations, struggling merely to survive and unintentionally abusing their environment in the process.[26]

HISTORY OF THE ENVIRONMENTAL MOVEMENT

Historical, as well as modern, thinking about environmental policy has been shaped by our DSP. Historically, environmental awareness has influenced how environmental policy has developed. The history of the environmental movement may be best understood as having evolved through seven, often overlapping, phases: the period of dominance, the early awakening, early conservationist, later conservationist, the reawakening, complacency, what we term the "Little Reagan Revolution," and the post-Reagan resurgence.

Dominance

Throughout most of American history the environment has been viewed as hostile. Appreciation of the environment for its own sake was rare early in our history. Wilderness was to be conquered and used. Anything of no direct utility to humans was thought to be of little value.[27] This attitude dominated public perceptions of the environment and natural resources throughout the seventeenth, eighteenth, and most of the nineteenth centuries. However, beginning in the second half of the nineteenth century, American writers began to expound on non-utilitarian relationships with nature.

Early Awakening

In the age before mass communication, ideas circulated much more slowly. Important communicators of thought were, to a much greater extent than today, artists and writers who appealed to mass audiences. Nature writers, artists, and poets assisted the early environmental movement by drawing attention to natural areas and environmental problems. The drawings of George Catlin and the writings of Henry David Thoreau and Ralph Waldo Emerson were important catalysts in getting people to think differently about their relationship to nature. During the mid-1800s public reaction to the slaughter of bison on the Great Plains provided the impetus for the beginning of national concern with wildlife preservation.

One of the most influential writers of the period, George Perkins Marsh, published *Man and Nature* in 1864. This work brought to the public's attention environmental degradation and the impact of humans on the environment.

Early Conservationist

The later nineteenth century saw the emergence of the country's first environmentalists—those who, in addition to being concerned about environmental degradation, took up political action. These self-labeled conservationists, the most notable of whom was John Muir, a founder of the Sierra Club, would now more properly be labeled preservationists. The crusades of these conservationists to establish Yellowstone, Yosemite, and other parks were aimed at severely limiting, if not eliminating, human impact on the natural areas they sought to protect.

The early conservationists enjoyed a number of victories. By the time the National Park Service was created in 1916, 37 parks were included under its jurisdiction. Significantly, the early battles between conservationists and those that desired to hold land open for further development were won in great measure because the future national parks were often viewed as being worthless for anything other than sightseeing.[28] Hence the dominant view in government, if not society, was still one of conquering nature for resource use and exploitation.

By the end of the nineteenth century, conservationists could be divided into those who favored the planned use of natural resources and those who were interested in preserving them in an unspoiled state. We have labeled these individuals early conservationists and later conservationists, respectively.

Later Conservationist

Influenced by the work of George Perkins Marsh, President Theodore Roosevelt became an ardent proponent of resource conservation. However, unlike the earlier conservationists, conservation meant something different to Roosevelt and the first chief of the U.S. Forest Service, Gifford Pinchot. Conservation was redefined to mean multiple use or the management of resources so as to return the maximum benefits for people. For example, the maximization of water and timber produced in the forest.

In 1898 Pinchot was named the head of the Forestry Division of the Department of Agriculture, and in 1905 after a bitter struggle between the Department of Agriculture and the Department of Interior, Congress placed all forest reserves under the jurisdiction of the Department of Agriculture. Conservation, according to Pinchot, meant the use of natural resources for the benefit of humans. "The object of our forest policy is not to preserve the forests because they are beautiful ... or because they are refuges for the wild creatures of the wilderness ... but ... the making of prosperous homes ... every other consideration becomes secondary."[29] This attitude was both anthropocentric (the centering of one's views of everything around humans—still a common criticism of environmental policy) and utilitarian (concerned with the utility and practical uses of resources), but at least focused on preserving the forests for generations to come. Should values and uses other than those associated with humans be considered in the management of natural resources? These later conservationists thought not. This utilitarian perspective was in stark contrast to Muir's and the other preservationists' views of nature. "The frustrated advocates of wilderness preservation had no choice but to call Pinchot a 'deconservationist.'"[30] In 1908 when Pinchot organized a governor's conference on conservation of the natural resources, Muir and other spokespersons for the preservation of nature were not invited.[31]

The new conservationists and their resource policies dominated natural resource policy through most of the twentieth century. The influence of nature societies and clubs such as the Sierra Club and the Audubon Society was little felt until the late 1960s.

The Reawakening

A series of events in the 1960s brought environmental issues to the attention of the public and, eventually, policy makers. Rachel Carson published *Silent Spring* in 1962, focusing public attention on pollution, some say for the first time, with its eye-opening descriptions of the impact of chemicals, primarily pesticides, on the environment.

A number of sensational events also increased public awareness of environmental matters. When a sailor threw a cigarette into Cleveland's Cyahoga River in the summer of 1969, the river burst into flames. And on January 28, 1969, a Union Oil Company oil-drilling platform in the Santa Barbara Channel ruptured, sending hundreds of thousands of gallons of crude oil onto the beaches of Santa Barbara and adjacent communities.

By the late 1960s and early 1970s the environment had become a hot political issue. Politicians from every political persuasion claimed to be in favor of protecting the environment. On January 1, 1970, President Richard Nixon signed the National Environmental Policy Act, stating, "The 1970s absolutely must be the years when America pays its debt to the past by reclaiming the purity of its air, its water, and our living environment. It is literally now or never."[32]

On April 22, 1970, the country observed the first Earth Day. Twenty-two U.S. senators, thousands of students on college campuses, and millions of other people joined in the activities. The goal of Dennis Hayes, founder and organizer of Earth Day, was to keep environmentalism attractive to a broad spectrum of society. "There was a conscious decision in organizing Earth Day that 'environmentalism' would not be posited in a fashion that was ideologically exclusive; there was room for middle-class housewives, business executives, and radical college kids."[33]

From 1968 to 1972 the membership in many organizations, including the Sierra Club, the National Audubon Society, the Wilderness Society, and the National Wildlife Federation, increased dramatically, doubling and in some cases tripling.[34]

Thus, for the first time it appeared environmentalism was developing a broad base that cut across political ideology, and to a lesser extent, classes. This was in contrast to the earlier conservation movements, which were "hardly a popular movement. The achievements were made by the fortunate influence of a handful of thoughtful men upon a few receptive presidents ... [It was] ... the work of an elite—of a few particularly well-placed and influential individuals and small groups."[35]

As we see later, it was during this period that the primary environmental regulations dealing with air and water pollution were passed.

Complacency

Through the 1970s public concern about environmental issues leveled and slowly declined, as did the membership in many environmental organizations. But the decade also saw the establishment of new environmental organizations such as the Environmental Defense Fund and the Natural Resources Defense Council, with more specialized objectives—in these cases litigation. Even though President Jimmy Carter was considered a strong environmentalist who appointed representatives from environmental interest groups to positions of power in the Department of the Interior, Environmental Protection Agency, and U.S. Forest Service, some pundits in the late 1970s predicted that the environment as a driving issue in American politics was dead.

The Little Reagan Revolution

Ronald Reagan was elected president with what he claimed a mandate to "get regulators off our backs." The administration's early appointments made it clear that environmental regulations were a prime target. Although we deal with policies of the Reagan administration in subsequent chapters, it is important to note here that beginning in 1981, there was a public backlash to what was perceived as the administration's antienvironmentalism. Within a few years after the 1980 election, membership in major environmental organizations skyrocketed, mimicking the increases seen during the 1960s and early 1970s.[36]

The 1980s also saw further splintering and growth of new types of environmental groups. For example, so-called radical action groups, such as Earth First! and the Sea Shepherd Conservation Society, developed. Some members of these groups engaged in activities such as spiking trees (driving steel spikes into tress, making their harvesting extremely dangerous), lying down in front of bulldozers, and sinking whaling ships.[37]

The 1980s saw the change in the makeup, organization, and tactics of some of the more traditional environmental organizations. The growth of major environmental organizations had, in some cases, made coordination of efforts on all levels problematic. This growth led to decentralization so that some organizations, such as the Sierra Club and the Audubon Society, operated semi-autonomously, with central offices mainly providing information and services. The strategies of some mainline groups also shifted subtly. Many groups began to feel little could be gained from obstructionism; to have a long-term impact, in addition to pointing out environmental problems, they must provide practical solutions that consider the concerns of government and polluters. This approach has been referred to as the new environmentalism.[38]

Post-Reagan Resurgence

After the federal government's poor environmental record under the Reagan administration, Presidents Bush and Clinton took a much less confrontational stance toward environmental policy.

President Bush, who proclaimed himself the "environmental president," oversaw environmentally significant efforts, such as the amending and reauthorization of the Clean Air Act. However, the Bush administration did not go as far as many environmentalists had hoped in supporting environmental protection policies.

Much environmental fanfare accompanied Bill Clinton's election to the White House in 1992. The Clinton administration placed environmental protection policies at a higher priority than its immediate predecessors. Clinton was praised by the environmental community for his appointments of Bruce Babbitt as Secretary of the Interior and Carolyn Browner as Director of the Environmental Protection Agency. As Clinton's tenure in office lengthened, his attention to environmental affairs waned. The apathetic approach toward environmental policy that characterized the latter part of the Clinton administration may be the result of another period of public complacency towards environmental concerns.

The election of President George W. Bush in 2000 signaled a shift back toward less federal involvement in environmental protection. For example, less than a year into his administration, Bush lifted a ban on logging in roadless national forests, fought to weaken clean air standards, and opposed curbing greenhouse gas emissions via the Kyoto Protocol. Bush was closely aligned with the energy industry and moved to allow oil drilling in federally protected Arctic National Wildlife Refuge (ANWR).

INTEREST GROUPS

It is interesting to note that during the two periods in American history of greatest natural resource/environmental concern, the early conservation movement and the late 1960s and early 1970s, the issues that were first raised by people who, at the time, were considered to be "radicals," later came to be accepted and adopted by the political mainstream. This included, to varying degrees, the business community.

Why did the membership of environmental interest groups grow in the 1980s, and why did additional groups form? Political scientists have developed a number of theories to explain interest group growth and development. David Truman in *The Governmental Process* argued that group formation was the result of two related factors: the growing complexity of society and political economic "disturbances."[39] Complexity or growth and change in society result in some groups or interests becoming more powerful and others less powerful. Technological developments, such as the ability to extract inexpensive fossil fuels from the earth, have in large part been responsible for the environmental problems we face today. Groups are created or grow in response to these developments. The second idea, that of disturbances, refers to political, social, or economic disruptions that upset the equilibrium in some sector of society and bring together the previously unorganized into an interest group whose goals are to deal with the problem that caused the disturbance.

Truman's theory would seem to explain why environmental interest groups were created and grew in the 1970s and 1980s. Technology and society changed, creating more environmental degradation and a series of disturbances such as the Santa Barbara oil spill. These events, and others, provided the catalyst for groups to form and people to join them. The theory has some problems, however. As Jeffrey Berry has pointed out, Truman's theory "is based on optimistic and unjustified assumptions about all people's ability to organize.... Equally damning ... is that many groups have formed without a distinct, identifiable disturbance.[40]

Robert Salisbury has developed what he calls "an exchange theory of interest groups," which attributes group organization and growth to group leadership ability and the delivery of one of three types of benefits that group leaders can use to get members to join groups: *purposive benefits* associated with ideological goals without individual material reward; *material benefits* such as the expected increase in income that induces many to join professional associations such as the American Medical Association; and *solidarity benefits*, or the social rewards one can expect from interacting with a group of people with whom one shares interests.[41] According to this theory the rise in environmental interest groups would have been in large part a function of the activities of group leadership in presenting to potential members the benefits that could come from group membership (primarily purposive benefits). Although environmental groups did seek publicity and try to attract new members during the 1970s and 1980s, much of the growth in many groups was not the result of recruiting but due to external factors (some groups didn't do any advertising or recruiting and still grew).

Responding to the argument that formation takes place according to the ability of the group to grant selective material benefits to its members, Steven Davis has postulated that extenuating circumstances, such as the grassroots (and limited) financing of many environmental interest groups, preclude the influence of selective benefits in recruiting members.[42] Anthony Nownes and Grant Neely agree with Davis that the power of selective benefits to lure members to join interest groups is inoperative. Nownes and Neely cite low-startup costs, an increase in patronage, and rapid societal change as factors that truly spur the formation of interest groups. Also, the authors agree with Davis, most other interest group formation is closely tied to highly visible events that create societal disturbances.[43] As social disturbances attributed to a specific policy area decline, public interest in these areas tend to decline as well.

What form will the next phase of the environmental movement take in the United States? Surely a series of environmental disasters, as occurred in the late 1960s, could trigger widespread demands by the public for increased environmental action. Consequently, it is difficult to predict with any certainty what future environmental policies may develop. However, an examination of public opinion, and particularly how public opinion has changed since the early 1970s, is illuminating for what it says about the depth and importance that environmental issues have for the public.

PUBLIC OPINION AND THE ENVIRONMENT

One of the most important indicators of the salience of environmental issues to the public has been the shift of the public's attitudes toward environmental regulations from the late 1970s to the 1990s. In 1979 when the Roper Organization polled the general public, only 5 percent would agree that environmental regulations had "not gone far enough" to protect the environment. By 1983 the percentage of the public agreeing with that statement had increased to 48 percent.[44]

A series of Cambridge reports taken in the late 1970s and 1980s found similar results. When asked whether or not we should "sacrifice economic growth for environmental protection" in 1979, 37 percent of the population were in favor of sacrificing environmental protection whereas 23 percent were in favor of sacrificing economic growth for the benefit of environmental protection. When asked again in 1988, 19 percent of the public was in favor of sacrificing environmental protection and 58 percent were in favor of sacrificing economic growth. A similar study performed in 1991 by the Gallup organization found that 71 percent of Americans would favor sacrificing economic growth for environmental protection.

The Cambridge survey also asked respondents if they think "there is too much, too little, or about the right amount of government regulations and involvement in the area of environmental protection." In 1982 35 percent of the public indicated there was too little environmental protection, and in 1986 the percentage indicating there was too little protection had climbed to 59. Gallup's 1991 poll found that 88 percent of the public favored at least some increase in environmental policy action.

In 1987, 1988, and 1989, Cambridge Reports asked a national survey to identify the "two most important problems facing the United States today." Only 2 percent named the environment as one of the two most important problems in 1987. By 1988 the number of people identifying the environment had increased to 6 percent and in 1989 this jumped to 16 percent.[45] A CBS News/*New York Times* Poll asked the public to agree or disagree with the statement that environmental protection "cannot be too high" and should be pursued "regardless of the cost." In 1981 the public was nearly evenly divided, with 45 percent agreeing that environmental standards cannot be too high and should be pursued regardless of cost and 42 percent disagreeing with this statement. By 1984 66 percent were in agreement and 27 percent were in disagreement. This reflects the public backlash to perceptions of Reagan administration anti-environmentalism. In 2001 57 percent of respondents agreed that we should protect the environment at the risk of curbing economic growth, whereas 71 percent agreed in 1990.[46]

In 1995 a Gallup poll attempted to assess the progress made over the last 20 years. They found that the public's overall concern for environmental protection had begun to level off. In 1991 57 percent of the public agreed with the sentiment that life would be able to continue without major environmental disruption only if "immediate and drastic actions" were taken to preserve the environment. In 1995 only 35 percent agreed, and by 2001 this figure was down to 27 percent.[47] The number of persons who identified themselves as environmentalists declined from 78 percent in 1991, to 63 percent in 1995.

It would appear that the leveling off of environmental concern might be due to the perception that environmental policies have been successful to a point that the government may begin to focus on other issues. In 1990 and 1991 18 percent of the public claimed that the government had made "great" progress in environmental protection since 1970. In 1995 that number jumped to 24 percent and by 2001 25 percent concurred.[48] These figures seem to indicate that the public may again be entering a period of complacency.

What makes these poll results interesting is that social scientists generally are in agreement that public opinion does not often change much in the short term. As Robert Erikson, Norman Luttbeg, and Kent Tedin wrote, "[O]ur review of the results of opinion surveys has disclosed a few instances in which the distribution of opinion on an issue has changed somewhat over time. But these shifts ... can best be seen over a span of many years. In the short run, opinion distribution on long standing issues is generally quite stable."[49]

How can we explain these shifts in public attitude toward the environment in the 1980s that then leveled off in the 1990s and into the new millennium? As we see later, there were a number of highly publicized environmental problems in the 1980s. Acid rain received more attention during the decade than it had previously. The disaster at Chernobyl certainly alerted many to potential drawbacks of nuclear power, and every few months in the 1980s it seemed there were new revelations about hazardous or toxic waste and the pollution of water resources.

Another reason for the shift in public attitude in the 1980s could be attributed to the perceived anti-environmentalism of the Reagan administration. Reagan's first Secretary of the Interior, James Watt, was openly hostile toward environmentalists, reportedly refusing phone calls, and repeatedly referring to environmentalists as "extremists." The first administrator of the Environmental Protection Agency (EPA) in the Reagan administration, Anne Burford, was openly and repeatedly criticized for ignoring environmental concerns and currying favor with industrial polluters. Furthermore, she even lobbied Congress to cut funding to her own agency—very unusual indeed. Although backlash to the Reagan administration policies surely played some role in the percentage shifts just noted along with the reports of environmental disasters, it is not entirely clear why public attitudes shifted so dramatically.

A closer examination of public opinion with respect to environmental issues reveals several interesting trends. First, until the 1980s, most analysts thought that environmentalism was an upper-middle-class or elite issue. A number of studies conducted during the 1980s found, however, that although the membership of environmental *organizations* is drawn disprotionately from the middle class (members of the environmental organizations are likely to have higher educational attainment, incomes, and greater occupational prestige that the general public), that same upper-middle-class bias does not extend to environmental concern in the public at large.[50]

In a thorough review of studies that dealt with environmental concern, Kent D. Van Liere and Riley Dunlap found that the correlations between environmental concern and income, education and occupation were very weak. The strongest correlations were with education and environmental concern, but even these were inconclusive.[51]

Van Liere and Dunlap also found that among the public there was very little relationship between environmental concern and political party; however, among elites who also happen to be policy makers, and among the college-educated public, Democrats were found to be significantly more environmentally concerned than Republicans. Self-identified liberals were also found to be more environmentally concerned than conservatives. Still, a 1999 poll revealed that nearly half of Republican primary voters considered themselves "environmentalists," and over 90 percent claimed protecting the environment was important in deciding their vote.

In addition, when comparing the environmental concerns of urban residents with rural residents, with some exceptions, urban residents are generally found to be more concerned than their rural counterparts.[52]

Another demographic, age, is a good indicator of environmental concern. People between the ages of 20 and 24 years old register the greatest concern over environmental issues of any age group. However, environmental activism and participation, measured by involvement in environmental organizations, is not the highest among 20 to 24 year olds—the most active group are those in their early 40s.[53]

Van Liere and Dunlap's assessment is supported by a 1995 Gallup Poll that found that though younger (18 to 29 years old) Americans support the sacrifice of economic growth on favor of environmental protection, middle and older aged (above 30 years old) Americans are more apt to consider themselves "strong" environmentalists.

What impact do environmental attitudes have on elections? This is a difficult question to answer. Judging from public attitudes in the early 1980s as their concern for the environment and the dramatic increase in the percentage of the public that was perturbed about the amount of environmental regulation, one might expect that environmental issues would play a major role in national elections. President Reagan's landslide victory in 1984 over Walter Mondale suggests otherwise. This seeming inconsistency is probably best explained by examining the salience of environmental issues vis-à-vis other issues. Simply stated, although the public registers high levels of environmental concern, there are other issues, such as unemployment and inflation, that, when it comes time to vote, are more important. Evidence of this was found in a CBS News/*New York Times* exit poll taken after the November 1982 election that asked voters "Which of these issues were most important in deciding how you voted for the U.S. House?" The voters were handed a checklist that contained nine issues but were only allowed to check two of them. Only 3 percent of those polled checked "the environment," making it the least often decided item in the list.[54]

This is not to suggest that environmental issues are not important in elections. During the 1988 presidential election both candidates, George Bush and Michael Dukakis, thought it prudent to incorporate environmentalism in their platforms and campaigns. President Bush used the backdrop of polluted Boston harbor in Dukakis' home state of Massachusetts to announce he wanted to be the "environment president." Similarly, during the 1992 presidential elections both President Bush and Bill Clinton professed to be "environmentalists," although as an issue the environment seemed to play a minimum role in the election. The same was true during the 1996 presidential election between President Clinton and Robert Dole. This was also true to a somewhat lesser extent in the 2000 elections.

Surveys from September 2000, just prior to George W. Bush's narrow victory over Vice-President Gore, found that 71 percent of adults thought the candidates' position on the environment would be "extremely" or "very important" in deciding how they would vote. However, the environment was still only ninth highest priority (of 14) for these potential voters. From 1992 to 2001 never more than 4 percent of the American public believed the environment was one of the two most important issues facing the nation.[55]

As we see later, the Reagan revolution in environmental regulation was largely successful and—receiving no immediate threat to existing regulations—many of those concerned with the environment may feel free to vote on other issues. Also environmental issues frequently play an important role in the state and local elections. For example, zoning controversies and waste disposal selection are primarily local concerns that frequently play an important role in local elections.[56]

Though public opinion is very important in terms of how we as a society deal with the environment, public opinion is shaped by how we talk about the environment. John Dryzek and David Schlosberg stress the significance of environmental discourses, or how we communicate and think about the environment. According to Dryzek, how we see the world and thus frame environmental problems guides us to specific and limited solutions or perhaps to even denying the problems altogether.[57]

It is through language that we understand complex issues like the environment; some may argue this constitutes our reality. Imagine trying to explain environmental problems without words, and you begin to understand the importance of discourse. Now we must consider the tools we use to manipulate language and derive meaning. To talk about something means to not talk about something, that is, we must limit our scope to focus on a certain subject. If you are reading this, you are probably not paying attention to other people, books, or even the environment around you. That is, environmental discourses recognize certain natural and human entities while ignoring others. They make assumptions about natural relationships, who environmental players are, and what motivates them to act. They also use various metaphors to convey their outlook on the world.

A few should illustrate the point. When you look over the land, do you see swamps or wetlands? Are other animals food and clothing or extensions of God? Do forests exist or are they simply collections of timber? Do you see wilderness and beauty or wasted, undeveloped land? Is nature a machine, a goddess, its own, unique, organic life form, or simply a figment of our imaginations? The answers to these questions can produce extremely different, yet all internally logical environmental policies. At the risk of oversimplification here is a summary of Dryzek's nine environmental discourses. These are presented here not as the only ways we view the world—humans are much too complex to distill everything into nine worldviews. They are useful shorthand, however, to categorize many of the ways people view environmental matters.

Survivalism

First is the discourse of survivalism, known to some as "gloom and doom environmentalism." Here, the basic scope is that modern economic and technological patterns of growth, development, and obsolescence (consumerism) will inevitably lead to ecological catastrophe and hence the downfall of humanity. Population growth and resource use/pollution are growing exponentially and since nature is seen as a finite storehouse of resources, societal and environmental collapse must occur if major changes are not effected immediately.

New technologies and human ingenuity cannot be relied upon to solve every crisis resulting from previous technologies and ingenuity. Human values including a respect for nature with ensuing political and social upheaval are necessary to avoid disaster, and these changes will not be easy or fun. Survivalists think in terms of limits, population curves, and past environmental disasters. Ultimately, a disposable, materialistic, market-driven capitalist society cannot sustain itself. Only through science and tough political and social sacrifices can we endure. Humanity today, with its capitalistic, selfish, growth-oriented way of life, is a cancer growing on and feeding off the earth that will not stop until its host is dead.

##Prometheans

Prometheans, on the other hand, hold that humans can solve any problem they are faced with, as we always have in the past. If we run out of some resources, we will develop ways to use others. Prometheans believe in economics and capitalism. Further, because price reflects scarcity (diamonds cost more than corn), and all commodities since the Industrial Revolution have continually become cheaper, it is illogical to worry about resource depletion. Standard of living is up the world over since the nineteenth century, we have longer life spans, and we have plenty of resources. So what makes anyone think we are on the road to catastrophe rather than even greater prosperity? In addition, because survivalists cannot prove the sky is falling, why should we simply take their word for it and destroy our useful, versatile economy just to hold it up?

Prometheans hold that capitalism and markets improve rather than harm life. Nature is seen only in its utility to humans and has no intrinsic value. Left in its wild state it is nothing; it "needs" us to be something more. A rock is just a rock unless we make it part of a house. Moreover, Adam Smith's "invisible hand" will always allocate resources more efficiently than bureaucrats or elitists can.

Ultimately we were put on earth by God to cultivate it and flourish. Because self-interest will always dominate human behavior, it should be exploited fruitfully and efficiently within our current economic framework. Engineering is our savior, for it seeks to learn how the intricate machine of nature works and allows us to tweak it to our full advantage.

Administrative Rationalism

Dryzek also discussed the more moderate Administrative rationalists. They believe in data, cost-benefit analyses, and rational, scientific management (of people and nature) under government. We simply need to break down environmental problems into their parts and let our experts handle them. The liberal-capitalist state, as we know it, is workable but does need some fine-tuning. The technocrats of our administrative state can effectively manage the environment, so long as greedy corporations and noisy politicians stay out of their rational way. NEPA was a big step in this regard, as is the establishment and prominence of expert advisory committees. The objective administrative mind (the collective expertise of technocrats) can save us all from ruining the environment and our economic and political institutions.

Democratic Pragmatism

Democratic pragmatists take a different approach that is also very practical but incorporates much greater levels of public participation to help guide the technocrats. This discourse sees public hearings as right-to-know legislation like the TRI (Toxic Release Inventory) as superior tools to regulate the environment for the best public use. Democratic pragmatism emphasizes open communication and equality and looks at democracy not just as an institution, but also as the process that can best solve problems, environmental or otherwise. In a sense this is a meta-discourse in that it seeks to reconcile other discourses and values within a democratic framework.

Ultimately, we live in a world of extreme complexity and uncertainty, and a handful of experts cannot come close to knowing every problem or solution; however, collectively we can approach this capacity. Flexibility, plurality, and experimentation with constant, open feedback are the keys to solving environmental problems. Public policy is the outcome of myriad forces constantly colliding with each other, and thus is like a physics experiment; adaptive management has become a buzzword. If we carefully examine the results of various policy experiments and how the parts interact, we can come as close as possible to understanding the "public will" and what is the most effective means of regulating the environment.

Economic Rationalism

Economic rationalists take yet a different direction. Also known as market liberalism, this discourse believes market incentives, privatization, and tradable pollution permits are the best solutions to our environmental problems. This discourse holds that the tragedy of the commons only exists because there is a commons. If we make citizens real stakeholders of the former commons, where they have legal ownership as well as control over their resources, and financial incentives to use them wisely, they will. Public bureaucrats get paid whether they lease the public's land to be grazed for pennies or use it in the best "public interest." Further, industry will continue to pollute the river next door as long as it is free to do so.

Our political system is set up to encourage public officials to give away public resources to special interests. Politicians love to see narrow interests profit handsomely when the costs are small and diffuse; this wins friends and produces no enemies; again, if there is no public land for politicians to give away, this problem is solved. Finally, people only care about what they own. People also know what is best for them and their possessions. Humans are first and foremost Homo economicus, and once we establish clear property rights, free markets will guide us to environmental quality. Competition and self-interest motivate people, not regulations, so let's use what works in all other aspects of life to protect the environment.

Sustainable Development

A discourse popular among those working on international environmental treaties is sustainable development. The goal here is to meet the needs of the present generation without compromising the ability of future generations to meet their own needs. We need economic prosperity but we must also recognize our limits and ensure distributive justice. Environmentalists must work more closely with economists because their problems and solutions are intractable. With cooperation we can play a positive-sum game where we have material goods as well as a healthy environment.

We need democracy and capitalism, but the global North must change its consumptive patterns while the South must limit its population growth, and this can only occur through new, more globally oriented political participation; that is, we need less focus on nation-states and more emphasis on the global community. The North also is going to have to pay the South to develop in a more sustainable manner. The wealthier developed nations all went through a very dirty industrial revolution that is the next step in the progression of less developed economies. The North has no right to tell the South they cannot develop the same way the North did. If development is truly to be sustainable, the North must share in its wealth to prevent the environmental mess developing industrial economies in the South would otherwise go through; this means donating cleaner technologies and industrial processes.

Finally, development does not imply growth that tends to continue indefinitely in unchecked capitalism. Sustainable development requires economic improvements and efficiencies guided by democracy, where constant growth only occurs in human and environmental health education.

Ecological Modernization

Ecological modernization is a discourse that emphasizes a systems approach to capitalism and democracy. These institutions do require some reorganization, but this can be accomplished in a "win-win" situation for business and the environment; indeed this must be the case, because environmental protection and economic prosperity literally go hand in hand. Neither the "invisible hand" nor the command-and-control will solve environmental problems. What we need is a viable economy that produces environmental goods. Since business only responds to money, they must be shown how environmental goods can help them earn more. In the end, we need a cleaner, more efficient capitalism that is guided by market incentives, sound science, and democracy. For example, less pollution can come from more efficient production that uses fewer raw materials. Further, ignoring environmental problems will not save money, but will be much more costly in the future; spending a few thousand dollars today on some cleanup efforts is better than a billion dollar lawsuit tomorrow. A cleaner environment also means happier, healthier (and thus more productive) employees. Finally, pollution abatement and "green" products are a growing and profitable new segment of the economy.

Environmental protection is not a lost cost, but an investment. It is not a luxury but a necessity for continued economic progress and an adequate quality of life. The role of government is not to let economic agents act as they please, but to impose the collective will on them, including the internalization of former externalities. Ecological modernization transforms and then uses the language of markets and the logic of efficiency to achieve environmental ends.

Green Romanticism

Taking a much more radical turn is green romanticism. This discourse prefers to think in terms of "ecosophy" rather than ecology; that is, they stress feeling and personal insight over science and technocracy.[58] Their locus of change is the individual and his or her consciousness rather than on institutions. Dominating nature, which our current system is based upon, is fundamentally wrong, just as is dominating women, the poor, or minorities. Our exploitation of the environment is nothing short of rape, and when we dominate "others" we are in fact limiting our full cooperative potential and ourselves. Our hubris has led us to believe we can live better through conquering nature and fulfilling material desires, but there is a natural order and harmony to which we must return and which cannot be improved upon.

Rationality has become an end in itself and this along with science and "objectivity" alienates us from that which we wish to understand and need to exist. Radical reform is required that recognizes all life has equal value and a potential beyond mere human utility; it is our moral obligation to see to it that this fundamental right of self-realization can be achieved by all.[59] We must turn from our anthropocentric ideology to a biocentric or ecocentric philosophy. Finally, we must seek totally decentralized control within small, self-sufficient communities where we can recognize our ignorance and smallness (insignificance) while achieving balance in all its meanings.

Green Rationalism

This leads to Dryzek's final discourse, which he calls green rationalism. It can be defined as an "ecologically guided radicalization of Enlightenment values."[60] The emphasis is back, however, on social and political institutions and how they can be rationally restructured to meet more or less radical "green" ends. This discourse is a more humanist and rational version of green romanticism. Still, humans are nothing without nature, and thus we are ultimately subservient to it.

A subsection of green rationalism is social(ist) ecology, such as that espoused by eco-anarchist Murray Bookchin, who tells us that hierarchy always leads to domination, oppression, alienation, and destruction. Unfortunately, our society and bureaucracies are based on hierarchy. Yet we find no such hierarchy in the nonhuman natural world, and this is why it has been in balance and has flourished for eons. Our collective freedom ultimately lies in cooperation within grass roots, localized, self-sufficient communities, or "radical municipalism." This also means abandoning capitalist owned, centrally run nation-states.

As the survivalists contend, there are limits, but balance must be obtained via environmental justice movements, for example, rather than oligarchic bureaucracies. Humans are indeed special, as we are nature's way of knowing itself, but this does not give us license to dominate and destroy. In fact, our special privilege of advanced intelligence demands that we repay our gift with environmental stewardship and protection.

Although Dryzek's nine discourses are not meant to be a definitive list of how people think about environmental matters—real people may incorporate elements of several discourses in their thinking—nonetheless they are a useful way of categorizing the different points of view.

SUMMARY

As you have seen, the dominant social paradigm, which has itself been shaped by historical influences, in turn affects the electoral choices made by the American public. More broadly, the DSP in the United States has driven our history and our attitudes toward environmental regulation. It will continue to shape public policy responses to environmental policy. What limitations will our DSP have on our ability to respond appropriately to future environmental problems? Does our DSP prevent us from making environmental progress, or is it the only way it can be achieved? Will we ever be able to collectively change, and if so, how will that change come about?

In this chapter we have examined the nature and implications of our DSP. Historical attitudes toward individual liberty, property rights, economics, religion, and other values have impacted the history of our policy relationship to the environment as well as contemporary public opinion on environmental issues. The regulatory constraints, assumptions, and discourses used in the environmental policy-making process also have a significant impact on environmental policy outcomes. That regulatory environment is the subject of the next chapter.

NOTES

1. If you are confused about how these ideals fit with a U.S. history that includes slavery and the treatment of blacks and women as personal property, remember that the founding fathers, and many of the political philosophers who influenced them, had somewhat different notions of equality than we do today. For John Locke, governments were established by the rich and serve the interests of the rich. As French philosopher Paul d'Holbach wrote at about the time our government was

being formed, "[B]y the word people I do not mean the stupid populace. ... Every man who can live respectably from the income of his property and every head of a family who owns land ought to be regarded as a citizen." Quoted in George H. Sabine, *A History of Political Theory* (New York: Holt, Rinehart and Winston, 1961), p. 570.

2. Riley E. Dunlap and Kent D. Van Liere, "Commitment to the Dominant Social Paradigm in Concern for Environmental Quality," *Social Science Quarterly*, 65 (4) (December 1984), pp. 1014–1028.

   Furthermore, many scholars (Catton 1980, Rifkin 1980, Drengson 1980) have argued that the DSP has a direct relationship to public policy responses to environmental problems. See, for example, William R. Catton, *Overshoot; The Ecological Basis of Environmental Change* (Urbana: University of Illinois Press, 1980), pp. 221–240; Dennis Clark Pirages, *Sustainable Society* (New York: Prarger, 1977); and Jeremy Rifkin, *Entropy: A New World View* (New York: Viking, 1980).

3. Fifty percent recycling is considered an optimistic goal and even then recycling is not 100 percent efficient. Some resources—such as the iron loss to rust prior to recycling—are not recoverable.

4. William Ophuls, *Ecology and the Politics of Scarcity* (San Francisco: Freeman, 1977), p. 170.

5. Quoted in Sandra Postel, "Toward a New 'Eco'-Nomics," *World Watch*, 3 (5) (Sept./Oct.1990), p. 20.

6. Ophuls, *Ecology and the Politics of Scarcity*, p. 169.

7. The final problem of substitution with the market distribution of goods and services raised by some critics concerns efficiency in the marketplace. Efficiency for economists is usually described in terms of "pareto-optimality." A Pareto improvement can be made when a voluntary exchange results in at least one party being better off and no party being worse off. A situation is Pareto optimal when it is impossible to enact an exchange that will not make some party worse off. As philosophers Donald Van De Veer and Christine Pierce point out, "We may have some serious moral reservations about even maximally efficient situations. For example, suppose I am your master and you are my slave. There may be no way to alter this arrangement so that one of us can be better off and no one worse off. That is, it may be pareto optimal or maximally efficient." Donald Van De Veer and Christine Pierce (eds.), *People, Penguins, and Plastic Trees: Basic-Issues in Environmental Ethics* (Belmont, CA: Wadsworth, 1986), p. 211 The same point can be made about any social organization (country, corporation, etc.) in which all rights and privileges are held by a ruling elite.

8. Paul Erlich, and Anne Erlich, *Betrayal of Science and Reason* (Washington DC: Island Press, 1996), p.176.

9. Ibid., p. 180.

10. Richard B. McKenzie and Gordon Tullock, *The New World of Economics* (Homewood, IL: Irwin, 1978), p. 7.

11. Ophuls, *Ecology and the Politics of Scarcity*, p. 167.

12. White, Lynn, Jr., "The Historical Roots of Our Ecologic Crisis," *Science*, 155 (March 10, 1967), pp.1203–1207.

13. However, it is believed that the overuse of antibiotics has led to the evolution of more resilient disease varieties that are harder to control, thus requiring the introduction of new, and more powerful, antibiotics.

14. Kenneth R. Hammond (ed.), *Judgement and Decision in Public Policy Formation* (Boulder, CO: Westview Press, 1978), p. 5.

15. There is a presumption of objectivity in science that may or may not be accurate. Some have argued that the values science pursues color and lead to conclusions that if not preordained are at least not value-free. See, for example, Hillary Rose and Steven Rose, *The Political Economy of Science* (London: McMillan, 1976).

16. Wade L. Robinson, *Decisios in Doubt: The Environment and Public Policy* (Hanover, NH: University Press of New England, 1994), p. 3.

17. What this means in terms of policy might be the requirement of "proof" from industry that their actions will not cause serious environmental harm before we (government, the people) allow them to proceed; this is along the lines of an EIS. Another step might be to require corporations to put up a bond whenever a project could possibly harm the environment. If it does not, the state refunds the money with interest, but if environmental harm does occur, the perpetrators can easily be held accountable and their bond spent on reparations. Ultimately, if an activity could hurt the environment and thus all of society so a few can profit, it is best to avoid this activity. Some critics, such as the late Aaron Wildavsky, believe the precautionary principle is ridiculous as well as dangerous. Since when do we live in a society that puts the burden of proof on private entities rather than government? Moreover, looking throughout world civilization and history one notes that the wealthier a

people are the healthier they are. In addition, so long as people have to worry about where their next meal is coming from, or which bill to pay, protecting the environment will never be a priority for them. Thus, any unnecessary impediment to economic progress is also a detriment to human health and possibly the environment itself. Industry and economists, then, will likely hold that the precautionary principle is more harmful than helpful in environmental policy. Rachel's "The Precautionary Principle," *Environment and Health Weekly*, 586, 1998, Annapolis, MD: Environment Research Foundation. See also Aaron Wildavsky. *But Is It True?* (Cambridge, MA: Harvard University Press, 1995).

18. Paul Feyerabend, *Science in a Free Society* (NLB, London: 1978), p. 88.
19. Some have also argued that the research priorities are skewed given that most research is carried out for purposes of profit, often defense profits, or social control. See Hillary Rose and Steven Rose (eds.), *The Radicalization of Science* (London: McMillan, 1976).
20. Brian Martin, "Antichrist Science Policy," *Raven*, Volume 7, No.2, (Summer 1994), p. 140–141.
21. Ibid.
22. Anne and Paul Ehrlich, "Ecoscience," *Mother Earth News*, 72 (Nov./Dec. 1981), p. 198.
23. E.J. Mishan, "The Growth of Affluence and the Decline of Welfare," in Herman E. Daly (ed.), *Economics, Ecology, and Ethics: Essays Toward a Steady State Economy* (San Francisco: Freeman, 1980), p. 281.
24. Ibid., p. 277.
25. For a further discussion of Minamata Bay and other environmental problems in Japan, see Norie Huddle, Michael Reich, and Nahum Stiskin, *Island of Dreams: Environmental Crisis in Japan* (Rochester, VT: Schenkman Books, 1987).
26. Joseph W. Meeker, "The Assisi Connection," *Wilderness*, 51 (180) (Spring 1988), p. 63.
27. Hans Hughs, "The Aesthetic Emphasis," in Roderick Nash, (ed.), *Environment and Americans: The Problem of Priorities* (New York: Holt, Rinehart and Winston, 1972), pp. 24–31.
28. Alfred Runte, *National Parks: The American Experience*, unpublished Ph.D. dissertation, 1976, University of California, Santa Barbara.
29. Grant McConnell, "The Failures and Success of Organized Conservation," in Nash, *Environment and Americans*, p. 49.
30. Roderick Nash, "The Conservation Schism," in Nash, *Environment and Americans*, p. 71.
31. Ibid.
32. Robert L. Sansom, *The New American Dream Machine* (New York: Anchor Books, 1976), p. 4.
33. Peter Borrelli, "Environmentalism at the crossroads," The Amicus Journal (Summer 1987), p. 28.
34. Riley E. Dunlap, "Public Opinion on the Environment in the Reagan Era," Environment, 29 (July-August 1987), p. 35.
35. Grant McConnell, "The Failures and Successes of Organized Conservation," *Environment*, in Nash, Environment and Americans, p. 47.
36. Riley E. Dunlap, "Public Opinion on the Environment in the Reagan Era," *Environment*, 29 (July-August 1987), p. 35.
    Membership in the major national environmental organizations rose significantly from 1980 to 1989. Defenders of Wildlife membership went up from 44,000 to 80,000 (average annual increase of 9 percent). The Environmental Defense Fund from 45,000 to 100,000 (average annual increase of 14 percent); National Audubon Society from 412,000 to 575,000 (average annual increase of 4 percent); Natural Resource Defense Council from 42,000 to 117,000 (average annual increase of 20 percent); Sierra Club from 180,000 to 496,000 (average annual increase of 20 percent); and the Wilderness Society saw a membership increase in the 1980s from 45,000 to 317,000 (an average annual increase of 67 percent). See Robert Cameron Mitchell, "Public Opinion and the Green Lobby: Poised for the 1990s?" in Norman J. Vig and Michael E. Kraft (eds.), *Environmental Policy in the 1990s* (Washington, DC: Congressional Quarterly Press, 1990), p. 92.
37. Borrelli, "Environmentalism at the Crossroads," p. 35.
38. Frederick D. Crupp, "The Third Stage of Environmentalist," EDF (Environmental Defense Fund) *Newsletter*, 17 (3) (August 1986), p. 4.
39. David B. Truman, *The Governmental Process* (New York: Knopf, 1951).
40. Jeffrey M. Berrry, *The Interest Group Society* (Boston: Little, Brown, 1984), p. 69.
41. Robert H. Salisbury, "An Exchange Theory of Interest Groups," *Midwest Journal of Political Science*, 13 (February 1968), pp.1–32.
42. Stephen Davis "Environmental Politics and the Changing Context of Interest Group Organization," *Social Science Journal*, (October 1996), p. 343.

43. Anthony Nownes and Grant Neely. "Toward an Explanation for Public Interest Group Formation and Proliferation: "Seed Money," Disturbances, Entrepreneurship, and Patronage." *Policy Studies Journal*. (Spring 1996), p. 74.

44. Riley E. Dunlap. The information reported from these polls was taken from "Public Opinion on the Environment in the Reagan Era," *Environment*, 29 (July-August 1987).

45. Mitchell, "Public Opinion and the Green Lobby: Poised for the 1990s?," p. 84.

46. Gallup Poll: Environment, April 2001. www.gallup.com/poll/indicators/indenenvironment.asp accessed September 5, 2001.

47. Ibid.

48. Ibid.

49. Robert S. Erikson, Norman R. Luttbeg, and Kent L. Tedin, *American Public Opinion* (3rd ed.), (New York: Macmillan, 1988), p. 67.

50. See, for example, Paul Mohai, "Public Concern and Elite Involvement in Environmental-Conservation Issues," *Social Sciences Quarterly*, 66 (4) (December 1985), p. A20; Robert Cameron Mitchell, "Public Opinion and Environmental Politics in the 1970s and 1980s" in N. G. Vig and M. E. Craft (eds.), *Environmental Policy in the 80s: Reagan's New Agenda* (Washington, DC: Congressional Quarterly, 1984), pp. 51–73; Kent D. Van Liere and Riley Dunlap, "The Social Basis of Environmental Concern," *The Public Opinion Quarterly*, 44 (2) (Summer 1980), pp.183–197; and Denton E. Morrison and Riley E. Dunlap, "Environmentalism and Elitism: A Conceptual and Empirical Analysis," *Environmental Management* 10 (5) (1986), pp. 581–589.

51. Kent D. Van Liere and Riley Dunlap, "The Social Basis of Environmental Concern," *The Public Opinion Quarterly* 44 (2) (Summer 1980), pp. 183–197. See also Paul Mohai, "Public Concern and Elite Involvement in Environmental-Conservation Issues," *Social Sciences Quarterly* 66 (4) (December 1985), p. A20; and Robert Cameron Mitchell, "Public Opinion and Environmental Politics in the 1970s and 1980s," in N. G. Vig and M. E. Craft (eds.), *Environmental Policy in the 80s: Reagan's New Agenda* (Washington, DC: Congressional Quarterly, 1984), pp. 51–73.

52. Ibid.

53. Paul Mohai and Ben W. Twight, "Age in Environmentalism: An Elaboration of the Buttel Model Using National Survey Evidence," *Social Sciences Quarterly* 68 (4) (December 1987), pp. 789–815.

54. Dunlap, "Public Opinion on the Environment in the Reagan Era," p. 35.

55. Gallup Poll: Environment, April 2001. www.gallup.com/poll/indicators/indenenvironment.asp accessed September 5, 2001. See 48.

56. For example, the politics of water importation dominated water control board and county elections in Santa Barbara County in the late 1970s and the early 1980s; an initiative petition that would have prohibited the building of a luxury hotel on the Big Island in Hawaii played an important role in the 1988 County of Hawaii elections; and the location of a permanent nuclear waste repository was an important issue in the Washington State 1986 U. S. Senate elections. Finally, in the 1998 city council elections in Flagstaff, Arizona environmental issues, notably growth control, played an important role in the electoral loss of incumbent councilperson, Zachary Smith.

57. John Dryzek, *The Politics of the Earth: Environmental Discourses* (New York: Oxford University Press, 1997).

58. John Dryzek, and David Schlosberg, *Debating the Earth* (New York: Oxford University Press, 1998).

59. Ibid.

60. John Dryzek, *The Politics of the Earth*, p. 172.

The Regulatory Environment

THE REGULATORY CONTEXT

Our dominant social paradigm has a significant impact on the scope and force of regulations that have been devised to deal with environmental problems. In this chapter we explore varying approaches to environmental regulation, including the impact of the assumptions of science and risk analysis, and we examine the accepted role of government regulation on environmental policy. We conclude with an overview of environmental law.

Scholars of regulatory theory use several models to explain when and under what conditions government regulates business. The *economic theory of regulation,* exemplified by the work of George Stigler, holds that regulations are driven by the needs of business and are acquired, designed, and operated primarily for the benefit of business in a manner, not surprisingly, that protects the profits and competitive environment of regulated business.[1] (This is also called the "self-interest" theory of regulation.) In contrast, other scholars, notably James Q. Wilson, have argued that regulations are best understood as arising out of the *political incentives* that operate on policy makers. Examining the "costs" and "benefits" associated with different regulations and their distribution, we can determine under which conditions government is more likely to regulate industry. For example, if benefits are concentrated and costs diffused, then organized groups are likely to persuade policy makers to regulate and thereby institutionalize the benefit. Usually, in this example, there will be little political opposition to the regulation.[2] Finally, adherents of the *public interest theory of regulation* hold that policy makers regulate in response to broad social movements or crisis situations and act to protect the public from undesirable business practices. The public interest theory is most often used by policy makers themselves to explain the introduction of environmental regulations.

Each of the theories just described contain some truth, but all fall short in explaining the emergence of environmental regulations. Certainly, some environmental regulations have been developed by public-spirited policy makers in response to constituent demands that undesirable business practices be curtailed, as the public interest theory holds. On the other hand, other environmental regulations, such as uniform auto emission standards or energy efficiency ratings for appliances, have been sought by industries to stabilize markets and protect themselves from a variety of state regulations or from regional competitors operating under more lax state laws. The most appropriate regulatory theory for environmental regulations would seem to depend on the politics surrounding a given regulation. With this in mind, let us move on to looking at the role of science and risk analysis and the accepted role of government in environmental policy, for both of these are fused with politics.

Science and Risk Analysis

Regardless of the specific environmental policy or regulation, an assessment must be made of the environmental impacts of human activities. All the major health and environmental agencies in the United States engage in some kind of risk analysis or risk assessment.[3] Risk is inherent in any activity. The question of acceptable risk involves the personal decisions and trade-offs that individuals are willing to make in their own lives. However, in environmental management, there may be what are called *involuntary risks,* risks over which the individual has no control. In these situations, government organizations or other third parties make the assessment of risk for society as a whole.

For practical, political, and economic reasons, it would be impossible to eliminate all forms of pollution from the environment. Zero discharge, as attractive as it might sound, is, in most instances, nearly impossible to obtain. Furthermore even when zero discharge is obtainable the cost of removing the last few remaining units of a pollutant from the environment can be astronomical. Therefore, acceptable levels of pollution and the risks to human health contained therein are required for any form of environmental management. For example, a flowing river has a natural capacity to cleanse itself and hence can absorb a certain level of nontoxic pollutants. The determination of that level is part of what we mean by acceptable risks.

What is an acceptable level of risk? For some substances, for example, carcinogens (cancer-causing agents), it is widely accepted there is no safe threshold of exposure. Reflecting this, the Delaney clause of the U.S. Food, Drug and Cosmetic Act stipulates that no substances found to be carcinogenic will be allowed in food, drugs, or cosmetics in the United States. However, risk analysis is fraught with uncertainty and experts disagree on the appropriate level of exposure to many substances.

Three points are important to remember when examining risk analysis and environmental policy: (1) analysis is as political as it is scientific; a conflict of values must be considered over and above scientific information; (2) because of a lack of data or the appropriate methodology, science often lacks information to make risk assessments with any degree of certainty; (3) there is often disagreement within the scientific community itself as to the harm or risk involved in a given level of pollution or exposure to a chemical substance.

Ronald Brickman, Sheila Jasanoff, and Thomas Ilgen, in a four-country comparison of the regulation of the herbicide 2,4,5-T, concluded that the experience in the four nations

> [I]llustrates how regulatory procedure interacts with science to produce different assessments of risk. Yet it also suggests that, in the case of genuinely controversial products, political pressure ultimately overwhelms scientific evaluations and forces similar outcomes in very different policy making environments.[4]

Although the layperson might assume that objective scientific analysis would determine acceptable levels of risk, such is not the case. In another study of environmental risk assessment, Larry Silver concluded, "[R]isk selection and resolution is not objective, but inevitably is subject to the result of the political process. It is policy making at its essence."[5]

The political nature of risk analysis is inherently tied to the uncertainty involved in the process. "Sufficient information will rarely be available to permit an accurate assessment of environmental health risks. Generally, the uncertainties as to the degree of risk are substantial, and many issues in assessing the risk can be estimated only judgmentally.... Uncertainties arise at all stages of risk assessment."[6] This uncertainty means risk assessment is naturally both a scientific and a political process. Under such conditions of uncertainty most environmental policy analysts would agree that policy makers tend to err on the side of regulation. This uncertainty may have the effect of distorting the nature and importance of certain environmental risks. For example, the EPA found that its own prioritization of environmental issues has had less to do with real risks to the public health than with the public's perceptions of problems based on well-publicized, though perhaps scientifically negligible, risks. A study conducted by the EPA in 1987 titled *Unfinished Business* found that the scientific information used to assess environmental risks was extremely poor and that the agency placed the value of public opinion in agency decision making at an exceedingly high level, to the detriment of the natural environment itself.[7]

The result of this introspective analysis was the re-examination of priorities within the agency, and the redefinition of risk to include the health of the environment as well as that of the public. Richard N. L. Andrews argues that this redefinition of risk assessment generalized the language of political debate concerning environmental priorities, as well as implied that these priorities could be arrived at through precise technical means, rather than through political choice. An EPA study conducted in 1990 found the agency to be lacking in direction and mission. However, political constraints, such as the EPA's detailed, prescriptive, and fragmented appropriation statutes, have prevented attempts to fundamentally reorient the agency's priorities.

Attempts by the Occupational Safety and Health Administration (OSHA) to set workplace exposure levels for benzene illustrate both the political aspects of risk assessment and the scientific uncertainty involved. OSHA developed regulations lowering the maximum workplace exposure level for benzene from 10 parts per million to 1 part per million. In a U.S. Supreme Court case involving a challenge to the new regulation, *Industrial Union Department, AFL-CIO v. American Petroleum Institute,*[8] the Court found that OSHA had no direct evidence of a link between benzene exposure at 10 parts per million and adverse health effects. OSHA did know, however, that benzene could cause leukemia in humans at high levels of exposure, that it was absorbed rapidly into the human body through inhalation, and that other toxins were carcinogenic at low levels of exposure. Lacking more solid data with which to make a decision, the choice of setting the exposure level at 10 or 1 part per million was a matter of judgment. In this kind of a decision-making environment, we would anticipate that the actors who have a stake in risk assessment will actively attempt to influence the assessment process through the courts, legislators, or administrative agencies. Uncertainty in and of itself has not been found to be grounds for invalidating regulations.[9] And, to repeat, the system is fraught with uncertainty. As former EPA Director William Ruckelshaus once commented that "Our scientists told me that we can defend any standard between 150 and 250 parts per million. So pick a number."[10]

Faced with uncertainty, environmental regulators have an incentive to guess on the side of safety.[11] Environmental groups support this position and often argue that no chances should be taken with the well-being of a human life. However, the regulated industries would naturally prefer risk assessments that maximized their options by setting more lenient exposure levels.

Related to issues of uncertainty is the question of unanticipated consequences. As we see later, many environmental policies have had results that were both unanticipated and sometimes undesirable. For example, federal regulations that required minimum fleet averages for gasoline mileage in automobiles had the impact of stimulating automobile manufacturers to build lighter and more fuel-efficient cars. A study by the Harvard School of Public Health and a Brookings Institution economist found that as a result, many American and Japanese cars were 500 pounds lighter than they would have been without federal regulations. The study concluded that fatalities would increase due to the decreased safety factor of the lighter cars and estimated the increase in fatalities would total 20,000 in a ten year period.[12]

Uncertainty naturally leads to disagreement within the scientific community over what is acceptable environmental risk. For example, in 1985 the Universities Associated for Research and Education in Pathology published a report on an 18-month study of health effects related to exposure from chemicals in toxic waste dumps. They found, among other things, that "[T]here's little scientific evidence that chemical disposal sites have had serious impacts on the health of populations residing near them."[13] A year earlier, a study of a chemical waste disposal plant in Wales found that the number of babies born with abnormalities in the vicinity of the disposal plant was significantly higher than the average for the rest of the country.[14] In 1978 a report released by a group of well-known scientists representing three U.S. federal research institutions estimated that 20 percent of all cancer was caused by occupational exposure and that this figure "may even be conservative."[15] Although Samuel Epstein, in *Politics of Cancer,* endorsed the 1985 report and President Carter's Toxic Substances Strategy Committee accepted these estimations with minor qualification[16], this study was denounced in an editorial in the magazine *Science* as being "flimsy" and was reviewed in the British medical journal *Lancet* with the comment, "[I]t is sad to see such a fragile report under such distinguished names."[17]

For a more detailed examination of problems in risk assessment, you are referred elsewhere.[18] For the purpose of understanding environmental policy and the regulatory process, it is important to remember that a faith in science and technology is a part of our dominant social paradigm.[19] Risk assessment is not, however, an objective science, and determining acceptable levels of pollution or exposure to potentially dangerous chemicals involves as much politics as science. Subsequent chapters dealing with air and water pollution control measures illustrate this interaction of science and politics.

Closely related to the subject of risk assessment is the use of benefit-cost analysis in setting priorities among policies. Basically, benefit-cost analysis, as the name suggests, involves the weighing of the costs and benefits of different activities. Designed to accomplish a certain objective, benefit-cost analysis might be used, for example, to determine which among competing methods of pollution control will accomplish the same objective at a lower cost. Benefit-cost analysis is also used to measure and compose the costs and benefits associated with a given activity. Benefit-cost analysis may be applied in the arena of policy making to evaluate either newly proposed regulations or existing policies. The goal is to help target the most efficient distribution of resources to accomplish a certain task.

The implications that benefit-cost analysis has on environmental policy making are very serious, especially in relation to risk assessment. As stated, most environmental policy analysts agree that a zero pollution level is impossible to attain. The abatement cost attributed to the first 50 to 75 percent of a given pollutant may be considered fairly reasonable. However, as we approach zero tolerance of a given pollutant, the cost of further pollution reduction rises dramatically. This is the economic concept of marginal utility. Marginal utility dictates that at a certain level, the costs begin to outweigh the benefits of an action. At this time, resources will be shifted to other activities in which resources will result in greater benefits and less costs.

Examples of benefit-cost analyses may be unsettling, especially where a monetary value is placed on human life. In a study conducted in 1987, 132 EPA regulatory decisions, concerning the carcinogenic potential of different chemicals made from 1976 to 1985 were compared. Those chemicals found to have an individual cancer risk greater than 4 chances in 1,000 were regulated. Those chemicals found to have an individual cancer risk of less than 1 in 1 million were not regulated (with one exception). Between these two levels, cost-effectiveness was used as the deciding factor. In economic terms, chemicals were regulated if the cost per life saved was less than $2 million; if the cost exceeded $2 million, the chemical was not regulated.[20]

Another study conducted in 1994 by the U.S. Office of Management and Budget, which calculated simple risk assessment ratios, found that the cost of avoiding one human fatality (basically zero exposure) in relation to compliance with the EPA regulation on dichloropropane in drinking water was $653 million. The figure jumps to just over $92 billion in the case of the chemical atrazine. It is amounts such as these that beg the question of whether resources should be put to use in areas that seem to pose greater threats to a greater percentage of the public, or should chemicals readily identifiable as toxic hazards be pursued over those substances whose environmental effects are mired in uncertainty.

It is wrong, however, to assume that cost-benefit analysis is predisposed to an anti-environmental orientation. The reintroduction of wolves into a region in the northwest corner of Arizona was preceded by an extensive cost-benefit analysis in which maximum favor was given to the fears of area ranchers, who feared the effect of the wolves on their livestock. It was found that the environmental benefits of the reintroduction far outweighed the costs attributed to the detrimental effects the wolves might have on neighboring human populations. Similar cost-benefit studies were conducted in the mid-1970s to assess the probable benefits of removing lead from gasoline. The public health benefits were found to be much higher than the cost of removing the harmful pollutant.

These examples do lead us to question how a cost-benefit analysis may be performed when the value of certain benefits must be placed in quantifiable units. How does one place a value on the health of the land or on the psychological effects of breathing clean air? This is one of the problems of cost-benefit analysis. Another problem, related to the first, is the lack of information that policy makers have at their disposal to help place value on benefits and costs. Responses to these concerns include the argument that the use of cost-benefit analysis will help encourage objectivity among the bureaucracy in formulating and implementing regulations based on legislative statutes.

Every administration, from Reagan to the present, as well as congressional leadership has agreed that cost-benefit analysis should be utilized when considering policy alternatives. President Clinton's Executive Order 12866 reaffirmed the institutionalized use of the cost-benefit analysis to assess the economic impact of proposed regulations in an effort to help inform decision making. Similar executive orders were passed by both the Reagan and Bush administrations. Cost-benefit analysis will continue to play a powerful role in governmental decision making in all policy areas, including the environment.

The Role of Government

Although our dominant social paradigm plays an important role in the form and content of environmental policy, there are important differences in the approaches government takes to environmental regulations. These differences may be best understood as the orientation of a policy maker to the role of government (including the level of government activity, that is, national, state, or local) and the role and use of market forces in the implementation of environmental policy.

For purposes of analysis, it is useful to describe policy orientation toward the role of government as lying on a continuum. At one end there is no government involvement, that is, total free-market control, and, at the other end, total national government control over environmental policy. In between the complete free market approach and total national control are the various combinations of market forces and government controls (see Figure 3–1).

None of these policy orientations characterized American environmental policy until the mid-nineteenth century.[21] As we saw in our summary of the history of environmental policy in the United States, pollution was not perceived as a problem early in American history; nature was a force to be conquered without concern for environmental consequences. The establishment of Yellowstone National Park in 1872 is early evidence of the acceptance of a role for government in controlling the U.S. environment.

Today, for all practical purposes, much of international environmental management, notably management of ocean pollution, is essentially free-market man-

FIGURE 3–1

1———————2———————3———————4———————5

1. Free market.
2. Use of market forces with some government controls.
3. Government controls on the state and local level (which may or may not utilize market or market-like mechanisms).
4. Government controls developed on the national level and implemented on the state and local level.
5. Controls developed and implemented on the national level—total national control.

agement. But most countries are engaged to some degree in the management of the environment to prevent pollution.

Although it is not a popular position, those in the United States who advocate no role for government in environmental protection often use the argument that corporate self-interest provides the necessary environmental safeguards. The Reagan and Bush administrations, as we see in our discussion of energy, came close to a totally free-market approach to energy policy.

The second step on the continuum of the role of government and environmental policy is the utilization of market forces. As we see later, some environmental policies are designed to limit government involvement in implementing controls by using market mechanisms to produce desired outcomes. One way this has been done is through tax incentives or pollution charges. This category includes a number of quasimarket arrangements with varying degrees of governmental influence. For example, the EPA, through the use of a bubble concept (see Chapter 5), allowed manufacturing plants to determine their own mix of pollutants admitted into the atmosphere from a given plant. Although not a market mechanism, the bubble concept allows polluters to choose the areas within a plant on which to concentrate their pollution control efforts. This is in contrast to a regulatory scheme in which government regulators make those determinations.

Government intervention in the form of state and local control over environmental regulations, both in the formulation and implementation process, was the primary form of environmental regulation in the United States up to the early 1970s. In 1964 California was the first government in the United States to begin regulating automobile emissions. Solid waste management and land-use planning continue to be primarily a local government concern. In some other countries—for example, Canada—the national government's role is severely limited, leaving primary responsibility for pollution control with the provinces.

Beginning in the early 1970s, environmental regulations in the United States were formulated by the national government and implemented primarily by state and local governments. This pattern of regulatory control has been adopted by many other countries as well. Total national control over the formulation of environmental regulations and their implementation has only been attempted on a very limited basis in the United States, for example, in regulating nuclear power.

These descriptions of varying types of governmental control and the use of market forces in environmental regulations provide the framework for understanding differences in the types of environmental regulations that we discuss later. Clearly no correct formula is best in all circumstances. Combinations of national, state, and local control, and market forces may be used in different situations, and often different combinations work better in some cases than in others.

Approaches to Regulation

Our orientation toward the proper role of government in the free market colors our perception of what is good or bad environmental regulation. The common pool nature of environmental problems tells us that without some type of regulation or self-control we will, in pursuing our own interests, destroy common pool resources—the air, water, or land.

There are four general approaches to dealing with common pool problems, each of which to varying degrees relates to the role of government in environmental management as we discussed earlier. The first approach is essentially the free-market option, a reliance on self-interest and volunteerism with no government intervention to correct for common pool resource problems. Decades of human experience, as well as much current practice, tells us that volunteerism is not a reliable solution to common pool problems.

The second means of dealing with common pool problems is a "standards and enforcement" or "command and control" system of environmental regulation. Essentially, some governmental unit determines what the appropriate level of a given pollutant or activity is, sets the standards, and establishes a way to enforce these standards. This is the primary means of environmental regulation in the United States and includes permitting, setting standards for discharges (and other types of rule making), and requiring that information on discharges be reported. In addition, in the United States pollution is regulated by banning certain activities, zoning to isolate undesirable activities, and, when necessary, adjudication.

There have been a number of criticisms of the command and control system of environmental regulation including the following: (1) uniform national standards ignore varying local conditions; (2) national standards may or may not provide an incentive to find the least costly method of pollution control; (3) once a standard is set, there is no incentive for pollution discharges less than the established amount; and (4) standards limit the flexibility that might allow polluters to reduce the total amount of emissions at the lowest cost.

In defense of the command and control system of regulation, it has been argued that: (1) a uniform standard produces equity in implementation, since all polluters are, theoretically, treated alike; (2) it is less expensive to administer because time and energy are not necessary to investigate individual cases; and (3) it is less susceptible to political influence and manipulation.

A third approach to dealing with common pool problems, and an alternative often suggested to command and control strategies, is the use of taxes or effluent charges or some other type of monetary measure that would provide polluters with an incentive to find the most cost-efficient means of limiting their pollution. As an example of how an effluent charge might work, imagine a lake surrounded by three manufacturing plants. All of the plants wish to discharge their waste into the lake.

Assuming none of the potential discharges was toxic, the government could estimate the total amount of discharge that could be accepted and biologically
processed by the lake without causing sustained damage. For example, let's set that
amount at 3 million gallons a day. Under these circumstances, each of the manufacturing plants might be given a permit to discharge 1 million gallons a day into the
lake with the stipulation that for every additional gallon of discharge the company
would be charged a fee. If the fee was high enough, this would theoretically prevent
any of the plants from discharging above the limit that would damage the lake. On
the other hand, if the fee was too low, the plants might find little incentive to hold
discharge below the limit and merely pay the tax. The primary benefit of an effluent
tax regulatory system would be that the polluter—the manufacturer in this example—would have an incentive to find the least costly way within the plant to limit
discharges. In addition, if the effluent tax started at a relatively low rate on the first
unit of pollution and then gradually increased to a high rate on units of pollution
above a standard acceptable for the lake, the polluter would then have an incentive
to reduce discharges even further than the acceptable standard.

Finally, another way to deal with the common pool problem is through establishing property rights in the commons. The essential idea here is to divide the commons, giving individuals a stake in the appropriate use and management of their
now private resources. In short, it would no longer be common property. This is obviously not possible for many common pool resources such as air, but it is frequently advanced as a means of managing forests. A *Wall Street Journal* editorial
on private ownership of U.S. forests illustrates this perspective: "[I]t would be in
the timber companies' natural interest to properly harvest, reseed and nourish the
lands they manage."[22] Some argue, however, that the drive for short-term profits to
satisfy stockholders, pay off bonds used to finance corporate acquisitions, or to en-
hance the careers of upwardly mobile executives outweigh long-term profit and loss
considerations. Some ecologists argue, moreover, that we need to see a parcel of
forest as part of a larger ecosystem. Managing the parcel without regard to the
larger system could result in a substantial decline in the sustainability of the ecosystem as a whole (which would affect the health of parcels owned by others).

Related to the privatization of common pool resources is the idea of creating
private enforceable rights to a clean environment. In common law, the "nuisance"
doctrine has been available to varying degrees when the activities of one individual
cause harm or damage to another. For example, if your neighbor decided to put a
hog farm in his backyard, which resulted in a stench that caused you personal dis-
comfort and reduced your property value, you might have a cause of action under
the nuisance doctrine. In modern environmental law, nuisance suits have been replaced by regulations that limit such activity, such as agricultural zoning regulations. Other regulations, such as the Clean Water Act, have provisions that allow
individuals to sue polluters or force EPA to sue for compliance with existing
regulations.

It would be possible to establish enforceable rights to clean air and water
whereby citizens might use the courts to protect themselves for many infringements
upon those rights. One potential problem with this approach is that an individual
might have little incentive to pursue an action on his or her own. The cost of a lawsuit is high, and an individual, when calculating personal cost and benefits, may
find the expense is not worth it. In such situations, the common legal remedy is the

class action suit wherein a group of individuals, each of whose personal injuries may be relatively small, can represent a whole class of persons that have been damaged. Unfortunately, for a variety of reasons, the federal courts, and many state courts, have procedural requirements that make the bringing of such suits very expensive.[23] Although subsequent chapters will summarize specific environmental statutes here, we will survey the fundamentals of environmental law as they relate to regulations.

FUNDAMENTALS OF ENVIRONMENTAL LAW

The legal foundation for environmental, as well as other federal, law is found within Article I, Section 8 of the U.S. Constitution. It is this provision of the Constitution that reserves for the federal government the power to regulate interstate commerce. Known as the Commerce Clause, this provision was originally intended to prevent individual states from undertaking policies intended to have adverse effects on other states within the union. Over the past 200 or so years, the clause has been interpreted in ways which broaden its scope significantly.

Environmental law, as with all other types of law, is primarily concerned with the allocation of resources. Essentially, environmental protection boils down to two actions: preventing the dispersement of pollution into the natural environment, and preventing the damage and depletion of natural resources. In order to address these two feats, a reallocation of resources, or a limit on distribution of resources, is required.

Based on the principles of English common law, the American justice system is based on the idea of private property preeminence, as well as an adversarial-based justice system. Traditionally, the concept of private property preeminence provides the property owner with the right to pollute his or her land as much as he or she wishes, as long as the pollution does not carry over onto another's private property. In resource use situations, common law private property rights allow the individual to use whatever resources are on the land to whatever extent desired. Hence the owner of land, under the common law, may pump water from the land regardless of the impact such pumping has on adjacent landowners. The primary principle at work here is the protection of each individual property owners' rights. Most environmental protection measures seek to limit the absolute rights of private property owners.

The second principle of English common law, on which our own legal system is based, is the adversarial justice system. This system, in contrast to the inquisitional systems commonly found in Europe, requires that the two parties involved in legal dispute bring their own supporting information to the court, rather than the court conducting its own investigation. In many cases environmental litigation involves more than two parties whose rights are not clearly defined. Hence, critics argue, our legal system is fundamentally ill-equipped to address the intricacies of environmental protection questions. The regulatory process is an attempt to correct some of the primary failings of the English common law.

In order to understand environmental law, it is important to remember that most environmental statutes require the executive branch to develop regulations. Consequently, the courts have primarily been concerned with the development and enforcement of environmental regulations. And in our system, court-made law is just as real and enforceable as laws made by legislatures.

The foundations of environmental law and regulation in the United States as created by legislators, require the presence of three basic mechanisms:

1. established legislative policies and directives
2. prescribed methods of executing these policies and directives.
3. prescribed methods of resolving disputes that arise from the execution of policies and directives.

The first of these mechanisms is the duty of the Congress to pass laws. The second involves the power of the executive to execute these laws through the formulation and implementation of regulations. The third mechanism is the oversight of this regulatory process to ensure that the executive is carrying out their legislative mandate in proper accordance with the relevant statute.

Of most concern to students of the environment are the last two mechanisms. The formulation and implementation of regulations is primarily governed by the Administrative Procedures Act (APA). This act sets forth the framework for creating and implementing regulations, as well as other rule-making capabilities. The laws that pertain to, and govern, administration and bureaucratic government actions are referred to as administrative law. The process that resolves the regulatory disputes of executive agencies is referred to as judicial review.

Before the courts will conduct a judicial review of a regulation, the plaintiff must first exhaust all administrative remedies available that the court deems appropriate. This procedure is known as the "Exhaustive Doctrine," and although there are some exceptions, it requires that polluters, or others contesting regulations, seek every available avenue of appeal within the administrative agency before going to court. The Exhaustive Doctrine is not universal; what is required of the parties is usually defined within the relevant statute.

The next step in the adjudication process is judicial review. Judicial review carries with it numerous limitations that define which cases the court will and will not hear. Below are some of the primary qualifiers that decide who shall be heard by the court.

The scope of review concerns which parts of the relevant administrative actions the court will address. Some statutes may have provisions that define their specific scope of review, though scope may also be found in similar statues, as well as prior court findings.

Standards of review define the degree of scrutiny that the court may take in examining a challenged agency action. Again, this may be defined within the relevant statute. Other sources for determining the standard of review include the APA and prior court rulings. More often than not, courts defer to agency discretion or expertise in adjudicating challenges to agency actions. However, the exceptions to this include agency actions that are clearly without legal foundation, actions that are arbitrary and capricious, and actions that are not supported by substantive evidence.

One of the most important limitations on judicial review is judicial standing. In a nutshell, judicial standing concerns who can and cannot bring a suit before the court for judicial review. The plaintiff must satisfy two requirements to qualify for standing. First, they must prove a concrete interest in the matter before the court. Based on previous court cases involving environmental protection, this is taken to mean that the plaintiff must prove imminent injury in fact (that is, that they were personally injured by the action in question). Second, the court must be able to remedy the situation in some way.

The issue of standing in relation to environmental protection may be seen in the 1970 case *Sierra Club v. Morton* in which plaintiffs contested a decision by the U.S. Forest Service to grant the Disney Corporation the right to build a resort in Mineral King Valley in the Sierra Nevada Mountain region of California. The court denied the plaintiffs standing because they could not show imminent injury in fact. The Sierra Club was arguing against the development based on the organization's role as a public interest group dedicated to the long-term preservation of the environment, rather than as individual hikers whose *individual* and *personal* experience would be ruined by the development. Court cases that followed *Sierra Club v. Morton* fleshed out the requirements of standing in environmentally focused issues. (See *Lujan v. National Wildlife Federation* 1990 and *Lujan v. Defenders of Wildlife* 1992) In recent years, standing for plaintiffs arguing for environmental protection has been much easier to obtain.

The utility of environmental litigation as a tool in the regulatory process is not to be underestimated. As environmental groups have garnered greater success in challenging administrative decisions, agencies have begun to follow a much more cautious route in their formulation and implementation of regulations. As such, the final recommendations are often the result of more thorough interaction with environmental interest groups. As we shall see in the next chapter, the power wielded by interest groups plays a major part in the regulatory process.

SUMMARY

Clearly, not all regulatory systems are created equal. Different regulatory systems affect different interests or groups in different ways. The type of regulatory system adopted to deal with environmental problems depends, to a great extent, on the influence of affected interests on the policy-making process. In this chapter we have seen some of the problems associated with developing environmental regulations. Science is not always exact (or as we often say, "hard"); hence, determining acceptable levels of risk is difficult. In addition, the need for and type of regulation, including appropriate levels of market control, are matters for political debate. The type of regulation developed for an environmental problem and the interests that are benefited by the regulation are, to a large extent, determined by the ability of participants to exercise influence on the policy-making process. Many of what we call the paradoxes of environmental policy are the result of political outcomes (which become regulations) that are not well-suited for dealing with an environmental problem. This is because political actors can influence the process in ways that produce policies that are to their benefit, but may not be the most environmentally desirable. The ability to exercise influence on the policy-making process is the subject of the next chapter.

NOTES

1. George J. Stigler, "The Theory of Economic Regulation," *The Bell Journal of Economics and Management Science,* 2 (1) (Spring 1971), pp. 3–21.
2. See James Q. Wilson, "The Politics of Regulation," in *Social Responsibility and the Business Predicament* (Washington, D.C.: Brookings Institution, 1974), pp. 135–168.
3. Ronald Brickman, Sheila Jasanoff, and Thomas Ilgen, *Controlling Chemicals: Politics of Regulation in Europe and the United States* (Ithaca, NY: Cornell University Press, 1985), p. 41.
4. Ibid., p. 212.
5. Larry D. Silver, "The Common Law of Environmental Risk and Some Recent Applications," *Harvard Environmental Law Review,* 10 (61) (1986), p. 96.
6. Chris G. Whipple, "Fundamentals of Risk Assessment," *Environmental Law Reporter* 16 (August 1986), pp. 10192–10193.
7. U.S. Environmental Protection Agency, Office of Policy, Planning and Evaluation, Office of Policy Analysis, *Unfinished Business: A Comparative Assessment of Environmental Problems. Volume I. Overview.* February, 1987.
8. 448 U.S. 607, 100 S.Ct. 2844, 65 L.E.2nd 1010 (1980).
9. See Silver, "The Common Law of Environmental Risk and Some Recent Applications."
10. Walter A. Rosenbaum, *Environmental Politics and Policy,* 3rd ed., (Washington, D.C.: Congressional Quarterly Press, 1995), p. 161.
11. Whipple, "Fundamentals of Risk Assessment," p. 10191.
12. "High Fuel Mileage Requirement for Autos Is Tragic Mistake, Researchers Report," *Houston Chronicle,* March 27, 1988, p. 14, sec. 1.
13. Cited in David J. Hanson, "Little Serious Health Damage Linked to Waste Sites," *Chemical and Engineering News 63* (March 25, 1985), p. 29. This research was funded, incidentally, by a consortium that included the Chemical Manufacturers Association, U.S. Chamber of Commerce, National Agricultural Chemicals Association, National Association of Printing Ink Manufacturers, and the National Paint and Coatings Association. Ibid., p. 30.
14. "Birth Defects Up Near Waste Unit," *European Chemical News,* 43 (October 15, 1984), p. 27.
15. Cited in Brickman, Jasanoff, and Ilgen, *Controlling Chemicals: Politics of Regulation in Europe and the United States,* p. 190.
16. Samuel S. Epstein, *The Politics of Cancer,* rev. ed. (New York: Anchor Press, 1981), p. 18.
17. Brickman, Jasanoff, and Ilgen, *Controlling Chemicals: Politics of Regulation in Europe and the United States,* p. 191.
18. See Whipple, "Fundamentals of Risk Assessment."
19. A survey of the U.S. public undertaken in 1986 found that 72 percent felt that science and technology will do more good than harm in the future. "Living Dangerously," *U.S. News and World Report,* May 19, 1986, p. 19.
20. U.S. Environmental Protection Agency, Office of Policy, Planning and Evaluation, Office of Policy Analysis. *Unfinished Business: A Comparative Assessment of Environmental Problems. Volume I. Overview.* February, 1987.
21. One could argue that American environmental policy until the mid-nineteenth century was one of a free-market approach. My point here is that there was no governmental policy per se.
22. "Burning Yellowstone," *Wall Street Journal,* August 30, 1988, p. 18.
23. Zachary A. Smith, "Class Action: State Notification Requirements After Eisen," *Western State University Law Review,* 8 (1) (Fall 1980), pp. 1–20.

4

The Political
and Institutional Setting

THE INSTITUTIONAL SETTING

Formal Institutions

The Judicial System

Environmental battles are often fought in the courts. This is particularly true of interest groups lacking the resources necessary to fight in more traditional arenas, such as legislative bodies. But this is also true of regulated industries when they challenge regulations. As we have seen, there are a number of longstanding common law judicial remedies for those concerned with the environment, notably the public nuisance doctrine. But since the early 1970s, the most common legal challenge used by *environmental* organizations has been to enforce the environmental impact statement requirements of the National Environmental Policy Act (NEPA). Most often, environmental impact statements are challenged on the grounds that they do not sufficiently assess environmental impacts or their alternatives.

As we see in Part Two, a number of environmental statutes, notably the National Environmental Policy Act and the Clean Water Act, have provided environmentalists with opportunities to use the judicial branch of government to enforce environmental laws. Early in the history of the contemporary environmental movement, access to court systems was limited somewhat by questions of legal standing (discussed in the previous chapter). Standing means a party has a right to represent an interest in court. For example, to bring a lawsuit, a person or organization must show (1) that it suffered an injury and (2) that the injury can be remedied. Standing has not been a major obstacle to use of the judicial system by environmentalists since the early 1970s, when the Supreme Court began taking a somewhat more liberal view of standing in environmental cases.[1]

The use of the courts in environmental matters and the benefit to be derived from pursuing a court action vary depending on the interests involved. For instance, if a lengthy lawsuit will allow the maintenance of the status quo (such as continuing to pollute), then clearly the polluting party is advantaged by pursuing its interest in the courts at length. Thus the utility of initiating court action will vary depending on a group's objectives and its available resources.

There are a number of considerations that make the use of the judicial system an attractive alternative—considerations that are different from those considered in dealing with the other branches of government. For example, there is the question of time. Lawsuits take time. Relatively new interest groups might be concerned with simple organizational maintenance and hence would avoid undertaking commitments of resources to lawsuits when the benefits to be achieved are long term and uncertain. Moreover, groups with few monetary resources would avoid lawsuits for fear of not being able to see them through to their conclusion. The decision by an interest group to pursue its environmental policy goals through the judicial system then will be influenced by a number of variables. These include the group's relative strength in other stages of the policy-making process, the desirability of seeking a short- or long-term solution to the problem, and the nature of the dispute. For example, if the court is the only currently feasible forum, this may play a part in the decision of group leaders to use the courts.

Also, the decision by environmental organizations to use the courts may be affected by which court has jurisdiction over a case. The courts in some states are much less likely to find in favor of environmental interests than are the courts of other states. On the federal level, Lettie Wenner, an expert on environmental litigation, found that federal courts in the Northeast, Midwest, and on the West Coast have, since the 1970s, been favorably disposed toward environmental litigants, whereas federal courts in the Southeast, Southwest, and Rocky Mountains have been more likely to favor economic and development interests.[2]

The Legislative Branch

Generally, environmental groups often find legal systems useful in pursuing their policy interests. This is partly because some environmental statutes provide for judicial remedies. Perhaps more importantly, environmental organizations traditionally have lacked the political resources useful for exercising influence in the legislative or executive branches of government.

It is important to remember that legislatures are, for the most part, decentralized in their organization and operation. In the U.S. Congress, for example, the major work is done by committees and subcommittees. As we see, decentralization has a number of effects on the policy-making process. The committee system and the bicameral nature of legislatures in all the states except Nebraska make it much more difficult to pass legislation than to block it. Consequently, those interests that are benefited by the status quo have an advantage in the policy-making process in the United States. Because there are so many different points in the legislative process where a bill can be defeated, those attempting to influence legislation must follow it closely through each stage. Some groups have the resources to closely monitor legislation by attending hearings, or to influence discussion by providing research, whereas other groups do not.

One of the most important aspects to consider when examining the policy-making process in legislatures is that legislators are, in large part, motivated by a desire for reelection.[3] Although there are a number of different demands on the attention of a legislator and a variety of incentives not directly related to reelection that are important to legislators, most analysts have concluded reelection is a primary motive for legislative behavior. Thus legislators are likely to be influenced by the forces that impact their ability to be reelected.

The late Jesse Unruh, who was speaker of the California Assembly (1961–1969) and state treasurer (1974–1987), once remarked, "[M]oney is the mother's milk of politics."[4] In practical terms, this means money is necessary for reelection and that groups with the money to support politicians in their bid for reelection are most likely to have influence in the legislative process. Although it is difficult to show a direct causal relationship between contributions and influence, there is widespread agreement that campaign contributions buy access to the legislative policy-making process. Access is a very valuable commodity. Because of limitations on a legislator's time, and given the large number of issues a legislator must address, access provides a crucial opportunity for influence.

Although money is important, a large membership can be a source of influence as well. Interest groups with a large and motivated membership are likely to be more influential in the legislative policy-making process than groups without these resources. Members vote, campaign, and can be enlisted to attend hearings.

The Executive Branch

The executive branch of government on the federal level is responsible for administering federal environmental regulations through a variety of federal agencies. The Environmental Protection Agency (EPA) is perhaps the most important regulatory agency concerned with environmental matters. The EPA was established in 1970 through a reorganization that consolidated pollution regulatory activities from a variety of different departments into a single agency. The EPA is responsible for a wide variety of environmental regulations, including the Clean Air Act, the Clean Water Act, the Toxic Substances Control Act, the Safe Drinking Water Act, the Resource Conservation Recovery Act, and the Federal Insecticide, Fungicide and Rodenticide Act.

Another federal agency involved in environmental matters is the Interior Department. Within the Interior Department are the Bureau of Land Management, the National Park Service, the U.S. Fish and Wildlife Service, and the Office of Surface Mining. Additionally, the U. S. Department of Agriculture is an agency involved with environmental policy making. Both the U.S. Forest Service and the Soil and Conservation Service are located in the Department of Agriculture. Finally, the Department of Energy includes the Federal Energy Regulatory Commission (FERC) and deals with various nuclear, fossil fuel, and environmental issues.

Informal Institutions

The resources that help provide access to the chief executive of a governmental body are similar to those resources needed by groups working with the legislative branch, such as a large or motivated membership or any resources conducive to providing electoral support. The needs of career bureaucrats, the individuals primarily responsible for the implementation of policy, are, however, somewhat different than those of the chief executive or political appointees. Public administrators, particularly those working in state or local governments with little support staff, have limited resources for acquiring information. Interest groups often provide that information.

Interest Groups-Support Networks

Administrators also need political support from interest groups. They are often concerned with maintaining organizational autonomy and integrity. This is accomplished, among other ways, by developing networks of support within the legislature and among the public. Public support is most often cultivated among the individuals or groups in the public that the administrative organization serves. It is often developed by the provision of a particular service. We might expect, therefore, administrative organizations to be most responsive to groups that are the beneficiaries of whatever service or function the organization performs, and that these groups will have more access and influence with bureaucrats than other groups. To illustrate, the National Park Service enjoys the support of the National Parks and Recreation Association and other supporters of the National Park System during its budget hearings. In return these organizations enjoy increased access to the agency and prompt responses to their inquiries.

What develops from these informal support systems can be referred to as an "iron triangle" or "subgovernment." Here, interest groups, bureaucrats, and legislators become wedded in a sometimes useful, sometimes destructive, triangle of support and need. Legislators need the bureaucrats to implement their policies and are rewarded for this with funding. In turn, the bureaucrats provide electoral support by making interest groups happy and will also take the fall if policies do not work out. The interest groups need the bureaucrats to provide them with services, so they support the bureaucracies in front of legislators. The cycle continues where one group depends on the others for support, funds, votes, or work but also provides these things to the others.

A concrete example of this can be found in what has been deemed the "military-industrial complex." Here, industry helps the military (bureaucracy) by lobbying Congress for more money for research, development, and, of course, new weapons produced by industry. The military rewards industry for their political support by also requesting more funds and weapons, which are bought from the profiting industry. This support network continues with a "revolving door" where retired military officials get jobs in the weapons industry for their inside track to the military's and Congress's ear. Congress provides more and more funding for more and more weapons because they get the political support of the massive military and weapons industry lobby.

Similarly, subgovernments form that control specific segments of public policy. Subgovernments often shy from the otherwise bright lights of mainstream politics and media attention. They require an industry dominated by a few firms that grow rich with government help through subsidies, price supports, tax breaks, government contracts, public land, bailouts, or protective tariffs.

Members of subgovernments are not democratically elected, yet they rely on the same "pluralism" formal government offices do. They come from one industry's corporate and trade association executives; their lawyers, lobbyists, and publicists; its trade papers' journalists; congressional subcommittee members and staff; and the relevant agency's employees. Examples abound and include the mining industry "donating" campaign support and lobbying on behalf of regulators to continue to receive public lands and the underlying minerals for free. The Forest Service has a long tradition of selling lumber at a loss to keep the timber industry/lobby happy. ADM, an agribusiness giant, gave former President Bush (technically the Republican Party) $652,000 in 1988 and the next year got a $3.4 billion ethanol subsidy.[5] Perhaps it is in the "public interest" to give tax dollars to corporations to keep them happy so they will spur the economy and provide employment. Maybe subsidies taken from middle-class taxpayers and given to corporate shareholders and executives are necessary to keep America running. Whether or not it is good or bad public policy, this is how many subgovernments operate and how our pluralist democracy operates in certain cases.

Environmental Interest Players

There are a variety of types of environmental interest groups. Each will have its own unique membership, motives, and resources. For example, there may be a group of *consumers or citizens* who band together to protect their favorite fishing hole from development or from an industrial site being built near their residences. These groups are usually less well funded and organized, but often contain large numbers, so if they are stirred to unusually high motivation they can be extremely effective.

Then there are *business or trade union* groups that only care about their narrow work environments, success, and profits. Often the environment is a tool for them to provide jobs, profits, and taxes. While many such groups are increasingly sensitive to their environmental public relations image, their core motivations stay the same, regardless of the advertisements they purchase to cloak them.

There are also NPOs or NGOs (nonprofit or nongovernmental organizations) established by concerned scientists, journalists, or former government employees to protect more diffuse and intangible interests such as ecosystem services, the "rights" of organisms other than humans or future generations of them. Funding can be a problem with these groups, too, especially if the experts running them alienate a more diverse public than may be otherwise willing to support their cause.

The divergent motives and viewpoints on the environment of these groups can make discourse, let alone compromise, difficult. Further, the form of pluralist, interest group democracy we utilize pushes these groups to take the stances they do. Together, though, business, personal, or nonprofit type interest groups heavily influence public policy. We now turn to how they can achieve or block the implementation of that policy.

Implementation

An important resource for influence in the administrative process is familiarity with the implementation process and the informational needs of the organization. Paul Culhane, in a study of interest group influence in the Forest Service and Bureau of Land Management, found that "[Forest Service administrators] expected public participation to be professional; that is, they expected comments and public participation forums to present new information about the subject under consideration that they had overlooked."[6] Those participants in implementation that have backgrounds and training similar to organizational members will be advantaged in interaction with the organization, as opposed to participants that do not have such experience.

Implementation is a long-term process. Battles won today in the legislature may be lost in the implementation process if mandates are ignored or misinterpreted. Consequently, to influence the implementation process it is necessary to have the resources to monitor the process on a continuous and long-term basis. This is particularly important in environmental policy where in many areas once the environmental side loses the battle it has lost the war. Accordingly, groups lacking the resources to send well-prepared spokespersons to agency hearings and to follow up agency action are disadvantaged.

In summary, resources most useful for influencing the implementation stages of the policy-making process are the traditional resources of money, political support, and information and expertise that are useful to promote interaction with bureaucrats. Finally, these resources must be adequate and channeled in such a way that groups can stay involved in the implementation process for the long haul.

Interest Groups in the Policy-Making Process

Although different groups may choose to exercise their influence at different stages of the policy-making process, it is clear in all cases that monetary resources are very beneficial either for initiation or follow-through of a group's policy goals. Given the inherent advantages that private-economic interest groups have in fundraising (discussed later), it should not be surprising to find that in all stages of the policy-making process, these groups have a certain advantage. This is not to suggest, of course, that private-economic interest groups always win out in environmental battles with public-noneconomic interest groups. However, it is clear that in policy formation they start with an advantage. As we see next, the policy process is not only driven by the concerns that have been detailed in this section. There are numerous examples in American history where, because of the volatile or intense nature of a policy debate, the incentives that traditionally operate on policy makers have, so to speak, gone out the window. Indeed, much of the major U.S. environmental legislation that was passed in the early 1970s provides examples of how the status quo and traditional incremental forms of influence can give way in the face of widespread public support for environmental regulations. Nevertheless, in the day-to-day operation of government, nonincremental change is the exception rather than the rule.

INSTITUTIONAL BIASES

Incrementalism

It is widely accepted among scholars of the American policy process that policy is made incrementally. Incremental theory, or simply incrementalism, may be summarized in the following manner:

1. Only some of the possible alternatives for dealing with a problem are considered by the decision maker. Either by virtue of limitations on information, ability, time, or because of the desire to achieve a consensus, a comprehensive evaluation of all alternatives is not undertaken.
2. The alternatives considered and the option ultimately selected will differ only slightly or incrementally from existing policy.
3. Only a limited number of consequences for each alternative are evaluated.
4. The problem being evaluated is continually redefined with adjustments being made to make the problem more manageable.[7]

There are practical and political reasons why policy is made incrementally in the United States. Practically, it would be impossible to consider all the numerous alternatives to a decision and the consequences of each alternative. Given the nature of pluralism, the numerous parties that are involved in the policy-making process, and the inherent limits on human ability to comprehensively analyze all the alternatives and the ramifications of policy options, it may be that incremental decision making is inevitable. Given limited capacity and information, it makes sense to simplify decision making to facilitate some kind of action. In political terms, incrementalism makes sense because it allows participants in the battle over policy in a given area the advantage of being able to work from past policy agreements and shared assumptions. Since politics inherently involves trade-offs, bargaining, and compromise, we should not be surprised to find decisions are often made in relatively small increments that do not differ greatly from past decisions. It is easier to reach agreement on matters when the modifications being discussed in a given policy vary only slightly from prior agreements.

Whether incrementalism is inevitable or desirable, it is a fact that many environmental policy decisions are made on an incremental basis. To cite one example, which we discuss in more detail later, the national debate on the appropriate means of protecting water quality has always centered on evaluation of existing standards, procedures, and means of enforcement. Rarely have federal policy makers seriously considered simply eliminating the entire "standards and enforcement" approach to water quality and substituting, for example, some kind of market-incentive mechanism. Incrementalism means that new, unique, or seemingly radical policy alternatives are rarely, if ever, given serious consideration.

The incremental nature of the policy-making process in the United States has important consequences for environmental policy. First, policies are rarely comprehensive in the sense that they thoroughly evaluate, question, and analyze all the possible options available to decision makers. During the policy process, it is likely to be assumed that past decisions and policies were fundamentally correct and, if anything, may only need fine-tuning. Given the interrelated and interdependent nature of many environmental problems, the incremental approach increases the likelihood that a solution will address only part of the problem. Second, the incremental nature of the policy-making process virtually assures that the established relationships and alliances, which enabled programs to develop, remain and guide subsequent policy adjustments.

In many policy areas, the attributes of incrementalism give stability to the process. Although stability is clearly a benefit for political systems, at times it may be necessary to take quick and decisive action inconsistent with past policy decisions. As we see later, sometimes the system has been able to respond quickly to an environmental emergency. Unfortunately, however, most of the time constraints inherent in the policy-formation system, including incrementalism, prevent the development of policy to address short- and long-term problems.

Decentralization

Policy making and implementation in the United States are decentralized. Many policy decisions are made at the state and local level. Within governments, at all levels, decision making and influence are divided up among committees, commissions, boards, and various executive branches.

For example, environmental regulatory standards are established by the federal government and enforced by state and local governments according to federal regulations. This can make management of environmental programs problematic.

Decentralization brings with it certain challenges. For example, David Brian Robertson and Dennis R. Judd have traced the development of political conflicts over the establishment of a national environmental policy within a federal structure. They point out that state and local governments charged with enforcement of federal regulations face many obstacles, including the following: (1) limited resources to carry out legislative mandates (especially since the 1980s when federal grants-in-aid for pollution control were reduced); (2) the need for cooperation among various state and local agencies that deal with such diverse areas as highways, land use, natural resources, and economic development—all of which have environmental impacts; (3) direct economic dependence on local industries to be regulated; and (4) interstate cooperation on environmental problems that cross state boundaries.[8]

In a variety of ways the decentralized nature of policy formation affects which groups will be successful in pursuing their policy goals. Decentralization helps or hurts some organizations and their interests. For example, it is helpful to those with influence in a state legislature, but who do not have influence in the U.S. Congress.

Short-Term Bias

If given a choice between two policy options that will both accomplish the same goals over the same period of time, rational political actors will select the option with the lowest short-term cost. To illustrate, imagine you are a congressperson considering two competing bills designed to deal with the problem of acid rain. The first bill, which we will call the Anderson bill, is estimated to cost approximately $5 billion a year for each of the first 5 years and then $25 billion for each of the next 20 years. The total cost of the Anderson bill is $525 billion. The competing bill, which we will call the Jones bill, has an initial cost of $25 billion for each of the first 5 years with subsequent costs of $5 billion for each of the following 20 years. The total cost of the Jones bill over the 25-year life of the program is estimated at $225 billion. Which bill would you support?

Although such a decision might seem relatively easy, if you were a member of Congress faced with a decision between these two policy actions, the rational and the logical choice for society may not be the rational choice for you. Election cycles, those two-, four-, or six-year periods in which politicians must run for reelection, require that politicians be responsive to constituent demands in the short term. When deciding between two competing programs, one with low short-term costs and high long-term costs and another with high short-term costs and low long-term costs, it is easier for politicians to select the program that is less costly over the short term. The average voter may not follow particular votes closely, but voters are sensitive to tax increases. The electoral cycle and the pressures of reelection do not always function to push policy makers toward policy options that are attractive only in the short term, but, as we see in Part Two, this has often been the case in environmental policy.

Related to the short-term bias of the policy-making process is the tendency of both policy makers and regular citizens to discount the future in their calculations of current options. In individual behavior this is evidenced by those who smoke cigarettes or purchase on credit, to give only two examples. In the policy-making process this results in decisions that defer costs into the future or assume that technological advances or other changes will mitigate any undesired future consequences of decisions made today. Hence the short-term bias in the system is driven not only by the politicians' attention to the electoral cycle but also by shared cultural assumptions about a society's and the scientific community's ability to cope with future problems.

Ideological Bias

Throughout most of America's history, an ideological bias in the system has favored growth and development, an important part of our dominant social paradigm. Assumptions that are considered normal in a capitalist system about production and consumption may or may not be consistent with the rational stewardship of natural resources and the environment. Without passing judgment on the appropriateness or necessity of such assumptions, it is important to remember that an orientation toward growth and development underlies much of the policy-making process in the United States.

For example, when communities plan for future development, rarely is zero growth a serious option. Instead, the question is the acceptable percentage of growth. But for any community, and ultimately for the planet, there has to come a time when the development of new housing tracts on agricultural land, for instance, comes to a halt, thereby limiting growth significantly. This is rarely one of the seriously considered options. The same orientation was evident in energy planning through the 1950s and 1960s. In making their predictions for demand, utilities frequently employed linear projections based on past and current usage and ignored variables that might affect future demand. During the same period, many municipalities employed the same type of projections in their planning for future water resource needs.

Politicians have a number of incentives to heed the call for increased growth. For one, the businesspeople who make up the local chamber of commerce, who want to sell more newspapers, cars, or whatever the product or service, naturally see an expanding market as directly related to their future well-being. These local businesspeople are also the people who are most often in contact with elected officials, who make campaign contributions, and share similar backgrounds. Further, they are most likely to interact socially and officially, formally and informally, with elected officials. Labor unions and, to a certain extent, representatives of minority groups, are also often proponents of economic expansion. Both groups understandably perceive economic growth as the way to provide additional employment. It should not be surprising, therefore, to find that many policy makers share an orientation toward expanding production, increasing development, and expanding economic opportunity.

Finally, there's strong evidence throughout the twentieth century of an ideological bias toward increased energy consumption. Often it has been assumed that increased energy consumption is necessary for maintaining or expanding the country's gross national product and the overall quality of life. Although strong evidence indicates little relationship between prosperity and energy consumption,[9] as we see in Chapter 7 the debate over energy development has often been reduced simply to how we can produce more energy.

Private Nature of Public Policy Making

Most of what elected officials do escapes public attention. Although major issues may generate headlines, the details related to these issues are largely ignored by the public. Furthermore, though we may know how elected officials vote from roll call and recorded vote figures, we know much less about what motivates them to vote one way or the other. Many decisions are made outside of the public spotlight. Much new legislation and many refinements in existing legislation receive very little, if any, attention from anyone other than the parties directly involved in the legislation.

Considering the resource-raising advantages of private-economic interest groups and the resource and organizational disadvantages of public-noneconomic interest groups, these facts skew the less controversial or less visible decisions to the advantage of private-economic interests. It is estimated that in excess of 70 percent of the bills Congress votes on are not even contested by two parties or interests on opposite sides of the issue.[10]

Crisis and Reforms

Although policy for the most part is developed and redeveloped in an incremental fashion, the system does seem to respond reasonably well to a crisis or an emergency. The bargaining, compromise, and give-and-take that characterize the policy-making process during normal times can be suspended during times of crisis. A notable example is the Great Depression. During Franklin Roosevelt's first 100 days in office, the policy process was streamlined both by a sense of urgency and through the force of Roosevelt's personality. In more recent times, due largely to congressional fears that U.S. forces had been attacked in Vietnam, President Lyndon Johnson was able to secure swift passage of the Tonkin Gulf Resolution. More recently, in response to the terrorism tragedies of September 11, 2001, President Bush was able to create a new cabinet-level agency overnight. The new Office of Homeland Security was the first to be created since the Department of Veterans' Affairs in 1989. Congress gave the President unusual discretion and support with little debate. Clearly, under such circumstances things can and do get done more quickly and with much less compromise.

Similarly, we have every reason to believe the policy-making system will respond to urgent environmental problems perceived to require immediate action. The Three Mile Island nuclear reactor accident resulted in relatively swift change in the policies of the Nuclear Regulatory Commission. Much of the major environmental legislation passed in the early 1970s in the United States represented a significant departure from past environmental policies. This was due, in part, to a sudden frenzy of public support on myriad environmental issues. Not only were academics and authors proclaiming the end of civilization as we know it, but the first images of Earth from space gave us all an acute sense of smallness and finiteness. When Earth Day hit in 1970, followed by the Stockholm Conference in 1972, the momentum of the environmental movement was in full swing and could not be accommodated in the regular incremental fashion.

Although the system can and does react to crisis or emergency situations, most environmental problems do not present themselves as urgent. The discovery of the toxic dump in Love Canal, New York, and related health effects in that community surely added impetus to the passage of the Comprehensive Environmental Response, Compensation, and Liability Act, otherwise known as the Superfund, in 1980. Nevertheless, the Superfund, in its passage and undoubtedly in its implementation, has followed the incremental process that typifies the policy-formation process.

Many environmental problems, such as global warming and the greenhouse effect, the discovery of polluted groundwater, the depletion of fossil fuel resources, and the pollution of a river basin, progress slowly without noticeable or dramatic change from one month to the next. This slow progression is ideally suited to incremental decision making and also does not disrupt or challenge the short-term bias of elected policy makers or the ideological bias toward growth and development. In short, environmental problems often lend themselves to incremental solutions.

Unfortunately, the slow, cumulative nature of many environmental problems means these issues are not perceived as urgent by the public or by policy makers. Hydrologists and water resource managers, for example, may be concerned about declining groundwater levels and that farmers are ceasing to irrigate in parts of the Southwest, but to many in the public and to many policy makers, these are viewed as unfortunate yet isolated or unrelated incidents. And the news that another lake in Canada has been found to be devoid of life may spark concern among the public as well as policy makers, but such news is unlikely to provide the necessary incentive for effective action to deal with acid rain.

As we will read later, nonincremental policy options are available today that may provide long-term and inexpensive solutions to many environmental problems. These options may not be available in the future when it becomes politically feasible to act on environmental issues in a comprehensive manner. It may be that environmental policy in some policy areas is doomed to failure if the system is unable to respond appropriately or in time. However, as we have seen under FDR, Johnson, Nixon, and G. W. Bush, nonincremental change can occur under the right circumstances, notably either when the public or relevant interest groups almost unilaterally get behind an issue or in times of crisis.

THE POLITICAL SETTING

Pluralism

Although some scholars would disagree, for purposes of our discussion in this chapter we will assume that the United States is a pluralist democracy.[11] An assumption of pluralism is that public policy is determined, in large part, through the bargaining, compromise, and negotiating of various interest groups in society. Although group activity is not the only explanatory variable in determining public policy, according to most scholars who have studied the policy-making process it is a very important part. As V.O. Key wrote, "[A]t bottom, group interests are the animating forces in the political process; an understanding of American politics requires a knowledge of the chief interests and their stake in public policy."[12]

The notion that groups compete over the nature of public policy is as old as the republic. James Madison's analysis of interest groups (which he called "factions") in essay 10 of *The Federalist* remains, in the words of political scientist Jeffrey Berry, "the foundation of American political theory on interest groups."[13] Madison defined a faction as "a number of citizens, whether amounting to a majority or minority of the whole, who are united and actuated by some common impulse of passion, or of interest, adverse to the rights of other citizens, or to the permanent and aggregate interests of the community."[14] The tendency toward faction, according to Madison, was "in the nature of man" and would lead people, when possible, "much more disposed to vex and oppress each other than to co-operate for the common good."[15] Madison feared that a tyrannical faction would come to dominate others in society but felt a republic form of government (incorporating checks and balances), combined with the many and diverse interests competing with each other in a large country such as the United States, was good insurance against the dominance of one faction.[16]

The contemporary focus of study on interest groups was first emphasized by sociologist Arthur Bentley in *The Process of Government,* published in 1908.[17] Bentley argued that "there are no political phenomena except group phenomena" and that politics "reflects, represents, the underlying groups."[18]

Bentley's work appeared at a time when the study of government was oriented toward formal institutions; hence scholars were not quick to adopt a group approach to politics. During the 1920s and 1930s, several important works contributed to the development of pluralist theory. These were primarily case studies providing insights into interest group activity.[19] However, perhaps the biggest boost for pluralist theory was the publication of *The Governmental Process* by David Truman in 1951.[20] Group activity for Truman, particularly interest groups, had a significant impact on policy. "[Interest groups] are so intimately related to the daily functioning of those constitutionalized groups—legislature, chief executives, administrative agencies, and even courts—that make up the institution of government that the latter cannot adequately be described if these relationships are not recognized as the weft of the fabric."[21]

Since the publication of *The Governmental Process* a number of political scientists have expanded on, defended, and criticized pluralist theory. Robert Dahl, in *Who Governs?*, a study of political influence in New Haven, Connecticut, confirmed and gave a boost to pluralist theory by finding that policies in New Haven were influenced by different groups of people acting in different policy areas.[22] Other scholars, such as Terry Moe and Zachary Smith, have examined the organization, incentives, and behavior of interest groups.[23] Among the critics, Jack Walker and Theodore Lowi have argued that pluralism maintains the status quo by making it more difficult for newer organized groups to influence the policy-making process.[24] The greatest weakness of pluralism, as a *normative* theory of politics, is in the failure of all groups and interests to be represented in the bargaining and policy-making process. In environmental policy, for example, how are the interests of your grandchildren represented in the process? What about the interests of inanimate objects such as trees? And even when these interests are represented by "public interest" groups, these groups are, as we have seen, at a serious disadvantage vis-à-vis economic interests when competing in the policy formation and implementation arena. However, just because pluralism is not useful as a normative blueprint for the policy-making process does not mean it is not valuable as a descriptive tool. Although the behavior of interest groups is not the sole force influencing the policy-making process, groups and group activity, according to most scholars of American politics, do have a significant impact on the policy outputs of American democracy.

Group Types

A distinction can be made between types of interest groups by examining their goals and the resources they have available to achieve these goals. Although not all interest groups fall into one of the two following categories, the distinction sharpens our analysis and enables us to better understand the advantages of some groups in participating in the policy-making process.

The first type of group is the "private-economic" interest group. This is the kind of organization we typically think of when we hear the term *interest group.* Characteristically, private-economic interest groups pursue noncollective benefits, or benefits the group seeks for its membership that are not available to society at large. Examples of private-economic interest groups would include associations of oil and gas producers, fishers, cattle or timber producers, or any organization that regulates a business or profession and simultaneously attempts to influence government policy.

The second type of group is the "public-noneconomic" interest group, which pursues collective benefits that cannot be withheld from society at large. Examples of such benefits include clean air, clean water, and a strong national defense. Examples of such groups include most environmental and conservation organizations, consumer organizations, and associations that are involved in nonspecific foreign policy or defense issues.

In contrast to the private-economic interest group leader, the leader of a public-noneconomic interest group, when soliciting contributions, is unable to hold out any specific individual advantage for members who participate through their contributions. Some have argued, therefore, that it is illogical for members of such groups to contribute or participate in the activities of noncollective groups.[25] When soliciting contributions for a public-noneconomic interest group, the group leader might hold out the benefits of an expanded national park system or a coastline free of oil platforms; however, the rational member of a public-noneconomic interest group quickly realizes that these potential benefits may be available whether or not he or she decides to contribute to the group. This is a major fund-raising disadvantage for public-noneconomic interest groups.

By virtue of their organization and the incentives operating on members and leadership, private-economic interest groups have several advantages when attempting to influence the policy-making process compared to public-noneconomic interest groups. First, private-economic interest groups are advantaged in their fund-raising ability. Given the noncollective nature of their benefits, private-economic interest groups can offer benefits to members in return for their support. For example, the head of a state oil and gas association can solicit contributions from their membership with promises the money will be used to lobby for additional taxes on imported oil. The relationship between the contribution and the potential benefit is straightforward.

The difference between public and private interest groups in their ability to raise money is important. As we soon see, although groups have many different types of resources and these resources have varying utility for influencing the policy-making process, money is a very important part of the process, due primarily to the role it can play in campaign contributions and public relations.

Interest Groups and the Policy Cycle

In describing the policy-making process, a number of scholars have identified stages through which policies pass. Characterizations of the policy-making process almost always describe the process as (1) agenda setting, or having an item up for the serious consideration of policy makers; (2) policy making, or having action taken on the item; and (3) implementation, or the carrying out of a given policy.

The "agenda" is commonly defined as the listing of items for governmental action. Agenda setting is obviously a prerequisite to any policy action. Proficiency at agenda setting means the ability to get your issue on the list of items to be taken up by policy makers.

Policy making in government involves the desired action or nonaction on an item that has been placed on the public agenda. It can take place in any one of the three branches of government. It is important to know that inaction, or the continuation of the status quo, is also a form of policy making. As we see later, proficiency at policy making requires different skills and resources depending on the type of policy involved and the location of decision-making authority over the policy issue.

Policy implementation is, in large part, the purview of the bureaucracy. Administrators have discretion in implementing programs. Discretion is power. Even seemingly minor administrative decisions can have a significant impact on how a general legislative mandate is translated into governmental action. For example, the decision about when and where to hold public hearings can have a significant impact on who participates in those hearings. Hearings conducted by the U.S. Forest

Service for its first Roadless Area Review and Evaluation (RARE 1) to determine, among other things, the extent and location of wilderness areas on Forest Service lands, were held in the Pacific Northwest. The hearings were often held close or adjacent to logging communities, and large numbers of loggers participated in the hearing process. This was significant in that the RARE 1 hearings in the region generated an abundance of testimony against establishing additional wilderness areas.

Agenda setting, policy making, and implementation are all important in different ways. For a major public policy such as the Clean Water Act to be successful, there must be success at each stage of the policy process. For example, water must become an issue that policy makers, in this case the U.S. Congress, are interested in addressing; the interested parties and their representatives in Congress must be able to agree on a policy; and some organization, such as the Environmental Protection Agency, must have the incentives and resources to carry out the policy. Failure at any one of these stages in the policy-making process will prevent the objectives of the policy from being realized.

Like any organization, interest groups vary significantly in terms of their size, organization, assets, and other measures. Some groups have combinations of attributes or resources that enable them to participate effectively in any stage of the policy-making process. For example, the oil industry in the United States in the 1950s and 1960s and their associated groups and supporters were influential enough to have most of their policy objectives dealt with favorably in the U.S. Congress.[26]

The resources that are useful for influencing a particular stage of the policy-making process vary. For example, bringing an issue to the attention of policy makers and thereby getting it on the public agenda requires a different set of resources than having the issue acted upon favorably. Hence different groups, based on the types of resources they possess, have different levels of strength and influence when attempting to have an impact on a particular stage of the policy process.

The ability to attract media attention is one important preliminary step in the agenda-setting process. By virtue of their strategy, tactics, or their available resources, some groups are more likely to use the media for getting their items on the public agenda. Media managers, particularly of broadcast media, have incentives to produce salable, interesting, attention-attracting news. Some groups pursue policy goals that are better suited for satisfying that need. For example, the news that community drinking water supplies are threatened by toxic substances is much more likely to be reported than the release of a study showing that toxic residues in water are below U.S. public health standards.

Tactics that are conducive to attracting media attention include disclosure of the unusual, frightening, or bizarre. A case in point was when an antinuclear activist jumped into Hilo Bay in front of a U.S. Navy nuclear destroyer to protest nuclear weaponry in the early 1980s. Another attention-attracting tactic is protest activities, such as demonstrations or picketing. Also, the perception that a group is an "underdog" fighting the "big boys" or "the establishment" will attract attention.

In each of these cases the group using a particular media-attracting tactic is likely to lack resources necessary for more conventional means of getting their policy issue on the public agenda. An example of conventional agenda setting in the U.S. Congress would be having a sympathetic congressperson introduce a bill and lobby on the bill's behalf in the hope that it is passed by Congress and signed by the president.

Accordingly, groups that are influential and are able to get their items on the public agenda are either those groups that can attract the attention of the media or that possess the conventional resources necessary for influencing the policy-making stage of the policy formation process. Environmental organizations are more likely to use media-grabbing tactics than are organizations that have the resources for influencing the other stages of the policy-making process.[27] Therefore, if an organization is successful in influencing the policy-making stage of the process, then the group is also likely to have the resources necessary for influencing the agenda-setting stage of the process.

Group Resources and Policy Making

The relationship between group resources and interest group influence is important within each of the three branches of government and at every stage of the policy process. Policy making means many different things to different people and can be difficult to define. To illustrate, when the Organization of Petroleum Exporting Countries (OPEC) decides to raise the target price for its oil, there may be a variety of related consequences that affect the world's economy and environment. Consequently, it is often difficult to distinguish between what is strictly public policy making and what is private sector policy making. Here, however, we limit our discussion to policy making traditionally defined as the activity that takes place in legislative bodies, the executive branch, and the judicial systems. It will be useful for you to remember, however, that there is a close relationship between what goes on in the private sector and what ultimately happens in the public policy-making arena.

The Regulators

Although the laws and agencies that govern environmental management are discussed throughout the text, we identify here the major participants in the process and present an overview of one of the most significant environmental laws in the United States: the National Environmental Policy Act (NEPA).

In 1969 Congress passed the National Environmental Policy Act (NEPA). Although relatively simple and straightforward, NEPA eventually became the most litigated of all federal environmental statutes. Unlike other federal legislation in the environmental area, NEPA exerted control over federal agencies themselves in an attempt to make them more responsive to environmental concerns and values.

In the opening section of the act, NEPA declares its purpose as follows:

> [T]he Congress, recognizing the profound impact of man's activity on the interrelationships of all components of the natural environment, particularly the profound influence of population growth ... industrial expansion, resource exploitation, and new and expanding technological advances, and recognizing further the importance of restoring and maintaining environmental quality to the overall welfare and development of man, declares it is the continuing policy of the federal government ... to use all practicable means and measures ... in a manner calculated to foster and promote the general welfare, to create and maintain conditions under which man and nature can

exist in productive harmony, and fulfill the social, economic, and other requirements of present and future generations of Americans.[28]

To back up these lofty goals, "action forcing" procedures were developed in Section 102 of the act.[29] The most important requirement of NEPA was that an "environmental impact statement," or EIS, accompany "major federal actions significantly affecting the human environment."[30] NEPA directed that an EIS contain the environmental impact of a proposed federal action, any adverse environmental effects that cannot be avoided should the federal action proposed be implemented, any alternative to the proposed action, and any irreversible commitments of resources that an action would involve should it be implemented.[31]

NEPA also established the Council on Environmental Quality (CEQ) within the executive branch. Although the primary purpose of the CEQ was to advise the president about environmental matters, the CEQ became influential by developing regulations governing the EIS process and its implementation by federal agencies. Although the CEQ could not legally stop a proposed agency action that it deemed inappropriate, the council could delay the action by asking for reassessments. The U.S. Supreme Court has recognized the authority of the CEQ in developing regulations for the implementation of NEPA.[32] During the administrations of Ronald Reagan and George Bush, environmentalists charged that the CEQ had been stripped of its power. President Reagan wanted to eliminate the CEQ, and during both the Reagan and Bush administrations funding for CEQ operations was significantly reduced. In a similar vein President Clinton, in the first month of his presidency, announced his intention to abolish the CEQ and create a White House Office on Environmental Policy (OEP). The new office was designed to strengthen the hand of Vice President Al Gore in shaping environmental policy, thus signaling the Clinton administration's intentions to give environmental issues priority in the executive branch.[33] Although the CEQ was not abolished (the Clinton administration learned that presidents cannot unilaterally eliminate statutorily created offices) the OEP was merged in 1994 with the CEQ in conjunction with plans to elevate the Environmental Protection Agency to cabinet status through legislation. Although the EPA legislation never passed, the office created by merger of the CEQ and OEP continues to advise the President on matters of environmental policy.

The EIS provisions of NEPA are binding on all federal agencies. Early agency reactions to these provisions were mixed. Some agencies were quick to adopt a thorough environmental impact statement process, whereas others were slow to respond, as evidenced by numerous lawsuits forcing agency action. Consequently, much of what NEPA has come to mean in practical terms has been decided by the courts.

NEPA requires that an EIS be circulated among state, local, and federal agencies as well as the public. The act itself has no enforcement provisions; however, the courts, through a number of decisions, have provided enforcement mechanisms.[34]

Two bills introduced in 1969, House Resolution 6750, introduced by Congressman John D. Dingell, and Senate Bill 1075, introduced by Senator Henry Jackson, became the basis of NEPA. In a House-Senate conference committee, the final version of NEPA emerged with an important component deleted. The Senate bill had provided that "[E]ach person has a fundamental and inalienable right to a healthful environment. . . ."[35] In the final version, these words were changed to, "[E]ach person should enjoy a healthful environment." The inclusion of the original language might have given citizens legally enforceable environmental rights.

The conference report on NEPA indicated the intent of Congress when it stated, "[A]ll federal agencies shall comply with the provisions of Section 102 to the fullest extent possible, . . . [T]hus it is the intent of the conferees that the provision, to the fullest extent possible, shall not be used by any federal agency as a means of avoiding compliance with the directives set out in Section 102."[36] This report suggests that Congress had intended NEPA to be interpreted as an act that could affect the *substance* of agency decisions and was not intended to be only a procedural requirement.

Three major questions have been before the courts in NEPA litigation: (1) the determination of whether an EIS is necessary, (2) finding that it is, what the EIS should contain, and (3) when it should be prepared. Concerning the first issue, according to NEPA an EIS is required when a federal action is major and has a significant environmental impact. The cases revolve around determining what constitutes "major" and what is a "significant environmental impact." An action is a federal action if a federal agency has some control over that action or if the action is carried out by the agency itself. For example, since the federal government is involved in licensing nuclear power plants, an EIS is required for their construction. The determination of whether or not an act is "major" generally involves any substantial commitment by the government of money or other resources.

While Supreme Court decisions over the nature of major federal actions have been fairly clear, more activity has focused on determining what constitutes "significant environmental impact." First, according to NEPA, the environment does not refer to just woods and streams. The language of NEPA requires that the public in all locations be provided "safe, healthful, productive, and aesthetically and culturally pleasing surroundings."[37]

To illustrate, a New York federal court found that the construction of a new jail in downtown New York involved an impact significant enough to require an EIS.[38] In another case, the Supreme Court found that "[E]ffects on human health can be recognizable under NEPA, and that human health may include psychological health."[39]

To determine whether or not an impact is "significant," a two-step process has been developed that involves assessing the degree of change from the current use of land and the total quantity of the impact involved.[40] The EIS process starts at the time of a proposal for a federal action. In 1975 the U.S. Supreme Court found that "[W]here an agency initiates federal action by publishing a proposal and then holding hearings on the proposal, the statute would appear to require that an impact statement be included in the proposal and to be considered at the hearing."[41]

The first step in the EIS process is the preparation of an "environmental assessment," or EA. If no significant impact is found, then the agency is required to make a "finding of no significant impact," or FONSI. In the cases where the impact is found to be significant, the second step is to prepare an EIS.

When an EIS is created, it must take into consideration the environmental impacts of the total project, not just one particular component of that project. For example, an Atomic Energy Commission EIS for a single breeder reactor was found to be inadequate, and a federal circuit court held that an EIS was necessary to cover the entire breeder reactor program.[42]

Writing the EIS

The elements that need to be included in the EIS vary from situation to situation and should be determined through the scoping process. Scoping, as the name suggests, determines the scope and breadth of an EIS. The lead agency preparing an EIS is responsible for identifying members of the public and other agencies that may have an interest or stake in the project under consideration. Notices are mailed, posted, and published describing the proposed action and requesting input by a certain date. The discovery process is designed to determine the priorities in an EIS. The fundamental questions include: significant environmental impacts of a project; the geographic or physical parameters of the study areas; possible alternatives to the proposed action; and any other activity or actions in the study area or any other relevant factors that might impact the project.

The components of a completed EIS will depend significantly on the nature of the proposed project. Clearly a project located on a shoreline, for example, would entail considerations different from those of a project located in an urban area. A well-known source book used by environmental professionals for EIS preparation divides the components of an EIS into two categories: the natural environment and the built environment. Table 4–1 identifies what constitutes each environment.[43]

The items in Table 4–1 do not all have to be addressed in the EIS. To the list could be added several caveats and qualifications. For example, the courts have made it clear that agencies need to proceed with the EIS process even when they lack complete information necessary to fully assess the impacts of a project.[44] In addition, environmental impact statements need to include the direct effects of a proposed action, that part is clear, but more significantly (and more problematic), the EIS should also contain indirect impacts that are reasonably foreseeable.[45] There are limits, however. Though an agency is required to include in the EIS any information necessary for a reasoned decision, it is not required to obtain that information when the cost is exorbitant.[46] If it is determined that some data is too costly or difficult to obtain the EIS must indicate what is missing and evaluate its relevance to any reasonably foreseeable adverse impacts.

Generally speaking, an EIS prepared under NEPA will contain the following:

Contents of an EIS

1. Cover sheet.
2. Executive summary, to describe in sufficient detail (10 to 15 pages) the critical factors of the EIS so that the reader can become familiar with the proposed project or action and its net effects, the alternatives and major conclusions.
3. Table of contents.
4. Purpose and need for the action.
5. Alternatives considered by the applicant (proponent), including the do-nothing alternative. The applicants (proponents) preferred alternative shall be identified. There must be a balanced description of each alternative.

TABLE 4–1 Components of an EIS
Natural Environment

Earth:	Geology, Soils, Topography, Unique physical features, Erosion
Air:	Air Quality, Odor
Climate:	
Water:	Surface water improvement/quality/quantify; Run off/absorption; Floods; Groundwater movement/quantity/quality
Public Water Sources:	
Plants:	Unique or sensitive (threatened or endangered species); Number or diversity of species
Animals:	Unique or sensitive (threatened or endangered species); Habitat for numbers or diversity of species; Fish/wildlife migration routes
Energy and Natural Resources:	Amount required, rate of use, efficiency source/availability; Non-renewable resources; Conservation and renewable resources

Built Environment

Environ. Health:	Risk of explosion; Releases or potential releases to the environment affecting public health such as toxic or hazardous materials
Land and Shoreline Use:	Relationship to existing land use plans
Housing:	
Light and Glare:	
Aesthetics:	
Recreation:	
Historic and Cultural Preservation:	
Trans.:	Transportation systems; Vehicular traffic waterborne, rail, and air traffic; Parking movement/circulation of people or goods; Traffic hazards
Public Services/ Utilities:	Fire, police, schools, parks or other recreational facilities maintenance, communications, water supply, storm water, sewer, solid waste

6. The affected environment. The affected environment on which the evaluation of each alternative was based to include such matters as hydrology, geology, air quality, noise, biology, socio-economics, energy, land use, archeology, and history. The total impacts of each alternative shall be presented for easy comparison.

7. Coordination. Full consideration must be given to the objections and suggestions made by local, state, and federal agencies, by individual citizens and environment groups.

The results of public participation through public meetings or scoping meetings shall also be included. A list of persons, agencies, and organizations, to whom copies of the EIS have been sent shall be included.

8. List of preparers of the EIS, and their qualifications. Persons responsible for a particular analysis shall be identified.
9. Index, commensurate with the complexity of the EIS.
10. Appendices.
11. Material incorporated into an EIS by reference shall be included in a supplemental information document, available for review on request.
12. The format used for EISs shall encourage good analysis and clear presentation of alternatives, including the proposed action, and their environmental, economic, and social impacts.
13. The text of a final EIS shall normally be less than 150 pages, and for proposals of unusual scope or complexity shall normally be less than 300 pages.
14. EISs shall be written in plain language with readily understood graphics.[47]

The preceding paragraphs describe the technical characteristics of an EIS. Such considerations, well known to people in and out of government who prepare EIS's, will satisfy the procedural requirements of NEPA. But they may, and often do depending on how the EIS is prepared, lack any substantive force.

Although NEPA contains both procedural requirements (for example, the EIS), and a number of substantive recommendations (for example, to maintain a clean and healthy environment for all Americans), the courts have not enforced any of the substantive language. In effect this means that once the procedures have been followed and the EIS prepared, an agency may then go forward with its plans regardless of the negative impacts these plans may actually have on the environment. As Matt Lindstrom and Zachary Smith have written in their history and analysis of NEPA, *The National Environmental Policy Act: Promises Unfufilled,*

> The executive and judicial responsibilities for implementing, enforcing, and interpreting NEPA's broad policy objectives are where NEPA's execution has faltered. Rather than recognizing the comprehensive core and the long term view of NEPA, most presidents, courts, and agencies have taken a very narrow and myopic view in implementing NEPA.[48]

This is not to suggest the EIS process is pointless. The mere identification of environmental problems, sometimes coupled with public reaction to these problems, has caused many government plans to be changed or dropped.

Environmental Administration

In the United States, all three levels of government, national, state, and local, are involved in some capacity in environmental management. Most states have several agencies that are involved in environmental protection. State agencies may go under the name of the environmental protection agency or may be identified by function such as Department of Health, Department of Water Resources, or Water Quality Control. At the local level, there are a variety of air and water quality management districts in cities and counties. Larger cities often have environmental quality control departments or, more often, cities have health or public service agencies that have some responsibility for environmental quality control. Also on the local level there are various special districts or single-purpose districts that have responsibility over environmental quality control. Special districts are local government units organized to perform one or a limited number of functions, such as park and recreation development or mosquito abatement.

Preferences differ as to the appropriate level of government for the development and implementation of environmental regulations. There is no "correct" level of government for environmental regulation, and the appropriate regulatory authority may vary depending on the issue and the problem. However, certain interests have preferences for the location of regulatory authority. In addition, certain environmental problems have traditionally been handled in one level of government. For example, land-use planning, with minor exceptions, has been a local government concern in the United States. On the national level, nuclear power, again with minor exceptions, has primarily been the responsibility of the federal government.

Interest groups prefer that decision making over public policy be made in an arena where they feel they have the most influence. For example, in a state like Hawaii, in which a particular agricultural activity plays a dominant role in the state's economy, agricultural interests might prefer that pesticide regulation over pineapple and sugar cane be centered in the state government. In another example, the coal mining industry in West Virginia prefers strip mine reclamation to be on the state level.

On the other hand, major manufacturing companies with nationwide distribution systems often prefer environmental regulations to be implemented on the national level. The consistency and uniformity possible through national regulation costs the companies less than several different types of regulation in different states. In the face of multiple and sometimes conflicting state auto emission requirements, the automobile industry preferred the establishment of national standards to avoid the necessity of producing numerous types of cars for sale in states with differing air pollution control laws. In the late 1980s, refrigerator manufacturers lobbied for national energy efficiency guidelines to head off numerous and potentially conflicting guidelines being considered in state legislatures.

Environmental Protection Agency

The Environmental Protection Agency (EPA) has the primary responsibility for enforcing environmental regulations in the United States. President Richard Nixon, through an executive order in 1970, reorganized environmental administration in the United States, grouping together numerous programs throughout the federal bureaucracy under the direction of the EPA. "[The EPA is] designed to serve as the public's advocate for a livable environment."[49] The agency engages in research, the setting of standards, and monitoring and supporting similar activities on the state and local level.

The EPA is basically organized around programs over which Congress has given it enforcement authority. The agency is headed by an administrator with nine assistant administrators. There is also a general counsel, an inspector general, and ten regional offices. The regional offices are the primary contact points for the agency with state and local officials. Administrative units with substantive policy responsibilities include divisions of water, solid waste, air and radiation, pesticides and toxic substances, and research and development.

One of the potential problems with this type of organization is that it ignores the interrelationship of environmental problems. For example, the water division might not interrelate with the solid waste division. The agency refers to the overlapping of related problems as "multimedia" management. Although the term *media* correctly refers to the affected environmental media such as air, water, and land, the agency uses the term to refer to "media programs" or the major statutory programs under the administration's jurisdiction. As former EPA administrator Lee Thomas described multimedia solutions, "[Y]ou look at a problem on a geographic basis instead of pollution and air, water, or land. That way, you don't just pull the pollution out of the air and flush it into the water, or pull it out of the water and dump it out onto the land."[50]

Enforcement of environmental regulations within the EPA is the responsibility of the assistant administrator for enforcement and compliance, which includes an office of criminal enforcement; each of the major program areas, for example, water, pesticides, toxic substances, also has an enforcement office and/or an office of compliance monitoring. The EPA has special agents who work within the agency's Office of Criminal Enforcement. These agents are required to have at least six years of experience investigating organized crime, white-collar crime, or major felonies. Coming to the agency from police departments, the FBI, and the Treasury Department, EPA agents have jobs very much like the law enforcement agencies from which they come—serving warrants, collecting evidence, and occasionally getting shot at.[51]

The EPA was criticized for being lax in its enforcement efforts during the Reagan administration. For example, the Federal Water Pollution Control Act Amendments of 1972 directed the EPA to develop regulations to prohibit the discharge of toxic pollutants. During the three years that followed the passage of the 1972 Act, the EPA developed effluent standards for only six pollutants. By November 1987, the EPA had published standards for 63 toxic pollutants discharged by organic chemical plants, but it was not anticipated that standards for the pesticide industry would be developed until sometime into the 1990s.[52] In 1986 a U.S. General Accounting Office (GAO) report criticized EPA enforcement of the Superfund as being unsystematic and uncoordinated and stated that enforcement decisions were not uniform between the EPA regions or even within the same region. Representative James Florio, who requested the GAO report, remarked that EPA management of the Superfund was characterized by "delay after delay with no effective enforcement."[53] Another GAO study found in 1983 that 3,400, or about half, of the nation's major manufacturing plants had broken the law for discharging pollutants into water for at least six months of the previous year.[54]

EPA enforcement of its regulations has at times been motivated as much by political considerations as by any real intention to elicit compliance. For instance, in 1987 the EPA imposed construction limits on major new sources of pollution in 10 areas that were not in compliance with the Clean Air Act. EPA administrator Lee Thomas, anticipating the public reaction, commented at the time, "I think there will be a real uproar."[55] The EPA's action was seen as an attempt to put pressure on Congress to amend the law. Representative Henry Waxman from Los Angeles, one of the affected areas, remarked, "I think what the EPA is doing is trying to shift the burden to Congress to deal with the Clean Air Act. I find this somewhat unfortunate because for the last six years they've failed to use the law to force the kind of reductions in air pollution that might have been achieved."[56]

The politics of enforcement has always been an issue in EPA management. The EPA has enjoyed at various times to varying degrees the support of both political parties. As an attorney with extensive experience representing clients before the EPA wrote, "[B]oth Republicans and Democrats have enforced the environmental statutes, requested and obtained additional statutory authority, and issued new regulatory controls to improve the environment. ... [T]he differences between administrations in the environmental enforcement area are merely of degree."[57] And as the former EPA administrator during the Carter administration remarked, the Environmental Protection Agency has "always enjoyed a strong degree of bi-partisan support."[58]

The first administrator of the EPA was William Ruckelshaus, a former Indiana politician and attorney for the U.S. Justice Department. Ruckelshaus quickly built a reputation for himself and the EPA as being aggressive in the enforcement of environmental statutes. Although often at odds with the EPA, President Nixon wanted to draw attention to the environmental activities of his administration in an effort to prevent potential Democratic presidential nominee Edmund Muskie from using the issue in the 1972 elections. Within weeks after assuming the administrator's job, Ruckelshaus moved against Atlanta, Detroit, and Cleveland, threatening federal court action to prevent the discharge of untreated sewage. These cities all had Democratic mayors. It was part of Ruckelshaus's early strategy, and the EPA's strategy through most of its institutional history, to go after highly visible polluters in an effort to generate publicity. Early in his term, Ruckelshaus took action against Republic Steel, Jones and Laughlin, and the Kennebec River Pulp and Paper Company.[59] As a press officer for the EPA at the time of Ruckelshaus's tenure remarked, "[Ruckelshaus was] anxious to bring the big polluters into line, [so] he used the press to instill fear in their hearts by holding up a few of them as bad examples."[60]

Throughout the 1970s, the EPA continued to enjoy bipartisan support and a reputation for strong enforcement of environmental statutes. The Reagan administration brought a new approach to the management of the EPA. Reagan's first EPA administrator, Anne Burford, sought to ease the enforcement of environmental laws and place more emphasis on voluntary compliance. Uncharacteristic of typical agency behavior, Burford sought smaller, not larger appropriations for her agency and, atypically for EPA administrators, her main priority was relief for regulated industries. During the first two years of the Reagan administration, the EPA's enforcement budget was cut by 45 percent. The number of cases referred by the EPA to the Department of Justice for prosecution had hovered at about 200 per year prior to the Reagan administration, dropping to 50 during the first year of his administration.

The journal of the Natural Resources Defense Council editorialized that "[A]bout all that has mattered has been the sight, smell, and taste of politics. Although the President failed in his promise to weaken environmental laws, through rhetoric, appointments, and budget constraints, his administration has succeeded in blunting their effectiveness."[61]

Appointments to major offices within the EPA, like other environmental appointments during the Reagan administration, often came directly from the regulated industries. For example, the first general counsel of the EPA was formerly a lawyer for Exxon Corporation. Burford's chief of staff was formerly with Johns-Manville Corporation (a building material manufacturer), and the assistant administrator in charge of air quality was the former lobbyist for Crown Zellerbach Corporation (a paper and pulp manufacturer).[62]

The emphasis on voluntary compliance and the primacy of politics in the EPA created an atmosphere within the agency that apparently was conducive to political abuses of environmental administration. The head of the Superfund during Burford's tenure at the EPA was Rita Lavalle, a former campaign worker for President Reagan when he was running for governor of California. In 1983 Lavalle was discovered to have used her office to further the chances of Republican congressional candidates in the 1982 elections. Lavalle was distributing Superfund cleanup monies in ways that might be seen as politically advantageous for Republicans.[63]

The combination of Lavalle's problems and accusations of politicized environmental enforcement leveled against Burford and the EPA generally led to a great deal of turmoil within the agency early in 1983. According to agency officials, the EPA was "demoralized and virtually inert."[64] Both EPA administrator Burford and Superfund administrator Lavalle were forced to leave the EPA in March 1983.[65] Lavalle was accused of perjury and obstructing a congressional investigation of EPA management of the Superfund. The charge concerned at what point she learned her former employer, Aerojet General Corporation, had been a user of the Stringfellow Dump in California. When dismissed from office, Lavalle's staff "went into a flurry of removing sensitive documents from her office."[66] In December 1983, Lavalle was convicted of perjury and sentenced to prison.

To the delight of environmentalists, Anne Burford was replaced by William Ruckelshaus. Though he had spent the previous eight years as an executive for Weyerhaeuser Corporation, environmentalists remembered the assertive action Ruckelshaus had taken as the first EPA administrator and were optimistic he would continue with that style of management. Many of the hopes of environmentalists were realized. Ruckelshaus replaced most of the EPA's top administrators with people who had wide experience in environmental policy and science. This was in contrast to many of Burford's inexperienced appointees.[67]

The EPA administrator who succeeded Ruckelshaus when he resigned in 1985 was Lee Thomas, formerly the head of the Federal Emergency Management Agency (FEMA). Earlier he had assumed control of the toxic waste division of the EPA from Rita Lavalle at the time of her departure. On most issues, Thomas was much more aggressive in implementing EPA's mandate than was administrator Burford. An article in *Business Week* magazine reported,

> [U]nder Rita Lavalle's stewardship, environmentalists charge, the Toxic Waste Cleanup Program was rife with political favoritism and soft on polluters. After her ouster, business leaders say the agency compensated by taking too hard a line, forcing some companies to pay the full cost of cleanups even when they were responsible for only a portion of the waste.[68]

A change in management strategy in the EPA was evident by the increased number of enforcement actions referred from the agency to the Department of Justice for prosecution.[69]

During the election of 1988, George Bush promised to be the "environmental president." His EPA administrator, William K. Reilly, pushed through the 1990 amendments to the Clean Air Act. However, at the same time, Vice President Dan Quayle's Council on Competitiveness and the Office of Management and Budget were working to weaken implementation of the 1990 amendments as well as other environmental regulations in the name of economic efficiency. While the Council had no statutory authority, it did have the ear of President Bush, and, as such, provided a format for businesses seeking regulatory relief. The *Sierra* magazine characterized the council's attack on the 1990 Clean Air Act Amendments as follows: "[T]he Competitiveness Council has pecked at the act ever since its passage, handing out exemptions like candy to power plant operators, automobile manufactures, and newspaper publishers, among others."[70]

Early in the Clinton administration, the President moved to abolish the Council on Competitiveness. Clinton appointed Carol Browner as the new EPA administrator. Browner was a former member of Vice President Gore's Senate staff and headed the Florida Department of Environmental Regulation. Environmental organizations generally applauded her appointment.[71]

The 1994 elections saw a wave of dramatic shift in the control of Congress. Conservative Republicans, led by Newt Gingrich (R-Georgia) came to power with promises of government reform in general and environmental reform in particular.

The mid-1990s saw the EPA become an example of what most perceive to be wrong with most federal bureaucracies. As Walter Rosenbaum, a scholar of environmental policy who spent a year working in the EPA, wrote, "Despite significant accomplishments, the agency often appears to regulate in slow motion, to labor unproductively, and to write too many costly and impractical regulations after more than twenty-five years as the nation's most important environmental regulator."[72] Even the White House has conceded that the EPA needs to reform its policies and organizational structure. Vice President Al Gore's report "Re-inventing Environmental Regulation," released in March of 1995, argued for an assessment of current regulations in order to better provide for the future protection of the environment.

One of the primary problems within the EPA is the fragmented way in which it regulates various programs. As discussed, the agency tends to focus too much on specific media, without much consideration of the interrelations among media. Reformers argue that the agency needs to consolidate some of its pollution abatement programs in order to become more administratively, as well as economically, efficient. Rosenbaum suggests a greater emphasis be placed on risk assessment and benefit-cost analyses to cut costs and administrative burden, while still providing for environmental protection.

Christie Whitman, former governor of New Jersey, now heads the EPA under President G. W. Bush. She defends a go-slow approach to environmental regulation and initially did not favor reducing CO_2 emissions (which was consistent with the president's decision not to support the Kyoto CO_2 treaty).[73] Still, it seems a Reagan-era regression is not likely to happen again soon. In September of 2001 the President's choice for top law enforcement official at EPA, Donald Schregardus, withdrew his name after scathing criticism he has done poorly enforcing the environmental laws of Ohio.[74]

However, clearly G. W. Bush will not be the "environmental president." Early indications suggest that his administration is likely to drop pollution lawsuits against power plants that were built prior to 1970 (and do not meet Clean Air Act standards). These coal-burning plants mostly in the Midwest produce up to ten times more SO_2 and NO_x than modernized plants.[75]

In addition the EPA received strong pressure from Vice President Cheney's energy task force to review environmental regulations that may slow energy production or make it more expensive.[76]

Overall, the EPA has organizational problems outside of its political leadership. First, even with 18,000 employees and a $7 billion budget, the EPA cannot regulate what it does not understand. For example, water quality assessment data are available for only 6 percent of the nation's shorelines, 19 percent of rivers and streams, and 40 percent of its lakes.[77] Furthermore, for the 476 chemicals that EPA identified as most in need of testing under the Toxic Substances Control Act, only ten (2 percent) have been measured for human exposure. However, EPA has begun a partnership with the Department of Health and Human Services to improve this area.[78]

To better protect human and environmental health EPA will have to enter into more partnerships to reduce costs and duplication or contradiction of effort across regions and states. It will need to adopt a more flexible regulatory strategy with less paperwork and fill in important gaps in data so it fully understands what environmental problems it is dealing with. Steps it has taken include the High Production Volume Challenge Program that began in 1998 to get industry to voluntarily report the effects of the chemicals they produce. As of June 2000 over 400 companies agreed to compile and report such data on 71 percent of the 2,800 high-volume chemicals produced in the United States.[79] Administrator Whitman has also vowed to streamline the Clean Air Act without diminishing its effectiveness.[80]

In summary, the politics of the Environmental Protection Agency may best be described as bipartisan and, depending on the issue and the administration in power, aggressive on enforcement. The early Reagan administration and the EPA administration of Burford was an exception to this trend, and once the political liabilities of a politicized EPA soft on enforcement became apparent, was short lived. Only time will tell if G. W. Bush's administration will attempt to follow suit and if so what the repercussions or backlash may be.

Department of Interior

The Department of the Interior was established in 1849 by combining the Treasury Department's General Land Office, the War Department's Office of Indian Affairs, which later became the Bureau of Indian Affairs, the Patent Office, the Pension Office, and the Census Office. In its first year of operation, the department had a permanent workforce of 10 people and a budget of $14,200.[81] Today the Department of Interior has extensive responsibility over environmental and land management. The Department of Interior houses the National Park Service, the U.S. Fish and Wildlife Service, the Bureau of Land Management, the Minerals Management Service, the Office of Surface Mining, the U.S. Geological Survey, the Bureau of Reclamation, and the Bureau of Mines. The department is organized with a secretary and five assistant secretaries covering each of the major substantive areas within the department's jurisdiction.

Traditionally, major Interior Department appointees, which include the secretary and the assistant secretaries, have had ties to the West and, to a lesser extent, the Midwest.[82] Although the agency has known its share of scandal, the Department of the Interior and many of its component agencies, such as the National Park Service, enjoy a long institutional history and tradition and a well-developed interest group support system.[83]

Consistent with their western roots and the conservation goals of many of the agencies within the Department of Interior, secretaries of the Interior have, for the most part, been conservationists themselves. However the management pattern we saw in the EPA early in the Reagan administration also occurred in the management of the Department of Interior. President Reagan's first secretary of the Interior, James Watt, came to the department from the Mountain States Legal Defense Fund, an organization that had been active in suing the Interior Department over the management of western lands. As Patricia and Robert Cahn, contributing editors to *National Parks Magazine,* wrote, "[W]ith the advent of James Watt and the Reagan administration in 1981, came the attempt to make drastic changes. The Watt team brought an anti-government 'sagebrush rebellion' philosophy to the department and a tilt toward development and privatization, which they aggressively sought to impose. . . ."[84]

Secretary Watt put the Interior Department on a path away from conservation and toward greater development of federal resources. These activities included the opening of the outer continental shelf to additional oil company bidding; the rapid acceleration of coal, oil, and gas leasing, including the opening of wilderness areas for mineral exploration; and an end to spending for the acquisition of additional park lands.[85] Watt immediately drew criticism from environmental organizations for both his actions and attitudes. The Secretary did not shy away from controversy nor was he willing to appease environmentalists. Watt regularly referred to environmentalists as "radicals" and compared those in the environmental movement to "communists" and "Nazis."[86] A staunch conservative, Watt, in his own words, felt "[T]he contest between liberals and conservatives . . . is a moral battle. It is a contest over who's right and who's wrong."[87]

Watt's outspokenness eventually led to his resignation. The Secretary had become a political liability for Republicans in the 1984 elections, and on October 10, 1983, President Reagan accepted the Watt's resignation.[88] In addition to attacks on environmentalists, Watt alienated other Interior Department constituent groups. For example, the Secretary had called the department's Bureau of Indian Affairs an example of the "failure of socialism," and when characterizing the makeup of an Interior Department's coal advisory board, described the board as being "well balanced," including "a woman, a black, a Jew, and a cripple."[89] This comment turned out to be the fatal blow to his Interior Department career.

Ironically, many in the environmental movement as well as some Democratic Party leaders did not welcome Watt's resignation. The controversy caused by Watt's tenure helped fuel the rapid rise of membership in environmental organizations and, undoubtedly, was a catalyst for increased public support for environmental regulation. There is also some irony in the fact that Watt actually accomplished very little, in spite of his rhetoric. By drawing attention to his actions, he undermined the resource development and privatization goals he sought to achieve.

Watt was replaced by Interior Secretary William Clark, who was replaced in 1985 by Donald Hodel. Both Clark and Hodel assumed relatively low profiles and attempted, publicly at least, a more moderate form of management. Hodel, in what was seen variously as an attempt to either appease or divide environmentalists, suggested in 1987 that the Hetch Hetchy Dam in Yosemite National Park be torn down and the valley be allowed to revert to its natural state. It was not, however, and the drive in the Interior Department for privatization and increased development on federal lands continued throughout the Reagan and Bush administrations.

President Clinton appointed former Arizona governor Bruce Babbitt as his secretary of the interior. The Babbitt appointment was widely praised by environmental organizations. In contrast to his predecessors, Babbitt came to office with ideas of reforming western resource policies, and a more balanced conservation ethic. During the spring of 1993 when Babbitt was rumored to be under consideration for appointment to the U.S. Supreme Court, environmental organizations lobbied the White House to keep the Secretary at Interior, which is what happened.[90]

Babbit's work was generally viewed as successful by environmentalists. Babbit's successor Bush appointee, Gale Norton, was the first woman ever to hold the post. She previously worked at the Department of the Interior, overseeing endangered species and public lands legal issues for the National Park Service and the Fish and Wildlife Service before becoming the Attorney General of Colorado.

Norton has some environmentalists concerned, however. She has gone on record saying that there was no energy or commercial use of public land she had a problem with. As has proven common in Republican administrations Norton has made numerous appointments of people with a background in the industry being regulated. Norton named Camden Toohey, a lobbyist for Arctic oil drilling, as her top official in Alaska.[91] Other Interior appointments have followed that trend. Prior to his appointment Deputy Interior Secretary Griles was a lobbyist for fossil fuel interests. Interior's new Solicitor William Meyers III has sued the federal government on behalf of grazing interests, and Lynn Scarlett, the new Assistant Secretary for Policy is former president of a libertarian anti-regulation think-tank.[92] Bush's dip into the anti-environmental lobby for key sub-cabinet positions speaks to his view on the environment as a collection of resources to be utilized by humans. It is still too early to tell what these appointments will mean in terms of environmental outcomes, though the direction for policy seems clear.

Bureau of Land Management. The Bureau of Land Management (BLM) created in 1946 through the consolidation of the general land office and grazing services, manages 270 million acres of public lands primarily in the Far West and Alaska, as well as 300 million acres where mineral rights are owned by the federal government.[93] After farmers had taken those federal lands they wanted for farming, prime forests were reserved in the U.S. Forest System, and the most spectacular or unique land was preserved in the National Park Service. What was left—those lands that no one wanted—became the responsibility of the Bureau of Land Management. Ironically, those "unwanted" lands are now the focus of much controversy in federal land management.

For most of the bureau's history, the agency has been criticized, correctly most analysts feel, for serving the interest of the ranchers that depend on bureau grazing permits to the exclusion of other interests. As one author wrote, "[F]or the first three decades after its creation in 1946 ... BLM did essentially what its parent bureaucracies had done: handed down land parcels, grazing leases, and mineral claims. It became a standard joke that BLM actually stood for Bureau of Livestocking and Mining."[94]

In 1976 passage of the Federal Land Policy and Land Management Act (or FLPMA) led to a change in BLM land management practices. FLPMA required the BLM to adopt the management principles of multiple use and sustain yield that were the mandate of the Forest Service. FLPMA also directed the BLM to examine its holdings to determine which were suitable for wilderness designation, giving the agency 15 years, until 1991, to complete the task. The early history of the BLM had consisted largely of agency validation of the existing arrangements and preferences of established local groups.[95]

After 1976 this was less the case, and in fact BLM offices both in Washington and in the field are staffed with professionals representing nontraditional values. Nevertheless, as one student of the BLM noted, "[P]rofessionals representing nontraditional values often complain that the values they represent are given short shrift in the planning process and that traditional values are still the dominant concern of many BLM managers."[96]

Still, the BLM has been attempting to reach out beyond the traditional ranching and grazing interests of the past. For example, in its wilderness planning for the southern California desert, extensive efforts were made to work with individuals and organizations that were concerned with protection of the desert environment. The BLM clearly has a self-interest in involving environmentalists in the agency's decision making. The exclusion of such interests in wilderness planning could result in a backlash in Congress and potentially the removal of some lands from bureau jurisdiction. The BLM has therefore been more sensitive overall to the concerns of environmental interests since the mid-1970s.

National Park Service.   The National Park Service, created in 1916, was directed to "promote and regulate the use of the federal areas known as national parks, monuments, and reservations ... the fundamental purpose of these parks ... is to conserve the scenery and the natural and historic objects and the wildlife therein, and to provide for the enjoyment of the same in such a manner and by such means as will leave them unimpaired for the enjoyment of future generations."[97] The inherent conflict between preservation and use is a major land-use problem for the National Park Service.

There are 376 areas within National Park Service jurisdiction, including national parks, monuments, historic sites, and recreation areas, which in total cover more than 80.6 million acres.[98] Park Service holdings expanded significantly in the 1960s and 1970s, growing from 176 units in 1960 covering 26.2 million acres to 333 units covering 77 million acres by 1980. In 1980 Congress passed the Alaska National Interest Lands Conservation Act, which more than doubled the acreage of the national parks system (adding 43.6 million acres).[99]

The growth of the park system has corresponded to growth in the number of visitations to National Park units. Due undoubtedly in part to increased visitation, the Park Service, unlike the other federal land management agencies discussed in this chapter, has enjoyed a considerable amount of public approval and support. In 1978 a Gallup poll found 95 percent of those responding gave the National Park Service a favorable rating.[100] The primary constituencies of the National Park Service are environmentalist and recreationalist. Environmentalists are primarily concerned with the preservation aspects of Park Service goals, whereas recreationalists are concerned with the use and enjoyment of the parks.

The Park Service, like all the federal land management agencies studied here, has fluctuated in its management philosophies from one segment of its public constituency to another. In an effort to provide more service for the public, the Park Service has been criticized by environmentalists for having a "Disneyland" mentality. For example, in the early 1970s, the Park Service and the Music Corporation of America (the concessionaire, at that time, in Yosemite National Park) together developed a master plan for Yosemite Valley that included, among other things, a significant expansion of visitor facilities, including the building of a convention center.[101] MCA produced and distributed promotional brochures outlining the corporation's commitment to preserving park values. One read, "[I]t's not just another American convention hotel. . . . [A]ll your worldly needs are provided for. . . . [T]his isn't no man's land or primitive wilderness. This is civilization."[102]

In terms of recent political events, some argue the new head of the National Park Service, Frances Mainella, is the only Interior appointee with solid environmental credentials. Even the National Parks Conservation Association that gives the G. W. Bush administration a "D" so far for park policies considers Mainella's appointment a victory. She was considered a success heading up Florida's massive array of parks for the President's brother, Governor Jeb Bush, and she is the first woman to hold this post. She intends to focus on environmental education, considering the national parks the world's greatest classroom.[103]

Forest Service.   The Forest Service was created in 1905 by the transference of federal forest reserves out of the Department of the Interior and into the Department of Agriculture. The Forest Service manages 156 natural forests, 19 national grasslands, and 17 land utilization projects in 44 states. Forest Service holdings cover 191 million acres.

The constituent groups that have had an influence on the Forest Service may be divided into two types: resource-using and recreation groups. The resource-using groups include timber, mining, and to a lesser extent, grazing interests. The recreation groups include environmental organizations and organizations of hikers, hunters, and fishermen. The management principle of Forest Service lands, and the Bureau of Land Management lands as well, is one of multiple use and sustained yield. For the Forest Service, the guiding principle is "the greatest good to the greatest number in the long run."[104]

Traditionally and historically, resource user groups have had the most influence within the Forest Service. The national forests have been seen as a kind of agricultural product to be used for the greatest amount of production in the furtherance of economic and consumptive use goals. This traditional orientation has worked to the advantage of and led to the growth and strength within the Forest Service of resource-using constituencies. This is not to suggest the Forest Service has ignored environmental or recreation concerns. Recreationalists in particular have been an important constituency for the Forest Service, and environmentalists have been placated somewhat by efforts of the Forest Service to create wilderness areas. These outcomes are discussed in more detail later.

Although the first assistant secretary of agriculture with jurisdiction over the Forest Service during the Reagan administration was a former counsel for a lumber company, the Forest Service did not undergo the same tumultuous administrative period that the EPA and the Department of Interior went through in the early 1980s.

The Bush administration is not seen as particularly environmentally friendly, as we have seen, due in large part to his choice of appointees to head federal agencies with environmental policy responsibilities. The trend continues in the Forest Service. Bush nominated Mark Rey for the top natural resources position at the Department of Agriculture, which has responsibility for the Forest Service. It would not surprise some to discover Rey has spent much of his career as a timber lobbyist. Similarly, Bush nominated Mike Parker to oversee the Army Corps of Engineers, which works closely with the Forest Service and many other federal agencies in natural resource management and environmental planning. Parker was quoted as saying he could not imagine any environmental interests that were more important than commercial interests.[105]

Forest Service management plans and problems along with those of agencies within the Department of Interior are discussed in detail in the chapters to follow.

U.S. Fish and Wildlife Service.   The Department of Interior's U.S. Fish and Wildlife Service was created in 1940 by combining the Bureau of Biological Survey, established in 1885 in the Department of Agriculture, with the Bureau of Fisheries, established in 1871, first as an independent agency and then later in the Department of Commerce. The Fish and Wildlife Service oversees 512 national wildlife refuges, 198 waterfowl protection areas, 50 waterfowl coordination areas, 65 national fish hatcheries, 9 major fish and wildlife research laboratories, and centers totaling more than 92 million acres.[106] By acreage, most of the national wildlife refuge system, about 88 percent, is in Alaska.

Department of Energy

Finally we have the Department of Energy (DOE). Its origins date back to the Manhattan Project and the race to develop nuclear weapons. In 1946 Congress passed the Atomic Energy Act creating the Atomic Energy Commission (AEC) and giving government a monopoly on atom-based research and technologies. Another Act was passed in 1954 encouraging the growth of commercial nuclear uses, especially for energy creation.

The AEC was in a precarious position because it was supposed to regulate nuclear energy to ensure public safety, but it was also supposed to foster the development of commercial nuclear use. When an agency is given responsibility to regulate an industry, but also promote its growth, problems inevitably arise. Eventually people began to realize such a mission created potentially dangerous conflicts of interest. That recognition combined with the greater environmental movement of the time led to the Energy Reorganization Act of 1974 and the split of the AEC into two agencies.

But the energy crisis of the 1970s brought to light the need for unified energy planning, and the Department of Energy Organization Act created a single Department of Energy (DOE) on October 1, 1977. During its early history the DOE was focused on energy development. Then with the rise of the Cold War the focus shifted to nuclear proliferation. The times have shifted once again and the Department today focuses on energy security, maintaining the safety and reliability of our nuclear stockpile while promoting nonproliferation, cleaning up the environment from the legacy of the Cold War, and developing innovations in science and technology.[107]

Despite these goals problems exist. The Departments of Energy and Defense are two of the largest polluters in the United States and the National Commission on Environmental Quality estimates they will cost the EPA specifically and American taxpayers in general over 150 billion dollars in clean-up costs over the next 25 years.[108] In addition, current Energy Secretary Abraham is seeking to overhaul the Clean Air Act to make energy exploration and production cheaper and easier. (It should be kept in mind that energy industries made very substantial contributions to the president's 2000 campaign.)

As should now be clear, political leadership and pressures can have at least as much if not more to do with environmental policy than department mission statements or specific language in enabling statutes. In that regard the political appointees tend to listen more to those interest groups that directly support them and this leads to a specific type of environmental policy.

SUMMARY

In this chapter we examined the regulatory process governing environmental policy in the United States. Fundamental to that process, as we have seen, is the concept of pluralism—or the bargaining that organized groups engage in when attempting to influence public policy outcomes. But all groups are not created equal. Because of differences in their ability to raise and spend money for political campaigns, as well as differences in the amount of other resources, some groups have the advantage when attempting to influence environmental policy. Generally, private-economic interest groups have more and better resources for influencing the process than do public interest groups—including most environmental groups. We also saw how incrementalism, decentralization, the incentives operating on policy makers to plan for the short term instead of the long term, ideological bias, and the crisis-response nature of policymaking all influence the policy formation process. These attributes of our political system often operate to produce policies that, as we see in greater detail in Part Two, do not do the job or do not accomplish what they were intended to achieve. In other words, they operate to help create the paradoxes of environmental policy.

We also introduced the National Environmental Policy Act and the federal agencies that have primary responsibility for implementing environmental policy. The federal agencies we discussed, the Forest Service, the Environmental Protection Agency, the Department of Energy, and the resource management agencies within the Department of the Interior, are the major governmental players in the environmental policy implementation process and are referred to throughout the book.

Part Two has seven chapters, which cover air, water, energy, toxic and hazardous waste, land management, international pollution problems, and international environmental management. Chapter 5, on air pollution, like most of the chapters in Part Two, begins with a description of the nature of the problem of air pollution, continues with a description of laws and regulations governing it, and discusses the successes and failures of those regulatory efforts.

NOTES

1. Although its impact is uncertain, a 1992 U.S. Supreme Court ruling (*Lujan v. Defenders of Wildlife*) found that in order to have standing an individual must have "personally suffered a specific injury or will be harmed immediately." The case involved the Endangered Species Act. The *Wall Street Journal* reported, "Justice Harry Blackmun, in a dissent joined by Justice Sandra O'Connor, accused the splintered majority of 'what amounts to a slash-and-burn expedition through the law of environmental standing.' " See Paul M. Barrett, "Environmental Lawsuits Face Tough Standard," *Wall Street Journal,* June 15, 1992, p. A3.
2. Lettie M. Wenner, "Contextual Influences on Judicial Decision Making," *Western Political Quarterly,* 41 (March 1988), pp. 115–134; Lettie M. Wenner, "Environmental Policy in the Courts," in Norman J. Vig and Michael E. Kraft (eds.), *Environmental Policy in the 1990s* (Washington, DC: Congressional Quarterly Press, 1990), pp. 189–210.
3. Numerous scholars have addressed the importance of reelection in motivating the behavior of legislators. See, for example, David R. Mayhew, *Congress: The Electoral Connection* (New Haven, CT: Yale University Press, 1974); and Gary C. Jacobson, *The Politics of Congressional Elections* (Boston: Little, Brown, 1987).
4. Charles G. Bell and Charles M. Price, *California Government Today* (3rd ed.) (Chicago: Dorsey, 1988), p. 69.
5. Nicholas Johnson, "Campaigns: You Pay $4 or $4000," *Des Moines Iowa Register.* July 21, 1996. The author is a professor of law and has been a top-level presidential appointee three times. He admits having been party to subgovernment quasicorrupt practices and now seeks to end them, in part, through elimination of soft money and public financing of campaigns.
6. Paul J. Culhane, *Public Lands Politics* (Baltimore: Johns Hopkins University Press, 1981), p. 234.
7. Taken from James E. Anderson, *Public Policymaking,* (3rd ed.) (New York: Holt, Rinehart and Winston, 1984), p. 9.
8. David Robertson and Dennis Judd, *The Development of American Public Policy: The Structure of Policy Restraint* (Boston and Glenview, IL: Scott, Foresman/Little, Brown, 1989), pp. 321–353.
9. Robert Stobaugh and Daniel Yergin (eds.), *Energy Future* (3rd ed.) (New York: Vintage Books, 1983), pp. 173–237.
10. Although this point may be found throughout the literature of political science, one of the most readable accounts may be found in Charles L. Clapp, *The Congressman* (Washington, DC: Brookings Institution, 1963).
11. Many scholars argue that the theory of elitism better describes policy formation in the United States. See, for example, C. Wright Mills, *The Power Elite* (New York: Oxford University Press, 1959).
12. V. O. Key, *Politics, Parties, and Pressure Groups* (5th ed.), (New York: Thomas Y. Crowell, 1964), p. 17. For a discussion of pluralism and alternative theories, see Kenneth Prewitt and Alan Stone, *The Ruling Elites* (New York: Harper & Row, 1973); and Jeffrey M. Berry, *The Interest Group Society* (Boston: Little, Brown, 1984).
13. Berry, *The Interest Group Society,* p. 2.
14. *The Federalist Papers* (New York: New American Library, 1961), p. 78.
15. Ibid., p. 79.
16. It should be pointed out that Madison was not as egalitarian as the forgoing might suggest. In fact, he was suspicious of majority rule and preferred the business of government to be conducted by the elite. Pluralist theorists, including Dahl, Truman, and others, have read Madison as a forerunner of pluralist participatory democratic theory. Although this would not be an accurate portrayal of Madison, he is historically interesting in this context for he identified potential problems with interest group influence early on which have now, in this author's opinion, come to pass.

17. Arthur Bentley, *The Process of Government* (Chicago: University of Chicago Press, 1908).
18. Ibid., pp. 222, 210.
19. See, for example, Peter H. Odegard, *Pressure Politics: The Story of the Anti-Saloon League* (New York: Columbia University Press, 1928); E. Pendelton Herring, *Group Representation Before Congress* (Baltimore: Johns Hopkins University Press, 1929); and E. E. Schattschneider, *Politics, Pressures and the Tariff* (Upper Saddle River, NJ: Prentice-Hall, 1935).
20. David Truman, *The Governmental Process* (New York: Knopf, 1951).
21. Ibid., p. 51.
22. Robert A. Dahl, *Who Governs?* (New Haven: Yale University Press, 1961).
23. Terry M. Moe, *The Organization of Interests* (Chicago: University of Chicago Press, 1980); Zachary A. Smith, *Interest Group Interaction and Groundwater Policy Formation in the Southwest* (Lanman, MD: University Press of America, 1985).
24. Jack L. Walker, "A Critique of the Elitist Theory of Democracy," *American Political Science Review*, 60 (June 1966), pp. 285–295; Theodore J. Lowi, *The End of Liberalism* (2nd ed.) (New York: Norton, 1979).
25. See, for example, Mancur Olsen, *The Logic of Collective Action* (Cambridge, MA: Harvard University Press, 1965).
26. See Martin V. Melosi, *Coping with Abundance: Energy and Environment in Industrial America* (New York: Knopf, 1985), Part Three.
27. Smith, *Interest Group Interaction and Groundwater Policy Formation in the Southwest,* p. 26.
28. National Environmental Policy Act, Section 101(a).
29. The first step in the EIS process is the preparation of an "environmental assessment" (or EA). If in the environmental assessment, which is relatively short, it is found that there is no significant impact, then the agency is required to make a "finding of no significant impact." The EIS process starts at the time of a proposal for a federal action. In 1975 the U.S. Supreme Court found that, "[W]here an agency initiates federal action by publishing a proposal and then holding hearings on the proposal, the statute would appear to require that an impact statement be included in the proposal and to be considered at the hearing." See *Aberdeen and Rockfish Railroad Company v. Students Challenging Regulatory Agency Procedures,* 422 U.S. 289 (1975).
30. National Environmental Policy Act, Section 102(c).
31. National Environmental Policy Act, Section 102(c) (i–v).
32. *Andrus v. Sierra Club,* 99 S.Ct. 2335 (1979).
33. Timothy Noah, *Wall Street Journal,* February 9, 1993, p. B6.
34. An early case, *Calvert Cliffs' Coordinating Committee, Inc. v. AEC,* found that NEPA "mandates a particular sort of careful and informed decision-making process and creates judicially enforceable rule duties." The Court went on to say that if the agency "decision was reached procedurally without individualized consideration and balancing of environmental factors—conducted fully and in good faith—it is a responsibility of the Courts to reverse." See *Calvert Cliffs' Coordinating Committee, Inc. v. AEC,* 449 F.2d 1109 (D.C. Cir. 1971).
35. U.S. Senate, Senate Report No. 91-296, 91st Congress, First Session.
36. 115 Congressional Record (Part 30) at 40417–40418.
37. National Environmental Policy Act, Section 101.
38. *Hanly v. Mitchell,* 460 F. 2d 640 (2d Cir. 1972).
39. *Metropolitan Edison Company v. People Against Nuclear Energy,* 103 S.Ct. 1556 (1983).
40. See *Hanly v. Kleindienst,* 471 F.2d 823 (2d Cir. 1972), *Cert. Denied* 412 U.S. 908 (1973); various other formulas have been adopted by other courts, but this is the one most often used.
41. *Aberdeen and Rockfish Railroad Company v. Students, Challenging Regulatory Agency Procedures,* 422 U.S. 289 (1975).
42. *Scientists' Institute for Public Information, Inc. v. AEC,* 481 F.2d 1079 (D.C. Cir. 1973).
43. This table is adapted from Diori L. Kreske, *Environmental Impact Statements: A Practical Guide for Agencies, Citizens, and Consultants* (New York: John Wiley and Sons, 1996), p. 281.
44. See, for example, *Scientists Institute for Public Information, Inc. v Atomic Energy Commission,* 481 F. 2d 1079, 1092 (D.C.Cir. 1973).
45. 30 C. F. R. Section 1500.1-.28 (1989) and A Worst case analysis: A continued requirement under the NationalEnvironmental Policy Act?@, 13 *Columbia Journal of Environmental Law* 53, 60 (1987).
46. 40 C. F. R. Section 1502.22 (1986).
47. Derived from NEPA and EPA regulations as reported in Alan Gilpin, *Environmental Impact Assessment (EIA): Cutting Edge for the Twenty-First Century,* (Cambridge: Cambridge University Press, 1995).

48. Matthew Lindstrom and Zachary A. Smith, *The National Environmental Policy Act: Promise Unfilled* (College Station, TX: Texas A & M Press, 2002), p. 4.
49. *U.S. Government Manual 1987–1988* (Washington, DC: U.S. Government Printing Office, 1987), p. 525.
50. "Reagan's Policy on Pollution," *Dun's Business Month,* 125 (June 1985), p.48.
51. Bill Adler, "Risky Business," *Sierra,* (November/December 1985) p. 21.
52. "The Quiet Crisis II," *The Amicus Journal,* 10 (1) (Winter 1988), p. 2.
53. "EPA Assailed on Enforcing Superfund Cleanups," *Chemical and Engineering News,* 64 (May 26, 1986), p. 24.
54. "Humpty Dumpty," *The Amicus Journal,* 10 (1) (Winter 1988), p. 14.
55. Larry B. Stammer, "EPA Takes a Harder Stand on Enforcing Clean Air Act," *Los Angeles Times,* April 24, 1987, p. 3.
56. Ibid., p. 32.
57. Patrick M. Raher, "How to Get Things Done at the EPA," *The Brief,* 15 (Winter 1986), p. 23.
58. Phillip Shabecoff, "Environmental Agency: Deep and Persisting Woes," *New York Times,* March 6, 1983, p. A1.
59. Joseph Bower and Charles Christenson, *Public Management* (Homewood, IL: Irwin, 1978), pp. 101–117.
60. Jim Cibbison, "The Agency of Illusion," *Sierra* (May/June 1985), p. 19.
61. "The Quiet Crisis II," p. 2.
62. Shabecoff, "Environmental Agency: Deep and Persisting Woes," p. A1.
63. Stuart Taylor, Jr., "Dingell Says That He Has Evidence of EPA Criminal Conduct," *New York Times,* March 3, 1983, p. A1.
64. Shabecoff, "Environmental Agency: Deep and Persisting Woes," p. A1.
65. The departure of Burford was greeted with joy by longtime high-level EPA staff–they threw a party.
66. "Aides to Ex-EPA Official Testify on Removal of Document," *New York Times,* November 23, 1983, p. A16.
67. "At EPA, Two Top Scientists Come on Board," *Science,* 223 (January 20, 1984), p. 262.
68. "The EPA Is Speaking Softly and Carrying a Bigger Carrot," *Business Week,* June 16, 1986, p.42.
69. "EPA Cites Action on Enforcement in 1986," *New York Times,* Dec. 17, 1986, p. 13.
70. Reed McManus, "Ambushed from Within: The White House Tries to Smother the Clean Air Act," *Sierra* (Sept.-Oct. 1992), p.45.
71. Curtis Lang, *The Amicus Journal* (Spring 1993), pp. 10–11.
72. Rosenbaum Quote on the EPA.
73. Douglas Jehl, "Members of Congress Begin Effort to Get U.S. to Join in Fighting Global Warming." *The New York Times.* July 27, 2001.
74. Katharine Seelye, "E.P.A. Enforcement Nominee Withdraws," *The New York Times.* September 18, 2001.
75. Richard Perez-Pena, (2001). "Possible Federal Pullout Clouds Northeast States' Pollution Suits," *The New York Times.* August 20, 2001.
76. *The New York Times.* August 22, 2001. Editorial "Retreat on Clean Air".
77. GAO Report, June 14, 2001. "Federal Rulemaking: Procedural and Analytical Requirements at OSHA and Other Agencies". p. 7.
78. Ibid., p. 14.
79. Ibid., p. 17.
80. *The New York Times.* August 22, 2001. Editorial "Retreat on Clean Air."
81. T. H. Watkins, "The Terrible Tempered Mr. Ickes," *Audubon* (March 1984), pp. 94, 96.
82. Dean E. Mann and Zachary A. Smith, "The Selection of U.S. Cabinet Officers and Other Political Executives," *International Political Science Review,* 2 (2) (1981), p. 223.
83. See Watkins, "The Terrible Tempered Mr. Ickes," p. 96. An example of the department's problems: Interior Secretary Albert B. Fall was found to have secretly leased portions of U.S. naval petroleum reserves in Wyoming and California in return for bribes well in excess of $100,000.
84. Robert and Patricia Cahn, "Disputed Territory," *National Parks,* 61 (5–6) (May-June 1987), p. 30.
85. Steven Weisman, "Watt Quits Post; President Accepts with Reluctance," *New York Times,* October 9, 1983, p. A1.
86. "Words Cited by Watt Critics," *New York Times,* October 10, 1983, p. D10.
87. "Saint James," *The New Republic,* 194 (March 24, 1986), p. 30.
88. Weisman, "Watt Quits Post; President Accepts with Reluctance," p. A1.

89. "Words Cited by Watt Critics," p. D10.
90. Alexander Cockburn and Bruce Babbitt, "Compromised by Compromise," *The Washington Post National Weekly Edition,* September 6–12, 1993, p. 24.
91. Timothy Egan, "New Priorities for Use of Public Land: Norton Charts a Different Course for the Interior Department," *The New York Times.* August 19, 2001.
92. Editorial "No Greens Need Apply," *The New York Times.* August 19, 2001.
93. *U.S. Government Manual, 1987–1988,* p. 352.
94. James Baker, "BLM Wilderness Review," *Sierra* (March-April 1983), p. 51.
95. Wesley Calef, *Private Grazing and Public Lands* (Chicago: University of Chicago Press, 1960).
96. Richard O. Miller, "Multiple Use in the Bureau of Land Management Cult: The Biases of Pluralism Revisited," in Phillip O. Foss (ed.), *Federal Lands Policy* (New York: Greenwood Press, 1987), p. 57. Unfortunately, the BLM still enforces outdated regulations like the 1872 Hardrock Mining Law and ridiculously low grazing fees. President Clinton made a number of significant mining regulation changes in 1997 and just before departing office, but his predecessor is in favor of weaker 1980 regulations and is instructing the Interior Department and BLM to repeal the Clinton changes. The 1997 regulations limited the scope of new mining activities by confining the size of new mills and dumping grounds. Since about 80 tons of rock needs to be disturbed to find one ounce of gold, miners, especially in Nevada, which is the world's third largest gold producer, were concerned. These interests also did not like the 1997 regulation's language allowing the BLM or the Secretary of the Interior to block any mining operation that might cause "substantial irreparable harm." In the name of economic efficiency, Bush, Norton, and the BLM will continue to allow miners to maim public lands for a nominal filing fee without paying any royalties to the owners of the land, i.e., American taxpayers. They also plan on continuing to allow miners like those in Nevada at the Cortez mine to dump two million pounds of cyanide into the land each year to leach out their gold. See Douglas Jehl, "Gold Miners Eager for Rollback of Rules," *The New York Times.* August 16, 2001.
97. National Parks Service Act of 1916.
98. *U.S. Government Manual, 1977–1978,* p. 1346.
99. Conservation Foundation, *State of the Environment: A View Towards the Nineties* (Washington, DC: Conservation Foundation, 1987), p. 278.
100. Alston Chase, "How to Save Our National Parks," *The Atlantic Monthly* (July 1987), p. 35.
101. U.S. House, House Committee on Appropriations, Budget Hearings, 94th Congress, First Session, p. 446.
102. *Natural History,* 86 (8) (1976), p. 59.
103. John Cushman Jr., "Public Lives: An Environmental Appointee Bush Critics Seem to Like," *The New York Times,* August 27, 2001.
104. *U.S. Government Manual, 1987–1988,* p. 130.
105. Editorial "No Greens Need Apply," *The New York Times,* August 19, 2001.
106. *U.S. Government Manual, 1987–1988,* p. 344.
107. Department of Energy website *http://www.energy.gov/aboutus/history/overview.hist.html* accessed September 21, 2001
108. Daniel Fiorino, *Making Environmental Policy.* (Berkeley: University of California Press, 1995.)

5

Air Pollution

Although some air pollution is generated from natural sources, such as volcanic eruptions, most air pollutants stem from human activities concentrated in urban areas. Forms of transportation, notably the automobile, are primary sources of air pollution. Other sources include power plants and factories, burning fossil fuels, and burning forests and grasslands for farming and grazing, which are common activities in the less developed world.

Although progress has been made to improve air quality in some categories of pollutants, the overall situation is not encouraging. International common pool characteristics make the search for solutions for globally generated air pollution difficult, particularly in the area of acid rain and the greenhouse effect. This chapter provides an overview of air pollution: its components, the laws and regulations governing air pollution, and the effects of air pollution on the environment locally, nationally, and internationally.

SOURCES

The most common forms of air pollution are carbon monoxide, sulfur oxides, nitrogen oxides, particulate matter, and ground-level ozone. Carbon monoxide causes about 67 percent of the measurable air pollution in the United States. Sulfur oxides and nitrogen oxides contribute about 15 percent, with suspended particulate matter and other pollutants making up the balance.[1] These pollutants originate from three primary sources: area sources (31 percent), which include homes and small businesses; mobile sources (39 percent), which include cars and airplanes; and point sources (30 percent), such as power plants.[2]

Carbon monoxide, the most common air pollutant, is a colorless, odorless gas that forms when fossil fuels burn incompletely. Two-thirds of carbon monoxide is produced by transportation (automobiles, trucks, etc.). In high concentrations, carbon monoxide is deadly. In lower concentrations, it can lead to drowsiness, slowed reflexes, and a reduction in the blood's ability to carry and circulate oxygen. EPA monitoring showed a decrease in the presence of carbon monoxide from 1970 through 1999, particularly in urban areas where the greatest carbon monoxide concentrations are found. Carbon monoxide continues to decline in atmospheric concentration, as well as emissions. Between 1980 and 1999, CO emissions dropped 22 percent with more than two-thirds of that occurring in the 1980s. Its concentration in the atmosphere fell 57 percent in that 20-year period, almost two-thirds of that coming in the 1990s.[3] This decrease was largely attributable to the Federal Motor Vehicle Control Program for New Cars (new car standards). As of 1999, motor vehicles accounted for 60 percent of carbon monoxide totals nationally and transportation generally accounted for over 77 percent.[4]

The sulfur oxides include sulfur dioxide (SO_2) and sulfur trioxide (SO_3). Sulfur dioxide is a colorless gas that can aggravate respiratory diseases in humans, reduce plant growth, and corrode metal and stone. Electric utilities generate 70 percent of the SO_2 emissions in the United States, with most of that coming from coal-fired power plants.[5] Power plants under the EPA's Acid Rain Program (established in Title IV of the 1990 Clean Air Act Amendments) have showed steady improvement. They reduced SO_2 emissions 29 percent from 1990 levels by 2000 and there was a 10 percent drop from 1999 to 2000 alone. During that same year utilization was up 2.7 percent, so the pollution control did not hurt energy production. The year 1999 was the first year of "Phase II" of the Program meaning the grace period of minor reductions beginning in 1995 was over. In 2000, only 9.97 million tons worth of "permits" were issued by the EPA, or 56 percent of what was emitted in 1980.

Utility emission levels of SO_2 in the United States decreased from 17.3 to 11.2 million tons from 1980 to 2000 due to the burning of lower-sulfur fuels, the installation of pollution control devices, and the Acid Rain Program. That is a 35 percent reduction in 20 years, and the decrease has been even greater since the program began in 1995. Between 1986 and 1995, national emissions of sulfur dioxide declined 18 percent and atmospheric concentrations declined 37 percent. From 1994 to 1995, the first year of the program, concentration levels dropped dramatically (17 percent), as did emission levels (13 percent). These declines may be attributed to the success of the EPA Program to combat acid rain, which is caused in large part by sulfur dioxide.[6] To highlight the impact of the program is the fact that sulfur dioxide atmospheric concentrations dropped 50 percent from 1980 levels and 36 percent from 1990 levels by 1999, while emissions are down 27 percent and 20 percent, respectively.[7]

Nitrogen oxides include nitric oxide and nitrogen dioxide. Like sulfur dioxide, emissions of nitrogen dioxide in the United States have declined slightly. From 1980 to 1999, average levels of nitrogen dioxide in the atmosphere decreased 25 percent, though no change occurred from 1998 to 1999. Average nitrogen oxide emissions have held fairly steady, however, increasing just 4 percent. Since Los Angeles finally met EPA attainment standards for NOx in July of 1998, the entire

United States now meets national air quality standards for this pollutant. Roughly 40 percent of all nitrogen oxides come from stationary fuel combustion sources, mostly utilities; much of the remainder comes from motor vehicles and jet-propelled aircraft.[8] Like sulfur dioxide, nitrogen oxides contribute to acid rain. Important to note here is the fact that with these pollution reductions, a 30 percent increase in electrical output has still occurred since 1990.[9]

Ambient suspended particulate matter, tiny fragments of liquid or solid matter floating in the air, has decreased 20 percent from the early 1970s into the mid-1980s, according to EPA measurements. These decreases were due in part to a reduction of industrial activities in the late 1970s and early 1980s, and the installation of pollution control equipment. Coal-fired power plants represent the largest source of particulate matter.[10]

In July 1987, the EPA revised its standards to monitor only those particles designated PM-10 (particulate matter with a diameter less than or equal to a nominal 10 microns). These particles are considered small enough to pose a health risk because their size allows them to penetrate the most sensitive regions of the respiratory tract. From 1988 to 1995, PM-10 concentrations have fallen 22 percent; emissions have declined 17 percent.[11] In 1996 the EPA reported that 78 areas still do not meet the standard for PM-10.[12]

In July 1998, the EPA promulgated new standards for the release of particulate matter and ground-level ozone. These new standards included regulations that address particulate matter four times smaller than PM-10, as well as the amount of time that particulate matter of certain sizes may be present in a specified area. In the case of ozone, the new standards would require assessments of attainability to take place over a much longer period. This allows for a much more accurate indicator of the ozone danger. The EPA considered these new regulations necessary to prevent 15,000 premature deaths, 350,000 cases of aggravated asthma, and 1 million cases of significantly decreased lung function in children.[13]

The year 1999 marked the first year the EPA received complete data on PM-2.5. Therefore, attainment data will not be available until 2005, so we must wait and see if we have successfully reduced this air pollutant. PM-10 air concentrations are down 18 percent from 1990 to 1999, and sulfates (that cause about half of PM-2.5 concentrations) are down 24 percent in the 1990s, so preliminary indicators for the successful regulation of this air pollutant are good.[14]

The American Trucking Association challenged the new EPA standards for PM-2.5 and ozone in 1999, claiming these new regulations were legislation, and Congress did not have the authority to delegate to the EPA this law-making function through the 1990 Clean Air Act Amendments. On February 27, 2001, the U.S. Supreme Court unanimously ruled that the Act is indeed constitutional and that the EPA can set NAAQS based solely on public health considerations, regardless of the potential cost to industry or others.[15]

Ground-level ozone (referred to by some as "smog") is not directly emitted into the air. Rather it is a poisonous form of pure oxygen that is created when sunlight reacts with nitrogen oxides and volatile organic compounds (VOCs) in the air.[16] VOCs come from three sources. Point sources or industries that use chemicals or solvents in their processing account for approximately 30 percent. Area sources that make up 20 percent of emissions are comprised of small emitters such as dry cleaners and print shops. Automobiles contribute 50 percent.[17] Anthropogenic (human-made) VOCs are down 31 percent from 1980 to 1999 and 14 percent from

1990 to 1999. Now industrial processes produce 44 percent of VOCs nationwide, and transportation sources account for 47 percent; solvent use alone contributes to 26 percent of total U.S. VOC emissions.[18] While many areas came close to meeting ozone standards in the mid-1980s, relaxed enforcement in the late 1980s resulted in 96 cities being categorized as nonattainment sites in 1991. Increased efforts during the early 1990s, however, have led to the decrease in nonattainment sites. In 1995 just 68 sites were in violation of national ambient air quality standards for ground-level ozone. As of August 2, 2001, 56 areas encompassing 241 counties that are home to 104 million Americans were in violation of ozone standards; 24 of these areas are considered "serious" or worse, with the remainder "moderate" or "marginal."[19] Overall, air concentrations of ozone are down 20 percent from 1980 levels, but only 4 percent in the 1990s. Seventeen cities actually have *higher* ozone levels in 1999 than 1990, whereas 14 cities have improved, and the rest have stayed fairly steady.[20]

Health Effects

Although it is difficult to establish a direct causal relation between a specific pollutant when it is in the atmosphere and a particular disease or death, many studies have shown that such relationships exist. Research has found air pollution to be associated with higher mortality rates and an increase in adverse health effects.[21] Strong evidence suggests that pollution from the burning of fossil fuels leads to the premature death of between 30,000 and 35,000 Americans each year.[22] The elderly, infants, and children are particularly susceptible to harm from air pollution as are adults with respiratory problems.

The interactive effects of pollutants in the atmosphere complicate the task of establishing direct links between air pollution and human health. "Synergistic interactions between various pollutants can lead to more harm than that of one acting alone, and the multiple causes and lengthy incubation times of diseases such as emphysema, chronic bronchitis, lung cancer, and heart disease" make it extremely difficult to establish direct causal relationships.[23] However, in extreme cases of air pollution, causal relationships between pollution and human health have been clear.

Several times severe thermal inversions have trapped pollution within an area allowing pollutants that would otherwise be blown away to concentrate.[24] In December 1952 the famous London killer fog led to 1,600 more deaths than ordinarily would have occurred. Similar events occurred in the Meuse Valley in Belgium in 1930 with 63 deaths and 6,000 illnesses and in 1948 in Donora, Pennsylvania, with 20 deaths and 6,000 illnesses.[25]

These tragedies are some of the easily identifiable adverse effects of air pollution on human health. However, as the figure of 35,000 premature deaths every year suggests, many more people are affected by air pollution than we realize. Although much is known about the relationship between National Ambient Air Quality Standards (NAAQS) and human health,[26] failure to meet those standards is an indication of a lack of progress toward cleaner and presumably healthier air. Nationally, the situation has improved slightly; it is estimated that only 2 out of every 5 Americans now live in cities where the air is unhealthful for part of the year.[27] The American Lung Association (ALA), on the other hand, estimates 141 million (about half of all) Americans live with unhealthful air, up from 132 million in 2000.[28] They go on to say 50,000 to 100,000 Americans die annually from complications due to air pollution, not to mention the millions who suffer from asthma attacks or other acute respiratory symptoms. The Reason Public Policy Institute, however, estimates the ALA's figures are up to 60 percent too high.[29] Whatever numbers you are inclined to believe, the fact remains that air pollution is directly linked to a number of persistent and expensive health problems.

Internationally, the situation is much worse. In Calcutta, India, it is estimated 60 percent of the city's population suffers air pollution-related diseases. Sao Paulo, Mexico City, Cairo, and New Delhi all have serious air pollution problems that border on being hazardous. And in Athens, Greece, air pollution claims as many as 40 lives a year.[30]

The health effects of air pollution provide a good example of the paradox of environmental policy. Some argue there is a lack of scientific evidence for any link between a pollutant and a particular illness. Even in the case of killer fog in London, as an illustration, evidence of the impact on human health was derived from death rates comparing the killer fog period with other periods. The relationship was not as direct as to be absolute proof, but the degree of probability of a connection was overwhelming. While more specific evidence of the impact of air pollution on human health would lead to greater support for regulation, as a leading environmental science textbook points out, "[I]nstead of establishing absolute truth or proof, science establishes only a degree of probability or confidence in the validity of an idea, usually based on statistical or circumstantial evidence."[31] In air pollution policy this uncertainty has, at times, resulted in a "go slow" approach to new regulation.

Although health effects may be our most immediate and personal concern, air pollution can also cause significant damage to crops. Air pollution can cause a 10 to 15 percent reduction in yield, and even go so far as to cause the complete loss of crops.[32] In the United States the EPA and U.S. Department of Agriculture have estimated that air pollution has reduced crop yields from 5 to 10 percent—representing a loss of between $3.5 and $7 billion.[33]

Ozone causes more damage to plants than all other air pollutants combined. Spring and summer O_3 concentrations in the southeastern United States usually average between 50 and 55 ppb (parts per billion in the air) every year. Cotton, peanuts, and soybeans demonstrate a 10 percent crop loss at such levels compared to O_3 concentrations at 20 ppb or less. When O_3 reaches 60 ppb crop yields for these important agricultural products drop 20 percent and fall by a third at 80 ppb. Parts of southern California sometimes exceed 80 ppb.[34] Further, yield reductions in the United States due to ozone in the late 1980s were estimated to be about 5 percent of total national production. If the United States reduced ground-level ozone by 40 percent that would yield a $3 billion increase in agricultural revenue.[35]

On the global market, crop yields of winter oilseed rape, a common crop in the UK, fell by as much as 14 percent when plots were exposed to high levels of ozone. Similar field trials on winter wheat, another major UK crop, produced a 13 percent loss in yields. In eastern Spain, watermelons showed a 19 percent drop in yields where ozone levels were double the guidelines set by the United Nations Economic Commission for Europe. When ozone levels were five times the guideline, there was a resulting 39 percent loss in crop yields.[36]

Recall that policy makers have incentives to pursue short-term solutions with low immediate costs, without regard for the long-term costs. Since air pollution problems rarely present themselves as a "crisis," policy makers can politically afford to move slowly and incrementally. Unfortunately, some air pollution problems require immediate and costly investment, which is not likely to be made without an apparent "crisis" and will be very expensive when the problem presents itself in crisis proportions.

Many representatives of polluting industries have argued over the years that air pollution is a relatively minor problem. The Ford Motor Company, while lobbying a Los Angeles county supervisor in 1953, wrote, "[T]he Ford engineering staff, although mindful that automobile engines produce the exhaust gasses, feels that these waste vapors are dissipated in the atmosphere quickly, and do not present an air pollution problem."[37] Although automobile companies are now willing to concede that cars contribute to air pollution, the lack of scientific certainty on the exact magnitude of the impact, which make control requirements difficult to quantify, is still used as an argument against regulation. The president of a major utility in the southern United States, when arguing for a "go slow" approach to the control of acid rain, made the point that "[T]he roster of respected scientists who have pointed out how much we don't know about acid deposition would fill at least a page of fine print."[38]

With respect to acid rain, as well as other air pollution problems, it is true scientists do not speak with a single voice. That is to be expected where science is not in the business of establishing *absolute* truth or proof but the probability of such effects. However, the negative impacts of air pollution are well established. The problem of developing policy to mitigate these negative impacts is compounded by scientific uncertainty, the nature of scientific proof, and the fact that the atmosphere does have some natural assimilative capacity. The air can accept some pollution without necessarily having a negative impact on life on earth. However, the question remains as to what is the appropriate level of air pollution control.

Motor Vehicles

Motor vehicles are a primary cause of air pollution in the United States and globally. The EPA estimates motor vehicles account for about one-half of all the hydrocarbon and nitrogen oxide precursor pollutants, up to 90 percent of the carbon monoxide, and over half of the toxic air pollutants in the United States.[39]

The Department of Energy (DOE) estimates that 40 percent of the growth in greenhouse gas emissions through 2015 will come from cars and the rest of the transportation sector. The half a billion cars out there today cause 20 to 25 percent of total global greenhouse gas emissions.[40] Cars, trucks and other mobile sources account for almost a third of the total air pollution in the United States.[41] Motor vehicles as a class are likely the single largest source of air pollution, and they cause an estimated $93 billion in health and environmental damage annually in the United States. Though Americans have the strictest air quality standards in the world, about 30,000 Americans die annually from respiratory illness related to car exhaust.[42] This is despite the fact that 2000 model year cars are about 96 percent cleaner than 1960s models, and the auto industry spends $18.4 billion annually to make cars cleaner and safer.[43]

The proportionate increases in air pollutants discussed at the beginning of this chapter are surprisingly low given the increase in motor vehicle production in the

United States and worldwide since the early 1970s. From 1970 to 1986, the number of passenger cars sold in the United States, for example, increased 51 percent. Sales in the then noncommunist industrial world increased by 71 percent.[44] However, it should be noted that since the 1970s, pollution abatement initiatives within the automobile industry have decreased automobile pollution levels about 90 percent. This dramatic decrease may be attributed to changes in automobile design (addition of the catalytic converter) as well as in gasoline composition (reductions of aromatic chemical compounds like sulfur, benzene, and the elimination of lead). The EPA is currently advocating the production of reformulated gasolines (RFGs) that are estimated to allow for the reduction of total automobile emissions by 20 percent by 2000 from 1990 levels.[45]

The jury is still out on the effectiveness of RFGs in reducing pollution. "Oxygenates" such as MTBE were supposed to decrease CO emissions, but there is evidence that MTBE can severely contaminate ground and surface water, cause other health problems, and it may not substantially decrease CO emissions. The EPA and Centers for Disease Control (CDC) asked the Health Effects Institute (HEI) to conduct a study on MTBE to settle the issue. Current levels of MTBE found in ecosystems seem to be negligible, and MTBE reformulate gasoline's environmental effects are about the same as with regular gasoline. However, they did note MTBE's continued use could lead to concentrations in water supplies that are dangerous. Now the EPA is looking into banning MTBE under the Toxic Substances Control Act.[46]

Parts of the country utilize other RFGs, though. The Midwest has favored a gasoline additive called ethanol produced primarily from corn. It is not clear that this RFG is a cleaner alternative to regular fuel either. In fact, it takes much more energy to farm the corn and turn it into ethanol than is gained by adding it to gasoline, so its overall environmental impact could be detrimental regardless of how much cleaner (if any) it makes gas burn in cars.[47] In any case, ethanol will likely continue to be an important part of motor vehicle fuel in the Midwest because of its strong congressional lobby and (primarily corn farmers) resultant heavy subsidies.

The cost of fighting air pollution through the use of reformulated gasoline is "far lower" than some earlier estimates. A 1998 study compared the pump price of regular unleaded gasoline to cleaner burning fuels that include additives and found that the RFG cost an average of just 2.89 cents more per gallon. Using the cleaner fuel costs the typical family only about $25 a year.

The total cost of motor vehicle emission abatement, which included the cost of equipment as well as increased fuel cost and maintenance, has been estimated at approximately $8 billion a year.[48]

This is a fraction of the cost to society for continued air pollution from automobiles.[49] Many hidden costs (or negative externalities) exist, such as the destruction of rubber on automobiles and equipment and corrosion of stone and iron on buildings and statues. In some countries another hidden cost is the political instability that results from a dependence on foreign sources of oil. The reduction of crop yields and timber harvests, increased health costs, and the destruction of buildings are additional factors. Researchers at the University of Miami estimated the hidden cost of gasoline consumption is approximately 80 cents per gallon of gasoline burned.[50]

Gasoline costs disappear from consumer view in a number of ways. First, there are direct oil company subsidies, and then government-funded research for these corporations. There are also lower than average sales taxes applied to gasoline, and, of course, the hidden environmental damage burning gas causes. Federal corporate income tax is at an effective rate of 11 percent for the oil industry, compared to 18 percent for non-oil industries. Without those tax breaks, the oil companies would have to find that $2 billion from its customers to keep profits at present levels. In addition, state and local government sales taxes for gas are also about half of what they are for other goods, and this means state and local governments are giving up between $2.7 billion and $4.1 billion annually of what they would otherwise collect in sales taxes. Finally, the environmental externalities are estimated to cost Americans between $54 billion to $232 billion annually.[51]

All this is not surprising given the political and economic might of the auto and oil industries. One in every seven jobs in the United States is tied to the automobile industry, and lobbyists ensure that every legislator knows that. They are also aware that jobs in this sector are among the highest paying in the world. Because political job security is often tied to economic performance, and whether or not local constituents have well-paying or any jobs, it will be extremely difficult to fight corporate subsidies for these industries let alone force them to internalize the costs of environmental externalities.

It is important to note that the above numbers are subject to interpretation based on various assumptions, but the majority of energy experts agree the current cost of gasoline does not come close to the true cost primarily because of negative externalities. For example, in an Energy Project report at Harvard Business School, the researchers concluded the external cost of oil ranges from $65 to $165 a barrel.[52]

Even if these hidden costs were widely known, the obstacles to reducing pollution from motor vehicles remain enormous. Again, automobile production plays such an important role in the economy of the United States that auto executives know any threat to the industry (real or perceived) will be taken seriously by policy makers. During the debate over passage of the 1970 Clean Air Act, auto executives used this fear to manipulate policy makers to the betterment of the auto industry. Lee Iacocca, as vice president of Ford Motor Company, warned that were the proposed bill to become law, U.S. auto production could come to a halt after January 1, 1975. Even if production were to continue, Iacocca argued, the bill would force "huge hikes in car prices and do irreparable damage to the American economy." Iacocca continued that the act would produce "only small improvements in the quality of the air."[53]

Soon the debate focused on the capacity of auto manufacturers to meet the act's requirements. Senator Edmund Muskie, who sponsored the 1970 Clean Air Act, responded to industry charges with the argument that the auto industry already had the technology to meet the 1975 standards. "Representatives of that industry," Muskie said on the Senate floor, "whose great genius is mass production, are trying to tell us that what can be done in the laboratory cannot be converted to mass production in five years."[54] Although Muskie prevailed in 1970, the industry subsequently convinced Congress and the EPA that limits could not be met and the auto makers were granted extensions. Ironically, extensions were granted to American automobile manufacturers at the same time foreign producers were meeting and exceeding the EPA's requirements.

The 1990 Clean Air Act amendments contain several measures designed to reduce motor vehicle pollutants. The phaseout of lead, scheduled for January 1, 1996, has been attained. In some nonattainment areas, gasoline will have to be reformulated to contain fewer VOCs, and detergents in gasoline to prevent engine deposits will be required. During winter months, oxyfuel, which contains increased oxygen to make fuel burn more efficiently to reduce carbon monoxide release, will also be required in cities with the worst air pollution problems. Finally, the 1990 amendments also increase the number of areas that must implement inspection and maintenance programs for automobiles.

AIR POLLUTION: LAW, REGULATIONS, AND ENFORCEMENT

Air pollution regulation in the United States represents both the best and the worst of environmental policy making. On the one hand, air pollution regulation has consisted of a relatively rare nonincremental approach to a policy problem, which has represented a positive approach. For example, the Clean Air Act, passed in 1963 and amended in 1967, 1970, 1977, and 1990, has changed past practice in several ways. On the other hand, subsequent tinkering with these laws, primarily through exemptions and extensions, provide instances of incrementalism in the policy-making process, which has led to less than desirable air pollution control outcomes.

The federal response to the problem of air pollution began in 1955 with Congress offering technical expertise and financial assistance to the states. The Clean Air Act of 1963 was the first major federal involvement in air pollution. The Clean Air Act empowered federal officials to intervene in interstate air pollution matters only at the request of state governments. However, the apparatus for enforcing pollution abatement was so cumbersome as to be ineffective. Between 1965 and 1970, only 11 abatement actions had been initiated under the 1963 Clean Air Act.[55] Congress eventually amended the Clean Air Act by passing the Air Quality Act of 1967. This legislation directed the Secretary of the Department of Health, Education and Welfare to establish Air Quality Control Regions (AQCRs). Within each region, states established air quality standards and emission standards for regulated pollutants. Unfortunately, by 1970, of a projected 91 AQCRs in the country, only 25 had been designated by the federal government.

These early acts deferred to state governments with respect to air pollution control enforcement. Due to the common pool nature of environmental pollution problems, deference to state government creates a special regulatory dilemma. Without federal guidelines backed by federal enforcement for uniformity, states have an incentive to compete with each other for industry by using pollution control, or a lack of pollution control, as an inducement to bring industry within its borders. Under such circumstances, all states in the region are environmental losers. A state that wishes to limit polluting activities suffers from pollution generated by its neighbors. Air pollution does not respect state borders. For this reason, some industries pushed for exclusive state pollution control. However, many other industries, particularly those doing business in several states, argued in support of federal pollution control. For example, the automobile industry initially fought strenuously against any auto emission regulation. After it became clear the states would act individually to limit automobile emissions, thus producing many separate regulations, the industry pushed for uniform national emission regulations.

The Clean Air Act of 1970 and subsequent amendments in 1977 and 1990 represented significant increases in federal involvement in air pollution regulation, addressing some of the common pool problems associated with local control of air pollution. The act directed the EPA administrator to establish "national ambient air quality standards" (NAAQS) (see notes).[56] Primary standards represent "ambient air quality standards the attainment and maintenance of which in the judgment of the administrator, based on such criteria and allowing an adequate margin of safety are requisite to protect the public health."[57] Secondary standards are those necessary to protect the public welfare from adverse effects associated with air pollution.

Pollutants emitted directly into the atmosphere are classified as primary pollutants. Secondary pollutants are formed after emission as a result of a reaction with substances already in the atmosphere. Pollutants that consist of tiny fragments of liquid or solid matter are classified as particulates. Gaseous pollutants, which can be further divided into inorganic or organic gasses, are the final classification of pollutants.[58]

The 1970 act required uniform national standards of performance to be developed for new stationary sources of air pollution and for preexisting sources that were modified in a manner that increases the emissions of any pollutant. It also required uniform national standards for "hazardous" air pollutants, defined as "[A]ir pollution which may reasonably be anticipated to result in an increase in mortality or an increase in serious irreversible, or incapacitating irreversible, illness."[59]

The 1970 Clean Air Act originally required that primary air quality standards be met no later than December 31, 1975. This deadline, like other air quality deadlines, was extended once and then again. Nine months after the development of NAAQS, the states were required to submit to the EPA their state implementation plans (SIPs), which, when promulgated by the EPA, represent the legally binding strategies to be implemented to meet the National Ambient Air Quality Standards. The Clean Air Act requires that SIPs lead to attainment of NAAQ Standards "as expeditiously as practical but ... in no case later than three years from the date of approval of such plan." However, a two-year extension is possible under certain circumstances. There is no specific time for the achievement of secondary standards other than a "reasonable" time. Initially, the EPA established standards for carbon monoxide, particulates, sulfur dioxide, nitrogen dioxide, hydrocarbons, and photochemical oxidants.

The Clean Air Act of 1970 also directed the EPA to establish minimum emission standards for stationary sources called "new source performance standards." These standards (the NSPS) are to be established on an industry-by-industry basis, taking cost into consideration. New source performance standards are to use the "best available control technology."

The Environmental Protection Agency uses a number of classification schemes in its implementation of the provisions of the Clean Air Act. Emission sources are divided into "major" or "minor" and are found either in "attainment areas" or in "nonattainment areas," depending on whether or not air quality goals have been met. Sources are "new" or "existing," depending on if the source of emission was in place when permits were first issued. Regulations vary depending on whether a source is major or minor, in an attainment area, or new or existing.

The 1977 amendments to the Clean Air Act divided each type of Air Quality Control Region that was attaining the standard into three classes. Class I regions include national parks, wilderness, and similar areas. Little, if any, deterioration in air quality was allowed in a Class I region. Class II areas are those areas where moderate increases of air pollution are allowed, as long as the resulting pollution does not exceed the NAAQS. States were allowed to reclassify a Class II area as a Class I area or as a Class III area to allow for industrial development, provided air quality standards would not be violated. Class III designation allows air quality degradation up to the NAAQS.

The 1977 Clean Air Act Amendments also established emission standards for automobiles and trucks requiring a 90 percent reduction in carbon monoxide and hydrocarbon emissions by 1975 and nitrogen oxide emissions by 1976, as measured against 1970 emission levels. The act empowered the EPA administrator with the authority to extend these deadlines, and extensions were granted by either the EPA or Congress in 1973, 1974, 1975, and 1977.

The 1977 Clean Air Act Amendments also required states to develop plans by 1982 that would bring air quality for ozone, carbon monoxide, and other pollutants up to EPA standards by December 31, 1987. When the deadline passed, approximately 60 of the 247 Air Quality Control Regions that had been established at that time within the country did not meet EPA standards. The EPA had the authority to ban construction of new major stationary sources within these 60 regions if an approved State Implementation Plan (SIP) was not submitted by 1979. In addition, those areas that had either not submitted SIPs for approval or had submitted plans that did not have inspection and maintenance plans were subject to mandatory highway sanctions. This occurred in California, Kentucky, and New Mexico. Anticipating difficulty in meeting with the standard mandated in 1977, Congress debated over amendments to the Clean Air Act to reduce the standards or grant extensions every year from 1981 to 1990.

In the event that state implementation plans were not submitted to the EPA or did not meet EPA approval, the 1970 Clean Air Act amendments provided that federal implementation plans could be imposed on a region. The EPA has been very reluctant to develop its own plans for political reasons. As a result of several lawsuits by environmental organizations, initially in Phoenix, Arizona, but also in the metropolitan Los Angeles area; Bakersfield, Sacramento, Ventura, and Fresno, California; and Chicago, Illinois, the EPA was forced to develop federal air pollution plans (FIPs).

The passage of the 1990 Clean Air Act amendments ended more than 10 years of congressional stalemate over the reauthorization of the Clean Air Act. Environmental policy formation is often directed (or thwarted) by coalitions or subgovernments composed of interest groups, elected officials, and bureaucrats that dominate policy making in their area of interest. During the 1980s, a coalition of utilities, labor unions, Midwestern politicians, and auto and oil interests successfully prevented any strengthening of the Clean Air Act. President Ronald Reagan and Senate majority leader Robert Byrd (from coal-producing West Virginia) opposed new legislation to control air pollution. The election of George Mitchell of Maine as majority leader, a proponent of a stronger Clean Air Act, and President Bush led the way to tougher legislation. President Bush proposed a clean air package in 1989 that would reduce emissions of sulfur dioxide and nitrogen oxide. For the first time in 10 years, the Reagan/Bush administration indicated its willingness to support tougher legislation. When the 1990 Clean Air Act amendments were being debated, Midwestern politicians found themselves isolated against other sections of the country, which did not want to pay for cleaning up pollution from utilities in the Ohio Valley. These politicians had joined with the oil and auto industries and successfully prevented previous clean air bills from passing in the 1980s. However, in 1990 a combination of rising public support for environmental legislation (detailed in Chapter 2) and the perception among politicians up for reelection that it was not a good time to vote against the environment led to passage of the 1990 amendments.[60]

The 1990 Clean Air Act Amendments (CAAA) have 11 major sections, or titles, and run about 800 pages. This reauthorization carries with it implementation plans through 2005.

Title I, often referred to as the "nonattainment of ambient air standards title," deals with those states and localities that chronically exceed EPA's ground-level ozone limitation standards. As we noted previously, the 1970 Clean Air Act required the EPA to set health-based ambient air standards for certain pollutants. The 1990 CAAA revised regulations for six criteria pollutants: ground-level ozone, carbon monoxide, sulfur dioxide, nitrogen dioxide, lead, and particulate matter (PM-10). Title I designated nonattainment status for three of these criteria: ozone, particulate matter, and carbon monoxide.

For ground-level ozone, states are required to develop an ozone abatement strategy in revised SIPs based not only on ozone but on its hydrocarbon and nitrogen oxide precursors as well.

The nonattainment status for areas designated by Congress is also classified by severity. For ozone, there are five classifications, ranging from marginal to extreme. Each classification carries with it increasingly more stringent abatement measures. Carbon monoxide and particulate matter have only two classifications, moderate and serious. Title I also redefines "major" stationary sources according to the nonattainment level of their location.

Other titles of the 1990 CAAA deal with air toxics, protecting stratospheric ozone, and acid rain. We discuss them later. However, there is one new key component of the act that attempts to link all CAAA compliance programs for major sources and all other sources covered by federal regulatory programs. It was argued that SIPs were too difficult to revise or enforce because they required rule making at both the state and federal levels. In an effort to simplify revisions and enforcement, Title V establishes an operating permit program. Based on the National Pollutant Discharge Elimination System (NPDES) of the Clean Water Act, this program requires sources to provide information on which pollutants are being released, in what quantities, and to provide plans to monitor levels of pollution. Theoretically, the permit would contain all the detailed information required by all sections of the CAAA. For instance, an electric power plant could be covered by nonattainment for the ozone, acid rain, and toxic pollutant parts of the CAAA. The EPA has delegated NPDES monitoring and enforcement authority to 40 states. NPDES permits within the remaining ten states are administered by the EPA through its regional offices.[61]

Regulatory Innovations

Since the mid-1970s, the EPA has introduced a number of innovations in the implementation of the Clean Air Act. These innovations primarily involve various types of emission-trading systems. Trading systems are classified as netting, offsets, bubbles, or banking. Each of these systems is designed to allow polluters flexibility in meeting emission limits. Trading is based on the assumption that the polluters are in the best position to understand their own sources of pollution and how to make the most cost-effective reductions in pollution. Although the EPA establishes broad goals and regulations, the responsibility of administering trading systems falls to state and local agencies.

Netting, which began in 1974, sums the total output of pollution from a given plant or plants and allows management to reduce the output of pollution in one aspect of the plant's activities while increasing it in some other aspect or some other area.

Offsets, which have been used since 1976, allow a polluting plant to start operation in a nonattainment area. Basically, this means the new polluter must reduce pollution from existing sources within the nonattainment area. For example, an energy company desiring to build a refinery in a nonattainment area may be required to purchase and install pollution control equipment in the refineries of competitors in the region. Although the offsets are theoretically allowed only when there will be a net decrease in the amount of pollution in the nonattainment area, in practice, the reductions in pollution from offsetting, as well as from other emission-trading devices, have been minimal.[62]

Counted as a success among critics, the U.S. Acid Rain Program has shown promising results in the "cap-and-trade" system of emissions trading. This program, established in 1990 to reduce sulfur dioxide emissions from heavy industries, performed much better than estimates had predicted. A study of the effectiveness of the program showed that in 1995 one-third of the industries involved complied at a profit.[63]

Bubbles, first used in 1979, allow a polluter to total the emissions from a plant and thus allow adjustments in the source of emissions within the plant, as long as the aggregate emission levels are not exceeded. Bubbles are similar to netting except that external trading may be allowed between plants in an air quality region.

Banking, also developed in 1979, is used in conjunction with the bubble policy and allows for the saving of emission reduction "credits" for future use. Bubbles and banking have led to markets in emissions credits for particular pollutants in nonattainment areas across the United States.

The banking system in Chicago, Illinois, has been held up by many critics of air pollution policy as a model for the emissions credit banking system. The bank, which was the first to be established by a municipality in 1994, encourages industries to donate their credits in return for potential tax breaks. The system works like this. When a business uses credits from the bank in order to pollute, it must commit to retiring 30 percent of those credits. The ERC Bank also requires companies to complete an environmental project that benefits the local community. Companies that reduce emissions beyond what air quality regulations require can deposit unused credits in the ERC Bank. These donors then become eligible for federal tax benefits, while Chicago has more credits to lend out to businesses.[64]

The first company to purchase emission-credits from the bank, Wheatland Tube Company, also initiated an environmental program that included donating $7,500 for new landscape projects in their community, as well as $7,500 worth of materials to the local chapter of Habitat for Humanity. The availability of an emissions-credit bank allowed Wheatland to initiate a $12 million expansion of their operation, which will ultimately include $2 million for environmental improvements.[65]

Emission Reduction Credits (ERCs) are required for new major emission sources, or sources undergoing major expansions, by various state air agencies in regions that do not meet the EPA's national ambient air quality standards (NAAQS). The 1990 CAAA do indeed require a market-based approach to facilitate the attainment of the mandated milestones and goals of Title I.[66]

The goal of emissions trading, or the buying and selling of "Emission Reduction Credits" (ERC), is to achieve cleaner air at a lower cost. Evidence suggests that emissions trading has lowered the cost of pollution control to industry, but it has had a negligible effect on air quality.[67] Theoretically, pollution reductions are achieved by the requirement that the purchase of an offset or credit from a polluting source be for a right to pollute less than the original amount of reduction. The "offset ratio" determines how much reduction in total emissions there will be as a result of an emission trade. So, for example, an offset ratio of 1:1 would result in no net reduction in pollution, whereas a ratio of 2:1 would result in a 50 percent reduction of a particular emission from the original source when it was traded.

Although emissions trading sounds tidy and efficient in theory, there are a number of practical problems in its administration. First, emissions trading requires careful monitoring of plant emissions to determine the amount of pollution output. The states' implementation of EPA policy varies significantly in the quality of their air quality monitoring data, some requiring detailed data while others require little or none.[68] In addition, offset ratios vary significantly. For example, in California, the Bay Area Air Quality Management District has required an offset ratio of as high as 2:1 when based on the average annual emissions of a source, provided a net air quality benefit can be demonstrated from the trade. In contrast, other jurisdictions, such as Connecticut, Illinois, and Virginia, have offset ratios at or near 1:1, which even in the best of situations would lead to little or no net air pollution reduction.

The emissions-trading market has developed in nonattainment areas across the country. ERCs are bought, sold, and auctioned. Shopping for ERCs can be as or more important than any other aspect of a manufacturer's business. For example, the president of a spa company in Chino, California, remarked, "I spend a lot of time shopping for ERC's—for us, they are a matter of life and death."[69] Josh Margolis, an ERC broker who works for AER*X, which stands for Air Emission Reduction Exchange, based in Washington, D.C., described how the exchange process should work to reduce total air emissions. "If you have a credit of 250 tons of oxides of nitrogen per year and sell it to the plant around the corner, they can only admit 225 tons."[70] Credits are sold on the open market and, consequently, they can fluctuate wildly based on general economic conditions. For example, in Los Angeles hydrocarbon credits sold for around $1,000 a ton in 1984 and had more than doubled two years later.[71]

Most criticisms of the marketing of emission reduction credits center around two primary concerns. First, the use of emission reduction credits enshrines the holder with a right or entitlement to pollute. That is, by allowing a permit to pollute, polluting industries are effectively given property rights to air resources. In turn, these rights are withheld from private citizens who also are entitled to use the air. ERCs also legitimate the polluter's "right to pollute" at the expense of the public's right to enjoy a pollution free environment.

The command and control techniques that have historically characterized pollution reduction tend to emphasize the presumption that pollution is not acceptable, at any price, when it harms the environment or human health. Such a perspective places the value of public and natural health above economics. Second, there is the concern that emission reduction credits do not result in aggregate decreases in pollution. This is in contrast with best available technology or technology-forcing requirements that seek to reduce the overall amounts of pollution. Only if the market supply of emission credits is gradually reduced may the trading schemes work. In this market, it is important that demand not control the system.

Environmentalists have been wary about emission reduction credit trading. One national environmental organization, the Natural Resources Defense Council (NRDC), has labeled the bubble concept "one of the most destructive impediments to the cleanup of unhealthy air."[72] The NRDC and other environmental groups have argued that emissions trading essentially allows current levels of pollution to remain the same in nonattainment areas. Some state and local officials have also been skeptical of emissions trading, repeating the concern that trading in nonattainment areas often prevents the reduction in total air pollutants within the area.[73]

However, as emission-trading programs develop, some environmental groups are beginning to recognize the potential value of emission-trading programs. In the summer of 1997, EPA officials, law makers, and environmentalists agreed that emission-trading systems, established under the Clean Air Act, should be expanded to include other programs oriented toward the reduction of greenhouse gases and particulate matter.[74]

The primary argument in favor of emissions trading is not that it reduces air pollution, but rather it allows corporations to determine where they can cut back internally on their polluting activities. In general, industries that are major stationary source polluters strongly favor the bubble concept. Exactly why they favor emissions trading is no mystery. Netting and offsets provide greater flexibility and allow firms to seek the least costly pollution solution available.[75] A potential problem for a firm attempting to establish a plant in a nonattainment area is that competitors may attempt to freeze new firms out of the market.[76]

Regulatory Issues

One significant problem in implementing air pollution regulations is having sufficient and accurate information. The EPA and state environmental agencies responsible for implementing air pollution regulations depend on the firms they are regulating for a great deal of information. This information is often incomplete or inaccurate and even when available, regulators may have difficulty interpreting it to determine its accuracy.[77] Furthermore, because of inadequate staffing, both on the federal and state level, universal enforcement is virtually impossible. Consequently, regulators often go after the most obvious and gross violators. This is a major problem in air pollution regulation as it is in environmental management generally. Undoubtedly, better enforcement of existing regulations would decrease air pollution significantly.

The EPA has a great deal of flexibility and discretion in administering the Clean Air Act. For example, when establishing new source performance standards, the agency is directed to require the best available control technology to be applied to new stationary sources of air pollution, taking into consideration the cost of a reduction along with health, environmental, and energy impacts.[78] The 1990 CAAA required various levels of control depending on the pollutant and its source including "reasonable available control technology," "lowest achievable emission rate," and the "maximum achievable control technology." What do these mean? In one extreme, they *could* be interpreted in some situations to mean "the best system of continuous emission reduction" or zero emissions. We do, after all, have the technical ability to reduce air pollution to close to zero. However, such reductions would be expensive and, because of the ability of the atmosphere to absorb some pollution without harm to humans, may be unnecessary. At the other extreme, related to the scientific uncertainty and the EPA's possible sympathy to hardship arguments of polluters, the agency might conclude that restrictions on new stationary sources in attainment areas should be minimal. The discretion lies in determining what limits need to be imposed between these two extremes.

Administrative discretion is, in and of itself, not a bad thing. In fact, given the complexity of air pollution and other regulatory problems, discretion is necessary. It is the exercise of regulatory discretion—in the implementation or formulation of environmental policy—that becomes a problem. Since much of air pollution regulation is implemented on the state level, industries that are influential on the state level or in a particular locality may be able to prevent meaningful pollution control.

This discretion, according to some analysts, has led to inadequate levels of air pollution controls. In their book *Air Pollution and Human Health,* Lester Lave and Eugene Saskin conclude that the federal standards for particulate matter are too lax, and the standards approach in general, which assumes there is an acceptable level of exposure to air pollutants as determined by the EPA, ignores the negative health effects from exposure below the federal standard.[79] Even if there were no problems with the measurement of pollution or the willingness, or the lack thereof, of federal or state regulators to implement emission standards once established, there is still the problem of lack of certainty as to the harmful effects of air pollution:

> [The] scientific research into the harmfulness of air pollution has been much too little. . . . In short, there is a great deal we do not know about the hazardous effects of many air pollutants. Part of the problem is due to inadequate government research funding and the lack of any incentive, monetary or regulatory, on the part of industry to undertake air pollution impact research.[80]

As we saw earlier in the comments of a utility executive on acid rain, scientific uncertainty works to the advantage of those who argue for a go-slow approach to pollution control. The precautionary principle has not caught on in the United States.

The use of administrative discretion in environmental regulations is well established in law. For example, in *Natural Resources Defense Council v. Environmental Protection Agency,*[81] the NRDC claimed that the EPA, in accordance with the Drinking Water Act and the Safe Drinking Water Act Amendments of 1986, must not set emissions levels for possible or known carcinogens (in this case VOCs) above zero. If uncertainties exist concerning the carcinogenic potency of a toxin, the NRDC felt that the EPA should prohibit any emissions of the toxin. The EPA argued it could set emission levels based on cost and available technology; that is, emissions may be set to the "lowest level feasible," in the EPA's determination. In effect, the court was condoning broad administrative discretion.

The courts have generally upheld EPA administrative discretion. In a 1990 case involving the NRDC and EPA, the courts held the EPA must identify toxic sources of pollution, but they may regulate them as they see fit.[82] Another case in

1991 again determined that the EPA had discretion in when to hold mining operations accountable under the Clean Air Act, and what methods they may use to make such a determination.[83] Finally, in 1994 the courts upheld EPA's right to judge what can be considered a "hazardous" material.[84]

Other major issues in air pollution control include the cost of emission controls, who should pay those costs, and whether regulatory expectations in light of costs and benefits are realistic. In passing the Clean Air Act, Congress engaged in "technology forcing" by developing standards that were impossible to comply with, given the then existing technology. Congress assumed technological breakthroughs would lead to developments that would allow the standards to be met—forcing technology with little concern for cost. Technology forcing has occasionally been effective.[85]

The overall cost of air pollution control has always been a controversial issue. As we have seen, the auto industry first argued that automobiles are not a major source of air pollution. Then they argued pollution control is prohibitively expensive. Yet pollution control devices in use in 1990 have reduced the emissions of some pollutants in excess of 90 percent from 1970 levels. In 1993, the cost of air pollution abatement was estimated at $31 billion annually.[86] Annual *capital* expenditures on air pollution abatement exceeds $4.3 billion; and air pollution abatement *operating* costs may be more than double that amount.[87]

Four air pollution problems have attracted a great deal of attention in recent years: acid rain, the greenhouse effect, the thinning of the ozone layer in the stratosphere, and toxic air pollution. Acid rain, ozone, and the greenhouse effect share international common pool management characteristics and problems and hence present special, perhaps insurmountable, problems. These are air pollution problems both domestically and internationally; hence they will be discussed in this chapter as well as in Chapter 10 on international environmental issues. All four of these problems are discussed in detail next.

Toxic Air Pollution

Although some would make technical distinctions, for our purposes we have to conclude that the terms *toxic* and *hazardous* are essentially synonymous and may be used interchangeably.[88] A chemical referred to as toxic in one statute may, and frequently is, referred to as hazardous in another. Typically, a toxic substance is something that causes serious human health problems even in very small amounts. While most of the discussion over toxic or hazardous waste problems center around water pollution, it has become increasingly apparent that toxic airborne pollutants pose a serious environmental threat.[89]

In the Clean Air Act, a hazardous air pollutant is defined as "[A]n air pollutant which no ambient air quality standard is applicable [to] which in the judgment of the administrator causes, or contributes to, air pollution which may reasonably be anticipated to result in an increase in mortality or an increase in serious irreversible, or incapacitating irreversible, illness."[90] Although the Clean Air Act has provisions for designating an air pollutant as hazardous and establishing an emission standard for that pollutant, the EPA has been slow to develop such standards. By 1990, nearly 20 years after the passage of the Clean Air Act, only seven substances had been regulated under the hazardous emission provision of the act.[91] The 1990 Clean

Air Act Amendments sought to overcome this problem. Title III of the 1990 CAAA, often referred to as the "air toxins" section, specifically listed 189 toxic or hazardous air pollutants, and set a schedule requiring EPA to develop standards for all major sources over a 10-year period. A major source is one that emits more than 10 tons per year of a single toxin or more than 25 tons per year of any combination of the 189 toxins listed.[92]

The EPA must further identify categories of the major sources and then develop "maximum achievable control technology" (MACT) for each category. These standards are to be based on technology that has already been proven to provide the best pollution control. Thus there are no technology-forcing aspects to this section. It is hoped the MACT standards will provide incentives for pollution prevention. By only setting standards for levels of toxic emission reductions, the act allows industry to substitute nontoxic substances for the current toxic chemicals. Also, sources that reduce emissions by 90 percent before MACT standards go into effect have six additional years to comply with the remaining 10 percent.

On July 16, 1992, EPA published an initial list of source categories for which it intends to establish national emission standards for hazardous air pollutants (NESHAPs). Of the 174 source categories, 166 are for major sources categories and 8 are for area source categories.[93] These additions set as an overall goal up to 90 percent reductions in the emissions of toxic air pollutants by 2003.[94]

These are admirable goals. Although it is too early to tell how successful the 1990 amendments will be, we can anticipate many of the regulatory problems that have come to be associated with command and control regulatory systems (see Chapter 3 for a discussion of regulatory systems), including the incentives of polluters to delay compliance.

There are a number of reasons why so few hazardous pollutants were identified for regulation by the EPA. The identification and verification process is long and complicated and made more so by the lack of monitoring equipment sophisticated enough to detect some pollutants. Furthermore, during the Reagan administration a combination of the decrease in EPA's budget and a lack of enthusiasm among agency leadership for increasing regulation resulted in a situation that was not conducive to expanding hazardous air pollution regulation. Also, there is a lack of data on the human effects of pollutants. These studies take many years to complete and are very costly to conduct.

For example, asbestos, a hazardous air pollutant, has attracted attention of the EPA and state and local air pollution regulators. However, another air pollutant, lead, although not regulated under the hazardous air pollution regulations, is hazardous and has also attracted a great deal of attention. Humans may be exposed to lead through food or through exposure to lead-based paints, but exposure is most likely to occur from lead that is mixed in gasoline to improve octane ratings. Exposure to lead can lead to convulsions, anemia, and kidney and brain damage.[95] Use of lead has declined roughly 40 percent since the early 1970s, due to a ban on lead-based paints and restrictions on lead in all grades of gasoline. Fortunately, because of restrictions on leaded gasoline and the retiring of older automobiles that burned leaded gasoline, hazardous lead pollution in the air went down more than 70 percent from the early 1970s to the early 1990s.[96] In the late 1970s the EPA estimated that the average American's blood lead level was 50 percent higher than it would otherwise be without auto emissions.[97]

Asbestos is "one of the few substances with essentially irrefutable evidence demonstrating that it causes cancer in humans."[98] Although latency periods vary depending on the amount and duration of exposure, asbestos-induced cancer can occur after a relatively low dose and short latency period (the amount of time between the initial exposure to the cause of a disease, in this case airborne asbestos, and the actual onset of the disease).[99]

Asbestos is used in brake and clutch linings, some paper and plastic products, paint, cement, and roofing and flooring tiles. Today, the greatest asbestos exposure problem occurs in classrooms with deteriorating asbestos surfaces, particularly ceilings. Children are six times as likely as adults to develop cancer from exposure to asbestos. It was estimated in 1984 that one-third of all school classrooms in the United States had asbestos problems. In 1986 Congress required schools to inspect for asbestos-containing materials and develop a removal plan where necessary.[100] Congress did not, however, appropriate the funds necessary for effective asbestos removal, and many local governments, lacking the necessary funds, have been slow to act. The federal government's response to the problems of asbestos is typical of the environmental policy paradox. By recognizing a problem and subsequently passing legislation to deal with that problem, federal policymakers can take credit for having acted. However, to the extent the effort is not adequately funded, the credit may not be well deserved.

Toxic air pollution, especially carcinogenic substances, further illustrates the regulatory problems associated with risk assessment and economic trade-offs. In the case of asbestos, given the unusually strong evidence of a connection between even limited exposure and cancer, the risk question is not disputed. However, the economic issues are real and difficult. Asbestos is apparently the best material for use in clutch and brake linings. Therefore, any risk to the mechanic who repairs automobiles has to be weighed against automobile safety concerns associated with using other materials. Of greater concern is the extensive use of asbestos in home heating and insulation, as well as in most other types of construction such as office and apartment buildings. The problem is what to substitute and when to replace these noxious materials. Often problems can be avoided if asbestos-laden materials are simply left undisturbed. That type of balancing is troublesome at best.

It will cost billions of dollars to remove all asbestos from all schools, yet we know many children will develop cancer if the work is not completed. Delay in this situation is politically possible because the victims are unknown and the chance of any *individual* child developing cancer as a result of exposure to asbestos is very small. Yet, as a class of people, many children are at risk. This is the type of group that is unlikely to have influence in the policy process both because they are identified only as a class and because children as a class do not have the resources necessary for influencing the policy-making process.

Another group without the resources necessary to influence the policy process who have been victimized by a careless air pollution policy are the Native American miners on the Navajo reservation. For many years, the Navajo miners and their families have been exposed to inhalation of another acknowledged carcinogen, uranium, from open mines in the Arizona-New Mexico area. The danger was first recognized in 1949 when the U.S. Public Health Service conducted a study and decided not to tell the affected miners of the health dangers for fear many would quit and halt production, thus disrupting the nuclear armament program and posing an economic and a national security threat. These people were denied compensation in an unsuccessful suit against the U.S. government in 1979. "The Navajos are in a distinct position. The government not only didn't warn them, it was flagrant malpractice to do what they did," stated Stewart Udall, former secretary of the interior and the Navajo representative in the unsuccessful 1979 suit.[101] Only in the 1990s has this situation changed to some degree. The Radiation Exposure Compensation Act (RECA), sponsored by Senator Orrin Hatch and Representative Wayne Owens, was passed by the 101st Congress in 1990 to establish a $100 million trust fund to provide a $100,000 award to those miners who are victims of lung cancer and other diseases.[102] Though the Act was intended to compensate those whose health was damaged by exposure to radioactive materials as a result of their employment in the mining industry, extensive verification measures has placed much of the burden on potential recipients to prove their eligibility to receive funds. Those Navajo applying for compensation have run into a plethora of red tape that has proven very difficult to surmount; one reason for this is the absence of employment records that enable potential claimants to prove their eligibility. However, the Radiation Workers Justice Act of 1998 has amended the original Radiation Exposure Compensation Act of 1990. The hope is that this new legislation will allow easier access to compensation for impacted groups.

The 1998 Act extends coverage in several respects. Now above-ground miners and haulers of the radioactive ore are eligible, as are people who worked from 1942 to 1990, whereas RECA limited the range to 1947 to 1971. Also the minimum exposure levels have been dropped 80 percent and the maximum compensation doubled to $200,000. Perhaps most importantly, workers no longer have to prove they have illnesses directly related to uranium exposure; they are being compensated because their rights were violated.[103]

The George W. Bush administration has sent mixed signals on this topic, and a recent GAO report says the Justice Department is administering the program better since the 1998 Act, but is still not doing enough to reach out to victims to let them know they may be eligible for compensation. First, on July 24, 2001, President Bush signed into law PL 107-20 that appropriated an additional $84 million to the Radiation Compensation Exposure Trust Fund. This law also makes compensation an entitlement, so Congress cannot withhold payments or cut the program in budget battles. This has allowed more eligible claimants, but the money still is not flowing quickly. As of September 29, 2001, there were 275 people with nothing but IOUs from the government, and some have already died in the wait.[104] The Bush administration wants to further withhold payments until three separate studies are completed to ensure certain miners or haulers are not being (overly) compensated who may have become sick from other sources.[105]

This is an example of a weakness of normative pluralism. A group lacking the necessary resources to influence the policy process, the Navajo miners, did not have adequate influence early enough in the policy process.

Acid Rain

Many of the policy and regulatory problems that are associated with toxic air pollution are also present in acid rain concerns. Thanks to the popular press, nearly everyone has heard of acid rain, otherwise known as acid deposition because the acid and acid-forming substances that fall to the earth as a result of air pollution come not only in rain, but also snow, sleet, fog, dew, and even as dry particulate matter and gas. The term *acid rain* is used here, but you should remember it refers to acids deposited to the earth, regardless of their mode of transport.

Acid rain begins with emissions of sulfur and nitrogen oxide primarily from industrial plants and automobile exhaust. In the United States nitrogen oxides are emitted from fuel combustion (46 percent) and transportation (49 percent); most sulfur oxides are emitted from coal-burning power plants in the midwestern and eastern United States, and utilities and smelters in the western United States.[106] Sulfur dioxide and nitrogen oxides interact with water vapor and sunlight in the upper atmosphere to form acidic compounds. Over 80 percent of all sulfur dioxide emissions in the United States originate east of the Mississippi River with the heaviest concentrations coming from power plants in the Ohio River Valley.

Acidity is measured on the pH scale, which ranges from 0 to 14. A value of 7 on the scale is neutral; any grading below 7 is acidic. Readings above 7 are alkaline. Rainwater is normally acidic, primarily due to natural causes, measuring 5.6 on the pH scale. Although any pH reading below 5.6 is considered acid rain, damage to materials, plants, fish, and microorganisms in lakes and streams is associated with pH values of 5.0 and lower. The pH scale is logarithmic. This means acid rain with a pH of 4.0 is 10 times as strong as acid rain with a pH of 5.0, and only one-tenth as strong as rain with a pH of 3.0, all other things being equal.

Acidity levels of rainwater between 4.2 pH and 4.8 pH are common throughout the eastern United States and Canada. Acid rain has been a problem on every continent. Serious damage has been reported in Brazil, Australia, Thailand, South Africa, and China.[107] An estimated 6 million acres of forest in nine European countries has been damaged, as have 18,000 lakes in Sweden and 2,600 lakes in Norway. In Ontario, Canada, an estimated 300 lakes have become devoid of fish life due to acid rain; another 48,000 lakes are classified as "acid sensitive."[108]

Rain with an acidity of 1.4 pH, which is more acidic than lemon juice, has been recorded in Wheeling, West Virginia. Rain of 2.4 pH, about the same acidity as vinegar, was recorded in Scotland in 1974. A pH reading of 3.0, which is extremely acidic and does extensive damage over time to buildings as well as the natural environment, is common.[109]

One problem inherent in developing policies to deal with acid rain is that there is not always a direct relationship between the reduction of emissions and the reduction of acid rain. Local soil conditions, along with prevailing wind patterns, create conditions in which the threshold level of acceptable pollutants (the level beyond the natural assimilative capacity of the affected ecosystem) varies from place to place.

The impacts of acid rain over the long term can be devastating. As wildlife ecologist Anne LaBastille described, "My log cabin looks out over a lake that is becoming increasingly clear in recent years, with a strange mat of algae spreading across the bottom. Native trout are now scarce, as are loons, osprey, and otters. Bullfrogs are all but silent. As much as a third of the virgin red spruce around the lake have died."[110] Thousands of lakes and streams throughout North America and Europe have become acidified to the point where they no longer support aquatic life. If air emissions continue at 1990s' rates, many thousands of lakes, rivers, and streams worldwide will die, as will many millions of acres of forests.

In an effort to comply with U.S. air pollution emissions standards at ground level and decrease pollution in urban areas, tall smokestacks have been used on power plants so the emissions are discharged at altitudes high enough to pierce the thermal inversion layer and the pollution is carried to other regions or nations. For example, in the United States it is estimated that close to 40 percent of the acid rain deposited in the Northeast originates in the Midwest.[111]

Acid rain is a classic example of an international common pool management problem. Power plants in London belch fumes into the atmosphere that pollute and destroy forests, lakes, and streams in Scandinavia and Germany. More than three-fourths of the acid rain in Norway, Sweden, the Netherlands, Finland, Switzerland, and Austria is imported from other sections of Europe. Over half of the acid rain that falls on Canada comes from the United States.[112]

The production of sulfur dioxide and nitrogen oxides in the former Soviet Union and Eastern Europe are particularly troubling.[113] Most of the region is a net exporter of the airborne pollutants that contribute to acid rain. In many of these countries, governments are under domestic pressure to increase production of consumer goods. These governments will, understandably, be reluctant to restrain that activity and the pollution that results. Furthermore, since the region is a net exporter of airborne pollutants, the costs of these activities will not be fully felt by the nations emitting the pollutants.

Given the common pool nature of the acid rain problem, countries that are exporting their air pollutants have little incentive to restrict their polluting activities. International cooperation over acid rain has been limited, and even where attempted, has been ineffective. Indeed, there is no international organization that can provide the incentives through coercion or otherwise. In Europe, both the United Nations Economic Commission for Europe (ECE) and the 15-nation European Economic Community (EEC) have established guidelines for international cooperation in the control of acid rain. However, little progress has been made. The ECE sponsored a convention on Long-Range Trans-Boundary Air Pollution in Geneva in 1979, designed to address acid rain problems in both Eastern and Western Europe. The document produced contained language "so vague and general, and subjected to so many qualifications, that they do not impose on contracting parties any specific obligations with the respect to air pollution control policies."[114]

Since this initial agreement, there have been further attempts to strengthen air pollution regulations in Europe. In 1985 a protocol requiring SO^2 emission reductions of 30 percent from 1980 levels by 1993 was adopted without signature by the United States. Since then, federal legislation has been passed to reduce SO^2 emissions by 35 percent by 2000. A second protocol mandating a cap on NOx emissions at 1987 levels by 1994 was adopted in 1988; this treaty was renegotiated in 1999. Additionally, in November 1991, 21 members of the ECE signed a protocol for a 30 percent reduction in VOC emissions by the year 2000. Another protocol was arranged by the European Commission in 1999. National emission ceilings were set for member nations to, among other things, reduce acid rain. Compliance with the ceilings will reduce sulfur dioxide emissions 78 percent from 1990 levels by 2010, and nations in noncompliance will be forced to pay, though details are sketchy on how this will work. The program is estimated to cost 7.5 billion euros (6.7 billion U.S. dollars) per year, but is expected to yield 17 to 32 billion euros (15.2 to 28.6 billion dollars[115]) worth of benefits from increased agricultural production to decreased environmental maintenance costs.[116] As the European Union gains collective strength, it may be easier to hold individual member nations accountable. While these are positive steps, World Resources Institute editorializes, "There is little reason to believe that such reductions will cut acid deposition and ozone to the critical loads that ecosystems can tolerate."[117]

Totally independent sovereign states are not likely, on the other hand, to restrict their polluting activities voluntarily when they see no benefit or perceived burdens. The fact that the Convention on Long-Range Trans-Boundary Air Pollution is perceived to be weak should not come as a surprise. We do not expect altruism in individual personal behavior; capitalist economies assume the opposite, in fact. The behavior of sovereign states is no different.

The Midwestern United States, exporters of air pollution to the Northeast and Canada, out of self-interest are not likely to curtail their polluting activities voluntarily. Consequently, elimination of Midwestern air pollution necessarily will have to be by action of the federal government. In 1980 the U.S. Congress approved the National Acid Precipitation Assessment Program. This was a research program, which spent $500 million investigating the cause of acid rain. This research-only attitude was consistent with the position of the Reagan administration toward acid rain—more research is needed, better research is needed. Completed in 1989, the NAPAP drew much criticism for its lack of concern for policy matters connected to acid rain abatement. The oversight board concluded that NAPAP, "failed to pursue at all or with sufficient vigor a number of . . . questions that turned out to be important to policy decisions." The possible health impacts of acid rain, its long-term effects on soils and forest ecosystems, and the social and economic costs and benefits of alternative policies for curtailing acid rain were among the shortcomings cited by the NAPAP oversight board.[118] Overall, the primary indictment of NAPAP was pointed toward its reliance on research, to the detriment of broader policy concerns.

Great Britain shares this attitude toward the primacy of research when accused of contributing to acidification in Scandinavia. Although scientists do not completely understand the dynamics of acid rain and the interactions that involve chemistry, meteorology, geology, biology, botany, soil science, and other sciences, there is overwhelming agreement on a strong connection between airborne pollutants from sulfur dioxide and nitrogen oxide and acid rain. As Arthur Johnson, a contributing author to the 1986 National Research Council report on chemical pollutants remarked, "There is no longer reasonable doubt" about the relationship between aquatic ecosystems and sulfur emissions.[119]

Title IV of the 1990 CAAA is the first law in the nation's history to attempt to deal comprehensively with acid rain. It required that by the turn of the century, sulfur dioxide (SO^2) emissions be reduced approximately 40 percent from 1980 levels. In January 1993, the EPA issued its final rules to cut annual emissions of SO^2 in half, establishing a permanent national cap on utility emissions of just under a total of 9 million tons annually. Phase I began in 1995 and Phase II began in the year 2000 and utilizes a market-based allowance trading mechanism.[120]

Phase I affects 261 of the largest power generating plants. In 1991 the United States got more than 55 percent of its electricity from coal, consuming more than 750 million tons a year.[121] Sulfur dioxide, the most important contributor to acid rain, is produced when the sulfur in coal is released during combustion and reacts with oxygen in the air. The EPA, according to a formula based on the unit's average fuel consumption from 1985 to 1987, will issue allowances to emit sulfur dioxide to each of these plants. Each allowance will permit the plant to emit one ton of sulfur dioxide. If the utility is emitting more SO^2 than it has allowances, it has four choices. First, it can install pollution control equipment to reduce emissions. Second, it can try to buy allowances from other utilities nationwide. Third, it may choose to implement conservation measures to reduce both electric generation and emissions. The EPA will maintain a reserve of 300,000 special allowances for plants that develop qualifying renewable energy projects or use conservation measures. Finally, the plant can bid on a reserve of allowances (2.8 percent of the total each year) that EPA will put up for auction. Other than this, the EPA's role in allowance trading will be limited to tracking the trading.

Each plant is required to install emissions-monitoring equipment and keep track of both emissions and allowance trading activity on an operating permit that includes all applicable requirements under the 1990 CAAA. These permits will not have to be amended each time there is trading.

Phase II for sulfur dioxide began in the year 2000 and tightened emissions on these larger plants as well as nearly 2,000 other plants in the United States. Utilities that began operation in 1996 or later are not issued any allowances and have to purchase them from other plants. Phase II utilities in 2000 have decreased their sulfur dioxide emissions 29 percent compared to 1990 levels, and 10 percent from 1999 levels, though energy production is actually up.

Title IV also calls for a reduction of nitrogen oxide emissions of 2 million tons by 2000 to be implemented in two phases. Results are positive thus far. NOx emissions in 2000 were a million tons below the original target level. Units that have begun Phase II in 2000 have reduced these emissions 23 percent from 1990 levels and 7 percent from 1999 levels. Total NOx emissions from all Title IV affected units were 3 million tons below what they would have been without the Acid Rain Program in 2000, thus the goal of a 2 million ton reduction has been met and surpassed. What is crucial for the polluting industries and detractors who claim a better environment automatically means a damaged economy and productivity, these reductions have been achieved while electrical production in 2000, as measured by heat input, has increased 30 percent since 1990 and 2.7 percent compared to 1999.[122]

Stratospheric Ozone

The second major international common pool resource problem associated with air pollution is depletion of the stratospheric ozone layer primarily through the release of chlorofluorocarbons (CFCs).

Ozone in the stratosphere screens out more than 99 percent of the sun's ultraviolet radiation. Without this protection, the earth's atmosphere would not be conducive to supporting life as we know it.[123] CFCs have been used since 1955 in aerosol spray cans, refrigeration units, in industrial solvents and plastic foams for insulation, packing, furniture, and the plastic foam used in the manufacture of coffee cups and fast-food containers. Although CFCs in aerosol cans have been banned in the United States, Canada, and most Scandinavian countries since 1978, worldwide nonaerosol CFC production has increased.[124]

The increases in ultraviolet (UV) radiation due to ozone depletion have had a number of negative effects on humans. It is estimated that for every 1 percent decrease in ozone in the stratosphere, there is a 2 percent increase in UV intensity. In turn, each increase in UV intensity leads to a 2 to 4 percent increase in skin cancer cases. Currently more than 1.3 million skin cancer cases are diagnosed annually. Moreover, the EPA estimated that at 1991 rates of ozone depletion, skin cancer fatality rates in the United States could increase by 200,000 over the next 50 years.[125] Worldwide, a 236 percent increase in UV intensity has been detected at Ushuaia, Argentina, and a 285 percent increase at the Palmer Research Stations on Antarctica. These locations lay directly underneath the ozone hole. Still, during recent decades, stratospheric ozone thickness declined between 10 and 40 percent during winter and spring months over portions of the Northern Hemisphere, though some research indicates widespread, consistent global ozone depletion is currently around 3 percent.[126]

In addition, the increase in ultraviolet light can have a negative impact on the ocean food chain by destroying microorganisms on the ocean surface. Crops on land may suffer decreased yields as well. Putting these percentages in perspective, it was estimated in 1988 that since 1969, ozone losses have averaged between 2 and 3 percent over North America and Europe and as high as 5 and 6 percent over parts of the Southern Hemisphere. Over the United States the hole in the ozone layer that was first found only in winter and spring has recently continued in summer. The EPA estimates there was a 4 to 5 percent loss of ozone between 1978 and 1991.[127] For the Southern Hemisphere, it is estimated that skin cancers in Australia and New Zealand will increase approximately 20 percent because of ozone depletion by the year 2010.[128]

The discovery of the relationship between CFCs and stratospheric ozone depletion provides valuable insight into the environmental policy process both locally and globally. It is also an excellent illustration of the problems associated with international common pool resource management. F. Sherwood Rowland, then a chemist at the University of California at Irvine, working with research associate Mario Molina, discovered the relationship of CFCs and ozone late in 1973.[129] Early in their research Rowland and Molina found it difficult to believe the scope of the implications of their findings. "Our immediate reaction," Rowland told an interviewer, was "we have made some huge error."[130] Rowland went home one evening and told his wife that his research "is going well, but it looks like the end of the world."[131] Rowland immediately set out to educate the public and policy makers and to urge that CFCs be banned. In the process of doing so, he alienated the $28 billion CFC industry and found he was branded by some as "some kind of a nut." CFC manufacturers, as represented by industry scientists and executives, labeled the ozone hypothesis "nonsense," going so far as to claim, as the president of an aerosol manufacturing firm did, that CFC criticism was "orchestrated by the ministers of disinformation of the KGB."[132]

In the face of industry opposition, as well as seeming indifference by policy makers, little happened on the ozone front through the mid to late 1970s. A classic combination of scientific uncertainty, no immediate crisis or a single easily identifiable interest group suffering harm, coupled with strong industry opposition and the lack of resources necessary to make opposition felt in a political system that favors maintaining the status quo, predictably led to no action. Then, in 1979 a team of British scientists discovered a hole in the ozone layer over Antarctica. This hole, covering an area larger in size than the United States, continued to show up annually in late September or early October, staying longer each year. In 1987 the hole did not break up until late December. The total depletion in the region was 50 percent below normal levels, causing alarm among atmospheric scientists and others worldwide.[133] Then, in 1989 a hole was discovered in the Arctic ozone layer, adding credence to the argument that ozone depletion was occurring worldwide. Scientists estimated that with the right weather conditions, concentrations of ozone could be depleted up to 1 percent per day in the Arctic region.[134] Since the late 1980s, the size of ozone holes within the global stratosphere have grown larger than anyone had previously predicted. In 1995, the ozone hole over Antarctica was twice the size of the hole measured in 1994. Ozone depletion over North America prior to 1990 was estimated at 3 percent; during the spring of 1996, ozone depletion over North America reached as high as 45 percent. Though United Nations officials tout the successes of international agreements limiting the production of ozone-depleting materials, scientists argue that we are not out of the woods yet, and should more actively pursue limitations in the global production of ozone-depleting materials.[135]

The U.S. National Academy of Sciences studied the CFC-ozone link both in 1976 and 1979, essentially concluding that Rowland and Molina had been accurate in their estimates. The 1979 study estimated that ultimate ozone depletion would be somewhere between 15 and 18 percent.[136] The study had no major impact on policy makers, despite Rowland's five-year effort to urge a ban on CFC production. Even though studies had established a link between CFCs and ozone depletion, the U.S. congressional reaction was to ask for further study, in the form of National Aeronautics and Space Administration (NASA) reports every two years.[137]

As Rowland remarked of the period of the late 1970s, "That became the action item—to make a report rather than to have regulatory control."[138] The ozone problem is a classic example of the environmental policy paradox and problems associated with international common pool problems. Until the 1980s, despite strong evidence linking CFCs to ozone depletion and an understanding of the implications of that depletion, powerful interests—a $28 billion industry—had a stake in postponing action. A powerful lobby, coupled with the apparent noncritical, invisible nature of ozone depletion, made it easy for policy makers to defer action. In 1987 Reagan administration Secretary of the Interior Donald Hodel suggested the appropriate response to ozone depletion was to increase the use of a sunscreen and to wear head protection when out in the sun. (The proposal was labeled by conservationists as the "Ray-Ban Plan.") The interior secretary argued before the President's Domestic Policy Council that public awareness of ways to prevent skin cancer should be considered as an alternative to curbing CFC production. Although this is and was good advice, it clearly ignored or glossed over the more fundamental problem. Conservationists were outraged at the suggestion. A spokesperson for the NRDC charged that "[A]nimals, crops, fish and wildlife aren't going to wear hats and sunglasses."[139]

In 1985 NASA estimated that ozone depletion should be less than 1 percent over the United States, based on CFC production at 1980 levels. Total ozone depletion for the next century worldwide would be as much as 10 percent. Within two years, however, it was clear those estimates were much too low. Declines from 1969 through 1986 were estimated in 1987 to be an average of 2.3 percent in the Northern Hemisphere and, as we indicated, even higher in the Southern Hemisphere and over the United States.[140] A British discovery in 1979 led to a series of further tests of the Antarctic ozone and found the hole continually reappeared and was larger each time. A NASA ozone panel on March 15, 1988, confirmed that Antarctic ozone loss was attributable to CFCs and that ozone loss was detected at all latitudes. By then, worldwide attention had been focused on the ozone problem. Twenty-four nations signed what is known as the Montreal Protocol in September 1987. The protocol is designed to freeze production of five CFCs at 1986 levels and reduce total CFC production by 50 percent at the turn of the century. The U.S. Senate unanimously ratified the Montreal Protocol six months later. Shortly thereafter, Du Pont, the largest CFC producer in the United States, announced it had set a goal of "an orderly transition to the total phaseout of fully halogenated CFC production."[141] Du Pont was keeping a pledge it had made more than a decade earlier in full-page newspaper advertisements to phase out CFCs should they be found to be environmentally hazardous. Then, on March 2, 1989, environmental ministers from the European Economic Community agreed to a total phaseout of CFCs by the year 2000 and agreed to a 85 percent reduction in CFC production as soon as possible.[142] The next day President Bush called for a ban on CFC production by the year 2000, *provided* safe alternatives could be developed. This was a switch from the attitude of the Reagan administration. As the *Los Angeles Times* editorialized, "It is embarrassing for this country to be following someone else's lead on crucial environmental issues so much of the time, but Bush's reaction time was an improvement over the Reagan administration's response to such things. It probably would be calling for more study."[143]

The 1990 Clean Air Act amendments did, in fact, ban CFC production in the United States after the year 2000. In early 1993 the EPA proposed "speeded-up" phaseout dates for ozone-destroying chemicals. CFCs, carbon tetrachloride, and methyl chloroform production were listed for phaseout by January 1996, and halons production by January 1994.[144] Additionally, as of 1993, CFCs from car air conditioners, the biggest single source of ozone-destroying chemicals, must now be serviced using equipment that prevents release and recycles CFCs. This applies to all service shops, not just to the larger shops that had been required to start using this special equipment in January 1993. Hydrochlorofluorocarbons (HCFCs), CFC substitutes, are scheduled to begin phaseout by 2003.[145] Finally, the Montreal Protocol was amended in 1990 to create a $160 million fund to compensate developing countries for following a CFC-free path. The funding would come from the largest CFC users.[146]

It is tempting to conclude that initial efforts at ozone control, through the Montreal Protocol, elimination of CFCs in aerosol sprays, and other measures, provide an example of how the system can work to deal with environmental problems when they are identified. And in a sense progress has been made. Within eight years, from the start of the Reagan administration when then-EPA administrator Anne Gorsuch Burford dismissed ozone depletion as another environmental scare, the U.S. president had called for a ban on CFC production.[147]

Surface appearances may not, however, provide a complete picture, particularly in the international arena. First, the Montreal Protocol was designed to cut CFC production by only 50 percent over 10 years. Even if successful, the amount of CFCs still left in the atmosphere will have a significant impact on the environment—greatly increasing the incidence of skin cancer and damaging marine ecosystems. Furthermore, the Montreal Protocol allows less developed nations to increase

CFC use for a decade and is, of course, dependent on the good faith of the signatory nations for enforcement.[148] Finally, the Montreal Protocol does not address emissions of carbon tetrachloride, a chemical banned in the United States but commonly used in other countries with even greater potential to damage the ozone layer than CFCs.[149] As Rowland commented on the Montreal Protocol, "[It] does little to protect the atmosphere. Very little for a decade and then not enough."[150] And, as a spokesperson for the Natural Resources Defense Council remarked, "[The] Montreal accord and the proposed EPA rules will cut CFCs by less than 50 percent over 10 years. The world has *already* suffered more ozone depletion than EPA predicted would occur under that level of cuts by the year 2050. Safeguarding the ozone layer requires a rapid and total CFC phaseout, not just a ten-year halfway measure."[151] Progress has undoubtedly been made. Many observers feel, however, that more needs to be done.

In a similar manner, the ban on CFCs in aerosol propellants would appear to be a victory, and in fact it was. The ready availability of substitutes in aerosol propellants, at roughly the same cost, undoubtedly made this environmental "victory" easier to achieve. Despite this success, many countries that did not sign the Montreal Protocol continue to produce CFCs, albeit at a reduced level. Thus the protective ozone layer will continue to be depleted.

The incentives operating in international common pool resource management are such that many nations will be slow to act. When the CFC-ozone link was first established, skeptics in Europe argued that the theory was developed by American manufacturers desiring to have a corner on the market for substitutes for CFCs. CFC manufacturers also questioned the motives of Rowland and others who argued for a ban of CFCs. Unfortunately, the production of CFCs has continued to increase in many countries in spite of the mounting evidence of the damage being done to the ozone layer. In the United States, the production of most CFCs ended in 1995, though current stocks can still be used.[152] Although many nations have signed on to the Montreal Protocol for Ozone Protection, even member nations are still producing CFCs, and many developing nations are increasing production.[153] Under these circumstances, the outlook for the total worldwide ban on CFC production, before extensive damage is done to the ozone layer and our environment, seems slim.[154]

The Greenhouse Effect

> The gradual warming trend will likely go on.
> And the green belts begin to slide closer to the poles.
> The Plains States will be abandoned as giant dust bowls.
> Greenland and Antarctica will join the new Great Powers ...
>
> Let them have their little time in the sun,
> We'll say to ourselves as we begin to sway
> To the strains of our native beach band,
> Ignoring the hits from the Arctic on the radio.[155]

For over 100 years we have understood the possibility of atmospheric warming due to human carbon dioxide emissions. As early as 1896, Swedish chemist Svante Arrhenius predicted that a doubling of atmospheric carbon dioxide would raise average global temperatures by 9 degrees Fahrenheit.[156] The greenhouse effect, which is a natural occurrence and has allowed the development of life on earth, is thought by many scientists to have been radically altered by humankind's impact on the composition of the atmosphere. The problem lies in humans' effects on the dynamic nature of the heat exchange process of the sun, earth, and black space. These alterations threaten to transform the global environment. As one observer wrote, "The year is 2035. In New York, palm trees line the Hudson River ... Phoenix is in its third week of temperatures over 130 degrees ... Holland is under water. Bangladesh has ceased to exist ... in central Europe and in the American Midwest, decades of drought have turned once fertile agricultural lands into parched deserts."[157]

Problematic greenhouse gasses consist primarily of methane and carbon dioxide, according to recent studies. They also consist of water vapor and trace amounts of gasses including ozone, nitrous oxide, and CFCs. Greenhouse gasses prevent some of the sun's infrared radiation or heat from escaping the earth, similar to a greenhouse. As these gaseous levels in the atmosphere increase, greenhouse gasses trap more of the sun's heat in the earth's atmosphere, which has a number of effects on the earth's environment. Were it not for greenhouse gasses, most of the sun's energy would radiate back out into space, leaving the earth cold and lifeless with an average temperature of minus 18E C (0.4E F).[158] To illustrate the problem, under normal conditions, which for our purposes we define as before people started to burn fossil fuels releasing carbon dioxide in the atmosphere, global levels of carbon dioxide were around 275 parts per million (ppm). Carbon dioxide levels increased from 275 ppm to 346 ppm between 1860 and 1986, primarily due to the burning of fossil fuels and deforestation. By 1995 CO^2 concentrations had risen to 359 ppm, an increase of 170 billion tons from pre-industrial revolution conditions, and were estimated to be growing at 1.5 ppm each year.[159]

Plants convert carbon dioxide to oxygen and are one effective way to absorb carbon dioxide from the atmosphere. Deforestation has resulted in a reduction in the carbon dioxide to oxygen conversion. It is estimated that deforestation contributes 1 to 2.5 billion tons of carbon dioxide emissions annually.[160] It is thought that global levels of carbon dioxide in the atmosphere will reach 550 ppm sometime between 2040 and 2100; however, *most* analysts believe those levels will be reached closer to the middle of the twenty-first century.[161] In 1995, the International Panel on Climate Control (IPCC) released a report that chronicled the changes in global temperatures. During the last 100 years, the global temperature increased by about one degree Fahrenheit. It is estimated that over the next 100 years the temperature will increase 3.6 degrees Fahrenheit. Such a severe temperature change would most likely cause an increase in heat waves and drought, the spread of infectious diseases, and the disruption of ecosystems worldwide. Furthermore, increased temperatures would cause the expansion of seawater and the melting of ice in both polar regions, resulting in a rise in sea level, predicted by climatologists to be up to 1.5 to 3 ft by the end of the next century.[162] Such a rise is very significant if you consider that over the past 100 years, the sea level has risen only from 4 to 6 inches. A rise of 1.5 to 3 feet would devastate coastal areas around the world and cause hundreds of billions of dollars in damage. In 1987 the president of the Maldives, an island nation in the Indian Ocean, gave an impassioned plea to the United Nations to act on global warming. The estimated rising of the ocean due to global warming would completely submerge the low-lying Maldives Islands as well as most of the world's great seaports including New Orleans, Amsterdam, and Shanghai.[163] In 1995, the Alliance of Small Island States met in Berlin to discuss global warming and its potential to affect sea levels. The 30-member alliance pushed for a global 20 percent reduction of man-made greenhouse gas emissions from 1990 to 2005. The European Union's plan for greenhouse gas reduction is a bit less enthusiastic, calling for emission levels to be lowered 15 percent from 1990 to 2010. The United States is far behind the rest of the industrialized world; President Clinton advocated a plan that would hold emission levels steady at 1990 levels until 2008.[164] President George W. Bush has not pursued any additional initiatives in this area, and has expressly come out against the Kyoto Protocol to reduce carbon dioxide emissions that would slow the greenhouse effect.

Moreover, the increase in temperatures will also result in a negative impact on agriculture in a number of regions. In the midwestern United States, where much of the land is dependent on irrigation from groundwater, which in most places is a finite resource, farming could become impractical. All over the world food production would become erratic, reflecting the changed weather patterns. The impact on agriculture would be particularly severe, since most food is grown in the middle or higher latitudes of the Northern Hemisphere where the greatest impact from the greenhouse effect would be felt. Climate changes would be the least felt in the areas near the equator, where relatively little food is grown. As climatic zones shift northward, animals, and particularly plants, will have a difficult time adapting to the change. This would lead to a significant loss in species variety and loss of genetic diversity.

An EPA report to Congress in 1988 reads, "[T]he landscape of North America will change in ways it cannot be fully predicted. The ultimate effects will last for centuries and will be irreversible. ... Strategies to reverse such impacts on natural ecosystems are not currently available."[165]

Although the scientific community is never unanimous given the nature of scientific inquiry to question and to test, there is, in the words of John Firor, the director of advanced studies at the National Center for Atmospheric Research in Boulder, Colorado, "a spectacular convergence of scientific opinion on global warming." Firor noted, "[T]here is just no disagreement that we're in for a rapid heating. The only question is how much."[166] Numerous reports from NASA, the EPA, and the Department of Energy have confirmed we are headed toward a warmer climate because the greenhouse effect. Deforestation of rain forests largely for agricultural development is related to the greenhouse effect in several important respects. Deforestation is occurring in many parts of the world and is particularly intense in the less developed countries. Reforestation is the primary means of effectively reducing carbon dioxide in the atmosphere. Worldwide rates of deforestation are about 10 times the rate of reforestation. According to the World Resources Institute, approximately 27 million acres a year of forests are being lost.

Much of this deforestation occurs in the less developed regions, notably Brazil, Indonesia, and the Democratic Republic of Congo (Zaire), regions that rely on the forests for energy and increased agricultural production. Consequently the prospects for a dramatic end to deforestation are not encouraging.[167] Deforestation also has a dramatic effect on termite populations, increasing the number of termites by anywhere from three to ten times their predeforestation population. Termites give off methane gas. Increases in atmospheric methane, an important greenhouse gas, have been measured at between 1 and 2 percent each year, due in part, some scientists fear, to deforestation and the related increase in the termite population.[168]

The greenhouse problem is a classic example, and also one of the most frightening examples, of the environmental policy paradox. As an EPA policy analyst once wrote, "[G]lobal warming is an international problem that will require extensive and unprecedented cooperation ... [N]o single country, acting alone, will be able decisively to affect the problem."[169] Another author described the policy environment surrounding the greenhouse effect as "the catch 22 of the greenhouse."[170] Since there is some scientific uncertainty about the exact timing and nature of global warming and what impact it would have on a region-by-region basis, policy makers wait for additional research to be completed. Although there have been scientific conferences and international cooperation to study greenhouse gasses, the attitude of many governments has been one of "wait and see," and requests for further study. For example, the U.S. Congress passed the Global Climate Protection Act of 1987, which, despite its high-sounding title, basically called for a study and report on the greenhouse problem.[171] Some limited progress has been made internationally on the control of greenhouse gasses. At the 1992 UN Conference on Environment and Development in Rio de Janeiro (often referred to as the Rio Conference), 154 nations agreed to report each year on changes in their carbon emissions. Although this information will be useful and may lead to further attempts to deal with global warming, this is only a reporting requirement and hence is what we might expect when dealing with sovereign states managing an international common pool problem.[172] Herein lies the paradox. When the uncertainties have been resolved, it may be too late to prevent or prepare for the negative impacts of global warming.[173] The greenhouse effect also lends itself to incremental decision making. It is a long-term problem that does not have immediate identifiable effects on the public. Politicians are hesitant to ask for sacrifices now that will reap nonvisible present benefits and uncertain future benefits. Nevertheless, the scientific community is in agreement that we are headed for warming and the risks we take by ignoring the greenhouse effect are very great. Yet this is the policy of most governments—wait and see. What is needed is a crisis environment.

The summer of 1988, one of the hottest in recorded U.S. history, provided the crisis environment that is often necessary for policy makers to act.[174] Two bills were introduced to decrease fossil fuel use and in other ways deal with the generation of greenhouse gasses. In Congress, members were quick to sign up as cosponsors for the legislation. As one commentator noted, "[A]ll of this has politicians scurrying around to put themselves on record as firmly opposed to apocalypse."[175] The sponsor of one bill, Senator Patrick J. Leahy of Vermont, commented, "[T]here's too much at stake to let our normal cynicism—or realism—about congressional leadership hold sway. It is our job to worry about the long-term future of American agriculture and forestry. ... Congress can't seem to make up its mind about whether it wants a two year budget, let alone focus on the effects of global warming, which may not occur for several decades."[176]

Although the United States is the largest producer of carbon emissions from fossil fuels (per capita allocation twice that of Europe; five times that of the global average), carbon plays a comparatively minor role in the total U.S. gross national product.[177] In many parts of the world, notably China, Eastern Europe, India, and to a lesser extent Russia, fossil fuels are an extremely important part of the economy. From 1990 to 1994, carbon emissions have risen 16 percent in Brazil, 24 percent in

India, 44 percent in South Korea, and 13 percent in China. It is estimated that by 2025, China will surpass the United States in the production of carbon emissions.[178] Throughout Europe, coal is an important fuel, even more so since the Chernobyl disaster. Furthermore, carbon dioxide emissions in many parts of the world are a long-time and far-off threat, with many other problems such as food, sanitation, and health care more immediately pressing.

A long-term problem, more pressing immediate economic and social needs, the common pool nature of the problem, and the lack of certainty or recognition of long-term effects all suggest global warming is a problem that will not go away any time soon. All these arguments support those that benefit from fossil fuel consumption, or those who fear the negative political fallout from limiting that consumption, to argue against taking corrective actions.

James Hansen, head of NASA's Goddard Institute for Space Studies, told a U.S. Senate committee during the summer of 1988, "[It] is time to stop waffling so much and say that the evidence is pretty strong that the greenhouse effect is here."[179] After Hansen's Senate testimony, Joseph Mullan, a spokesman for the National Coal Association on environmental issues, told a *New York Times* reporter that perhaps there was no need to be concerned about the greenhouse effect because, Mr. Mullan explained, "[S]ince the earth faces another ice age within a thousand years or so one calamity might cancel out the other."[180]

Lester B. Lave from Carnegie-Mellon University, a strong supporter of using cost-benefit analysis in policy making, argues that since the damage and the cost of global warming are at present impossible to determine, "there is no way to justify spending tens of billion dollars a year" to prevent the greenhouse effect.[181] However, the real or perceived lack of cost-benefit analysis data in global warming or any other environmental policy should not lead us to conclude, as Lave suggests, that protective measures that take costs into consideration should not be attempted. One can be against the use of cost-benefit analysis and still be in favor of cost-effective environmental policies. Cost effectiveness only means selecting the environmental policy that will clean up the environment for the least cost. Furthermore, as we have seen, if we require absolute certainty about costs and causality then nothing will be done.

The greenhouse effect may be such a catastrophic problem that nations will be willing to undertake measures they perceive not to be in their best short-term economic interest. An international conference on global warming sponsored by the United Nations Environmental Program and the World Meteorological Organization, held in Geneva in late 1988, attracted representatives from 35 countries. The objectives of the group were to study scientific evidence and consequences of warming. The United States was one of a few nations that insisted the conference examine the causes of global warming. The majority were convinced that enough was known about causes. Nevertheless, an American official in attendance, Frederick Bernthal, the assistant secretary of state for international environmental and scientific affairs, allowed that, "[We] know that greenhouse gasses are accumulating and in principle, they should lead to global warming."[182] It remains to be seen if this effort will lead to corrective measures that will halt the pollution of the international commons that leads to global warming.

The most recent attempt at establishing a global initiative for the reduction of greenhouse gasses took place in December 1997, in Kyoto, Japan. One-hundred sixty-one countries participated in efforts to reach a multilateral agreement that would help reduce the threat of global warming, without unfairly affecting any one country's or region's economic growth. The United States, the European Union, and Japan were able to agree upon a reduction in carbon emissions of 7, 8, and 6 percent, respectively, from 1990 levels by the year 2012. However, the agreements reached are not binding for developing countries, including China and India, both major emitters of carbon pollution. Reaching the targets set forth in the conference will involve the trading of emission reduction credits, allowances for those countries with heavy forested regions (because trees absorb carbon dioxide), and penalties for those countries that do not make their reduction quotas.

In order to accomplish the reductions called for in the Kyoto agreement, drastic lifestyle changes are going to be required. Ron Gelbspan, an environmental analyst, argues that our society is going to have to mount an energy reform on the scale of the Manhattan Project. It is imperative that global economies gets the help they need to make the switch to more sustainable, more efficient forms of energy production. However, it is important to note that the modest 7 percent reduction in U.S. greenhouse emissions is nowhere near the 60 to 70 percent recommended by many atmospheric scientists. Such reductions would have a massive impact on the economy; it is estimated that abatement measures would cost up to $275 billion, and result in a loss of 2 million jobs in heavy industry.[183]

In any event the question is moot as far as the United States is concerned. One of the first orders of business early in President George W. Bush's administration was the announcement, to the astonishment of America's European allies, that the United States would not participate in the Kyoto agreement.

Air pollution, whether in the form of CFCs, greenhouse gasses, acid rain, or other forms of pollution provides numerous examples of the environmental policy paradox. We often understand the relationship between our polluting activities and the impacts these activities have on the environment. However, numerous factors operate to result in policies that do not fully address the problem.

There is a lot we can do as individuals to help clean the air. Carpooling, walking, bicycling, energy conservation, or anything that keeps fossil fuels from being burned is helpful. Rather than drive to the store that is only a block away, walk instead. Driving is a luxury and is expensive both in terms of operating the car and costs in damage to our environment. Paradoxically most people know these things. Fortunately, we as individuals *can* control our personal "policy" choices.

SUMMARY

This chapter provided an overview of air pollution, its components, health effects, laws and regulations, causes, and its effects locally, nationally, and internationally. In addition, we took a close look at toxic air pollution, acid rain, ozone depletion, and the greenhouse effect. Air pollution policy is, like much environmental policy, fraught with scientific uncertainty, particularly in regard to the lack of direct causal evidence of a relationship between particular airborne pollutants and human health. We do have strong evidence of human health impacts with some pollutants, but we have been slow to act. Congress debated amendments to the Clean Air Act through the 1980s, but regional and economic interests succeeded in preventing additional legislation to deal with air pollution. The 1990 Clean Air Act Amendments may go a long way toward cleaning the nation's air, or they may not. Initial results are encouraging, though, and the Acid Rain Program stemming from the Amendments has been effective thus far. Implementation has been and will continue to be the key. In any event, the failure to act throughout the 1980s, in light of the available evidence of air pollution damage, is a good example of the environmental policy paradox.

In the next chapter we examine U.S. water pollution policy and problems of water supply, use, and conservation. In water, as in air, uncertainties lead to policy paradoxes, and powerful vested interests make changing the status quo difficult.

NOTES

1. Statistical Abstract of the United States, Bureau of Statistics, Treasury Department (Washington D.C.: GPO, 1996), p. 237.
2. U.S. Environmental Protection Agency, *National Air Quality: Status and Trends Report* (1995), p. 26.
3. U.S. Environmental Protection Agency, *National Air Quality: Status and Trends Report* (1999).
4. Ibid., Chapter 2: Criteria Pollutants: National Trends, pp. 3–5.
5. U.S. EPA website, Acid Rain Program, Charts and Tables, Table A1, SO2 data *http://www.epa.gov/airmarkets/emissions/score00/score00a1.pdf*.
6. U.S. Environmental Protection Agency, *National Air Quality: Status and Trends Report* (1995).
7. U.S. Environmental Protection Agency, *National Air Quality: Status and Trends Report* (1999), Chapter 2: Criteria Pollutants: National Trends, p. 61.
8. Ibid., pp. 15–18.
9. U.S. EPA Website, "Compliance Results of Acid Rain Program, 2000" *http://www.epa.gov/airmarkets/cmprpt/arp00/index.html#so2compliancreslts*.
10. Lashof, "Earth's Last Gasp?" p. 53.
11. U.S. Environmental Protection Agency, *National Air Quality: Status and Trends Report* (1995).
12. John A. Paul, "Urban Air Quality: The Problem," *EPA Journal*, 17 (1) (1991), p. 24.
13. U.S. Environmental Protection Agency, *EPA's Updated Clean Air Standards* (1997). Available [online] *http://ttnwww.rtpnc.epa.gov/naaqsfin/naaqsfac.htm*
14. U.S. Environmental Protection Agency, *National Air Quality: Status and Trends Report* (1999), Executive Summary, p. 1–3.
15. Ibid., Chapter 2: Criteria Pollutants: National Trends, p. 41.
16. Paul, "Urban Air Quality: The Problem," p. 25.
17. Ibid., pp. 25–26.
18. U.S. Environmental Protection Agency, *National Air Quality: Status and Trends Report* (1999), p. 37.
19. U.S. Environmental Protection Agency Website, "Green Book: Ozone Nonattainment Area Summary," August 2, 2001. *http://www.epa.gov/oar/oaqps/greenbk/onsum.html*.
20. U.S. Environmental Protection Agency, *National Air Quality: Status and Trends Report* (1999), pp. 1 and 32.
21. Lester B. Lave and Eugene P. Seskin, *Air Pollution in Human Health* (Baltimore: Johns Hopkins University Press, 1987), pp. 235–237.
22. G. Tyler Miller, Jr., *Living in the Environment* (5th ed.) (Belmont, CA: Wadsworth, 1988), p. 432. See also Frederick G. Kappler and Gary L. Rutledge, "The Expenditures for Abating Portion of Emissions from Motor Vehicles, 1968–1984," *Survey of Current Business,* 65 (July 1985), p. 29. Some have estimated the number is well in excess of 50,000 in the United States.
23. Ibid., p. 433.
24. A thermal inversion is created when cool air is trapped within an air basin by overlying warm air.
25. Dean E. Painter, *Air Pollution Technology* (Reston, VA: Reston, 1975), p. 22. These numbers are subject to some dispute. The estimates are based on average numbers of deaths over the period compared to numbers of deaths during the period of the pollution period. The London killer fog has been estimated by some to have led to more than 4,000 deaths.

26. Much is known, since each NAAQS has a "Criteria Document" that presents all known health data for that pollutant.
27. Don Hinrichsen, "Computing the Risks: A Global Overview of Our Most-Pressing Environmental Challenges," *International Wildlife* (March-April 1996), p. 23.
28. American Lung Association Website (2001). "State of the Air 2001" *http://www.lungusa.org/air2001/.*
29. Reason Public Policy Institute, May 4, 2001. "Breathe Easier: The American Lung Association's Misleading 'State of the Air 2001' Report" by Joel Schwartz. Available at *http://www.rppi.org/rr102.html.*
30. Michael G. Renner, "Car Sick," *World Watch,* 1 (6) (November-December 1988), pp. 36, 38.
31. Miller, *Living in the Environment,* p. 433.
32. William H. Matthews, Frederick E. Smith, and Edward D. Goldberg, (eds.), *Man's Impact on Terrestrial and Oceanic Ecosystems* (Cambridge: Massachusetts Institute of Technology, 1971), p. 103.
33. National Acid Precipitation Assessment Program, *Interim Assessment: The Causes and Effects of Acid Deposition,* IV (Washington, DC: U.S. Government Printing Office, 1987). Cited in Lester R. Brown, "A New Era Unfolds," Lester R. Brown et al. (eds.), *State of the World* (New York: Norton, 1993), p. 13.
34. "Effects of Ozone Air Pollution on Plants" North Carolina State University and the Agricultural Research Service of the USDA. 1998. Raleigh, NC. Found at *http://www.ces.ncsu.edu/depts/pp/notes/Ozone/ozone.html* October 12, 2001.
35. M.R. Ashmore and F.M. Marshall, "Air Pollution Impacts on Crops" from the Regional Air Pollution in Developing Countries Website *http://www.york.ac.uk/inst/sei/rapidc/impacts/CropFS.html*
36. "Smog Spells Invisible Damage for Crops," Environmental News Network. June 27, 2000. Found at *http://www.cnn.com/2000/NATURE/06/27/smog.crops.enn/*
37. "Air Pollution," *Current History,* 59 (387) (July 1970), pp. 18–49.
38. Alvin W. Vogtle, Jr., "Investigate, Educate, Then Regulate: An Agenda for Dealing with Acid Rain," in Kent Gilbreath (ed.), *Business and the Environment Towards Common Ground* (2nd ed.) (Washington, DC: The Conservation Foundation, 1984), p. 245.
39. Richard D. Wilson, "Motor Vehicles and Fuels: The Strategy," *EPA Journal,* 17 (1) (1991), p. 15.
40. Hertsgaard, Mark. (1998). *Earth Odyssey.* (Broadway Books: New York), p. 91 and 94.
41. EPA's Green Vehicle Guide, FAQs *http://www.epa.gov/autoemissions/faq.htm#Control.*
42. Hertsgaard, *Earth Odyssey,* p. 95.
43. Alliance of Automobile Manufacturers Website *http://www.autoalliance.org/facts.htm.*
44. Renner, "Car Sick," p. 36.
45. U.S. Environmental Protection Agency, *Motor Vehicles and the 1990 Clean Air Act,* (August 1994). Available [online] *http://www.epa.gov/reg3artd/vehic/11-vehs.htm*
46. Charnley, Gail. (2000). "Enhancing the Role of Science in Stakeholder-Based Risk Management Decision-Making" from the Risk World Website *http://www.riskworld.com/Nreports/2000/Charnley/NR00GC04.htm.*
47. National Energy Information Center. July 2001. "A Primer on Gasoline Prices." *http://www.eia.doe.gov/pub/oil_gas/petroleum/analysis_publications/primer_on_gasoline_prices/html/petbro.html.*
48. Frederick G. Kappler and Gary L. Rutledge, "The Expenditures for Abating Portion of Emissions from Motor Vehicles, 1968–1984," *Survey of Current Business,* 65 (July 1985), p. 29.
49. Renner, "Car Sick," p. 36.
50. Ibid.
51. Union of Concerned Scientists Website, from the 2000 report "Money Down the Pipeline: The Hidden Subsidies to the Oil Industry." *http://www.ucsusa.org/vehicles/pipeline.html.*
52. Robert Stobaugh and Daniel Yergin (eds.), *Energy Future* (3rd ed.)(New York: Vintage Books, 1983), p. 66.
53. "Environment: Victory for Clean Air," *Time* (October 5, 1970), p. 46.
54. "Detroit's Battle with Washington," *Business Week* (December 5, 1970), p. 28.
55. Walter A. Rosenbaum, *The Politics of Environmental Concern* (New York: Praeger, 1973), p. 153.

56.

NATIONAL AMBIENT AIR QUALITY STANDARDS, U.S. ENVIRONMENTAL PROTECTION AGENCY.

PRIMARY (HEALTH-RELATED)

POLLUTANT	AVERAGING TIME	CONCENTRATION
Particulates (PM-10)	Annual arithmetic mean	$50\,\mu g.m_3$
<10 micrometers	24-hour	$150\,\mu g/m_3$
Particulates (PM-2.5)	Annual arithmetic mean	$15\,\mu g.m_3$
<2.5 micrometers	24-hour	$65\,\mu g/m_3$
Sulfur dioxide	Annual arithmetic mean	0.03 ppm
	24-hour	0.14 ppm
Carbon monoxide	8-hour	9.0 ppm
	1-hour	35.0 ppm
Nitrogen dioxide	Annual arithmetic mean	$100\,\mu g/m_3$ (0.053ppm)
Ozone	1-hour	$235\,\mu g/m_3$ (0.12 ppm)
	8-hour	$157\,\mu g/m_3$ (0.08 ppm)
Lead	Quarterly Average	$1.5\,\mu g/m_3$

SECONDARY (WELFARE-RELATED)

POLLUTANT	AVERAGE TIME	CONCENTRATION
Particulates (PM-10) <10 micrometers	Same as Primary	
Particulates (PM-2.5) <2.5 micrometers	Same as Primary	
Sulfur dioxide	Same as Primary	
Carbon monoxide	None	
Nitrogen dioxide	Same as Primary	
Ozone	Same as Primary	
Lead	Same as Primary	

Special thanks to Richard Foust.

57. U.S. Code Title 42, Section 7409 (b) (1).
58. Painter, *Air Pollution Technology,* pp. 3–9.
59. U.S. Code Title 42, Section 7412 (a) (1).
60. See Margaret E. Kriz, "Dunning the Midwest," *National Journal,* 22 (15) (April 14, 1990), pp. 893–897.
61. For an in-depth discussion of the NPDES permitting system, refer to John A. Veil, "NPDES permits have increased emphasis on control of toxic pollutants," *The Oil and Gas Journal,* (Jan 6, 1997), p. 46.
62. Robert W. Hahn and Gordon L. Hester, "The Market for Bads: EPA's Experience with Emission's Trading," *Regulation,* 3–4 (1987), p. 48.
63. Byron Swift, "A Low Cost Way to Control Climate Change," *Issues in Science and Technology,* (Spring 1998), p. 75.
64. City of Chicago Website. *http://www.ci.chi.il.us/Environment/AirToxPollution/EmissionReduction Bank.html*
65. Deborah Schwartz, "Chicago Uses Air Emission Trades to Boost Economy," *Planning,* (March 1998), p. 25.
66. National Transportation Library. "Guidance for Emission Reduction Credit Generation by Clean Fuel Fleets & Vehicles." January, 1993. *http://ntl.bts.gov/data/energy-env/air/00487.html*
67. See Hahn and Hester, "The Market for Bads: EPA's Experience with Emission's Trading"; see also Robert E. Taylor, "EPA Is Expanding Its Bubble Policy for Air Pollution," *Wall Street Journal,* November 20, 1986, p. 18.

68. Robert W. Hahn, "Trade-Offs in Designing Markets with Multiple Objectives," *Journal of Environmental Economics and Management,* 13 (March 1986), pp. 1, 7.
69. Roger Rapoport, "Trading Dollars for Dirty Air," *Science* 86 (7) (July/August 1986), p. 75.
70. Ibid.
71. Ibid. Examples of ERC trades include the sale of hydrocarbon credits to General Motors by B.F. Goodrich in Louisville, Kentucky. Mobile Oil in Renton, Washington, reduced its hydrocarbon emissions and sold the credits to Reynolds Aluminum. Arundel Corporation reduced its total suspended particle emissions in Sparrows Point, Maryland, and sold its reductions to Atlantic Cement.
72. Phillip Shabecoff, "EPA Sets Rules on Air Pollution Allowances," *New York Times,* November 20, 1986, pp. 1, 22.
73. Ibid. The Natural Resources Defense Council unsuccessfully challenged the bubble concept as a violation of the Clean Air Act. The U.S. Supreme Court upheld the EPA's authority to create bubbles. "Supreme Court Upholds Bubble Pollution Concept," *The Oil Daily,* 174 (8) (June 26,1984), p. 1.
74. Kimberley Music, "EPA, Lawmakers Back Expanded Emissions Trading," *The Oil Daily,* (July 10, 1997), p. 5.
75. See, for example, the discussion of EPA bubble policy and the steel industry in Bill Schmitt, "Revised Bubble Policy Might Be Tougher," *American Metal Market,* 94 (March 13, 1986), p. 1.
76. That reportedly was the case in northern California when existing firms refused to sell pollution permits to a potential competitor. See W. David Slawson, "The Right to Protection from Air Pollution," *Southern California Law Review,* 59 (May 1986), pp. 672, 729.
77. W. David Slawson, "The Right to Protection from Air Pollution," *Southern California Law Review,* 59 (May 1986), p. 727.
78. U.S. Code Title 42, Section 7411 (a) (1) (c). The statute reads in pertinent part: "reflect the degree of emission reduction achievable through the application of the best system of continuous emission reduction which (taking into consideration the cost of achieving such emission reduction, and any non air quality health and environmental impact and energy requirements) the administrator determines has been adequately demonstrated for that category of sources."
79. Lave and Seskin, *Air Pollution in Human Health,* pp. 312–316.
80. Ibid., p. 693.
81. Natural Resources Defense Council, Inc., *Petitioner v. Environmental Protection Agency.* 263 U.S. App. D.C. 231. Decided July 31, 1987.
82. Natural Resources Defense Council, *Petitioner, v. United States Environmental Protection Agency, Respondent.* 915 F.2d 1314. Filed with 9th Circuit Court of Appeals September 28, 1990.
83. *Natural Resources Defense Council, Inc., and Sierra Club, Petitioners v. U.S. Environmental Protection Agency, et al., Respondents.* 290 U.S. App. D.C. 323. Decided June 28, 1991.
84. *Natural Resources Defense Council, Inc., et al., Petitioners v. United States Environmental Protection Agency, Respondent.* 306 U.S. App. D.C. 357. Decided May 27, 1994.
85. This point has been the subject of some controversy. In conversations with EPA air quality officials, the point was made that the catalytic converter was developed. Also, advances were achieved in coating technology. It is argued that technology-forcing rules have probably gained more than other traditional regulations.

    However, given the history of the CAA to date, it would seem clear that industries that release harmful pollutants will not provide for better pollution controls unless legally compelled to do so.
86. Statistical Abstract of the United States, Bureau of Statistics, Treasury Department (Washington DC: GPO, 1996), pp. 233–240.
87. U. S. Bureau of the Census, Current Industrial Reports; Pollution Abatement Cost and Expenditures, 1992, MA200(94)-1; U.S. Government Printing Office; Washington, DC; 1996. Available at *http://www.census.gov/prod/2/manmin/ma200x94.pdf*
88. All air pollutants are potentially hazardous to human health though the law does distinguish between conventional and hazardous pollutants.
89. Conservation Foundation, *State of the Environment,* p. 135.
90. U.S. Code Title 42 Section 7412 (A)(1). (Note: It takes a special talent to write a sentence like that.)
91. "On the Regulation of Toxic Air Pollutants: A Critical Review Discussion Papers," *Journal of the Air Pollution Control Association,* 36 (1989), p. 990.
92. 42 U.S.C.A. section 7412 (b) (1).
93. George Siple, "HON Rule Targets Specialty Chemicals," *Environmental Protection,* 4 (6), (1993), p. 44.

94. The figures on the 1990 Clean Air Act Amendments reported in this chapter were taken from Keith Schneider, "Lawmakers Reach an Accord on Reduction of Air Pollution," *New York Times,* October 23, 1990, pp. A1, A11.

95. Conservation Foundation, *State of the Environment,* p. 152.

96. Ibid.

97. Ibid. Also see "Deadly Lead," *Environmental Action,* 17 (5) (1986), p. 20.

98. Conservation Foundation, *State of the Environment,* p. 154.

99. Latency periods make it easy for those who oppose air pollution regulations to minimize the health dangers of air pollution. Long delays frequently occur between exposure to the toxic pollutant that then triggers the disease process leading to later manifestation of disease symptoms. These lengthy delays make it difficult to pin the cause to the resulting effect. Decision makers cannot know beyond a doubt that exposure to asbestos, for example, will cause a schoolchild to develop cancer. Thus they are open to persuasive arguments from lobbies concerned with the cost of implementing restrictive regulations.

100. Asbestos Hazard Emergency Response Act of 1986, P.L. 99–519.

101. Ibid.

102. Brenda Norrell, "500 Navajo Mine Victims Pack Hearing," *Arizona Daily Sun,* March 14, 1990, p. 2. The act was passed and signed by President G.W.H. Bush in 1992. It provides for three levels of compensation: $50,000 for those downwind, $75,00 for those on site, and $100,000 for the miners themselves who satisfy damage criteria. The trust fund was not in the final version of the act but rather appropriations are being made on an annual basis. The first payouts began in 1992.

103. Radiation Workers Justice Act of 1998. Hearing Before the Subcommittee on Immigration and Claims of the Committee on the Judiciary, House of Representatives, One Hundred Fifth Congress, Second Session, on H.R. 3539 June 25, 1998. Available at *http://commdocs.house.gov/ committees/judiciary/hju59930.000/hju59930_0.HTM.*

104. WISE Uranium Project Website. September 29, 2001. "Compensation of Navajo Uranium Miners." Available at *http://www.antenna.nl/~wise/uranium/ureca.html.*

105. September 2001 GAO Report "Radiation Exposure Compensation: Analysis of Justice's Program Administration." **GAO-01-1043.**

106. U.S. Environmental Protection Agency, *National Air Quality: Status and Trends Report,* (1995).

107. Anne LaBastille, "The International Acid Test," *Sierra* (May-June 1986), p. 51.

108. Don Hinrichsen, "Computing the Risks: a global overview of our most-pressing environmental challenges," *International Wildlife,* (March-April 1996), p. 23.

109. Archie M. Kahan, *Acid Rain: Reign of Controversy* (Golden, CO: Fulcrum, 1986), p. 20.

110. LaBastille, "The International Acid Test," p. 51.

111. U.S. Office of Technology Assessment, *Acid Rain Transported Air Pollutants,* pp. 71–73.

112. G. Tyler Miller, *Living in the Environment,* (8th ed.) (Belmont, CA: Wadsworth Publishing, 1994), p. 579.

113. See Barbara Jancar-Webster, *Environmental Action in Eastern Europe* (Armonk, NY: M.E. Sharp, 1993); Peter Sloep and Andrew Blowers, (eds.), *Environmental Policy in an International Context: Environmental Problems as Conflicts of Interest* (London: Arnold Publishing, 1996), pp. 66–96.

114. Mark Pallemaerts, "The Politics of Acid Rain Control in Europe," *Environment* (March 1988), p. 42.

115. Conversion rate based on XE.com Universal Converter using live rates from October 24, 2001.

116. European Commission Website—Environment section. Com document (99)125. "Proposal for a Directive setting national emission ceilings for certain atmospheric pollutants" available at *http://europa.eu.int/comm/environment/docum/99125sm.htm.*

117. World Resources Institute, *World Resources 1992–1993* (New York: Oxford University Press, 1992), p. 199.

118. Leslie Roberts, "Acid Rain Program: Mixed Review," *Science,* (April 19, 1991), p. 371.

119. Conservation Foundation, *State of the Environment,* p. 77.

120. *Environmental Protection,* 4 (1) (1993), p. 10.

121. Ned Helme and Chris Neme, "Acid Rain: The Problem," *EPA Journal,* 17 (1) (1991), p. 19.

122. EPA Website. "Compliance Results of Acid Rain Program, 2000". Available at *http://www. epa.gov/airmarkets/cmprpt/arp00/index.html#so2compliancreslts.*

123. Another threat to the ozone layer may be presented by U.S. space shuttle flights. Experts in the former USSR claimed that every time the U.S. craft flies, it destroys massive amounts of atmospheric ozone. Calculations by Valeri Burdkov, one of the Soviet Union's leading geophysicists and

Vyacheslav Filin, deputy chief designer at the S.P. Korolyev Design Bureau, show that in "one flight, the space shuttle destroys up to 10 million of the three billion tons of atmospheric ozone. Three hundred launches is enough to do away altogether with the thin ozone layer which is already holed." The solid fuel used in the Titan rockets burns to produce hydrogen chloride, one molecule of which is said to destroy 100,000 molecules of ozone. The rocket emits 187 tons of chlorine and chlorine compounds as well as ozone-depleting nitrogen compounds (7 tons), aluminum oxides (177 tons), and 378 tons of carbon oxidizers. However, NASA maintains the shuttle is ecologically sound. See Nick Nuttall, "Russians say U.S. Shuttle Is Damaging Ozone Layer," *The Times* (London), December 20, 1989, p. 5.

124. Miller, *Living in the Environment,* p. 439.
125. William K. Reilly, "Statement on Ozone Depletion," U.S. Environmental Protection Agency, Washington, DC, April 4, 1991.
    Cited in Lester R. Brown, "A New Era Unfolds," Lester R. Brown et al. (eds.), *State of the World* (New York: Norton, 1993), p. 10.
126. Tom Fry, "Ozone Depletion Increases Skin Cancer Risk," *Environmental News Network.* August 28, 2001.
127. See Thomas H. Maugh II, "Ozone Depletion Far Worst Than Expected," *Los Angeles Times,* March 16, 1988, Pt. I, p.1; and "Ozone Depletion Worsens, NRDC Leads Drive for Total CFC Phase Out," *Newsline* (Natural Resources Defense Council), 6 (2) (May/June 1988), p. 1; and *The Plain English Guide to the Clean Air Act,* The EPA, (April 1993), p. 16.
128. Maugh, "Ozone Depletion Far Worst Than Expected," p. 1.
129. Edward Edelson, "The Man Who Knew Too Much," *Popular Science* (January 1989), p. 60. See also Lanie Jones, "He Sounded, Paid Heavy Price," *Los Angeles Times,* July 14, 1988, Pt. 1, p. 1.
130. Jones, "He Sounded, Paid Heavy Price," p. 18.
131. Edelson, "The Man Who Knew Too Much," p. 63.
132. Jones, "He Sounded, Paid Heavy Price," p. 1.
133. Maugh, "Ozone Depletion Far Worst Than Expected," p. 19.
134. The discovery was made by a group of scientists representing Canada, the United States, the then USSR, and several European countries. As reported on Cable News Network, February 15, 1989.
135. Mark Dowie, "A sky full of holes: why the ozone layer is torn worse than ever," *The Nation,* (July 8, 1996), p. 11.
136. Ibid.
137. Ibid.
138. Ibid.
139. Robert Gillette, "Hodel Proposal Irks Environmentalists," *Los Angeles Times,* May 30, 1989, Pt. 1, p. 2. When asked about the proposal a spokesperson for Bausch & Lomb, the manufacturer of Ray-Ban sunglasses, remarked, "Sounds fine with us. ... We'll be happy to set the Interior Secretary up as a distributor of Ray-Ban sunglasses." Ibid.
140. Maugh, "Ozone Depletion Far Worst Than Expected," p. 19.
141. Edelson, "The Man Who Knew Too Much," p. 102.
142. "EC Agrees to Ban All CFCs by 2000 in Surprise Move," *Wall Street Journal,* March 3, 1989, p. B2.
143. "Europe Takes Ozone Lead," *Los Angeles Times,* March 4,1989, Pt. 2, p. 8. See also Cathleen Decker and Larry Stammer, "Bush Asks Ban on CFC to Save Ozone," *Los Angeles Times,* March 4,1989, Pt. 1, p. 1.
144. *Plain English Guide to the Clean Air Act,* The EPA (April 1993), p. 16.
145. Ibid., p. 16.
146. World Resources Institute, *World Resources 1992–1993,* (New York: Oxford University Press, 1992), p. 152.
147. David D. Doniger, "Politics of the Ozone Layer," *Issues in Science and Technology,* 4 (Spring 1988), p. 86.
148. The agreement has provisions for trade sanctions against those who do not cooperate. The enforceability and utility of these sanctions is questionable, however.
149. "Ozone-Protection Plan May Have a Big Hole," *Honolulu Advertiser,* April 21,1989, Pt. D, p. 1.
150. Ibid.
151. "Ozone Depletion Worsens, NRDC Leads Drive for Total CFC Phase Out," *Newsline* (Natural Resources Defense Council), 6 (2) (May/June 1988), p. 1.
152. EPA Website. Ozone Protection Regulations. Available at *http://www.epa.gov/ozone/title6/609/.*

153. World Bank's Montreal Protocol Website, updated May 2001. *http://www-esd.worldbank.org/mp/home.cfm.*

154. A zero (0) indicates zero or less than one-half the unit of measure. Data are total of compounds F-11, which are about 94 percent of the chlorofluoromethanes produced. Chlorofluoromethanes are a group of carbon compounds. Data are available for the Chemical Manufacturers Association, which presents F-11 and F-12 separately. Data are composed of reports from 19 companies reporting to the Chemical Manufacturers Association's Fluorocarbon Research Program. Producers in USSR, Eastern Europe, and the People's Republic of China do not report data to the CMA-FPP, and are not included in this table. Source: Chemical Manufacturers Association, Production, Sales, and Calculated Release of CFC-11 and CFC-12 through 1985 (Washington, DC, 1986).

155. Carl Dennis, "The Greenhouse Effect," *Poetry,* 146 (August 1985), p. 266.

156. Christina M. Valente and William D. Valente, *Introduction to Environmental Law and Policy* (New York: West Publishing, 1995), p. 338.

157. Jeremy Rifkin, "The Doomsday Prognosis," *The Guardian,* August 21, 1988, p. 19.

158. Miller, *Living in the Environment,* p. 440.

159. Christopher Flavin and Odil Tunali, "Getting Warmer: Looking for a Way out of the Climate Impasse," *World Watch* (March-April 1995), p. 10.

160. Michael Oppenheimer and Robert Boyle, *Dead Heat: The Race against the Greenhouse Effect* (New York: Basic Books, 1990), p. 57.

161. Rifkin, "The Doomsday Prognosis," p. 19; and Miller, *Living in the Environment,* p. 441.

162. Colum Lynch, "The Mechanics of a Warming World," *Amicus Journal* (Winter 1998), p. 19.

163. William H. Mansfield, III, "With a Global Focus," *EPA Journal,* 15 (1) (January/February), p. 37.

164. Colum Lynch, "Stormy Weather," *Amicus Journal,* (Winter 1998), p. 16.

165. William Eaton, "Congress Urged to Fight Global Warming," *The Los Angeles Times,* December 2,1988, Pt. 1, p. 41.

166. Lester R. Brown and John E. Young, "Growing Food in a Warmer World," *World Watch,* 1 (6) (November/December 1988), p. 32.

167. Rifkin, "The Doomsday Prognosis," p. 19.

168. David M. Schwartz, "The Termite Connection," *International Wildlife* (July/August 1987), p. 38.

169. Linda Fisher, "The Wheels Are Beginning to Turn," *EPA Journal,* 15 (1) (January/February), p. 42.

170. Stefi Weisburd, "Waiting for Warming: The Catch 22 of CO_2," *Science News,* 128 (September 14,1985), p. 170.

171. Global Climate Protection Act of 1987.

172. Lester R. Brown, "A New Era Unfolds," Lester R. Brown et al. (eds.), *State of the World* (New York: Norton, 1993), p. 3.

173. Lewis M. Embler, Patricia L. Layman, Wil Lepkowski, and Pamela S. Zurer, "Social Economic Implications," *Chemical and Engineering News,* 64 (November 24,1986), pp. 36, 39.

174. It should be noted that during the summer of 1988 many felt that the unusual heat was related to the greenhouse effect. In fact there is little evidence this is the case.

175. "Shake or Bake," *The New Republic* (September 12, 1988), p. 5.

176. Eaton, "Congress Urged to Fight Global Warming," p. 41.

177. Christopher Flavin, "The Heat Is On," *World Watch,* 1 (6) (November/December 1988), p. 19.

178. Lynch, "Stormy Weather," p. 16.

179. "Notes and Comment," *The New Yorker* (August 29, 1988), p. 17.

180. Ibid., p. 18.

181. Ibid.

182. "35 Nation Conference Addresses Global Warming," *New York Times,* November 13,1988, Pt. 1, p. 11.

183. Lynch, "Stormy Weather," p. 17.

6

Water

The earth has no shortage of water. Seventy-one percent of the world's surface is covered with it, and total annual global precipitation is estimated at around 126,000 cubic miles. However, 97 percent of the earth's water is in the form of salt water and of the 3 percent remaining freshwater, only 0.003 percent is available as freshwater for human use.[1]

In this chapter we explore the paradox of environmental water policy. We start with a discussion of types of pollution. Then we examine the health impacts of water pollution and the laws and regulations governing water pollution policy.

Water moves through a cycle, falling to earth and returning to the atmosphere. It falls to the earth in the form of rain or snow. On earth, most water percolates into the soil where it remains or moves into rivers, lakes, and eventually the ocean. Some water is held by plants, which eventually release the water back into the atmosphere through a process called evapotranspiration. Other waters at the surface, in rivers, lakes, or in the seas, evaporate into the atmosphere to complete the water cycle.

In the United States, roughly 75 percent of freshwater comes from surface sources; the balance originates from the ground. Groundwater, that water stored in underground reservoirs called aquifers, is the primary source of water for major sections of the arid western United States, as well as large sections of northern and central Africa and other areas throughout the world. Since groundwater usually moves underground very slowly, it can take many years for water withdrawn to be naturally replenished and, as we see later, once polluted can be very costly to clean.

The source of water, surface or groundwater, and the way water is used are functions of the economy, level of development, and type of water resources available in an area. In more developed countries, large amounts of water are used for electric cooling and industry. For example, 38 percent of all water used in the United States is used for electrical cooling, whereas less than 1 percent of the water used in China is used for that purpose.[2] U.S. industrial and agricultural sectors account for 87 percent of freshwater consumption, and much of the water used by agriculture is for producing meat. Generally the less developed countries use more than 80 percent of their water for agriculture. Developed countries are also more intensive users of water for domestic purposes. The typical North American consumes 170 gallons of water daily, more than seven times the per capita average in the rest of the world, and almost triple Europe's consumption rate. The World Health Organization (WHO) says good health and cleanliness require a total daily supply of about 8 gallons of water per person.[3] Moreover, it is estimated that between 30 and 50 percent of the water used in the United States is wasted unnecessarily.[4] Simply by installing efficient showerheads and aerating faucets, the average American household would save 7,800 gallons of water annually.

According to the World Health Organization, approximately 1.5 billion people in the world do not have a safe supply of clean water. Around 1.7 billion people lack facilities for proper disposal of human waste. Two billion humans face chronic water shortages. The United Nations, in 1980, urged that $300 billion be spent to supply all of the world's people with safe drinking water and proper sanitation by 1990. In reality, only $1.5 billion was ever spent.[5]

In the United States many areas, most notably in the West, either are or will soon be suffering from water shortages; many others throughout the country are already experiencing serious water contamination problems.

SOURCES

When examining water pollution, the types of pollution are usually divided into point and nonpoint sources. Point sources of pollution are those that originate from some specific location such as a pipe, a sewer, or a ditch. Common point sources of water pollution would include factories, some sewage treatment plants, landfills, hazardous waste sites, and leakage from gasoline storage tanks. Common nonpoint sources of water pollution include runoff from irrigation containing salts and residue from pesticides, runoff from animal feedlots, salts from the salting of winter roads, and storm runoff from the streets of urban areas.

Until the late 1980s, the nation's water pollution abatement efforts focused on reducing pollution from point sources, primarily industrial and municipal sewage plants. The marked decline in point source pollution may be attributed to the $90 billion spent by federal, state, and local governments since 1972 to improve municipal sewage treatment plants.[6] The major problem areas in water pollution, however, according to most analysts, are nonpoint source pollution, particularly urban runoff and groundwater pollution. It is estimated that 60 percent of water quality violations are the result of nonpoint pollution.[7] We examine both nonpoint and groundwater pollution in some detail later.

In some areas, such as Lake Erie and the Willamette River in Oregon, water pollution has improved considerably since the 1960s. Overall, however, water pollution is still a very serious problem in the United States. Despite recent improvements, 96 percent of assessed Great Lakes shorelines are impaired; that is, pollutants in fish tissue are at unsafe levels. The EPA's 1998 Water Quality Inventory found that 40 percent of all surface waters are not safe enough for swimming or fishing. Two additional facts are clear. First, less than a third of all water bodies were actually studied, so the problem could be much worse due to limited resources and the expensive nature of water monitoring. Second, agricultural and urban runoff are the primary sources of water pollutants, and siltation, bacteria, nutrients, and metals are the leading pollutants.[8] Further, certain toxic metals, such as arsenic, cadmium, and mercury, as well as other contaminants including chlorides and nitrates, are increasingly sources of pollution of surface waters in many areas.[9]

A major problem area in the United States, particularly in surface water pollution, is municipal wastewater. Many municipal wastewater treatment plants do not meet the standards established in 1972 in the Clean Water Act. Wastewaters are treated in accordance with one of three levels of purity. Primary treatment basically removes whatever floats to the top or sinks to the bottom of collected wastewater. Primary sewage treatment removes about 60 percent of suspended solids, 20 percent of nitrogen compounds, 30 percent of oxygen-demanding waste, though few, if any, chemical pollutants.[10] Secondary treatment aerates sewage that has received primary treatment, causing a biological process that neutralizes and allows the removal of additional pollutants. Secondary treatment removes up to 90 percent of oxygen-demanding waste, an additional 30 percent of suspended solids, as well as an additional 30 percent of nitrogen compounds, 30 percent of most toxic metal compounds, and most synthetic organic chemicals.[11] Tertiary treatment further treats sewage that has been through the secondary treatment method by additional chemical and physical processes, which, depending on the process and the pollutant, can bring water close to or in excess of drinking water standards. Tertiary treatment plants are four times as expensive to operate as secondary plants and twice as expensive to build. Hence, tertiary treatment is used only when absolutely necessary. For example, in the community of Truckee, California, treated wastewater percolates into the ground and ultimately finds its way into the Truckee River and the water supply system for the city of Reno, Nevada. Tertiary treatment in Truckee is the only way to ensure the purity of Reno's water supply.

The Clean Water Act amendments in 1972 required that all municipal sewage treatment plants treat their sewage at the secondary level by 1977, with some extensions up to 1983. However, many municipal wastewater treatment plants have failed to meet these requirements and continue discharging wastewater that has only received primary treatment.

When asked why their surface water sources did not support designated uses, 19 state water officials identified municipal wastewater as the first reason, and officials representing 20 additional states ranked municipal wastewater as the second most important reason. Nonpoint sources of water pollution tied municipal wastewater as the primary cause of water pollution.[12]

Nonpoint Sources of Pollution

In the control of nonpoint sources of water pollution as well as groundwater, current laws are often either nonexistent or ineffectual. Nonpoint water pollution requires regulation of the land and its uses, specifically by the state and local governments.

While Congress directed states to address the issue in 1985—particularly coastal states—most have yet to do so. A notable exception is the state of Nebraska, which has established 23 special districts around watershed boundaries that are authorized to tax and enforce controls if necessary.[13]

Although the federal government invests about $3 billion annually to address nonpoint sources, the GAO estimates this spending is a "drop in the bucket." What's worse, some state officials estimate that federal government activities are the primary source of nonpoint source water pollution in half or more of their states' watersheds.[14]

Of all nonpoint water pollution, agricultural runoff is the most widespread source. The U.S. Fish and Wildlife Service and the EPA found that nonpoint agricultural water pollution was primarily responsible for adverse impacts on fish communities in 30 percent of the nation's lakes and rivers. In 60 percent of all states, state water officials identified agriculture as the most common source of water pollution.[15] Dibromochloropropane (DBCP), for example, is a pesticide that was banned by the EPA in 1979 but continues to be found in municipal wells in rural areas. The city of Fresno was forced to close 25 of its wells that exceeded the DBCP standard and it plans over 70 filtering systems to address the problem—at an estimated cost of up to $1 million each.[16] In some areas, blatant violations from farming are treated as "point sources" under regulations normally designed for industrial and sewage plants.

Nonpoint water pollution from urban storm water is second to agricultural runoff as a source of water pollution. In many ways, urban runoff is more serious than agricultural water pollution, primarily because the latter consists in large part of sediments whereas urban storm runoff contains many and diverse toxic substances as well as salts and oils. Urban runoff from streets, parking lots, and construction sites is estimated to affect 5 percent to 15 percent of surface waters and typically elevates temperatures (thermal pollution) in nearby streams, lakes, and reservoirs. It is no surprise urban runoff is an increasing nonpoint source water pollution problem. Since World War II, land devoted to urban areas in the United States is up 327 percent, and paved road mileage has jumped 278 percent.[17] Because paved areas block most water from seeping into the earth, it travels along its surface, picks up dirt and pollutants, and carries them to rivers and lakes.

Other nonpoint sources include projects such as dams that alter water flow patterns and sediment deposits; abandoned mines with their high acid concentrations and wastes; timber cutting and the soil erosion it encourages, as well as debris from the logging roads that end up in nearby waters; construction of highways and other land development projects; and land disposal of wastes, including leaking septic tanks.[18]

Groundwater Pollution

Roughly half of the U.S. population relies on groundwater for drinking water, and in some areas groundwater provides close to or all of the domestic water supply.[19] Threats to groundwater quality come from a variety of sources, including hazardous waste sites, landfills, wastewater disposal sites, leaking gasoline storage tanks, runoff from irrigation, salts from the salting of winter roads, seepage from septic tanks, and, on occasion, cemeteries. Twenty-five percent of all usable groundwater, and up to 75 percent in some areas, are considered contaminated.[20]

EPA studies have found that synthetic organic chemicals have contaminated 45 percent of the larger public water systems in the United States served by groundwater sources. The EPA estimates that contaminated aquifers in urban areas affect between 5 million and 10 million people—and many feel these estimates are conservative. Rural households that rely on wells, which are not required to undergo any kind of testing, were found to have violated at least one of the federal health standards for drinking water in two-thirds of the households surveyed.[21]

Serious as existing groundwater pollution problems may be, the future promises to be worse. In 1986 the EPA identified 24,269 abandoned hazardous waste sites in the United States that have either caused or have the potential to cause contamination of drinking water sources. In addition, there are over 15,000 municipal landfills receiving hazardous and nonhazardous wastes that were both unlined and located near or above aquifers. Since groundwater moves slowly underground, it can take decades or centuries for water to be replenished. Groundwater pollution, consequently, may go undetected for years. That is why the number of hazardous wastes sites that have been abandoned and the number of municipal landfills that are unlined and continue to be used suggest a frightening prospect for water quality in the future. A study in Arizona, for example, a state heavily dependent on groundwater, which in the past was lax in its regulation of the disposal of hazardous waste, identified 1,538 waste impoundment sites in the state. In examining these sites, the state of Arizona summarized what it termed "the average" surface impoundment and concluded that such an impoundment had a "strong potential to contaminate groundwater." The state described an average typical Arizona surface impoundment as

> unlined, and its purpose is to dispose of an unknown quantity of waste which is more hazardous to health than untreated sewage. Since the impoundment has no artificial barrier to prevent infiltration, the infiltration rate is controlled only by the vadose zone. It is located over ... a high yielding aquifer that is used as a drinking water source with at least one well located within one mile of the impoundment ... there is no groundwater monitoring at or near the impoundment to detect changes in groundwater chemical quality ...[22]

Although the numbers and the significance of pollution varies from region to region, the surface impoundment just described could be found anywhere in the United States.

Health Effects of Water Pollution

The health effects of chemicals that are commonly found in drinking water are numerous and frightening. Cancer; liver, kidney, and nervous system damage; sterility in males; genetic mutations; fetal damage; and infant death are among the effects associated with consuming chemicals that are commonly found in drinking water.[23] These are the consequences of the chemicals that we know about and have some idea of how they impact the human body. However, only a fraction of the chemicals found in groundwater are routinely tested or covered by federal water quality standards. Most people have no idea what is in their drinking water or what effect it will have on their health. Remarkably, neither do many government officials. In some communities, public attention to the risks of the water supply system has led to the widespread use of bottled water. For example, in the city of San Jose, California, more than half the residents in some areas either buy bottled water or have installed home purification systems.[24]

During April 1993, the city of Milwaukee suffered a Cryptosporidiosis outbreak, rendering the city's water supply virtually unusable. Cyptosporidium is a bacterium that originates in human or animal fecal matter. The disease is extremely dangerous to humans, especially those with decreased immune systems. During the outbreak, approximately 400,000 residents became ill, while 104 died from the waterborne disease. It is uncertain where the blame lies for this outbreak, though many potential sources have been identified. Among these are an illegal discharge from a stockyard less than 2 miles upstream from the city's water supply, inadequate quality controls in the city's water treatment plant, and the inadequacy of water quality regulations. This latter criticism is significant in that it represents a common problem among federal regulations: The regulations tend to be misdirected toward issues that don't deserve the high degree of attention given to them. In the case of Milwaukee, much more effort was spent on the elimination of lead. Because lead was a listed contaminant, while Cryptosporidiosis was not, it is not difficult to guess which was more likely to slip through quality control.

Even for those substances for which U.S. drinking water quality standards have been established, the determination of acceptable exposure levels can be as much an art as a science. Problems of risk analysis and scientific uncertainty make establishing safe exposure levels to chemicals problematic. The effectiveness of any drinking water standard, however, depends on the strength and effectiveness of water pollution laws and the feasibility to purify water to meet standards for consumption.

WATER LAW AND REGULATION

Although active federal involvement in water pollution control can be traced as far back as the late 1960s and early 1970s, Congress addressed the issue of water pollution control much earlier. In 1886 Congress passed the first bill forbidding the discharge of anything that would impede navigation in New York harbor. Then, in 1889 Congress passed the Rivers and Harbor Act prohibiting such discharges into all navigable waters. In 1899 the Federal Refuse Act prohibited the discharge of "waste matter of any kind or description whatever" into a body of water without a permit from the Army Corp of Engineers.[25] From 1899 until passage of the Clean Water Act in 1972, 415 permits were issued by the Army Corp of Engineers under the Federal Refuse Act. Half of these permits expired and were never renewed; in 22 states *no* permits were ever issued.[26]

A variety of federal water pollution control acts were passed prior to the 1970s. Major federal laws impacting water pollution were passed in 1912, 1924, 1948, 1956, 1961, and 1966. Although all these laws increased the federal role in water pollution control somewhat, they left the design and implementation of water pollution control programs to state and local governments.[27]

The fragmentation and decentralization that characterizes environmental policy generally is quite pronounced in water policy. Although the federal role in water pollution control has expanded significantly, states and localities still have primary responsibility for implementation of water pollution policy. At least 27 federal agencies are involved in some capacity in water policy. There are over 59,000 water supply utilities as well as thousands of state and local governments and water districts, improvement districts, and other special districts involved in some capacity in water quality and supply delivery.[28]

The three major laws regulating water pollution in the United States are the Resource Conservation and Recovery Act (RCRA), the Clean Water Act (CWA), and the Safe Drinking Water Act (SDWA). The RCRA, although important in water pollution control, is dealt with in more detail in Chapter 8 on hazardous waste, the main concern of that act.

Clean Water Act

Under the Clean Water Act, any discharge of a pollutant from a point source is only allowed pursuant to a permit issued by the EPA or by a state agency after EPA approval of a state plan.[29] The CWA defines "point source" to mean

> [A]ny discernable, confined and discreet conveyance, including but not limited to any pipe, ditch, channel, tunnel, conduit, well, discrete fissure, container, rolling stock, concentrated animal feeding operation, or vessel or floating craft from which pollutants are or may be discharged.[30]

Permits to pollute are issued under the Clean Water Act's National Pollution Discharge Elimination System (NPDES). Although more than 66,000 permits have been issued, the system has not lived up to its early promise. Budget cuts in the EPA, as well as in state environmental agencies, have forced officials to rely on industry for information necessary in establishing allowable discharges under the permit system. In addition, poor staffing has resulted in haphazard enforcement— pollution control agencies being forced to take action against the most visible permit violators while many other violators go undetected—and has led, particularly since the early 1980s, to the negotiated settlement with polluters that continue to violate their NPDES permits.

The Bethlehem Steel Sparrow's Point Plant on Chesapeake Bay provides an illustration of some of the problems with enforcement of the CWA. Between 1978 and 1983 Bethlehem Steel violated federal and state wastewater laws more than 700 times by pumping more pollutants into the Chesapeake Bay than its discharge permit allowed.[31] It is estimated that total discharges in excess of permit limits between 1979 and 1983 exceeded permit limitations in the amount of 4,500 tons. Daily discharges contained 11,860 pounds of oil and grease; 51,900 pounds of unspecified solids; 1,230 pounds of iron; and 990 pounds of zinc as well as other compounds.[32] Bethlehem Steel was able to circumvent the intent of the CWA by negotiating for implementation delays and using the courts to delay compliance. Furthermore, the numerous government agencies involved in the process added to the delay and confusion in efforts to seek compliance.

According to the National Resources Defense Council, "Bethlehem's flagrant violation of the law is not an isolated case." Violations are widespread and enforcement has been lax nationwide.[33] The U.S. General Accounting Office (GAO) issued a report in 1983 that substantially agreed with the National Resources Defense Council's position.[34] Since the GAO's study, EPA enforcement and federal laws did not change significantly through the 1980s and 1990s; hence it is reasonable to conclude the rate of compliance by industry with their NPDES permits has not accelerated much either.

The EPA has made some regulatory changes to NPDES recently, though. First, new large dischargers must obtain an offset of up to 1.5 times their proposed discharge before they can release *any* pollutants into impaired waters. Further, EPA now has the authority to require certain silviculture and animal feed and aquatic animal production facilities to obtain NPDES permits. The EPA can also choose not to renew some state permits to pollute into impaired waters where the permit conditions fail to meet federal standards. EPA estimates these NPDES regulations will cost industry $17.2 million to $65.2 million annually through 2015. Most of this will come from construction operations having to obtain offsets for their storm water discharges.[35]

The Clean Water Act (CWA), which on the surface provides mechanisms necessary to protect the nation's water, has not done so due to difficulty in enforcement. The NRDC reports, "[T]he reason is that the law's case by case application and its reliance on self-monitoring make it highly flexible, especially in the absence of aggressive enforcement.... [A]t this point, the punch has been so thoroughly baked out of the Clean Water Act's Enforcement Program that goals the legislature once considered basic had been made to appear unattainable."[36]

Industry is not the only source, or even the major source, of water pollution in the United States today. The CWA required municipal wastewater treatment plants to provide secondary treatment by 1977 with extensions to 1983. Through its construction grant program, over $45 billion has been distributed to municipalities for upgrading wastewater treatment plants. Initially, the federal government paid 75 percent of the cost of building these plants. In 1981 this was reduced to 55 percent, and in 1987 the program was converted from a grant to a loan program. As of 1991 the full cost of sewage treatment construction is paid by local governments. While the federal government was generous by initially providing 75 percent of building costs for the CWA construction grant program, no money was provided for operation and maintenance. This led to the result, in the words of Helen Ingram and Dean Mann, that "[C]ities have built Cadillac projects without the funds or technically qualified operators to maintain them, and some plants operate substantially below design capacity."[37]

In 1989 the EPA estimated that over two-thirds of the nations 15,600 wastewater treatment plants have "documented water quality or public health problems."[38] By 2003 the situation remains substantially the same. The bill for cleaning up the nation's waters will be enormous. According to the estimates by the Conservation Foundation, from 1972 until the mid-1980s government, business, and industry spent over $300 billion on water pollution control.[39] The future cost of water pollution abatement from 1997 until 2017 is estimated to be at least $139 billion.[40]

The EPA has estimated the cost of bringing municipal wastewater treatment plants up to secondary treatment levels would be at least $83.5 billion.[41] Many municipalities, particularly large urban areas, have suffered from eroding tax bases as people and industry move to the suburbs leaving behind a deteriorating infrastructure and high social service costs. These municipalities, and they include parts of nearly every major metropolitan area in the United States, will be hard-pressed to find the funds necessary for improved municipal wastewater treatment, though the Drinking Water State Revolving Fund (DWSRF, discussed in the following "Safe Drinking Water" section) will help.

Nonpoint sources of pollution are, for the most part, regulated by the states. Originally the CWA did not specifically address municipal runoff and storm water problems—two major sources of nonpoint water pollution. Using the definition of point source in the CWA, the EPA found that "these definitions combine to drag storm water runoff into the permit program. There are pollutants and storm water. Storm water systems, curbs, and parking lot burms all qualify as point sources.[42] The CWA amendments of 1987 limited this interpretation somewhat by not requiring permits for discharges composed entirely of storm water unless (1) a permit had already been issued; (2) a discharge was associated with an industrial activity; or (3) if the discharge was from a municipal storm sewer system serving a population of over 100,000.[43] If these provisions are vigorously enforced, a proposition that we explore in greater detail in the next section, the cost for local governments will run into the billions and billions of dollars.

The Reagan administration was hostile toward federal water pollution control regulations. Reagan vetoed the reauthorization of the Clean Water Act in 1986, arguing that water pollution regulations damaged the economy and gave too much control to the federal government. Reagan's veto was overridden by Congress early the next year. Contrary to the Reagan administration's position, many in the most polluting industries have supported the CWA. For example, in response to President Reagan's veto, a number of oil industry officials expressed disappointment. One official was quoted as saying, "[F]rom the standpoint of the programmatic part of the bill, it was a reasonable compromise among all the forces at play. It's the best we could have expected."[44]

The history of the Clean Water Act in the 1990s has been marked by a series of failed attempts at reauthorization. The Senate unsuccessfully tackled the issue in 1992 and 1994. These two attempts included components intended to address watershed protection and refinements to the NPDES system, among others. It was not until 1995, however, that Congress made a valiant effort toward amending the Clean Water Act.

A product of the Republican-controlled Congress, H. R. 961 was known to environmentalists as the "dirty water bill," or the "polluters' bill of rights." Included within the bill were provisions to transfer more funds to the states in order to help defer the cost of federal regulatory mandates, the inclusion of risk assessment and benefit-cost analysis within regulatory decision making, and the institution of a grant program for smaller communities to use in upgrading their pollution control infrastructure. Among the most controversial elements of the bill was the restructuring of wetland classification procedures, and an increase in the states' flexibility in dealing with polluters. Environmentalists claimed that the bill would favor economic development over water pollution prevention.

Unlike with the original 1972 CWA legislation, efforts during the 1990s to amend the act were extremely partisan in nature. The potential negative environmental impacts that the proposed amendments might have caused moved President Clinton to threaten to veto the bill if it made it to his desk. It never did, however, stalling in the Senate. In neither the 105th nor the 106th Congress were serious attempts made at reauthorizing the Clean Water Act. As of this writing, we are still without a reauthorization of the Clean Water Act.

The impact of the Clean Water Act over the past 30 years has been substantial. Since 1970, CWA regulations have reduced the discharge of untreated sewage into the nation's waterways by 90 percent. Within the last decade, the amount of wetlands lost annually has fallen by 200,000 acres, when compared to the annual loss from the mid-1970s to the mid-1980s. Still, 100,000 acres are lost every year to agriculture, road construction, and residential development.[45] It is estimated that the passage of the CWA in 1972 has prevented 1 billion pounds of toxic pollutants from being discharged into the nation's surface waters.[46] Still, there is much yet to accomplish.

Safe Drinking Water Act

The Safe Drinking Water Act (SDWA) regulates drinking water produced by public water supply systems. Initially, the 1974 act required the monitoring of and regulation of 22 different water contaminants. SDWA amendments in 1996 added 83 additional contaminants to those covered by the act as of 1991 and required public water systems to conduct a monitoring program for a variety of unregulated contaminants. An additional 25 contaminants are required to be added every three years. EPA regulations developed pursuant to the SDWA further specified criteria under which public water systems relying on surface water must install filtration equipment. As late as the 1980s, 20 of the nation's largest cities, including New York and Seattle, utilized some surface water supply systems that were unfiltered.[47] In response to this potentially dangerous situation, the EPA passed the Surface Water Treatment Rule (SWTR) that went into effect in 1993. It requires all inadequately protected surface water sources to be filtered and disinfected. By the time the rule became enforceable, 12 million Americans were using water from 1,000 community water systems not in compliance with SWTR. By 1995 these figures were down to 9.9 million people and 400 systems. At this rate, the EPA projects that these numbers will reach zero by 2005.[48]

Enforcement under the SDWA, as in the CWA, is a major problem. Recently, an important enforcement component of the SDWA and the Clean Water Act has been enacted which provides that citizens may bring suit to force compliance. Citizen suits allow any interested party to sue the polluter or even the EPA for failure to enforce the CWA. Although nearly every environmental statute passed or amended during the 1970s contains citizen suit provisions, most citizen suit activity has been focused on forcing compliance on polluters under the Clean Water Act.[49] In an effort to supplement enforcement efforts of the EPA, the CWA authorizes citizens to bring the action against persons or companies who are ". . . alleged to be in violation . . ." of their discharge permits.[50] Citizen suits are important for the opportunity they allow citizens or interest groups to influence the implementation of environmental policy.

After a citizen suit is filed, the EPA has the option to enforce the CWA, or whatever other environmental regulation is in question, thereby ending the issue. Should the EPA not act, citizens have several remedies available, including seeking injunctive relief, which means the polluter is ordered by the court to do a specific act, like shut down operations until it can comply with permit limitations and/or seek civil penalties in the form of monetary damages.

One advantage to permitting a citizen or citizen group to proceed is that the CWA provides for an award for reasonable attorney fees and expert witness fees.[51] In an article addressed to municipal wastewater managers, a former EPA official wrote, "[T]he Clean Water Act allows citizens suits. In recent years, there has been a large increase in citizen suit activity. They have been very successful and they have talked about changing their focus from industry to municipalities."[52] In essence, if municipalities do not comply with the CWA, then the EPA would be forced, through citizen suits, into seeking compliance from them.

In 1996, citizens were given another powerful tool with which to ensure their drinking water is safe from harmful contaminants. The Safe Drinking Water Amendments of 1996 require water suppliers to provide annual disclosure statements to their customers that identify the water sources drawn upon (surface, ground, etc.), a glossary of terms, and information that outlines contaminant levels. This latter requirement includes the maximum allowable contamination level, the local supplier's goals for contaminant reduction, and the actual level of contaminants present in the water supply. Critics of citizen suit provisions have argued that the "citizens" involved in these suits are usually environmental groups who, after courts have rewarded fees, benefit from stirring up litigation.

Besides the citizen disclosure provision, the SDWA 1996 amendments provide billions of dollars for water treatment infrastructure; regulations requiring that water quality personnel are properly trained and tested; new standards for a variety of pollutants, including radon, arsenic, and Crytosporidium; and strong economic incentives for states to ensure water suppliers within their borders are providing potable water. The 1996 amendments are generally viewed as a fine-tuning action intended to take into consideration variances that exist between large and small pollution abatement systems.

The federal government established a Drinking Water State Revolving Fund (DWSRF) to help meet community water health and infrastructure needs. That is, the federal government is helping smaller entities comply with its regulations. Congress authorized $9.6 billion for DWSRF for FY 1995–2003.[53] The first grants were distributed in 1997; Congress appropriated $1.275 billion and $1.255 billion of that was actually disbursed.[54] Through 2001, $4.42 billion have been appropriated, and the George W. Bush administration requested $823.2 million for FY 2002, though a billion is potentially available.

In addition, the 1996 SDWA amendments require the EPA to conduct a DWSRF needs survey that helps determine future funding. If the EPA's estimates are even somewhat accurate, these funding levels will be totally insufficient for future needs. In 2001 the EPA stated that $150.9 billion would be needed to spend on community water systems to meet federal standards over the next 20 years.[55] That's about $7.5 billion per year, or over nine times what the President is requesting for 2002.

It is important in understanding any of these acts to keep in mind the fragmented nature of water pollution control in the United States and the governmental overlap that exists in the implementation of water pollution policy. For example, water that comes in contact with hazardous waste, regulated under the RCRA, may find its way into a municipal wastewater treatment plant regulated by the CWA, which after treatment is discharged into a river and picked up by another municipality for drinking water, hence then subject to the requirements to the SDWA. As an EPA official responsible for monitoring water quality said, "[T]here's lots of overlaps ... different statutes have different deadlines. It's hard to coordinate our regulatory program."[56] In other instances the needed overlap is missing, such as the case of indoor radon gas, 1 percent to 5 percent of which is attributed to water in basements. The proposed drinking water standard for radon would only result in a 1 percent reduction in indoor air levels despite the extensive costs to achieve it. Meanwhile, no air pollution regulations address radon gas.[57]

Criticisms of Water Pollution Policy

Water pollution policy problems are both political and technical in nature. A criticism often leveled at water pollution policy, which is due to both political and technical concerns, is that we do not know the extent of the impact on humans of chemicals that find their way into our water supplies. Over 66,000 chemicals have been introduced in the environment since 1945, and only a few of these have been examined to determine their adverse health effects. As we have seen, the Safe Drinking Water Act only regulates 105 contaminants. Part of the problem, as former EPA official Arnold Kuzmack explained, is that, "[I]n many cases, there's not adequate toxicological data to determine the potential dangers of specific contaminants."[58] Even, however, when the potential dangers of the contaminant are known, they are not always regulated. For example, trichloroethylene (TCE) is a commonly used industrial solvent, which when ingested in humans can cause vomiting and abdominal pain in the short term, as well as liver damage and possibly cancer over a lifetime. TCE is measured as part of the Toxic Release Inventory (TRI), which determined that from 1987 to 1993, 100,000 pounds were released directly into America's waters, and almost twice that onto land. Drinking water standards prevent TCE concentrations from exceeding .005 mg per liter, though the EPA believes there is no safe level of exposure to TCE.[59] While TCE is regulated nationally by the Occupational Safety and Health Act, Clean Air Act, CWA, SDWA, TRI, and RCRA,[60] trichloroethylene was still detected in one-half of the wells tested in the San Fernando Valley; one-fourth of the wells in the San Gabriel Valley, with 10 percent exceeding state levels, and 1 percent targeted for Superfund cleanup; 19 Superfund-targeted sites in Santa Clara County's "silicon valley" from underground storage tanks; municipal wells in the city of Burbank, all of which were forced to close.[61]

The solution, on the individual level, would seem to be to drink only bottled water. However, even the safety of bottled or home-treated water has been called into question. Bottled water is regulated by the U.S. Food and Drug Administration, rather than the EPA, and is required to test for only 23 of the 30 chemicals for which municipal water supplies must check. Mineral water is not regulated by any regulatory agency. Individuals may use a number of techniques to treat their water at home, including active carbon filters, reverse-osmosis, and water softeners. It should be noted, however, that such treatment is expensive, and requires diligent attention to maintenance.[62]

A second criticism of water pollution policy concerns the role of state governments in pollution control, administration, and financing. When the Clean Water Act was debated in Congress in 1971, New York, California, as well as other states, and the Nixon administration, argued that the legislation vested too much power in the federal government.[63] Typically, state governments do not object to administering new programs, provided they are given the funds necessary for implementation with an appropriate amount of local discretion. In the case of water pollution policy, local discretion has always been limited, and, with changes in the construction grant program for municipal wastewater treatment plants, the so-called carrot of federal funding has disappeared as well (though DWSRF is a step in the right direction). In a report issued by the Council of State Governments on state water quality planning, the authors noted "in adopting what has proven to be an unrealistic timetable for the National Clean Water's Program, the Congress seriously overestimated both federal and state technical, institutional and environmental management capacity. However, at least in the view of the states, the most serious flaw in the national strategy was the dominant role given the federal establishment."[64]

In the area of groundwater protection, the states have always had, and continue to have, primary responsibility for water pollution control. The Safe Drinking Water Act of 1986 required states to identify "well head protection areas" or areas around groundwater sources that could lead to the contamination of groundwater. States are required first to identify well head protection areas and then propose a program to keep contamination of surface areas around groundwater from polluting waters that are used for drinking purposes. As one commentator noted, "[The] states will have enormous discretion in determining what is an adequate program [under the statute]."[65] The EPA also has the authority to designate an area as a "sole-source aquifer" in areas where the population is dependent on one aquifer for its drinking water. After being so designated, the EPA may act to refuse funding for any federal program that threatens water quality, such as a dam or a highway, over or near the aquifer. This is authority the EPA has rarely exercised.

Recently, citizen groups have begun reorganizing their efforts to push the EPA into actively forcing states to be mindful of water quality within their boarders. Rather than focusing on point pollution sources, however, activists have started to concentrate on watershed quality as a means to compel the EPA and the states to address problems of non-point pollution. The original CWA legislation instructs the states to measure local water quality broadly in order to gauge the success of discharge permitting, as well as to impose across-the-board limits on all pollution until reduction goals are met. Former EPA administrator Carol Browner has commented that this approach "is the cornerstone of how you deal with pollution watershed by watershed."[66] It remains to be seen what role, if any, the George W. Bush administration will take in terms of a heightened federal role in the management of non-point urban water pollution and overall watershed management. Nonetheless, for the foreseeable future watershed management in general and nonpoint pollution in particular promise to be important themes in water pollution policy.

The Paradox in Water Pollution Policy

In the areas where the primary water problem is one of sufficient quantities of water, a water policy paradox becomes apparent where, in most instances, simple conservation measures would assure adequate supplies. Yet water conservation is not the norm. The managers of most water distribution systems, in the United States as well as elsewhere in the world, do not charge for water itself but rather charge for storing, transporting, and treating the water.[67] As a result, water is often quite inexpensive to the consumer. The simplest conservation method both for domestic and agricultural use is to raise costs. Researchers in Israel, Canada, Great Britain, and the United States have found that domestic water use drops by 3 percent to 7 percent when prices increase 10 percent.[68] Furthermore, the true cost of developing water is often hidden and not reflected in the cost of water to consumers. In the United States municipalities often subsidize their water delivery systems through general taxes. Farmers, notably in the western United States, have water that is heavily subsidized by the federal government. For example, the U.S. Bureau of Reclamation supplies water to Arizona farmers for as little as $8 an "acre foot" (about 325,000 gallons), but municipalities developing water for distribution to residents in Arizona often find their cost to be in excess of $300 per acre foot. Agricultural subsidies of large western water projects are possible in part because the cost of developing the projects are spread across the nation as a whole. For example, a study of the Central Arizona Project (CAP) by the Congressional Research Service found that the cost of the project would be about twice any anticipated benefits to the nation.[69] In another case, the Garrison Diversion Project in North Dakota, one analyst found that with a projected cost of more than $1 billion, "[I]ts most expensive feature is $674 million for irrigation of about 400 farms totaling 131,000 acres. That works out to an investment of about $1.7 million per farm compared with average annual net benefits per farm of only $23,597."[70] Due to federal budget constraints, the era of large federal water projects has come to an end. Existing contracts, however, ensure the federal subsidy for agricultural water in the West well into the future. However, in conjunction with the general trend of shifting water allocation away from agriculture toward urban areas, many recommend that new irrigation projects be charged the "fair market value" for the water they use.

The situation in the United States is not unique. As one author concluded after an evaluation of global water supply and distribution, "Agencies often set water prices according to political expediency rather than in the cost of supplying it."[71]

Although manipulating cost is the easiest means of promoting conservation, few communities, as we noted, charge the full or true cost of water consumed. Some communities do not even meter water. Not metering water can lead to very wasteful water usage. A study in Boulder, Colorado, found that metering water caused water use for watering lawns to reduce by about half.[72]

The technology for increased water conservation is currently available. Flow reduction devices in showers, water-saving faucets, and appliances as well as other means are available and are currently in use in water-short areas. Toilets that typically use 5 gallons with every flush can be built to only use 1.6 gallons or less.[73]

Agricultural conservation of water is also technologically feasible, though expensive. Drip irrigation, where water flows through a pipe directly to a plant's roots, can deliver over 90 percent of the water used directly to the plant. Center-pivot irrigation systems, which are large sprinkler systems that rotate in a circle, can deliver water with a 70 percent efficiency rate, that is, with 70 percent of the water being used by the plant. Flood irrigation, which is used widely throughout the less developed world as well as throughout the United States, even in the arid West, can waste an average of 70 percent of the water.[74]

The paradox, then, in water policy in terms of water scarcity is why conservation measures are not being practiced if they logically would work. Part of the answer has to do with artificially low pricing, which, for political reasons, is not likely to change in the near future. For example, when serious shortage situations are reached in the future, prices will increase for municipal users but not, ironically, for many agricultural users who are the largest users of water (because of federal contracts and subsidies to agriculture).

What is often referred to as a water supply problem is often, in fact, a water distribution problem. Existing contracts, accepted uses, and support for farming and the political clout farmers enjoy in the policy-making process often protect existing uses and limit possible incentives for conservation.

Groundwater use also provides a good example of the environmental policy paradox and the politics that creates the paradox. Agriculture that relies on groundwater, notably in the West, has often pumped the water at rates that exceed natural recharge. This practice is known as groundwater mining and assures the resource will be depleted. Groundwater mining has already led to an end of irrigated agriculture in large parts of northern Texas and Oklahoma. If current practices continue, the loss of irrigated agriculture due to groundwater mining could result in serious disruptions in the Great Plains states. For example, it is estimated that Colorado could lose 40 percent of its wheat production by 2010.

In the United States, farmers and agricultural interests are still a potent political influence. Though government payments to farmers have fallen from a previous high of $16.7 billion in 1987 to $7.2 billion in 1996, they are on the rise again. Total payments in 2000 were well over $20 billion,[75] as various trade policies and global markets caused many commodity prices to plummet since 1998. Much of the increases of late have been emergency bailouts, such as the Agricultural Supplemental Bill signed the into law on August 13, 2001 by President Bush, giving farmers $5.5 billion in addition to funds from the 2001 Farm Bill. Although farmers enjoy an image of rugged individualism, working the land in relatively small family-owned farms, the reality has increasingly been one of agribusiness characterized by huge farm operations. The number of farms fell from 6.1 million in 1940 to just over 2 million in 1997, and at the same time the average size increased from 175 acres to 469 acres per farm.[76] Farmers are aided politically by other beneficiaries of the agricultural economy including pesticide and herbicide manufacturers, food packagers, exporters, and others. This combination of forces has allowed farmers to set their political agenda in some states and in the federal government, and assured a number of advantageous policies. These include liberal federal water rates, advantageous water rights laws, liberal regulation of pesticide use, and the ability to avoid policies that would force conservation measures designed to limit soil erosion, desertification, and the mining of groundwater basins. In each of these areas the problem is often that there is no policy in place.

Agricultural water subsidies made dubious economic sense. For example, in California 1,000 acre-feet of water might be used to support eight farm jobs, 3,300 urban industry jobs, or 17,000 high-tech jobs.[77]

A discussion of water scarcity should also touch on questionable uses of water in urban areas. Desert cities such as Phoenix and Las Vegas maintain beautifully landscaped water-intensive golf courses and housing developments. In Las Vegas housing developments with names like Mirage, Desert Shores, and The Lakes defy the reality of a desert environment. And water is not in abundance in Las Vegas. As Bruce Babbitt, former Secretary of the Interior, noted,

> Las Vegas is trying to take water at gunpoint from the rest of Nevada. The city's plan
> to tap water under the great underlying aquifer in central Nevada endangers vital water

connections all over the region, perhaps even disrupting springs in Death Valley. It is the most environmentally destructive project in the history of the West.[78]

In contrast, in water quality policy a major problem is that we have good regulations that are poorly enforced. All levels of government in the United States lack the resources necessary to monitor and test water for impurities or to build the wastewater treatment plants that are necessary. Even when quality problems are obvious to all concerned, the decentralization in water management and fragmentation of water quality regulations makes solutions—even obvious solutions—difficult to come by.

For example, in 1981 TCE, or trichloroethylene, was discovered in wells serving the city of Tucson, Arizona, which prompted local remedial action. Recall that the EPA believes there is no safe level of exposure to TCE. Those involved in the Tucson situation included Hughes Aircraft Corporation, three federal agencies, the city water department, and two state agencies. Two and a half years after the discovery of the contamination, Tucson, frustrated by conflicts over determining who was responsible for well monitoring, decided to put in its own monitoring wells. Also there was some question as to which state department would administer a feasibility study, paid for with EPA funds, of the Tucson situation. When it was decided the Arizona Department of Water Resources would be responsible for the project, as Bruce Johnson, the chief hydrologist for Tucson Water states, "Then the Department of Water Resources found out that they didn't have the legal authority to contract with the EPA. The city funded the initial startup of the feasibility study while they went back to the state legislature to get the enabling act language amended for the Department of Water Resources, allowing them to contract with the EPA."[79]

Risk management involves the managing of a pollutant to be sure it stays below levels determined during risk assessment. Assessment then management. But, like most things, nothing is as simple as it sounds—risk assessment and management involve trade offs (and as discussed in Chapter 3 trade-offs involve politics). Let us illustrate the problem the following way. Imagine we know that exposure to a particular substance, we'll call it pollutant x, is harmful to humans but we do not have strong data on exactly what level of x can cause what harms (a common situation in risk assessment). We do, however, have a fairly good idea how much it will cost to remove x from public drinking water supplies. (As with many pollutants the cost of removing a unit of x increases with the removal of each additional unit of x removed. Hence the cost of reducing the first 10 percent of x is a small fraction of the cost of removing the last 10 percent of pollutant x.)

Given what we know about x pollutant we might pick one of three possible risk management scenarios. In scenario "A" the annual cost of reducing x is $1 per household, the annual cost of reducing x in scenario "B" is $100 per household and in scenario "C" the cost is $1000 per household. Under scenario "A" we think the risk of death or serious harm to a human being is one in 10,000 exposures. Under scenario "B" we think the risk of death or serious harm is one in 100,000 and under scenario "C" the risk is one in one million. Which scenario would you choose? Table 6–1 illustrates the basic components of our decision problem.

Keep in mind the uncertainty of our knowledge about the level of exposure to x that humans can accept (in other words the estimations of the number of deaths

TABLE 6–1   Risk Management Scenarios for Reducing Pollutant X

Scenario	Annual cost per household	Risk of harm per exposure
A	$1	1 in 10,000
B	$100	1 in 100,000
C	$1,000	1 in 1,000,000

could be higher or lower in each scenario) and the fact that an expenditure for any-thing involves trade-offs—the $1,000 each year a family would spend under sce-nario "C" is $1,000 that won't be used for other things, like education or the cost or removing pollutant y or z.

Water management requires the weighing of certain levels of risk with the costs associated with cleaning the water source. As one author noted, "Risk man-agement assumes that, after a certain level of effort to clean up the water, additional effort would not be worth the cost in jobs and profit."[80]

As we noted previously, trace amounts of many chemicals, whose effects on the human body we do not know, have been found in water supplies. Given the costs associated with removing minute levels of pollutants from drinking water, many water professionals would like the public to be more accepting of pollutants in drinking water. As Ted Smith of the Silicone Valley Toxics Coalition put it, "[T]here's a very serious effort to get people to accept contaminants in drinking water the way people have come to accept contaminants in air."[81] In 1995, under the leadership of then House Speaker Newt Gingrich, the Congress passed a law requir-ing the use of risk assessment and benefit-cost analysis in policy making and rule making.

On an individual level, water quantity problems can be addressed by decreas-ing consumption and use of water. A plastic bottle in your toilet tank, not bricks that can dissolve and cause other problems, will save between 3,000 and 5,000 gallons of water a year. Flow restrictors on showers and faucets can save an additional 7,800 gallons. Further, it takes about 2,500 gallons of water to produce a pound of meat; comparatively, 25 gallons are needed for a pound of wheat. It takes as much water to feed a meat-eater for a month as it does a vegetarian for a year.[82] With re-spect to quality problems, we present ways to test and treat waters you suspect of being contaminated by hazardous waste in the hazardous waste section of Chap-ter 8. For example, properly disposing of household wastes such as motor oil, clean-ers, and solvents will help protect your community's water supply. Many service stations accept waste oil. For the location of disposal facilities for other toxic waste, contact your city or county department of public health or sanitation.

With respect to large polluters of water, as we have seen, there are citizen suit provisions in the Clean Water Act. You may not want to go to the trouble and ex-pense of going to court to enforce a polluter to cease a discharge, but if you en-counter what appears to be a source of serious water pollution, such as a discharge into a river that is obviously impure, contact your state or local environmental pro-tection agency. If they will not or cannot do anything, contact one of the major en-vironmental protection interest groups such as the Natural Resources Defense Council or the Sierra Club Legal Defense Fund.

SUMMARY

In this chapter we discussed types of pollution by source and location. In addition we examined the health impacts of water pollution, the laws and regulations governing water pollution policy, notably the Clean Water Act and the Safe Drinking Water Act. The environmental policy paradox in water policy is, as we have seen, twofold. The paradox in water policy in terms of water scarcity is why conservation measures, the most efficient way of increasing supply, are not being practiced. A variety of political factors, including cheap water due to government subsidies, artificially low pricing and incentives policymakers have to build things, all create, paradoxically, an environment in which conservation of water is often not aggressively pursued.

In the next chapter we discuss the history of energy use and development and examine the pollution problems associated with different sources of energy.

NOTES

1. Peter Rogers, "Water: Not as Cheap as You'd Think," *Technology Review*, 89 (8) (Nov.-Dec., 1986), p. 32; and G. Tyler Miller, Jr., *Living in the Environment* (8th ed.) (Belmont, CA: Wadsworth, 1994), p. 336.
2. Miller, *Living in the Environment*, 8th ed., p. 339.
3. The Center for a New American Dream Website. *http://www.newdream.org/monthly/aug00.html*.
4. G. Tyler Miller, *Living in the Environment* (5th ed.) (Belmont, CA: Wadsworth, 1988), pp. 213, 228.
5. Miller, *Living in the Environment* (8th ed.), p. 342.
6. Congressional Digest, "The Clean Water Act: Status of Current Programs," (December 1995), p. 291.
7. Ibid, p. 292
8. U.S. Environmental Protection Agency. 1998 National Water Quality Report. EPA-841-F-00-006.
9. Conservation Foundation, *State of the Environment: A View Towards the 90s* (Washington, DC: Conservation Foundation, 1987), p. xxv.
10. Miller, *Living in the Environment* (5th ed.), p. 478.
11. Ibid., p. 479.
12. Conservation Foundation, *State of the Environment*, p. 101.
13. Tom Arrandale, "The Pollution That Washes Off the Land," *Governing*, 5(11) (August 1992), p. 69.
14. News Release from Congressman Boehlert, Chair of the Subcommittee on Water Resources and Environment. March 10, 1999. "GAO Reports on Federal Role in Nonpoint Source Water Pollution." Available at *http://www.house.gov/boehlert/nonpoint.htm*.
15. Conservation Foundation, *State of the Environment*, p. 105.
16. Sue McClurg, "Drinking Water Quality, Western Water." Published by the Water Education Foundation, Sacramento, California (July/August 1992), p. 10.
17. GAO Report to Congress. June 2001. "Water Quality: Urban Runoff Programs," GAO-01-679.
18. Robert Griffin, Jr., "Introducing NPS Water Pollution: We Can't Write Permits on Parking Lots," *EPA Journal*, 17(5) (November/December 1991), p. 7.
19. See, generally, Zachary A. Smith, *Groundwater in the West* (New York: Academic Press, 1989).
20. Miller, *Living in the Environment* (8th ed.), p. 609.
21. Miller, *Living in the Environment* (5th ed.), p. 475.
22. Arizona, Department of Health Services, *Arizona Surface Impoundment Assessment—Draft* (December 1979), pp. I-1 and ii-2.
23. Substances known to cause cancer in humans (based primarily on tests with lab animals), which are commonly found in drinking water (and the effects on people in parentheses), include arsenic (cancer; liver, kidney, blood, and nervous system damage); cadmium (kidney damage, anemia, pulmonary problems, high blood pressure, possible fetal damage, and cancer); chromium (suspected

cancer from some forms such as chromate); lead (headaches, anemia, nerve disorders, birth defects, and cancer; mental retardation, learning disability, and partial hearing loss in children); mercury (nervous system and kidney damage; biologically amplified in food webs); nitrates (respiratory distress and possible death in infants, possible formation of carcinogenic nitrosoamines); Aldicarb (Temik) (high toxicity to nervous system); benzene (chromosomal damage, anemia, blood disorders, and leukemia); carbon tetrachloride (cancer, liver, kidney, lung, and central nervous system damage); chloroform (liver and kidney damage and suspected cancer); Dioxin (skin disorders, cancer, and genetic mutations); ethylene dibromide (EDB) (cancer and male sterility); polychlorinated biphenyls (PCBs) (liver, kidney, and pulmonary damage); trichloroethylene (TCE) (in high concentrations, liver and kidney damage, central nervous system depression, skin problems, and suspected cancer and mutations); vinyl chloride (liver, kidney, and lung damage, pulmonary, cardiovascular, and gastrointestinal problems, cancer and suspected mutations). Adapted from Miller, *Living in the Environment* (5th ed.), p. 459.

24. Peter Steinhart, "Trusting Water," *Audubon*, 88 (November 1986), p. 11.
25. "Water Pollution," *New Republic*, 168 (March 27, 1971), p. 8.
26. Ibid. See also Harvey Lieber, "Water Pollution," *Current History* (July 1970), pp. 26–28.
27. Ibid.
28. Rogers, "Water," p. 33.
29. 33 U.S.C. Section 1342 (a) (b).
30. 33 U.S.C. Section 1362 (14).
31. This case study has been taken primarily from Todd Oppenheiner, "Humpty Dumpty," *The Amicus Journal* (Winter 1988), p. 14.
32. Ibid., p. 16.
33. Ibid.
34. Reported in ibid.
35. Testimony presented to House Committee on Agriculture. June 28, 2000. Clean Water Act: Proposed revisions to EPA regulations to clean up polluted water. GAO/T-RCED-00.
36. Ibid., p. 17.
37. Helen M. Ingram and Dean E. Mann, "Preserving the Clean Water Act: The Appearance of Environmental Victory," in Norman J. Vig and Michael E. Kraft (eds.), *Environmental Policy in the 1980s: Reagan's New Agenda* (Washington, DC: Congressional Quarterly Press, 1984), p. 256.
38. Douglas Jehl, "Clean Water Cost Put at $83.5 Billion," *The Los Angeles Times*, February 15,1989, Pt. 1, p. 4.
39. As reported in Lyse Helsing, "Water Treatment: Solving the Second Generation of Environmental Problems," *Chemical Week*, 142 (May 18, 1988), p. 30.
40. Andrew G. Wright, "Still Room to Improve," *ENR* (October 1997), p. 30
41. Jehl, "Clean Water," p. 4.
42. Bill Diamond, "How EPA Plans to Move Ahead on Storm Water," *Nation's Cities Weekly*, 9 (December 15, 1986), p. 12.
43. 33 U.S.C. Section 1342 (p) (1) (2).
44. "Oil Officials Fear Stricter Water Act Provisions from New Congress," *Oilgram News*, 64 (218) (November 10, 1986), p. 2.
45. U.S. Environmental Protection Agency. June 2000. National Water Quality Report to Congress: 1998. EPA-841-F-00-006.
46. "Happy 25th birthday, Clean Water Act—and many more," *Amicus Journal* (Fall 1997), p. 15.
47. G. Wade Miller, John Cromwell, III, and Frank Dombrowski, "Drinking Water's New Guidelines," *The American City and County*, 101 (November 1986), p. 41.
48. U.S. Environmental Protection Agency. June 1996. Index of Watershed Indicators (IWI): Population Served By Unfiltered Surface Water Systems at Risk from Microbiological Contamination. Available at *http://www.epa.gov/iwi/help/indic/fs2.html*.
49. Citizen suit provisions are found in the Federal Water Pollution Control Act, Section 505, 33 U.S.C. Section 1365; Clean Air Act Section 304, 42 U.S.C. Section 7604; Marine Protection, Research, and Sanctuaries Act Section 105(g), 33 U.S.C. Section 1415(g); Noise Control Act Section 12, 42 U.S.C. Section 4911; Endangered Species Act Section 11(g), 16 U.S.C. Section 1540(g); Deepwater Port Act Section 16, 33 U.S.C. Section 1515; Resource Conservation and Recovery Act Section 7002, 42 U.S.C. Section 6972; Toxic Substances Control Act Section 20, 15 U.S.C. Section 2619; Safe Drinking Water Act Section 1449, 42 U.S.C. Section 300j-8; Surface Mining Control and Reclamation Act of 1977 Section 520, 30 U.S.C. Section 1270; and Outer Continental Shelf Lands Act Section 23, 43 U.S.C. Section 1349(a).

50. 33 U.S.C. Section 1365 (a).
51. 33 U.S.C. Section 1365 (d).
52. Diamond, "How the EPA Plans," p. 12.
53. U.S. Environmental Protection Agency. SDWA 1996 Amendments Website. *http://www.epa. gov/safewater/sdwa/summ.html#4.*
54. U.S. Environmental Protection Agency. 1999: 25th Anniversary of SDWA. Drinking water costs and federal funding. EPA 810-F-99-014. *http://www.epa.gov/safewater/faq/costs_funding.pdf.*
55. Congressional Research Service Report, redistributed by the NLE (National Library for the Environment). Safe Drinking Water Act: State Revolving Fund Program. 97–677. Available at *http://www.cnie.org/nle/crsreports/water/h2o-25.pdf.*
56. Laurie A. Rich and Reginald Rhein, "How Water Is Regulated," *Chemical Week*, (February 12, 1986), p. 45.
57. Sue McClurg, "Drinking Water Quality," pp. 5–6.
58. Barbara Quinn, "The Cost of Pure Water," *American City and County*, 101 (June 1986), p. 54.
59. U. S. Environmental Protection Agency. Drinking Water and Health pages. National Primary Drinking Water Regulations. Technical Factsheet on: Trichloroethylene. Available at *http://www. epa.gov/OGWDW/dwh/t-voc/trichlor.html.*
60. Environmental Defense Website. 2001. Scorecard: About the Chemicals: Regulatory Coverage: Trichloroethylene. Available at *http://www.scorecard.org/chemical-profiles/regulation.tcl? edf_substance_id=79%2d01%2d6.*
61. Sue McClurg, "Drinking Water Quality," pp. 10–11.
62. G. Tyler Miller, *Living in the Environment* (8th ed.), p. 616.
63. "Pressure Against a Pollution Bill," *Business Week*, 2203 (November 20, 1971), p. 70.
64. Council of State Governments, *State Water Quality Planning Issues* (Lexington, KY: Council of State Governments, 1982), p. 6.
65. John M. Winton et al., "Water Treatment: The State's Zero in on Groundwater Regulation," *Chemical Week*, 140 (February 11,1987), p. 34.
66. John H. Cushman, Jr., "Courts Expanding Effort to Battle Water Pollution," *New York Times* (March 1, 1998), p. 1(N) col. 6.
67. Rogers, "Water," p. 33.
68. Ibid., p. 469.
69. Cited in William Sander, "Shooting the Political Rapids of Western Water," *Wall Street Journal*, April 13,1987, p. 26.
70. Ibid.
71. Rogers, "Water," p. 33.
72. Ibid., p. 40.
73. William S. Bergstrom, "Water, Profits Won't Go Down Drain of This Toilet," *The Arizona Republic*, April 30,1989, p. E-2.
74. Rogers, "Water," p. 34–35.
75. U.S. Department of Agriculture. Economic Research Service. "Agricultural Outlook: June/July 2001." Available at *http://www.ers.usda.gov/publications/agoutlook/june2001/AO282h.pdf.*
76. U.S. Department of Agriculture, *Agricultural Statistics—1997* (Washington, DC: GPO, 1997), p. 1x-2.
77. *Hydata* (July 1992), p. 5. Taken from an article by Carl Boronkay, general manager of the Metropolitan Water District of Southern California in *Focus* 2 (1992).
78. Frank Graham, Jr., "Gambling on Water, Las Vegas Raises the Stakes on Development in the West," *Audubon*, 94 (4), (July-August 1992), pp. 65–69.
79. Quoted in Fisher, "Rx. for Clean Water," p. 38.
80. Steinhart, "Trusting Water," p. 11.
81. Ibid.
82. Vegan World Website. "Can We Afford NOT to Change Our Diet?" Available at *http:// home.rochester.rr.com/veganworld/change.html.*

Energy

Energy makes life on earth possible. All energy, except nuclear and geothermal energy, is derived from the sun.[1] The fossil fuels the world has come to rely on were once ancient plants that depended on the sun's rays for photosynthesis. The food that plants produce is the fundamental energy source for all animals in the food chain. The sun's heat evaporates water, causing rain and snow, which result in rivers that can be tapped for hydroelectric power. Uneven heating of the earth's atmosphere by the sun causes winds, another useful form of renewable energy. And the sun can be harnessed directly to produce heat and electricity using modern solar technology.

Humankind's ability to harness different forms of energy has played a large part in homo sapiens becoming the dominant species on the planet. The exploitation of fossil fuels has provided the means to support a rapidly expanding population. These fuels have also caused extensive pollution, which, as we have seen, threatens the world with catastrophic climatic changes.

Our dependence on nonrenewable fossil fuels has put us in a precarious position. Eventually fossil fuels will run out. The quality of life we will enjoy in the future is directly related to how carefully we manage our finite fossil fuels today. Energy experts are in agreement that a transition from fossil fuel dependence to renewable sources of energy is inevitable. Agreement notwithstanding, we seem, paradoxically, to be doing little to prepare for this eventuality.

There are two important ways, illustrated by Amory Lovins, that one can think about energy: the "hard" path and the "soft" path. Hard energies include coal, oil, gas, and nuclear energies. These are what we primarily rely on now, though they are nonrenewable and environmentally destructive. The dominant hard energy industries have traditionally focused on producing as much energy as possible in any way possible, understanding that they would be subsidized, as all people and businesses rely on them, and that they could externalize their environmental costs.

The soft energy path reframes the energy problem. After all, we do not need energy per se; we just want the resulting end products, such as lighting, heating and cooling, and torque. The soft approach becomes one of "end use-least cost." Instead of relying on the old maxim of increasing sales to increase profits, soft energy companies can reduce sales that lead to input and capital reductions that can actually lead to greater profit margins. The government, too, can step in to subsidize soft energies from the efficient use of any energy source to promoting renewable and minimally or nonpolluting energies and technologies.[2]

Though public policy can and should play a pivotal role in energy, it is ultimately businesses that drive energy markets. They have the knowledge, expertise, creativity, and motivation (profit) to become energy efficient and renewable. Public policy can guide markets in the right direction to create a sustainable energy economy, or a "natural capitalism" that considers the value of ecosystem services.

Public policy steering business down the soft energy path may take numerous forms. For example, government could shift subsidies to only soft energy sources like wind, solar, and fuel cells. Government could also decouple regulated energy company profits from sales. This means that energy companies would be rewarded for helping customers save energy instead of the common situation of selling more yielding greater profits.

As it turns out, power companies can actually earn greater profits by encouraging their customers to save energy. (We focus here on electricity generation since it is the costliest source of energy, and power plants burn a third of the world's fuel.) This is because the cost to increase supply, building new power plants, is huge as well as risky. Demand-side management (end use-least cost) reduces costs and conserves energy, whereas the "hard" style of simply selling as many electrons as possible encourages waste.[3] More on the hard-soft discussion and specific problems and success stories regarding these approaches will be presented throughout this chapter.

In this chapter we discuss the history of energy use and development starting with fuelwood and coal. We also examine the pollution problems associated with different sources of energy. Finally, we look at the long-term implications of energy use and production and make suggestions for policy changes that will help ensure sustainable energy in the future.

This chapter has a somewhat unique place in the book. Energy per se is neither pollution nor, in its final form, a natural resource like the others discussed in this book. Yet the production of energy is, arguably, the primary cause of most of the planet's pollution (for example, deforestation for fuelwood or almost all transportation related air pollution) and most energy production involves the use of natural resources. For these reasons the subject of "energy" deserves its own chapter.

The following section, history of energy development, draws heavily from the work of environmental historian Marvin Melosi. If you are interested in the history of energy use, be sure to read the extensive notes that accompany this chapter.

HISTORY OF ENERGY

When ancient humans discovered fire could be used for warmth, cooking, and heating, they adapted this form of energy to their purposes. Human ingenuity led to the harnessing of the wind and water to power sailing ships and to turn mills. However, fuelwood remained the most important source of energy for heating, cooking, and manufacturing in Europe and the United States until the dawn of the Industrial Revolution in the 1700s and 1800s. Huge tracts of land on continental Europe and over much of Great Britain were denuded for their fuelwood. In the less developed nations, fuelwood is still the primary source of energy—with similar environmental consequences.

Industrial Revolution

With the Industrial Revolution, techniques were developed for mining and transporting coal, an energy source that enabled people to undertake industrial projects that would not have been possible otherwise. The use of coke, a coal derivative, as a substitute for charcoal led to the mass production of high-quality iron and then steel. Coal was also convenient for stoking the boilers of steam locomotives and by 1880 accounted for 90 percent of locomotive fuel in the United States. In addition, coal was used to power steamboats and other machinery along with its use as a popular heating fuel.[4]

Coal utilization led to America's first major modern environmental crisis. The use of soft bituminous coal led to extensive smoke pollution in industrial cities, causing respiratory diseases, corroding marble statues, and depositing black soot on clothing, buildings, and streets. The toxic smoke compounded by overcrowded living conditions, traffic congestion, and inadequate sewage and solid waste disposal systems led to the first environmental protests and the realization that progress had its drawbacks.[5] An alternate source of energy at this time was hydropower, which had been used since the 1800s for producing electricity.[6] But coal was the most important source of energy for industrializing the America of the 1800s, while oil was destined to become the premium fuel of the twentieth century. The petroleum industry grew rapidly after the first commercial oilrig hit black gold in Titusville, Pennsylvania, in 1859. Within a decade of the strike, oil production had increased tenfold.[7] The gigantic strikes in the Southwest and California in 1890 and 1901 transformed the nation west of the Mississippi by creating a new source of wealth. Unlike eastern oil, which was used mostly for a lubricant and illumination, this new oil was well suited for powering locomotives, steamships, and eventually automobiles. Thus it came into direct competition with coal.[8]

Oil and War

The era of oil began with World War I. The war effort was dependent on motorized transport, and oil played an essential role. In the words of Lord Nathaniel Curzon of the British War Cabinet, "The Allies floated to victory on a wave of oil."[9] The low cost of oil, well-financed and efficiently managed oil companies led by Standard Oil, and the ease of shipping gave oil an advantage over the cumbersome, financially weak, labor-intensive coal industry.[10]

After the war, the dismantling of the war bureaucracy caused confusion and a temporary shortage of oil in the United States. At the same time, overseas development of petroleum expanded significantly for the first time.

Fueled by oil and a maturing electrical industry, America experienced unprecedented prosperity after the war. Industrial output in the United States during the 1920s grew twice as fast as the population. Demand for oil more than doubled during the 1920s.[11] The temporary shortages experienced after World War I stimulated production and led to overproduction and intense competition as hundreds of producers entered the market.[12] The big producers began to recognize the dangers of indiscriminate drilling as prices and profits fell.[13]

During World War II oil was again the indispensable fuel for a successful Allied effort.[14] Access to oil and oil transport were essential strategic considerations for all warring nations. The naval vessels of all nations and 85 percent of merchant ships relied on oil for fuel.[15] The war prompted, after much controversy and delay, construction of two major transcontinental pipelines.[16]

The war demand for oil, gasoline, and lubricants for military vehicles and aircraft led to shortages in the United States and the development of synthetic fuels and synthetic rubber. The federal government, seeking to maximize production, introduced new subsidies, favorable tax provisions, and eased antitrust activity against energy companies. This general atmosphere of cooperation between the government, the military, and business would leave a legacy of economic advantages for the oil industry and establish a military-industrial complex as a major economic and political force in the nation.

Although Middle Eastern oil did not make a critical contribution to the Allied war effort, the importance of this region as an oil-producing area was recognized and firmly established during the war. The political, economic, and military interests of the United States had become clearly linked to the international oil market. The interests of American multinationals, which had exploited oil resources in Mexico, Latin America, and, to a lesser extent, the Middle East and Asia, became intimately connected and aligned with the foreign policy goals of the United States during World War II.[17]

The United States emerged from the war as the premier world power. The nation's abundant energy and material resources played a crucial role in this development. The war effort was a miracle of modern industrial achievement and fortified Americans' faith in capitalism, technology, and continued economic growth. The war utilized those resources that America would continue to be dependent on—electricity, coal, natural gas, petroleum, and its refined products; it also opened the door for the future development of nuclear power.[18]

Role of Personal Consumption

Just as the world wars had an impact on oil and energy policy in the United States, so did the development of personalized transit—the automobile. The emergence of the internal combustion driven automobile as a product for mass consumption began with Henry Ford's Model T in 1907. Before that time cars had largely been toys for the rich.[19]

The automobile industry was the most important segment of the manufacturing sector of the U.S. economy during the 1920s.[20] The automobile stimulated growth in all parts of the economy and was the major impetus to the petroleum industry in this century. And, as we have seen in other chapters, the widespread ownership of cars led to sprawling cities and suburbs and air pollution.

As people were buying cars they were also being introduced to the wonders of electricity—or more correctly, the wonders of electrical appliances and light bulbs. By the 1920s, electricity and electric appliances had become as important to the American people as the automobile. Mass communication facilitated advertising, which helped to create a mass consumer culture.

At the same time, giant utility companies came to dominate electrical generation, and the federal government gradually enlarged its role as regulator to curb abuses in the "power trust." The Securities and Exchange Commission (SEC) was formed in 1934 and provided with extensive authority to regulate the financing of utility holding companies and to break up monopolies formed by "tiering" one company on top of another. Utilities such as telephone companies were regarded as natural monopolies, and federal efforts were designed to protect the interests of the consumers while ensuring consistent and dependable service.

During the 1930s President Franklin Roosevelt promoted, in the face of heated opposition by private power generators, the concept of the public power ownership. Although public power holdings never approached the scale of those in the private sector, there were a few successes, notably the Tennessee Valley Authority (TVA), a public corporation with the flexibility of a private enterprise.[21]

Some of the private purveyors of electricity also produced natural gas. Initially treated as a nuisance by early oil producers, natural gas became an important fuel in the 1930s.[22] Since the establishment of pipelines was very expensive, holding companies combined gas enterprises with electrical systems, creating new monopolies and new abuses. The Natural Gas Act of 1938 granted the Federal Power Commission (FPC) the authority to regulate the interstate flow of gas and to establish the place and pace of pipeline construction.

After World War II natural gas became an essential fuel.[23] Since 80 percent of the country's natural gas was being produced in only four states, distribution of natural gas presented problems. Under the Natural Gas Act of 1938 *intrastate* prices were determined by supply and demand and *interstate* prices were determined according to production costs. As long as there was little difference in the two there were no problems. However, in the 1970s, prices in the intrastate market rose.[24] Rising demand in the interstate market was not being accompanied by rising prices, leading to market shortages. A day of reckoning was at hand as the country approached the oil "shock" of 1973.[25]

OPEC and the Oil Crises

By 1961 the Middle East had become the center of world oil production. Independents and host countries in the region were exerting increased control over their oil, and, in some instances, nationalizing oil industries. The Organization of Petroleum Exporting Countries (OPEC) was formed in 1960 largely because of dissatisfaction with price reductions by the major Western oil companies. Founding member countries were Saudi Arabia, Kuwait, Iran, and Iraq. Together they controlled 67 percent of the world's oil reserves, 38 percent of world production, and 90 percent of oil in international trade.[26]

The Yom Kippur War of 1973 provided the catalyst for OPEC's emergence as the undisputed world leader in crude oil pricing and production. When Egypt and Syria launched a surprise attack on Israel in October 1973, President Nixon fulfilled his promise to the Israeli state and airlifted weapons, tanks, and planes to its defense. The response was the Arab oil embargo of 1973. The days of cheap energy had passed.[27]

The Arab embargo lasted for six months, ending on March 18, 1974. The price increases and the shortage of fuel had shocked Americans. The past had suddenly collided with the future, as the realization came that the days of cheap abundant energy were slipping away and with them the foundation on which industrial America had been built. America's dependence on foreign oil became painfully obvious.

Increased domestic production of oil and natural gas was not a solution—only a stopgap measure. Oil started flowing through the Alaskan pipeline from the North Slope oil fields to the port of Valdez in July 1977. The crude created a temporary glut for California refineries and supported the illusion there was always more oil out there—all we had to do was find it. Americans failed to realize that several deposits the size of the North Sea and the Alaskan oil fields would have to be discovered each year to feed the voracious appetites of an energy-intensive society and to achieve energy independence.[28]

After the Arab oil embargo, President Nixon started "Project Independence," a program designed to decrease dependence on foreign sources of energy. Nixon emphasized the need to expand the nation's nuclear power generation, outer continental shelf development, and oil shale reserve leasing, but his message was largely unheeded. Nixon did eliminate oil import quotas in April 1973 and substituted fees, opening the door for more imports while making domestically produced oil more attractive.

Enmeshed in the Watergate scandal, the Nixon administration was unable to react effectively to the oil crisis. It engaged in crisis management by providing authority for gas rationing and maintaining price controls. Project Independence was a vague program that fell far short of its goal of eliminating America's dependence on foreign oil by 1980. In fact, by 1990 one-half of America's oil was imported. By 2010 the United States dependence on oil imports could reach as high as 70 percent.[29]

President Ford entered office with an ambitious plan to bring about energy independence through the deregulation of oil prices. Yet politically the only way to legitimize deregulation to a skeptical public, in the face of large profits for oil companies, was the enactment of a windfall profits tax. Congress failed to pass a windfall profits tax bill; hence Ford's energy policy and oil deregulation did not take place. Congress was likewise unable to pass legislation during the Ford administration that would have deregulated natural gas.

The Carter administration created the Department of Energy (DOE) in an attempt to address the problems associated with U.S. energy policy, or, rather, the profound lack thereof. The DOE replaced ERDA, FPC, FEA, and the Energy Resources Council. The DOE was overwhelmed with the dual mission of formulating and implementing a national energy plan and organizing a new superagency when the Iranian revolution set off the second oil shock of the decade. Weekend and even weekday shutdowns of gas stations hit the big cities. For a time, 90 percent of New

York gas stations were closed.[30] California was hit the hardest with gas lines extending for blocks. Fights broke out in lines and service station attendants were bribed as a panic psychology took hold. Shortages struck other populous states. The price of oil soared to $35 per barrel, bringing on a severe economic recession in the early 1980s. Gasoline prices approached $1 per gallon, which had previously been unheard of in the United States.[31]

The roller coaster energy ride was not over, however. As a result of rising prices, energy demand worldwide plummeted, which, ironically, produced an oil glut and declining prices beginning in 1982. OPEC was unable to maintain high oil prices and, as a result, the American economy benefited, bringing to an end the recession of the early 1980s.

When Ronald Reagan became president in 1980, he offered the public a panacea of "supply side" economics as a way out of the nation's economic woes. His vision was built on a faith that the productive capacity of the United States would resolve all energy crises. The potential for future shortages was dismissed, as some naively assumed the absence of a crisis meant the absence of a problem.

In August 1990 when Iraq invaded Kuwait and the United States sent troops into Saudi Arabia to prevent an invasion of that country (and to protect Western oil interests), the price of oil increased to $40 per barrel—as high as the price of oil had been during the peak of the Iranian oil crisis in 1979. President Bush responded, in part by selling off part of the oil that was stored in the Strategic Petroleum Reserve, a 500-million-barrel supply in storage established in 1975 to protect the United States in the event of a national emergency. The sale of this oil had little, if any, impact on world oil prices. Despite high prices during the Gulf War, after the war OPEC was unable to maintain production quotas. Production remains high, generating low prices. Cheap oil encourages unwise use of resources, a shift away from energy efficiency, and decreased domestic production.[32] U.S. dependence on oil imports is projected to increase to as much as 70 percent in 2010, and it is estimated OPEC will control 60 percent of the world's market share by the year 2020.[33] The DOE's most conservative estimate of U.S. reliance on foreign oil is 65 percent by 2020.

To put things in perspective, in 1973, when the Arab oil embargo hit the United States hard, America was only getting 36 percent of its oil from foreign sources. Today we are hovering around 55 percent, and much of that is from OPEC. The United States has economic sanctions on most of the OPEC nations for various human rights abuses, terrorist activities, drug trafficking, and the development of weapons of mass destruction. The State Department even has travel warnings for about half the OPEC nations.[34] If these nations are so unstable, and it is not safe for Americans to even visit these places, how wise is it to rely on them for our energy needs? National security and reliability are thus only two of the pitfalls associated with the hard energy path.

Development of Nuclear Power

The development of nuclear power was thought by many to be the panacea for solving the energy crisis. Nuclear power started with the development and use of the atomic bomb during World War II.[35] As the joy over the end of the war mixed with feelings of horror at the power of the unleashed atom, astute politicians realized warfare and international relations would never be the same.

In the United States, the federal government granted itself a monopoly over nuclear power with the passage of the Atomic Energy Act in 1946. The Atomic Energy Commission (AEC) was established as well as the Joint Committee on Atomic Energy (JCAE) in Congress. The AEC was a unique federal agency. It had total control over nuclear energy development, including ownership of nuclear fuels. It was also entrusted with the sometimes conflicting role of nuclear power regulator.

The Atomic Energy Act of 1954 gave a boost to commercial production of nuclear power. Private firms would be allowed to own reactors while the government would continue to retain ownership of the nuclear fuels.

This was not sufficient incentive, however, for private enterprise to become involved in a technology with an uncertain future and huge potential liability problems in the event of an accident. In an effort to address the liability issue, Congress in 1957 passed the Price-Anderson Act, limiting the liability from a nuclear accident of an individual company and providing governmental subsidies to cover damage above the liability limits. The Price-Anderson Amendments in 1988 raised the liability limits from $5 million per facility/per incident to $63 million per facility/per incident.[36] However, plant operators (or licensees) are not required to pay out more than $10 million in any one year in case of liability under the act.[37]

Although the Price-Anderson Act removed a major obstacle to commercial nuclear power, there were still inadequate incentives for the private sector to develop nuclear power. In 1963 Congress passed the Private Ownership of Special Nuclear Fuels Act, which would allow private ownership of nuclear materials for nonmilitary purposes. However, it was the environmental problems inherent in coal-fired plants and the great Northeast blackout of 1965 that gave an essential boost to nuclear power. It is ironic that environmental concerns helped to spawn an industry that would turn out to have serious long-term environmental repercussions of a different nature.[38]

The need for an alternative to polluting coal did not mean there were no organized environmental interest groups in opposition to nuclear power. In fact, the biggest threat to the vitality of the nuclear industry came from the new environmental movement, which recognized the potentially catastrophic impact of a major accident and the disposal problems of nuclear waste. Also nuclear power became associated in many minds with nuclear holocaust. The nuclear age had forced on the world the realization that humankind now had the power to destroy all life on earth.[39]

The 1973 energy crisis provided the nuclear power industry with an opportunity to promote their program as an alternative to oil and as protection from the whims of foreign oil exporting countries. By late 1974, orders for light water reactors (LWRs) reached a new peak. The market collapsed as quickly as it had risen as the demand for electricity dropped in reaction to the fivefold increase in the cost of oil.

By the late 1970s the future of nuclear power was uncertain. The energy crisis seemed over, thus eliminating one compelling reason to pursue the nuclear option, and cost overruns plagued the industry. In the late 1960s nuclear plants had cost twice what had been expected.[40] The year 1979 signaled the real decline of the nuclear power industry. That year the Three Mile Island (TMI) nuclear facility in Pennsylvania suffered a partial meltdown of one of its reactors. The accident made the headlines worldwide and caused many to question the desirability of nuclear power generation.[41]

The accident at TMI was a turning point for the nuclear industry. Not a single nuclear power plant has been ordered since that fateful day, and 117 have been cancelled including all orders placed after 1972.[42] Business-oriented *Forbes* magazine has called the U.S. nuclear power program "the largest managerial disaster in United States business history," involving $100 billion in wasted investments, cost overruns, and unnecessarily high electricity costs. The construction of a nuclear power plant in Seabrook, New Hampshire, for example, came on-line 14 years after it received its permit from the Nuclear Regulatory Commission at a final price tag of $6.6 billion (508 percent over budget). Public Service of New Hampshire, the utility company that built the plant, went bankrupt in 1988, two years before the plant came on-line.

Overall, nuclear energy is not any better than coal, oil, or gas. It poses very different but still equally damaging environmental and human health consequences. Though it is a newer and unique technology, nuclear power still continues along the hard path of producing more and more energy in a potentially disastrous way. That is, it only focuses on producing energy instead of how to reduce need, consumption, environmental or human health damage.

Development of a National Energy Policy

From wood to coal to oil to nuclear, the history of U.S. energy development has been market driven—without any national energy policy. The Truman, Eisenhower, Kennedy, and Johnson administrations failed to develop comprehensive energy plans. The pattern was crisis management substituting for a well-thought-out long-term program. This is, of course, consistent with what we might expect, given what we know about the informal incentives that operate on policy makers. Sacrifice, interference in the market, especially when that market is very profitable to an influential economic interest group, and planning are just not things our system does well. The specter of future scarcities loomed large even then, but little was done to plan for the future. The 1967 Arab-Israeli war and the subsequent oil embargo were not regarded as serious omens of future developments. When oil crises occurred, even as late as 1990, there was no real energy policy.

The Ford administration's most significant energy achievement was the dissolution of the Atomic Energy Commission (AEC) and the creation of the Energy Research and Development Administration (ERDA), which took over the research and development of all energy forms, and the Nuclear Regulatory Commission (NRC), which assumed the AEC's regulatory function over the nuclear industry.

President Carter attempted to formulate a long-range, comprehensive energy program for the country. On April 18, 1977, Carter announced his National Energy Plan (NEP). Carter emphasized the serious nature of the energy crisis by calling it "the moral equivalent of war." The President did not belittle the situation with the usual political pep talk and empty promises of prosperity. Instead he warned Americans that ignoring the increasing scarcity of petroleum "would subject our people to an impending catastrophe."

Conservation was at the heart of Carter's message, and for perhaps the first time, the soft energy path was placed on the national political agenda. It called for major improvements in energy efficiency for existing buildings and acceleration of the applications of solar technology. It asked for taxes and conservation incentives in information and transportation systems.

Further, the plan called for a reduction in average annual energy growth to less than 2 percent; reduction in natural gas consumption by 10 percent; and continued reductions in imported oil. This was a bold plan that called on Americans to make sacrifices.

Upon introduction in Congress, the NEP drew fire from all sides. Special interests attacked one of the most important parts of the bill—the Crude Oil and Equalization Tax (COET), which was designed to raise oil prices over the following three years to encourage the application of energy efficiency measures and thereby reduce demand. The revenues from the tax were to be diverted into several government programs. Without the price incentives, energy efficiency was much less likely to be recognized as an essential part of the national energy plan and its application was likely to be limited. Higher prices are necessary to spur consumers to conserve and engineers to develop better technologies.[43] The failure of the NEP to present a pricing strategy ensured only partial success of its goals.

The Natural Gas Act was one of the most controversial aspects of NEP. It eliminated the distinction between the inter- and intrastate markets with the government having a stronger, if only temporary, role.

The NEP also contained various conservation incentives, such as insulation credits, weatherization grants, energy audits, and loans for solar energy systems. It taxed gas-guzzling cars and prohibited the use of oil or gas in new electricity generation and new industrial plants and established voluntary electrical rate designs.

Members of Congress from virtually every region of the country attacked Carter's program. Northeastern representatives with constituents dependent on home heating oil, as well as westerners whose constituents used their automobile for extended travel, denounced various parts of the plan that would have increased the price of energy. The most ambitious aspects—those that would have led to the greatest energy savings—failed to pass Congress.

A major piece of legislation that did pass during the Carter administration was the Public Utilities Regulatory Policies Act of 1978 (PURPA). PURPA has been best known for its requirement that utilities purchase electricity from a class of independent generators known as "qualifying facilities" in order to encourage cogeneration and renewable resources for power production. In order to encourage the patronage of qualifying facilities, these firms were exempted from state and federal regulations. Utilities that wished to purchase power from qualifying facilities were required to pay what amounted to the utility's full avoided cost; that is, what the utilities would otherwise spend to generate or procure power.

PURPA led to a number of interesting developments. First, cogeneration became a growth industry. When written, PURPA was meant to protect independent energy producers using small turbines in existing steam plants. PURPA encouraged energy production by forcing utilities to purchase energy produced as a by-product (cogenerated) of some industrial or manufacturing process. Many newer power plants, however, were much larger and devoted most of their resources into generating power rather than producing heat for the parent factory.[44]

Another unintended consequence of PURPA is exemplified by the construction of a power plant in Michigan. A nuclear power plant faced bankruptcy. To meet PURPA requirements of independence from utility company ownership, investors were gathered from among the plant builders, suppliers, and large potential private customers. Investors formed a 51 percent privately owned company that was not subject to regulation by utility commissions. With the PURPA requirement that their electricity be purchased, bankruptcy was avoided; consumers, however, were forced to pay $1,700 per kilowatt hour for the power produced rather than the more typical rate of $600 dollars per kilowatt hour.[45]

According to the Reagan administration, free markets would satisfy current and future energy needs as profit-motivated investors sought to reap the economic rewards promised by future energy demands. Federal government spending on research and development of alternative energy sources were cut dramatically or eliminated entirely during the Reagan years. Market forces were more pragmatic, however, and energy usage as a percentage of GNP declined as more energy efficiency measures were adopted.

On October 24, 1992, President Bush signed the Comprehensive National Energy Policy Act (CNEPA). Among a multitude of provisions,[46] CNEPA creates a director of climate protection to oversee greenhouse gas research and policy making, foreign aid, and exploration of technology to combat global warming. CNEPA also targets a 30 percent increase in energy efficiency by 2010, a 75 percent increase in the use of renewable energy sources by 2005, and a decrease in oil consumption from 40 percent of total energy use to 35 percent by 2005.

The provisions included in CNEPA for promoting renewable energy sources and energy efficiency were a positive change from the past mode of crisis management, market solutions, and short-term policies. Efficiency standards, for example, were to be met by federal buildings and public housing. Standards were established for lights, showers, toilets, faucets, small motors, and commercial heaters and air conditioners. The federal government provided technical assistance with regional demonstrations of the latest technology. States were given incentives to update building codes to meet or exceed the new standards. The states are, for example, eligible for utility grants to promote efficiency and conservation; and they have access to aid in establishing revolving funds to increase efficiency in state and local government buildings. Grants are also available for industry to promote efficiency. Voluntary guidelines have been issued for homes along with a mortgage pilot program for energy-efficient homes and retrofitting.

There have been some criticisms of CNEPA, however. President Bush signed CNEPA in oil-producing Louisiana just before the election. Tax increases and gas mileage standards were absent from the legislation. CNEPA did include tax breaks to independent oil and gas drillers at an estimated cost of $1 billion over five years. Bush's earlier call for opening Alaska's Arctic National Wildlife Refuge for oil exploration was dropped from the final version of CNEPA.

Candidate Clinton raised hopes for environmental changes by choosing environmentalist Senator Al Gore as his running mate. During the first two years of the Clinton administration, not much was accomplished toward formulating a comprehensive energy plan for the United States. While an additional gasoline tax of 4.3 cents a gallon was enacted into law, it was part of an economic stimulus package and was not expected to affect consumption to any significant degree. Similarly, President Clinton publicly endorsed fuel efficiency standards and reduction of greenhouse gas emissions early in his administration but also endorsed voluntary compliance to achieve them. The White House Office on Environmental Policy (OEP) was created with an agenda to stress the economics of environmentalism, including creating jobs and new business opportunities for new technologies.[47] (See Chapter 4 for a discussion of environmental reorganization during the Clinton administration.)

Although research funding was dramatically increased in favor of renewable energy sources, the administration overall failed to link energy policy with other issues such as conservation and environmental protection. The inability of the administration to get a moderate tax on BTU usage through Congress would seem to characterize the lackluster approach taken by the new administration.

In the spring of 1998, however, the Clinton administration released the Comprehensive National Energy Strategy, intended to provide long-term guidance for the country's energy needs. Environmental protection components of the strategy include accommodations for the Kyoto protocol, which dealt with limiting the production of greenhouse gasses, and was grudgingly accepted by most developed nations in the fall of 1997. The five goals of the strategy are to improve energy efficiency; ensure against energy disruptions; promote energy production and use in ways that respect health and the environment; expand energy choices; and cooperate internationally. In order to achieve these goals, many specific initiatives are outlined, including: the development of affordable automobiles that use alternative fuels; the promotion of natural gas as a preferred alternative over other, more polluting, nonrenewable resources; and a proposed mandate requiring that electric utilities obtain at least 5.5 percent of their power from renewable resources by 2010.

The 1990s saw other changes in the regulation of energy. State governments, whose regulatory power over electric power suppliers was defined under PURPA, sought to increase competition among power companies by either repealing, or otherwise disabling the restrictions PURPA placed on electric utilities and how they obtain their power. It is believed that such deregulation could have a detrimental effect on the supply of renewable power that is created by the smaller, qualifying facilities. Deregulation would most likely increase competition greatly, and, as a result, would foster a market situation oriented toward short-term economic returns, rather than the long-term sustainability of renewable power resources. In California, such deregulation has already had the effect of decreasing advanced generation technologies by 88 percent from 1993 to 1995.[48] Then in 1996 Governor Wilson signed a law further restructuring California's energy markets to allow for competition in electricity generation to drive costs down. Flaws in the deregulation plan ultimately led to a power crisis in California beginning in June 2000 where prices skyrocketed and supply plummeted, causing consistent rolling blackouts.[49]

The major impetus behind the deregulation debate has been the proliferation of large independent power producers who are not considered qualifying facilities under PURPA. It is argued that the tax advantages given to qualifying facilities unfairly discriminates against these larger providers and stifles competition. An appeal has also been made on behalf of the consumer, who would most likely benefit financially from the lower prices that would result from increased competition. The perceived advantage of consumers being able to choose their own source of power, rather than being at the mercy of a single utility company, is one of the forces at the center of the deregulation debate. Finally, a general decrease in overall demand for power in the United States has led to a smaller market that must be shared by numerous utilities. From 1953 to 1973, the annual growth of power consumption was 7 percent. This growth has fallen to between 2 and 3 percent annually from 1973 to 1993. It is estimated that annual increases in demand will fall from 1 to 2 percent through 2013.[50]

Emerging trends also seem to indicate an overall unwillingness by the oil and gas industry, as well as some end-user groups, to pursue renewable forms of energy production as mandated in CNEPA. Of particular interest has been the requirement that 10 percent of the nation's petroleum based fuels be replaced with alternative fuels, accompanied by a phasing-in of alternative fuel compatible automobiles into federal, state, and local fleets by 1999. At the time of this writing, it is expected that the states, who have the responsibility of overseeing the phasing-in stage, will not be able to comply with this requirement.

The George W. Bush administration has made a few moves thus far in regards to energy policy. First, it has abandoned the Kyoto Protocol to cut greenhouse gas emissions, stating it would be devastating to the economy and that it is not fair that developing nations like India and China would not have to meet the same requirements as the United States. In addition, the President appointed Vice President Dick Cheney to head up the cabinet committee called the National Energy Policy Development Group.

The Vice President has made the Administration's energy position fairly clear. He makes a hard energy path case for the most part, by seeking, "to increase energy supplies from diverse sources, from oil and gas, renewables, coal, hydro and nuclear." It is unfortunate that the Vice President does not mention reducing demand, only increasing supply. He does state, "But it's not just a matter of cleaner use. We must become much more efficient in our energy use as well." The new President also signed an executive order requiring federal agencies to take extra steps in conserving energy.

Still the focus is on technological fixes, with the more immediate concern of increasing traditional energy supplies, including obtaining more energy from the American Arctic. The administration not only wants to drill for oil in ANWR, but is looking for more nuclear energy, as "conservation's important but it's not enough." Cheney prefers nuclear because it does not emit greenhouse gases, though he and the President need more research before believing global warming is really a problem they can do something about anyway. In fact the Vice President was adamant when he announced, "If you're really concerned about global warming and carbon dioxide emissions, then we need to come over here and aggressively pursue the use of nuclear power."[51]

This sounds like conservation and efficiency suddenly disappear from the argument, and we revert back to the hard path, where more nuclear power plants are the only solution. It seems that perhaps the Bush administration's position is that nuclear waste has no potential environmental or safety consequences. Time will tell if this administration is more serious about conservation and efficiency, or more concerned about increasing energy supply at almost any cost. Will the President steadfastly guide U.S. energy policy down a sustainable path, or will his administration simply default to the market, as has been the easiest course for the past 50 years?

NONRENEWABLE ENERGY SOURCES

Although it all comes out of the wall socket the same way, sources of energy vary significantly in terms of their negative impacts on the environment. In the following two sections we examine the various types of energy sources used in the United States.[52]

As we have seen, America's environmental awareness grew significantly in the 1960s. Industrial expansion was causing environmental damage that could not be ignored or rationalized as the cost of progress. Fossil fuels and nonfuel by-products, such as petrochemicals, were choking America's waterways, soil, and air with toxins. Although fossil fuels are the dirtiest source of energy, in fact all energy, its exploration, production, and use, has an impact on the environment.

Coal

Of all fossil fuels, coal has the most harmful immediate and long-term effects on the environment and human health. People who lived in the industrial cities of the nineteenth century knew that coal produced annoying and debilitating smoke, but they could not comprehend the magnitude of coal's impact on the environment and the human body. Today we have scientific measurements that show the extent of the destruction. Air pollution, thermal pollution, land devastation, groundwater pollution, acidification of streams and rivers, erosion, subsidence of land caused by underground mines, hazards to miners, and, of course, global warming are all recognized as part and parcel of coal's utilization.

Coal is the most abundant fossil fuel in the United States. As petroleum and natural gas have become more expensive and scarce, coal development has accelerated.[53] Identified reserves globally are expected to last about 2,000 years at 1994 consumption rates.[54] However, if all known reserves of coal were utilized, the consequences would be catastrophic for the environment (for example, significantly contributing to global warming). Acid rain caused by coal-fired electrical generating plants has also had devastating effects on the environment. Acid rain is covered in detail in Chapter 5. Other environmental costs are associated with the mining of coal. These include loss of lives and health of miners during the extraction, erosion, and pollution of waterways.[55]

The Surface Mining Control and Reclamation Act of 1977 (SMCRA) could have protected valuable ecosystems from the ravages of strip mining if it had been strictly interpreted and enforced. However, legal confrontations have delayed action, and the Reagan administration cut back the federal inspection force by 70 percent, making enforcement virtually impossible.

A key provision of SMCRA is the requirement that land be reclaimed after mining operations cease. Enforcement was to include withholding of mining permits for those who did not restore past sites. In a lawsuit against the government for lack of enforcement, the court ordered the federal government to install a computer system to better track violators. The resultant $15 million "Applicant/Violator System," which makes it harder for coal companies to conceal past offenses when they apply for new permits, was so flawed that half of the 660 permits in a six-month period were overturned by manual verification.[56] The Department of the Interior claims the system has been improved since its installation.

The SMCRA has had an impact, however. Even though enforcement is still spotty, some states have been much more aggressive in applying SMCRA than have others. For example, the state of Wyoming matches or exceeds SMCRA regulations for coal mining. Wyoming requires bonds up front that are returned only after revegetation is approved by the state Department of Environmental Quality (approximately a 10-year period in the arid West—if efforts succeed—as opposed to five years in the East). Reclamation costs in the West can range from $5,000 to $20,000 an acre.[57]

Demand for coal will remain strong into the foreseeable future. This is true for several reasons. First, it is projected that the use of coal to produce electricity domestically will increase; barriers to nuclear power (for example, cost and waste disposal) make short-term expansion of that source of power unlikely; worldwide demand for coal should be strong (especially in developing countries); President Clinton exempted coal exports from his failed BTU tax to ensure high production levels; and CNEPA promotes technological advances for "clean coal" promotion that can be exported along with the coal itself—all of which promise a bright future for coal.[58]

Oil

Oil causes many environmental problems as well. As we saw in Chapter 5, auto emissions contain nitrogen and sulfur oxides, carbon monoxide, hydrocarbons, ozone, nitrates, lead, and waste heat.[59] Carbon dioxide emissions contribute to the greenhouse effect. Oil also pollutes groundwater through the injection of brine solutions into aquifers.[60] All of these oil-related pollution problems are discussed elsewhere in the text. Although not as pervasive as air pollution from the burning of oil, one of the most attention-getting oil related pollution problems is oil spills from tankers and ocean platforms.

While it was not the first major incident, the Santa Barbara oil spill in 1969 was a major environmental crisis and focused national and international attention on the devastating effects of large oil slicks. The leak released 235,000 gallons of crude from Union Oil's Well A-21, creating a slick 800 miles long.[61] Since the blowout occurred on federal lease land, Washington responded—with investigations and studies. Congress reacted by revising the Outer Continental Shelf Act to tighten regulations concerning federal leases and clarifying the responsibilities of oil producers to assume liability for any accidents. However, no amount of federal legislation can make up for industry neglect.

The Exxon Valdez oil tanker spill in 1989 reportedly occurred because of the negligence of Exxon employees. Ample federal regulatory procedures were in place to prevent such a spill and, at least we thought so prior to the spill, to respond to and clean up after an accident. The Valdez released 10.1 to 12.6 million gallons of crude into Prince William Sound, Alaska, an area teeming with marine and bird life.[62] The largest oil spill in U.S. history spread out of control and covered 900 square miles within a week. Experts predicted that since the leak occurred in a closed body of water and there were no winds and waves to disperse the oil, particles would sink to the bottom of the bay to act as lethal time release capsules of toxic petroleum hydrocarbons, not only killing marine life but having the potential of destroying the local fishing industry.[63] For the thousands of waterfowl that use Prince William Sound as a summer nesting ground, the spill could not have come at a worse time. They returned in the summer of 1989 to find their home polluted and despoiled.

The Valdez spill provides several good examples of the paradoxical elements of environmental policy in the United States. Although what would have seemed to be adequate legislation was on the books, several things happened that theoretically should not have happened. First, the decentralized nature of the policy process was in evidence after the spill occurred. Several federal agencies as well as various Alaska state agencies were involved, but poor coordination hampered clean-up efforts. Furthermore, Congress was successful in getting the oil companies that would be shipping in Prince William Sound to give their assurances they would only sail double-hulled ships. Congress also established a fund to finance the clean up of oil spills.

These actions provided the public with tangible evidence of congressional concern on an important, and popular, public policy issue. However, the clean-up fund was found to be inadequate and, due to the lack of follow-through and enforcement, double-hulled ships were not the norm in Prince William Sound.[64]

There is no doubt we can now see the bottom of the oil barrel.[65] The largest oil discoveries of the 1970s—in Alaska, the North Sea, and Mexico—have only been of moderate size. U.S. oil extraction will continue to be dominated by deposits in the Southwest (which have already been heavily exploited), the Gulf Coast states, and Alaska's North Slope.[66] In order to maintain the level of fossil-fuel-supported activity in the world today, several deposits of oil comparable in magnitude to the North Sea and Alaskan North Slope discoveries would have be found each year.[67]

Natural Gas

About 95 percent of the natural gas used in the United States is derived from domestic sources.[68] Natural gas is the most clean burning of any fossil fuel and relatively inexpensive. Carbon dioxide is given off as it burns but in lower amounts per unit of energy produced *when compared to other fossil fuels*. From a cost-effective perspective, natural gas is a highly efficient source of energy with newer power plants approaching conversion efficiencies of 45 percent.[69] According to 1995 estimates, there are at least 4,900 trillion cubic feet of natural gas available worldwide, enough for 60 more years at current production rates. Natural gas is becoming increasingly important globally, though, and its consumption is projected to jump 85 percent from 1995 to 2015.

In its natural state, natural gas is easy to transport through pipelines, so domestic natural gas is simpler to transport. However, most natural gas supplies are found in remote areas of the planet like Siberia and the Persian Gulf. Pipes cannot be efficiently built across oceans, so an alternative approach is required.[70] Natural gas may be converted to a concentrated form—liquid natural gas (LNG) for transportation by refrigerated tanker ship. Although this is an efficient means of moving natural gas, LNG is highly explosive. An explosion on board a tanker could create a massive fireball, causing fires and third-degree burns as far as miles away.[71] LNG is increasingly important for developing nation exporters and importers like Japan; the United States accounts for less than 2 percent of this market.[72]

Geothermal Energy

One technology that has made impressive strides in recent years because of research and development (R&D) funding is geothermal power. With the possible exception of small amounts of wastewater and some unpleasant odors (when not properly controlled), geothermal energy is largely nonpolluting. In 1992 over 8 million megawatts of power were produced from geothermal sources by domestic utility companies. (Nonutility production figures are considered confidential due to the extremely competitive nature of the industry.)[73] Worldwide geothermal produces an estimated 1 percent of electricity produced.[74] Most geothermal resources are projected to last from 600 to 700 years.[75] Some geothermal resources such as those on the island of Hawaii in the state of Hawaii are perpetual and have the potential to supply large amounts of energy at a consistent rate.

Using only today's technology, geothermal energy has the potential to supply the world with over 70 thousand megawatts of electricity. Using technologies that are currently under development, that figure could almost double. This would amount to over 8 percent of global electrical output. North America (mostly the United States) has the potential to generate 200 million megawatt hours of electricity by geothermal means, which amounts to about 5 percent of total North American electrical output.[76]

Geothermal energy comes from the heat contained in underground rocks and fluids. About 10 percent of the world's landmass is suitable for developing this heat into usable energy. Currently there are about 20 countries that are exploiting geothermal deposits, supplying space heating for over 2 million homes in cold climates and enough electricity for 1.5 million homes.[77]

Most of the geothermal resources in the United States are located in the West. The Geysers steam field, the largest in the world,[78] located about 90 miles north of San Francisco, has been producing electricity since 1960.[79]

There are four types of geothermal energy resources. The Geysers field is known as a dry steam deposit—the most rare but desirable type because of its ease of extraction. Dry steam is a form of hydrothermal energy, and, along with geopressured energy, involves the extraction of subterranean hot water or steam that is then used for direct heating or conversion into electricity through the use of steam turbines. The other two types of geothermal energy involve the pumping of water into the ground through a piping system that is near a source of heat such as hot dry rock or magma (molten rock).[80] Naturally occurring wet steam and hot water geothermal deposits are most common but are more difficult and expensive to convert to electricity.[81]

Nuclear Power

The direct environmental problems associated with nuclear power are from a nuclear meltdown, the mining and storage of nuclear fuels, and disposal of nuclear waste. The world witnessed the consequences of a nuclear meltdown in May 1986 when the Chernobyl nuclear power plant in the Russian Ukraine blew up, sending a lethal cloud of radioactivity across Europe.[82] Regions of Europe were badly contaminated, and milk and other foodstuffs had to be thrown out. Sheep were quarantined in England. Reindeer were destroyed in Scandinavia. Thousands ultimately died from radiation poisoning.

Since the Three Mile Island (TMI) accident, there have been 30,000 mishaps at U.S. nuclear plants, some with the potential to have caused *more serious* disasters than that at TMI.[83] Although the potential for disaster from the production of nuclear-generated electricity is phenomenal, a realistic assessment of the true environmental costs of nuclear power must consider the entire nuclear fuel cycle from uranium mining at the "front end" of the industry to waste disposal at the "back end." These problems include radiation in mining, mine tailings or waste, and the potential for mishaps in the transportation and storage of radioactive materials. There are also potential security problems associated with the possibility that nuclear materials could find their way into the hands of terrorists.

Though nuclear power generation does not emit greenhouse gases, it produces tons of radioactive waste that will be deadly for hundreds of thousands of years. Standing a few feet away from uncontained nuclear waste would kill a human in seconds. Still there is no long-term (not even hundreds, let alone thousands of years) solution to radioactive waste storage. Much of the industry is pushing for "centralized interim storage" sites, where they would lock an estimated 85 thousand metric tons of irradiated fuel in a concrete slab in the ground, or perhaps buried in Yucca Mountain, Nevada. The "Yucca Mountain Solution" has been riddled with controversy. First, Yucca Mountain is in an earthquake zone, and 219 various organizations in December of 1998 asked the DOE to consider that site unsuitable. Second, even if a "perfect" site was located, where an earthquake or similar disaster was impossible, transportation would be a contentious issue. It would take anywhere from 15,000 to 80,000 separate shipments of nuclear waste to get it all to this central site. At least 50 million Americans live within a half-mile of likely transportation routes (rail and interstates) that would cross 43 states.[84] Many of these communities, like Flagstaff, Arizona, have protested the possibility of such shipments.[85]

Nuclear power plants could find themselves in a very unenviable position if the electric utility market is deregulated. In 1995, coal accounted for 55 percent of the nation's energy production; nuclear power provides approximately 22 percent. If deregulation were to occur, it is estimated that natural gas providers would benefit most. Technological advances have allowed for the invention of a natural gas fired turbine that can produce electricity at around 2.5 cents per kilowatt hour. The equipment needed is fairly inexpensive and compact, making the pursuit of natural gas very attractive. In 1994, coal cost approximately 7 cents per kilowatt hour. Although the actual generation of nuclear power costs little, it is the infrastructure and operation of a nuclear power plant that have made the plants not cost effective.

RENEWABLE ENERGY

As we learned at the outset of this chapter, eventually all energy will be renewable energy. Finite resources, such as fossil fuels, by definition run out. After the world's first major oil shock, progress toward developing new sources of renewable energy have met with mixed success. The 1986 oil price collapse further set back renewable programs by lulling citizens, businesspeople, and politicians into a dangerous sense of complacency that was only temporarily shattered by the "Persian Gulf Crisis" brought on by the Iraqi invasion of Kuwait in August 1990.

In the United States, uneven allocation of federal subsidies favors fossil fuels and nuclear power over renewables.[86] Since development of new technologies entails certain financial risks and requires sustained research, experimentation, and demonstration projects, governments typically pay a large share of these costs, while private investment increases as the project nears commercialization. The widely fluctuating research support for renewable energy as experienced during the 1980s makes long-term programs difficult to plan and implement.[87] Technologies with long-term potential that are in need of support by government monies are biochemical means of converting biomass feedstocks to energy, various solar thermal configurations, and systems that make use of the difference in temperature between surface and deep ocean waters. Development of an economical storage method that could stockpile electricity from solar and wind generators would be a great boon to those industries. In each case the private sector has not had adequate incentives to invest in the research and development necessary to make these sources of energy competitive with fossil fuels.[88]

The 1992 CNEPA did provide some remedy through tax credits for wind and biomass energy production and the general promotion of renewable energy sources. However, CNEPA included several unfunded mandates (for example, a phase-in of alternative fuels) that have not been popular with the petroleum industry, or states whose duty it is to supervise the transition from fossil fuels. It would appear that along with the proposed deregulation of the power industry through the repeal or reorganization of PURPA, the attack on CNEPA's unfunded mandates indicate a movement away from renewable resource development. Regardless, there have been many advances in the feasibility of sustainable energy sources from a scientific, as well financial, perspective.

Hydropower

Historically, hydroelectric power has several advantages over other sources of power. U.S. hydroelectric power plants produce electricity cheaper than any other source. One reason for this is that most of the large dams used in generating electricity were constructed between 1930 and 1950 when costs were low. Also the resource that powers the plants—falling water—is free.[89] In addition to these benefits, hydroelectric plants last 2 to 10 times longer than nuclear and coal-fired plants.[90]

However, hydroelectric power is not without its drawbacks. The disadvantages to hydropower include the following:

- Reservoirs created by dams flood valuable forests, farmland, and sometimes uproot entire communities.
- The spawning grounds of fish, such as salmon, are often ruined by hydroelectric facilities.
- Impounding a river drastically changes the surrounding ecosystem. Instead of nutrient-bearing sediments being deposited on agricultural floodplains and providing food for fish, they build up behind dams and lessen the capacity and power output of the facility. This reduces the fertility of valuable farmlands at river mouths and decreases the

amount of fish available for commerce, recreation, and religious reasons, as well as for mere species survival.

- Hydroelectric dams can alter the oxygen and temperature of downstream waters, having a negative impact on aquatic species.
- In some instances, the water pressure behind large dams has triggered earthquakes, creating a severe hazard for communities downstream.
- Seepage from reservoirs can raise the water table, bringing salty deposits with it, and thereby damaging soil fertility.
- Utilities value hydroelectric plants because they can increase capacity quickly. However, this causes fluctuations in river levels and consequential disruption of aquatic life.
- Large reservoirs in tropical countries can become breeding grounds for carriers of malaria, river blindness, and schistosomiasis.

Since constructing dams on the few untouched rivers in the United States will most likely create a storm of protest, much smaller hydroelectric projects are being contemplated and constructed. Many small-scale hydro sites that were abandoned in the 1940s and 1950s because of cheap abundant fossil fuels could be made serviceable again. Small systems, where turbines are turned by the natural force of water, only have a perceptible effect on the immediate area of the hydro site.[91] Small-scale hydropower could be a benefit on a local basis, but its contribution to total U.S. hydro production would not be great.[92]

Hydropower has many advantages over coal or nuclear-generated power, since the resource is free, relatively nonpolluting, and the lifetime of facilities is longer. Hydropower produced 86,616 megawatts of electricity in 1985, far outstripping any other renewable resource.[93] Globally, hydropower accounts for about 20 percent of electricity generation, and about 10 percent in the United States, or over 250 million megawatt hours. Norway's electricity is almost entirely from hydropower, and 75 percent of New Zealand's electricity is generated by hydropower. However, in the United States, which has the second largest installed hydroelectric capacity of any country (Canada is first),[94] not one new large dam has been approved since 1976. This is due both to the lack of suitable sites and opposition from environmental groups. Any large new sources of hydroelectric power for the United States will come from Canada.[95]

Hydropower is an important source of energy in many less developed countries. In 1986 Venezuela completed the Guri Dam, the largest in the world at that time, with a generating capacity of 10,000 megawatts. Currently, the largest dam is Itaipu on the border of Brazil and Paraguay, with a capacity of 12,600 megawatts. China is in the process of building an even larger one on the Yangtze River.[96]

Thousands of small generators are being installed on remote rivers and streams in less developed countries. Most hydro projects larger than 1,000 megawatts are also being constructed in developing countries, since industrial countries have already tapped their most useful hydropower sites. Dams proposed along the Danube River in Hungary and Czechoslovakia resulted in recordbreaking protests by 40,000 people in Hungary and 60,000 in Slovakia.[97] Critics argued the dams would cause the flooding of communities, the loss of agricultural land, and, more importantly, the potential contamination of Europe's largest drinking water aquifer. Advocates of the projects could be found among environmentalists in nearby Austria, who hoped to use Hungary as an electric colony.[98]

Solar Power

There are several ways to take direct advantage of the perpetual and cost-free sunshine that falls on the earth. Passive solar designs capture sunlight directly within a structure and convert it to heat.[99] According to some experts, climate-sensitive passive solar cooling and natural ventilation should be able to replace air conditioning units within all but the largest buildings.

Active solar systems either collect, concentrate, or convert solar radiation into useful energy. The most basic method uses collectors to absorb relatively low-temperature heat and then transfer it to water, air, or an oil-based liquid. Solar hot water heaters are the most popular use for this type of solar energy exchange. The United States was the world's largest market for solar collectors in the early 1980s. However, the fall in gas and oil prices in 1986 and the elimination of the residential energy tax credit caused the bottom to fall out of the U.S. solar energy market.[100]

Somewhat more complicated are systems that concentrate the sun's energy and focus it on a central receiver to produce high temperatures for steam used to produce electricity. The Luz International Ltd. complex in California's Mojave Desert is the largest example of this type of facility. The Luz complex is the source of 90 percent of the world's electricity drawn from the sun's radiation.[101] The third major category of solar technologies relies on the photovoltaic (PV) effect. This phenomenon causes electricity to be produced when sunlight strikes certain materials. First used to power spacecraft, the earthbound applications of this technology grew dramatically in the early 1980s.[102] Since then, the loss of tax credits, low energy prices, and slashed federal research funds led to a 6 percent loss in sales between 1983 and 1986 in the United States while Japan took over as the world's largest solar cell producer.[103]

Half of the photovoltaics sold provide power to areas that are too remote to be hooked up to electric utility distribution lines. The communications industry accounts for a large segment of this stand-alone market. The second largest category of PV use is for consumer products such as solar calculators, solar toys, and backyard lighting systems. Widespread use of PV for producing electricity in centralized systems depends on reducing significantly the cost of producing PV cells.[104] Recent research into photovoltaic technology has yielded promise toward manufacturing polymer-based cells that are much less expensive than conventional cells, though they are also only one-tenth as efficient.[105]

Cost per se is not the only issue affecting the development of solar energy. Political barriers stand as well. As discussed in Chapter 5, the oil industry pays only an 11 percent corporate income tax compared to 18 percent for all other industries, and state and local taxes for gasoline are only about half what they are for most other goods. If these billions of dollars of tax code subsidies were recouped and channeled toward solar energy, it would not likely be more expensive than oil. Citizens, as opposed to consumers, can make a difference as well. In Sacramento, citizens voted to shut down a nuclear power plant, which forced their energy company to rely on photovoltaics.[106]

Japan is leading the way globally with subsidies for solar power. The Kyoto train station is entirely solar powered, and the nation-wide "Sunshine" program seeks to put solar panels on all homes and schools.[107] Perhaps part of the impetus for this program is Japan's heavy reliance on imports for their energy needs.

Although the negative environmental effects of solar technologies pale in comparison to coal and nuclear power, they do exist. Without effective controls, solar cell manufacture produces hazardous waste. Solar thermal plants require the use of large amounts of land, causing disruptions in natural ecosystems and pre-empting other uses.

Ocean thermal energy conversion (OTEC) is yet another use of solar power that utilizes techniques similar to those in geothermal energy extraction. It is estimated that the 60 million square miles of ocean ten degrees north and south of the equator absorb solar energy equivalent to that released in 170 billion barrels of oil were burned every day.[108] The temperature of the oceans varies with depth, with the warmer water settling on the top, and becoming cooler as depth increases. Warm water is drawn from the top layers and used to vaporize some liquid with very low boiling point. This vapor is used to turn a turbine and create electricity. The vapor is then cooled by the lower, colder ocean layers and returned to the boiler. It is a closed system with minimal environmental impact. OTEC is a very attractive solar resource because it does not suffer from the problems of its cousins. Because the operation is based offshore, land use is not an issue. However, the cost of this type of solar power collector is very high; about three times that of power generated from oil. As an ocean-based facility issues also exist concerning the long-term security of the site, considering the possibility of poor weather.[109]

Wind Power

Among all the renewable energy sources, none has grown as rapidly into an important industry as wind power. Since 1981, California has been the site for a boom in wind power as over a dozen companies began "farming" the wind on a massive scale.[110] Other small wind farms are catching on in other parts of the United States. Vermont, Hawaii, Oregon, Massachusetts, New York, and Montana boast small wind farm operations.

Internationally, India has one of the most ambitious wind energy programs in the world. Denmark is on the cutting edge of wind power as well. Currently 12 percent of its electricity comes from the wind, the most per capita in the world. The Danes are even building giant windmills offshore. The primary Danish manufacturer of windmills is Vesta, with annual sales of $700 million. Even farmers and communities are banding together to purchase their own windmills. At $700,000 each they are not cheap, but the towers with 160-foot blades generate enough power for about 2,000 people, and costs are typically recouped in 10 years, though the windmills have a useful lifespan of about 20 years.[111]

The total amount of energy in the wind has been estimated to be extremely large, ranging globally from 250 million to 2,500 million megawatts of average continuous power.[112] Even if only 1 percent of that energy was harnessed, the world could shut down all nuclear and coal-fired power plants. However, there are serious obstacles to utilizing the wind. The first is the lack of an economical means to store electricity from wind generation. Wind power also requires backup from a utility company when the wind dies down.

A second obstacle is finding suitable sites. Many feasible sites are already in use and wind turbines are precluded. Turbines in the heavily populated Northeast, along coastlines and visible mountain ranges, would cause visual pollution. Excessive noise and radio and TV interference are also problems with large turbines. In some areas, turbines would interfere with the flight pattern of migratory birds, and sometimes causes death by impact with the windmills.

The cost of generating power from the wind has been brought into line with other traditional generating technologies in many markets. Costs are likely to be reduced further as Japanese firms begin to mass-produce turbines.

Biomass

Biomass, the product of photosynthesis, is plant matter that acts as a versatile fuel capable of providing high quality gaseous, liquid, and solid fuels as well as electricity. Forestry and wood products, crop residues, animal wastes, and energy crops are the most important sources of biomass-generated energy.

When assessing biomass systems, it is important to distinguish between those that convert waste products into energy, thereby increasing the efficiency of economic systems, and the type of biomass energy that requires the cultivation of special crops. The latter requires all the cost and effort involved in agriculture and/or silviculture.

Wood is by far the most widely used biomass energy source.[113] Over half the wood cut each year is burned to produce energy throughout the world.[114] Industrial uses of fuelwood are spread throughout the United States.[115] Each year the state of Virginia produces enough sawdust, logging residue, and unsalable low-quality trees to replace 42 percent of the oil and gas consumed in its industrial and commercial sectors in that state. Little of this potential has been exploited. However, as oil prices move upward, entrepreneurs are likely to take advantage of the opportunity.[116]

Crop residues can be a valuable source of energy when they are not being used for alternative purposes.[117] There are more than 70 developing countries that grow sugarcane whose residue (bagasse) can be used for power generation. Other crop residues that are and can be used extensively are rice hulls, coconut shells, cotton stalks and ginning waste, peanut and other nut hulls, fruit pits, coffee and seed hulls, and various kinds of straw and fiber. Alternative uses for these materials should be taken into account when assessing their relevance as energy sources. These materials are also useful for returning vitality to depleted soils. Robbing the land of life-giving nutrients is destructive; producing energy from a product that would be otherwise wasted is prudent and farsighted.

Some plants are grown specifically to produce energy. Fast-growing eucalyptus trees are being grown and harvested for this purpose in some parts of the world. The potential for fast-growing fuel plantations varies greatly among different countries. Use of marginal lands for this purpose makes the most sense.

The conversion of corn to ethanol is a beneficial use of biomass surpluses. Corn surpluses could replace 7 percent of the country's gasoline consumption.[118] More than 7 percent of the gasoline sold in the United States in 1987 was actually gasohol, a 1 to 9 blend of gasoline and ethanol.[119]

According to the DOE, by 1993 gasohol remained at approximately 8 percent of the nation's automobile fuel supply. Critics of ethanol, including the EPA, point to its increase in aldehyde emissions and ozone pollution without a significant decrease in imports. In addition, it takes more energy to produce ethanol from grain than the combustion of ethanol generates. It costs about $1.05 to produce the corn that would become one gallon of ethanol; this does not include the actual conversion costs.[120] Ethanol is required in some parts of the country during winter months. Critics attribute this law to a coalition of Archer Daniels Midland (producer of 70 percent of domestic ethanol); Ralph Nader's Citizen Action; the Sierra Club; Natural Resources Defense Council; and help from then corn-state senator Bob Dole.[121]

EPA's decision to endorse methyl tertiary butyl ether (MTBE) as the fuel additive of choice (rather than ethanol) was actually overturned by President Bush in October 1992.[122] Of particular concern to the Republican Party was the state of Illinois, a corn state of crucial importance to Republican presidential hopefuls.[123] The Clinton campaign criticized the action, and, when elected in 1996, President Clinton froze it and other last-minute orders from Bush.[124]

Brazil is proving that a biomass ethanol program can replace significant amounts of imported oil. In Brazil, sugarcane grown exclusively for fuel was converted into 10.5 billion liters of ethanol in 1986, providing about half of the nation's automotive fuel. The ethanol program in Brazil created about 475,000 full-time jobs in agriculture and industry and another 100,000 indirect jobs in commerce, services, and government. Cogeneration produced by the burning of bagasse powers mechanical cane crushers, produces electricity for on-site needs, and steam for alcohol distillation.

The Brazilian fuel program is not without problems, however. Runaway inflation and a large debt load have caused the Brazilian government to scale back its heavily subsidized fuel ethanol program, known as Proacool. The subsidies to the politically powerful sugar growers have allowed efficient producers to make huge profits and kept inefficient producers in business. Brazil's Institute of Technology recommends that subsidies be based on some minimum level of efficiency.[125] Furthermore, severe shortages of ethanol occurred in 1990 because of drought and higher prices on the world sugar market. Instead of being a gross exporter of ethanol, Brazil was forced to buy ethanol from the United States to alleviate this critical shortage.[126]

Due to protests against the resultant pollution in 1991, the Brazilian government decided to return to original mixtures of 22 percent alcohol and 78 percent gasoline rather than maintain the 12 percent alcohol levels of 1990. Brazil will need to import alcohol for the increased mixture levels. (Another problem facing Brazil is the bootlegging by sugarcane distillers of alcohol directly to the service stations, bypassing state control and taxes.)[127]

Even much less developed nations can reliably use this type of energy, as it can be cheap and clean. For example, in the Ho Village of Vietnam, energy for the kitchen has been supplied by extremely dirty coal patties. These villagers have been taught a low-tech solution to their power (and health) problem. They simply shovel their animal and other feces into a covered well near their homes, where it flows into a plastic bag to ferment. The result is methane, or natural gas that can easily be channeled into the home for cooking and heating. The minor capital investments are recovered in only two years.[128]

In any case, if biomass fuel stocks are managed properly, they are a reliable and sustainable energy resource that can replace significant amounts of fossil fuels and assist in reducing pollutant or greenhouse gas buildup in the atmosphere.

CONSERVATION AND ENERGY EFFICIENCY: SOME SUGGESTIONS FOR THE FUTURE

There are three energy strategies that need to be implemented in order to meet the impending shortfall of fossil fuels: subsidies to nonrenewable energy industries need to be removed, barriers to conservation need to be removed, and the price of energy should reflect its cost to society.[129]

First, institutional barriers prevent the rapid application of conservation and energy efficient technologies. These barriers favor technologies that are centralized, complex, glamorous, and backed by powerful constituencies. Solutions like conservation, which are mundane, simple, and lead to a decentralized power structure, are subjected to a far more rigorous set of economic tests and are left out of lavish subsidy giveaways to fend for themselves.

Market forces have inevitably given conservation some attraction, however. The oil crises of 1973 and 1979 forced the recognition of the rationality behind decreasing our dependence on all fuel sources simply by needing and using less energy. Conservation tends to create images of deprivation as people imagine having to turn down heaters in winter, turn off air conditioners in summer, and drive less. However, energy efficiency can mean continuing better or equal service with improved techniques and technologies. For instance, it can mean encouraging the establishment of mass transit facilities and building cars with maximum fuel efficiency.

There have been tremendous improvements in energy efficiency in the United States since the early 1970s. These have come about through subtle shifts in the economy, as new technologies are implemented—not by Americans driving tiny fuel-efficient cars or freezing in the winter.[130]

Even with these improvements, the United States has only just begun to reap the benefits of energy efficiency.[131] Efficiency has become a key ingredient in economic success. As a 1987 report of the International Energy Agency stated, "Investment in energy conservation at the margin provides a better return than investment in energy supply."[132] Though the United States is saving $150 billion to $200 billion worth of energy compared to 1973 efficiency levels, there are still $300 billion worth of energy wasted annually.[133] Most energy experts agree that conservation can, and should, play a major role in our national energy future. Fortunately, many such measures have been enacted into law under CNEP. Types of conservation and obstacles to conservation are discussed next.

Conservation in Homes and Buildings

In 1985 the buildings in the industrial countries of the world used the equivalent of 16.7 million barrels of oil per day, almost equal to the production of OPEC for the entire year.[134] The economic and environmental consequences of this level of energy consumption are staggering. This is not surprising considering buildings use about two-thirds of all U.S. electricity.[135] The ever-growing number of buildings, however, has used an almost constant amount of energy since the early 1970s.[136] Energy efficiency has filled the gap.[137]

Retrofitting, which means renovating to save energy, has proven to be an excellent investment.[138] In over 40,000 retrofits that have been monitored by U.S. utilities since the mid-1970s, energy use declined by 25 percent and homeowners received a 23 percent return on their investment annually.[139]

Energy efficiency is cheapest when built in from the start and so the efficiency potential in new buildings far exceeds those that must be retrofitted.[140] The key to these savings is superinsulation. This means doubling the normal insulation and building an airtight liner into the walls. These houses are so airtight that special ventilation systems must be installed to remove indoor pollutants.[141]

The most efficient new buildings are "smart buildings," which utilize computers to monitor indoor and outdoor temperatures, sunlight, and the location of people within the building. The system sends heat, light, and cooled air only where they are needed.[142]

Windows are also critical to energy savings in buildings. As much energy leaks through American windows every year as flows through the Alaskan pipeline.[143] There are several technologies available for doubling the insulating potential of windows that insulate as well as ordinary walls.

Windows are typically the weakest link in buildings in terms of energy efficiency. In colder climates, 10 to 25 percent of heat escapes through windows, amounting to $50 to $125 literally out the window each year for a typical home. Simple tasks such as caulking windows shut in the winter or lining them with plastic can greatly increase energy efficiency. Double-pane windows are much more efficient, and those filled with argon or krypton can increase efficiency 20 percent more. Though these are more expensive initially, they eventually recover their costs in energy savings.[144]

Many other types of energy-saving measures could greatly decrease U.S. energy consumption. For example, planting trees is an effective, inexpensive way to cool buildings in hot weather. Furnaces, air conditioners, appliances, and lights are also candidates for energy savings.[145] New condensing furnaces cut fuel use by 28 percent while reducing air pollution.[146] Integrating heating and cooling equipment can increase energy savings dramatically. Refrigerators and air conditioners produce as much heat as cold air. Directing this heat to hot water tanks saves energy. Integrating furnaces and water heaters also produces dramatic savings.[147]

Lighting, which accounts for 25 percent of U.S. electricity use, offers some of the most economical and easy to achieve energy savings now available; 20 percent of that energy is wasted running air conditioners to counteract the light's waste heat![148] Arthur Rosenfeld of Lawrence Livermore Laboratory estimates that 40 large power plants could be retired by installing the latest cost-effective lighting technologies.[149] Not only can more efficient light bulbs and such be used, but also simple, low-tech ideas like only lighting the area one needs lighted can help tremendously. If we do not need to cool the entire house to 40 degrees Fahrenheit to keep the milk cold, we do not have the light the whole house to read.

Moreover, the foregoing examples provide ample evidence that energy efficiency in the home or office is feasible and economical. Why, one might ask, are homeowners and others not adopting conservation measures in greater numbers? In part the answer has to do with the short-term economic incentives of energy conservation. Individuals, like government, often are attracted to options that have the lowest short-term costs—ignoring possible long-term savings. Consequently, government intervention, in terms of economic incentives or otherwise, may be necessary if we are to enjoy the full benefits of conservation. Since building designs shape energy policy for most of a century, strict efficiency standards could be made mandatory to ensure that maximum efficiency is built in from the ground up.

An alternative to regulating building efficiency codes would be to reward energy-wise buildings with cash bonuses from the utilities while fining energy gluttons. Additionally, the local authorities that set the building codes can also set targets for energy (and water) efficiency. Those that miss the per capita energy goals are fined, and those that exceed efficiency standards are subsidized with the money from fines. Going back one step further in the building process, architects could be rewarded for designing a building that exceeds previously agreed upon energy efficiency goals. Currently, architects and contractors are more likely to be rewarded for creating buildings that are cheaper to build than are energy efficient.[150] Moreover, consumer resistance to buying the most energy-efficient appliances and lights can be overcome somewhat through education and socialization and special energy-saving financing. Also, efficiency standards, such as those developed for refrigerators, can be developed and/or strengthened. The costs of retrofitting existing buildings might also be forwarded by providing special tax advantages. The market-oriented energy approach of both the Bush and Reagan administrations shunned government intervention to facilitate conservation. However, the mounting economic and environmental consequences of continued dependence on fossil fuels suggest further government intervention may be necessary.

Conservation in Transportation

Transportation is the largest single drain on world oil reserves. The United States burns 65 percent of its oil for transportation, especially for the private automobile.[151] The desire to own cars and trucks was not lessened by the oil crises of the 1970s. Buses, trains, and other mass transit systems, which require only 25 percent as much fuel to move each passenger the same distance, are avoided by many. People in American cities use more than twice as much gasoline as people in European cities and 10 times as much gasoline as people in Asian cities where walking is a popular way to get around.[152]

Part of the problem in convincing people to accept mass transit is that they often do not realize the true costs of private automobile use. There are both external costs that drivers do not pay (as discussed in the air pollution chapter) and also hidden subsidies that make private automobile ownership more attractive than it would otherwise be. The hidden costs of automobile ownership include road building and maintenance, traffic congestion, air pollution and environmental degradation, noise, and hazards to pedestrians. Elimination of the hidden subsidies of car ownership combined with the utilization of mandatory fuel efficiency standards that maximize fuel economy would be top priorities if we wanted to stem the flow of oil into transportation and out the tailpipe.[153] In Vancouver, public buses are run off fuel cells, which create energy, unlike batteries that simply store it. Cars for personal use are possible today that also run off fuel cells, and electric cars are currently available that are more efficient than their internal combustion engine peers; electric cars can even put energy back into their batteries when braking, as opposed to losing it in today's automatic transmission automobile.[154] Some even see full-size American cars getting 80 to 200 miles per gallon over the next few decades, without compromising, safety, comfort, or cost.[155] The oil industry will not take this lightly, however, and would likely rally its lobbyists against such efforts.

Strict sets of new fuel standards and taxes to boost fuel efficiency would go a long way toward reducing air pollution and dependence on foreign oil. President Clinton's BTU tax on gasoline was a first step in raising taxes in fuel, but it is still not designed to impact consumption. Fuel standards, even on a voluntary basis, are also a small step toward progress.

Conservation in Industry

Industrial energy use in the United States was 17 percent lower in 1986 than in 1973, despite a 17 percent increase in productivity. About 45 percent of this energy savings is attributable to a shift in the economy toward more service industries and fewer energy-intensive products.[156] For example, production of steel and cement has fallen while electronics industries have proliferated. Some energy-intensive raw materials are now imported from newly industrializing countries. The other 55 percent of the improvement is attributable to the application of energy efficiency technologies and processes.[157] In many industries, the economic benefits of energy efficiency have been recognized and pursued. From 1986 to 1992, however, industrial energy consumption was estimated at just 6.4 percent less than 1973 levels—indicating that industrial conservation, perhaps due to low energy prices in the late 1980s and early 1900s, is tapering off.[158]

Most energy efficiency improvements in the United States have been in petroleum refining, chemicals, cement, paper, glass, and clay—energy-intensive industries. Less intensive industries now use a growing share of total industrial energy.[159]

One of the greatest opportunities for improving industrial energy efficiency is cogeneration, the combined production of heat and electricity. The waste heat of electricity generation is made available for industrial processes by installing a small boiler and electric generator within a plant. Similarly, breweries in Copenhagen use the heat generated from their vats to energize the building itself, as opposed to just venting it outside.[160]

Due to the Public Utilities Regulatory Policy Act of 1978, which allowed industry to sell power to utilities at fair market value, industrial cogeneration has grown explosively in the United States.[161] The cogeneration industry now includes 20 kilowatt units in fast-food restaurants and apartment complexes as well as 300,000 kilowatt units in petrochemical plants. Studies show that by using cogeneration many plants can raise their total energy efficiency from 50 percent to 70 percent. As previously discussed, electricity production is projected to grow under the CNEPA expansion to cogeneration plants without the requirement for private ownership.

Industry as a whole is on the path to substantially decreasing energy use. Most industrial countries are unlikely to use as much energy in the year 2000 as they did a quarter of a century earlier.[162] However, programs to improve energy efficiency in industrializing less developed countries are essential to prevent the repetition of the wasteful practices of the more developed world. This means if the global North expects to make any progress in terms of energy efficiency and reduction of greenhouse gases, it will need to pay for the global South, or LDCs, to implement these more expensive (but cleaner) technologies. Many less developed countries suffer from subsidized energy prices as it is, as well as limited access to energy-efficient technologies and poor management. Policy changes and the transfer of relevant technologies are urgently needed. Enhanced energy efficiency is essential for economic success in a competitive world. Those countries that invest the most funds and education in energy efficiency now, and have the most developed system of renewable energy resources in the future, will be the world's economic leaders when we reach the bottom of the oil barrel.

Obstacles to Conservation

Instituting rational energy prices that reflect negative externalities and the cost of replacement of traditional energy sources with nonrenewable resources is necessary to discourage waste and create the conditions necessary for increased energy efficiency.

The chief obstacle to achieving sensible price controls and promoting energy efficiency is the instability of the price of oil. From 1973 until 1980, the price of oil increased sevenfold. Then real oil prices fell 75 percent between 1981 and 1986, hitting a low of about $12 a barrel before increasing again to $18 dollars a barrel in 1987.[163] The higher oil prices of the 1970s encouraged production and gains in energy efficiency. From the early 1980s to 1990, and again after the Gulf War, the world oil market was dominated by overproduction, creating the oil glut and falling prices. Low prices and fluctuating markets both work against efficiency, since policy makers become hesitant to undertake programs during conditions of energy uncertainty.

Although unpopular with voters, taxes are an effective way to encourage conservation and prevent cheap imported oil from undermining efficiency gains. An environmental tax such as a carbon tax on fossil fuels would bring the cost of energy closer to its real cost and reflect some of the hazards that burning those fuels represent. In Europe and Japan, fuel taxes are commonly used to raise revenues and discourage excessive driving. However, in the United States attempts to raise gasoline taxes have been defeated by the oil industry, consumer groups, and politicians reflecting constituent concerns.[164]

CONCLUSION

Before the invention of the steam engine and the discovery of coal, humankind had relied on energy resources that were recycled many times during a human lifetime. Humankind is now dependent on fossil fuel resources that have renewal times thousands to millions of times longer than the human life span. The discovery of fossil fuels and their utilization, compounded with breakthroughs in medical technology, have caused an unprecedented growth in population, furthering the strain on nonrenewable resources and hastening their ultimate depletion. Cultural and institutional inertia and obsolete myths about the limitlessness of finite resources have created an illusion of security and make the inevitable day of reckoning all the more certain and traumatic.

The carrying capacity of an environment is only sustainable if a balance is achieved between renewable resources and the population that is dependent on them. Humankind could overshoot the earth's carrying capacity. Our reliance on fossil fuels has allowed us to develop an energy-intensive society. Abundant and inexpensive energy has permitted intensified agriculture, heavily populated metropolitan development, and unsurpassed material abundance. When fossil fuels run out, our energy needs will have to be met through renewable energy sources. The transition from finite to renewable energy may be slow and gradual, with substitutions made in a manner that does not disrupt our lifestyles, or the transition may be abrupt—causing social unrest and disruption. Although the former is the desired course, many alternative sources of energy require, as we have seen, market subsidies in order to ensure their development. Business does not seem to be interested in investments with long-term payoff periods.

Policy makers, ever wary of increasing taxes, would rather put off tough decisions today and let tomorrow take care of itself. The general public is comfortable. Yet without development of alternative sources of energy, the transition to a steady state energy economy promises to be rough.

Whatever naysayers in oil or other industries may argue, energy transitions are a natural economic and social phenomenon. They end up in cleaner forms and in subsequent economic booms. The transition from biomass and wood to coal took about 70 years and led to great societal and industrial improvements. The exact same thing happened from coal to oil and natural gas. So it will likely go for solar and other renewable energy sources. However, never before have we been so aware of or close to our resource and environmental limits, so the sooner we can arrive at this sustainable future, the better.

SUMMARY

In this chapter we summarized the history of energy use and development in the nation and world. We also framed the energy situation in terms of a hard or soft path. The current mix of energy sources, renewable and nonrenewable, and the environmental problems associated with each were also discussed. Finally, we examined the promises of and obstacles to conservation. Conservation is the cleanest, least expensive, and most technologically feasible future energy alternative. Yet we are slow to seriously conserve. This is one of the paradoxes of environmental policy.

As we have seen, energy is not cheap. The by-products of energy production pose significant costs, or *negative* externalities, on society. We have paid these costs as part of the price for many modern technological developments that today we take for granted. Technological developments, such as new synthetic chemicals, have also generated significant environmental externalities in the form of toxic and hazardous wastes. That is the subject of the next chapter.

NOTES

1. David E. Fisher, *Fire and Ice: The Greenhouse Effect, Ozone Depletion, and Nuclear Winter* (New York: Harper & Row, 1990), p. 186.

2. Lovins, Amory and Lotspeich, Chris. Rocky Mountain Institute (RMI). "Energy Surprises for the 21st Century". Originally published in the *Journal of International Affairs*, Fall 1999, 53, no. 1. Available at *http://www.rmi.org/images/other/E-EnergySurprises.pdf*.

3. Lovins, Amory. "The Negawatt Revolution: Solving the CO2 Problem." Keynote Address at the Green Energy Conference, Montreal, 1989. Available at the Canadian Coalition for Nuclear Responsibility Website *http://www.ccnr.org/amory.html*.

4. Marvin V. Melosi, *Coping with Abundance: Energy and Environment in Industrial America 1820–1980* (New York: Newberry Awards Records, 1985), pp. 29–30.

5. By the 1920s more than 658 million tons of coal had been mined. At that time, coal represented more than 75 percent of the total energy consumption in the United States and exports exceeded 929,000 tons a year. Ibid., p. 33.

6. Electricity from hydropower peaked in 1946 while providing 35.1 percent of total generating capacity. Hydropower declined to 16.2 percent of total generating capacity by 1970. In 1984 hydroelectric supplied 14 percent of electricity and 5 percent of total energy consumption—a little more than nuclear power at that time. The contribution of hydropower to overall power consumption in the United States is predicted to remain relatively flat—at around 14 percent. High construction costs and a lack of suitable large rivers for siting the facilities are the primary limiting factors in the growth of hydroelectricity. G. Tyler Miller, Jr., *Living in the Environment: An Introduction to Environmental Science* (5th ed.) (Belmont, CA: Wadsworth, 1988), p. 403.

7. In 1890 total U.S. oil production for all years was 1 billion barrels. By 1929 U.S. production was 1 billion barrels annually.

8. Melosi, *Coping with Abundance: Energy and Environment in Industrial America*, p. 39.

9. Ibid., p. 97. During the war, 133 million barrels of oil were shipped to the Allies in Europe.

10. Ibid., p. 50. During the war the importance of oil as a military fuel gave oil producers leverage when dealing with elected officials. At the request of the industry in 1913, Congress granted the oil industry tax relief by approving an oil depletion allowance to increase production. This allowed producers to deduct 5 percent of the gross value of their oil and gas production against taxes. In 1916 the depletion allowance was changed so the 5 percent deduction could not exceed the annual costs of the discovery of oil. Then legislation was passed by Congress in 1918 that allowed producers "reasonable" deductions based on discovery costs or the fair market value of their properties. Since the market value of mineral properties greatly exceeded discovery costs, the oil industry became blessed with a major tax advantage that would last for decades. And this would not be the last time the oil industry would use the crisis of war to its economic advantage.

11. Ibid., p. 103.

12. The Great Depression beginning at the end of the 1920s could not have come at a worse time for the oil industry. Huge reserves in the East Texas fields were discovered in 1930 just as demand plummeted. The fact that the field was developed by small independents made it resistant to regulation. As production reached ridiculous heights, the Texas Railroad Commission (TRC) issued a prorationing order that attempted to limit production to expected demand. The Texas state legislature passed the Market Demand Act of 1932, which allowed the TRC to issue prorationing orders and thereby bring some stability to the industry. This kind of state initiative in Texas and later in Oklahoma preceded extensive involvement by the federal government in production controls. Oil had become essential to the economic well-being of the nation, and Congress limited its activity to antitrust legislation aimed at electrical utilities only. In a time of inexpensive energy, consumer protest was unknown and the oil industry emerged from the Depression on a firm financial footing.

13. Wasteful production and transportation practices were also causing pollution of rivers and coastal waters. Public attention led to congressional investigations into oil pollution problems and in 1924 Congress passed the Oil Pollution Act. Although inadequate enforcement procedures failed to halt the pollution caused from excess oil, this was the first attempt to deal with oil pollution at the federal level. It is interesting that this first federal effort at addressing oil pollution grew out of public response to a perceived crisis and resulted in congressional action and no enforcement. Thus federal policymakers were able to satisfy their constituents without alienating an important and influential economic interest group.

14. During the 1920s the coal industry had suffered from overproduction and low prices and had begun to limit production. Although coal was not the essential fuel for the war effort, it remained an important domestic fuel source and was needed for home heating, steel production, railroads, and electricity generation. Because of the war, the coal industry expanded and reached an all-time high output of 620 million net tons in 1944.

15. The U.S. Army Air Force alone consumed 14 times more gasoline during operations on the Western Front than were shipped to Europe between 1914 and 1918. Eight percent of the 7 billion barrels of crude oil used by the Allies between December 1941 and August 1945 was produced in the United States; hence long supply lines had to be maintained. By May 1942, 55 oil tankers that were servicing the eastern seaboard were sunk by German submarines. Ibid., p. 181.

16. The first pipeline dubbed "The Big Inch" carried crude 1,476 miles from the Southwest to Phoenix Junction, Pennsylvania. The second one was named "The Little Big Inch" and carried refined petroleum products 1,714 miles from Beaumont, Texas, to Linden, New York. Ibid., p. 184.

17. The conflict between domestic and imported oil flared up again after the Korean War with the ailing coal industry siding with the small domestic producers in demanding import quotas to stimulate sales of domestic energy. In the summer of 1956, imported oil was selling at $1.95 a barrel compared to domestic oil, which was selling for $2.75 a barrel. The vitality of the domestic market was at stake, and pressure was put on the Eisenhower administration to reverse its policy of no intervention in the oil market. Influenced by the national security threat represented by the Suez crisis and fearing that Congress would make the initial move in a way unfavorable to the administration, Eisenhower instituted mandatory controls in 1959.

   The Mandatory Oil Import Program (MOIP) was no panacea. Although it protected the domestic oil industry from foreign competition, it also created an artificial environment in which oil prices did not respond to international realities. Prices rose and consumers footed the bill. Ultimately, the MOIP had an impact on the ability of the United States to respond to the oil crisis of the 1970s.

18. A serious oil shortage occurred from 1945 to 1947 immediately after World War II. Until 1947 the United States had exported more than it imported. The year 1947 marked the transition of the United States as a net exporter to a net importer of oil. This created conflicts between domestic producers and the American multinationals, who were bringing in cheap foreign oil. Except during the Korean War, domestic oil supplies exceeded demand by a substantial margin. Small domestic producers called for quotas while the major companies, large independents, and the Truman administration supported voluntary controls. The preservation of the domestic oil industry was at cross-purposes with the administration's support of the multinationals and its reluctance to damage relations with Canada and Latin America by restricting imports. The Korean War and a booming domestic economy in the 1950s temporarily eased the tension as consumption rose to new levels. Consumption of oil increased by 80 percent between 1945 and 1959 and domestic production grew from 1.7 million barrels in 1945 to 2.6 million barrels in 1959. Ibid., p. 254.

19. The production of the Model T increased from 32,000 in 1910 to almost 735,000 in 1916. By 1921 the Ford Motor Company had reached the 1 million mark and by 1924 had produced 13 million cars. Ibid., p. 106.

20. In 1900 there had been only 4,200 cars in existence in the United States. By 1929 there were 5.6 million cars and trucks on the road. This was 1 car for every 5 Americans compared with 1 for every 43 British citizens, 1 for every 325 Italians, and 1 for every 7,000 Russians. Ibid., p. 108.

21. The TVA not only produces hydroelectric power but is also involved in flood control, fertilizer production, soil conservation, reforestation, inland waterway construction, and the promotion of regional growth. Ibid., p. 130. In 1936 Congress passed the Rural Electrification Act to establish nonprofit electrical cooperatives in those areas private utilities found uneconomical to service. The REA was a great success. In 1930 only 1 farm in 10 had electricity. By 1941 4 out of 10 had electricity and by 1950 9 out of 10 were receiving electrical power. Ibid., p. 136.

22. Much was wasted through flaring or burning it off.

23. Between 1945 and 1955 the number of households burning natural gas rose from 11 million to more than 21 million. Residential consumption increased from 607 billion to more than 2,000 billion cubic feet per year. Natural gas was clean burning and generated valuable consumer products such as solvents, films, plastics, adhesives, synthetic rubber, fiberglass, insecticides, gasoline additives, paints and drugs and was useful in the production of synthetic fibers such as nylon, orlon, and dacron. Ibid.

24. In 1971 90 percent of new gas production was going into the intrastate market representing 40 percent of total consumption.

25. World reserves of natural gas are estimated to last until 2033 at 1984 usage rates and to 2018 if usage increases by 2 percent per year. Miller, *Living in the Environment: An Introduction to Environmental Science*, (5th ed.) p. 349.

26. Melosi, *Coping with Abundance: Energy and Environment in Industrial America*, p. 249.

27. By December of 1973, price per barrel rose 130 percent to $11.65. By 1974 Arab oil exported to the United States was $12.25 a barrel compared to $3.65 a year before. Ibid., pp. 280–281.
28. William R. Catton, Jr., *Overshoot* (Chicago: University of Illinois Press, 1982).
29. Miller, *Living in the Environment*, p. 16.
30. Melosi, *Coping with Abundance: Energy and Environment in Industrial America*, p. 292.
31. The groundwork was being laid for a future energy crisis. The high oil prices of the early 1980s had encouraged depletion of some of the world's most limited oil reserves all outside of the Middle East. The high price of oil made it economical to drill for oil in dozens of non-OPEC locations, many of which will soon reach a point of diminishing returns.
32. Oil production in North America, Europe, and the Soviet Union is likely to begin falling steeply during the next decade. Fifty-six percent of proven oil reserves are still found in the Middle East. Sometime in the 1990s the center of world production should again move to the Middle East. Christopher Flavin, "World Oil: Coping with the Dangers of Success," *Worldwatch Paper* 66 (July 1985).
33. Louis Bley, "OPEC's Best Friend," *Euromoney* (June 1990), p. E49; and Peter Morton, "OPEC will Soon Produce Half of World's Oil, CERI Predicts," *The Oil Daily*, October 7, 1992, p. 3. Also Miller 1994, 16.
34. Senate Committee on Energy and Natural Resources, Senator Frank Murkowski, Chair. March 28, 2000. "Administration Fails to Meet Goal at OPEC Meeting". Available at *http://energy.senate. gov/press/releases/opec_response.htm*.
35. On August 6, 1945, the Enola Gay dropped an atomic bomb named "Little Boy" on the city of Hiroshima. A blinding flash of white light was followed by searing heat as a huge fireball with temperatures of several million degrees Centigrade rose in the sky. Thousands of people were instantly vaporized as 13 square miles of the city were flattened or set aflame. Over 140,000 people were killed or doomed to a slow death of radiation sickness or wounds. Of the 76,000 buildings in Hiroshima, 48,000 were totally destroyed and 22,000 had been damaged. Two days later, on August 8, the hellish debacle was repeated as a plutonium bomb named "Fat Man" was dropped on Nagasaki. Peter R. Beckman, Larry Campbell, Paul W. Crumlish, Michael N. Dobkowski, and Steven P. Lee, *The Nuclear Predicament* (Englewood Cliffs, NJ: Prentice Hall, 1989).
36. Price-Anderson Amendments Act of 1988 passed August 20, 1988 (P.L. 100-408) and extended coverage of the act to August 1, 1990. There are 114 reactors licensed to operate, with several operating reactors excluded, since the act only applies to reactors over 100 megawatts. Further, nine plants are in "deferred completion," with permits granted. An example is the Washington Public Power System where Units 4 and 5 were dropped with no construction being done after receiving licensing approval.
37. The Nuclear Regulatory Commission can, if loss is catastrophic according to certain criteria, assess a lesser amount than $10 million.
38. By the end of 1967, 75 nuclear power plants had been ordered. By the end of 1969, 97 nuclear plants were in operation, under construction, or under contract. However, by September 1968, only 14 plants were in operation. Melosi, *Coping with Abundance: Energy and Environment in Industrial America*, pp. 233, 239.
39. During the 1970s the conflict over nuclear power pitted expert against expert, creating a confusing amount of conflicting data and statistics about the safety of nuclear power generation. The battles were fought in the courts and in the streets as thousands joined in antinuclear demonstrations. In 12 states initiatives were introduced to block the expansion of nuclear power. Due in large part, no doubt, to the well-financed campaigns of the pronuclear forces, all but one failed. The successful initiative was passed in California, the voters there placing a moratorium on new nuclear plants until a solution was found for the nuclear waste problem.
40. Between 1971 and 1978 costs rose an additional 142 percent. Christopher Flavin, "Ten Years of Fallout," *World Watch Institute* (March/April 1989).
41. Although there had been several serious nuclear accidents before Three Mile Island (TMI) and many mechanical mishaps at nuclear facilities, TMI came close to a complete core meltdown with potentially catastrophic consequences. In 1957 the AEC had conducted a study on the worse possible consequences of a nuclear disaster. The report concluded that a meltdown of a light water reactor of 500 megawatt size located 30 miles from a major city would cause the immediate death of 3,400 people, injure 45,000, and cause $7 billion in property damage. A revised study by the AEC later concluded that it would be more accurate to predict that an accident of this magnitude would cause 45,000 fatalities and contaminate an area the size of the state of Pennsylvania. This is what

could have happened at TMI. Paul R. Ehrlich, Anne H. Ehrlich, and John P. Holdren *Ecoscience: Population, Resources, Environment* (San Francisco: Freeman, 1977).

After several months of study a presidential commission appointed to study the TMI accident concluded that the plant could be made operational again at a cost of $466 million. Ten years later and after an expenditure of almost $1 billion the project is still not finished. Plans to reconstruct the TMI plant were abandoned. Tons of radioactive debris have been sent by rail to a "temporary" federal dump in Idaho. The lower reaches of the reactor vessel are still so highly radioactive that special remote control tools must be used to protect workers, and the reactor's owners are trying to get permission to seal the radioactive debris inside for decades. Flavin, "Ten Years of Fallout."

42. Christopher Flavin, "The Case Against Reviving Nuclear Power," *World Watch Institute* (July/August 1988).
43. Demand tracks price. Before the oil crisis of 1973, consumption had been rising by 7 percent per year. When prices rose dramatically, demand slid to less than half the annual rate. Peter S. Nivola, *The Politics of Energy Conservation* (Washington, DC: The Brookings Institute, 1986).
44. Steve Wilhelm, "A Niche That Keeps Going: Cogeneration," *Puget Sound Business Journal*, 12 (9) (July 15, 1991), p. 3.
45. David W. Tice, "Risky Venture: A Utility's Cogeneration Project Still Has Woes Aplenty," *Barron's*, 71 (42) (October 21, 1991), p. 28.
46. This discussion is based on Holly Idelson, "National Energy Strategy Provisions," *Congressional Quarterly Weekly Report*, 50 (47) (November 28, 1992), pp. 3722–3731.
47. C. C. Sullivan, "Economy and Ecology: A Powerful Coalition," *Buildings*, 87 (5) (May 1993), p. 47.
48. Michael Zucchet, "Electricity Industry Restructuring: Renewable Resources in a Competitive Environment," *Congressional Digest* (August-September 1997), p. 202.
49. Pacific Gas & Electric. "A Concise Guide to California's Energy Crisis." Available at PG&E's Website at *http://www.pge.com/006_news/current_issues/energycrisis/index.shtml*.
50. Jonathan Weisman, "Nuclear Power's Fate on the Line in Utility Deregulation Debate," *Congressional Quarterly Weekly Report*, (Jan 11, 1997) p. 125.
51. 12th Annual Energy Efficiency Forum in Washington, DC, June 2001. Vice President Richard Cheney's speech and Q&A. Transcripts available at *http://www.eeforum.net/transcripts.html*.
52. Energy estimates are based, in part, on Chauncey Starr, Milton F. Searl, and Sy Alpet, "Energy Sources: A Realistic Outlook," *Science*, 256 (5059) (May 15, 1992), p. 982. Some have predicted greater increases in the use of electricity with its relatively low prices, which would mean an increased demand for coal to fuel the plants; such a course would also coincide with CNEPA's loosening of regulations on PURPA's cogeneration facilities. See Helmut A. Merklein, "The Case for Electric," *Industrial Investor*, 24 (13) (October 1990), pp. 504–505.
53. Some 10 trillion tons of coal—equal to more than 800 times the world's annual use of energy—are known to exist and may ultimately be recoverable. International Energy Agency, *World Energy Outlook* (Paris: Organization for Economic Cooperation and Development, 1982).
54. Miller, *Living in the Environment* (5th ed.) p. 292.
55. Between 1900 and 1985 underground mining in the United States killed more than 100,000 miners, permanently disabled another 1 million, and created over 250,000 cases of black lung disease, a severe form of emphysema caused by inhalation of coal dust. Surface mining of coal has devastated over 1 million acres of land in the United States causing erosion, acid runoff, and lowered water tables. Ibid., pp. 352–353. Tens of thousands of miles of streams have been polluted. Melosi, *Coping with Abundance: Energy and Environment in Industrial America*, p. 210.
56. Topper Sherwood, "Strip Search (Weak Enforcement of Surface Mining Control and Reclamation Act)," *Common Cause Magazine*, 15 (3) (May-June 1989), p. 9.
57. This is on land that may have originally sold for $200 to $300 an acre. See Anna Maria Gillis, "Bringing Back the Land," *BioScience*, 41 (2) (February 1991), p. 68.
58. Holly Idelson, "National Energy Strategy Provisions," pp. 3728–3730.
59. These chemicals can cause respiratory distress, destroy plants, rubber, textiles, and other materials. Residents of Southern California who vacation at Big Bear or Lake Arrowhead can see the dead pine trees by the side of the road. Ozone from Los Angeles smog has killed thousands of pine trees in the San Bernardino mountains. This is common throughout the United States. Lester R. Brown et al., *State of the World 1985* (New York: Norton, 1985).
60. Miller, *Living in the Environment* (5th ed.) p. 346.
61. Ibid., p. 268.

62. George J. Church, "The Big Spill," *Time* (April 10, 1989), p. 38.

63. Ibid., p. 39.

64. Note the similarities between the Valdez oil spill and the circumstances surrounding the passage and implementation of the Oil Pollution Act of 1924. It is interesting that in both cases the federal effort grew out of public response to a perceived crisis (waste and pollution from oil and an earlier major ocean oil spill, respectively) and resulted in congressional action with poor enforcement. Thus federal policy makers were able to satisfy their constituents without alienating an important and influential economic interest group.

65. Global-proven oil reserves increased rapidly after World War II rising from 76 billion barrels in 1950 to 664 billion barrels in 1973. Since the mid-1970s global-proven reserves have only increased by 5 percent even though high oil prices have encouraged exploration and extraction. Total estimates of world oil resources ranged from 1,600 to 2,400 billion barrels. Of this amount, 554 billion barrels have been consumed and 700 billion barrels of proven reserve have been discovered. It is estimated that approximately 350 to 1,150 billion barrels of oil remain to be discovered. At the rate of world oil consumption in the early 1990s, ultimate depletion of the world's oil reserves is between 50 and 88 years away. Christopher Flavin, "World Oil: Coping with the Dangers of Success," *Worldwatch Paper* 66 (July 1985), pp. 23, 25.

66. Ibid., p. 29.

67. Catton, *Overshoot*, p. 247.

68. G. Tyler Miller, *Living in the Environment* (8th ed.) (Belmont, CA: Wadsworth, 1994), p. 492

69. Ibid., p. 482.

70. "Worldwide Natural Gas Supply and Demand and the Outlook for Global LNG Trade." Article adopted from testimony from the Energy Information Administration Administrator to the Senate Energy and Natural Resources Committee on July 23, 1997. Available from the DOE at *http:// www.eia.doe.gov/pub/oil gas/natural gas/feature articles/1997/worldwide natural gas supply demand 2015/pdf/m08sr1.pdf.*

71. Miller, *Living in the Environment*, (5th ed.) pp. 348–349.

72. Ibid.

73. Telephone interview with DOE, October 25, 1993.

74. Hirokazu Hase, "Geothermal Programs Contributing to the Earth's Environment," *Japan 21st*, 38 (3) (March 1993), p. 43.

75. Miller, *Living in the Environment* (8th ed.) p. 472.

76. Karl Gawell, Dr. Marshall Reed and Dr. P. Michael Wright. Geothermal Energy Association. "Preliminary Report: Geothermal Energy, The Potential for Clean Power from the Earth." April 1999. Available at *http://www.geotherm.org/PotentialReport.htm.*

77. Ibid., p. 362. Almost all the homes, buildings, and food-producing greenhouses in Reykjavik, Iceland, a city with a population of 85,000, are heated by hot water drawn from deep hot water geothermal deposits. The hot salty brine pumped up from such deposits can be used to produce electricity in a binary-cycle system. The main problem is that the brine corrodes metal parts and clogs pipes.

78. Hirokazu Hase, "Geothermal Programs Contributing to the Earth's Environment," p. 43.

79. By 1987, it was producing 2 percent of California's electricity—enough to provide for a city the size of San Francisco at less than half the cost of a coal or nuclear power plant. Ibid., p. 362.

80. Congressional Research Service, "Renewable Energy Technologies," *Congressional Digest* (August-September 1997) p. 197.

81. Ibid., p. 364. The state of Hawaii has an aggressive plan to extract 500 megawatts of geothermal-generated electricity from hot brine on the island of Hawaii for export to the more populous islands of Maui and Oahu through an undersea cable. However, there has been well-organized protest against the project, since it would entail destroying a significant part of the only lowland rain forest in the United States, require extensive transmission lines through residential subdivisions, and be a potential source of air and groundwater pollution. Without adequate controls, there is moderate to high air pollution from hydrogen sulfide, ammonia, and radioactive materials as well as moderate to high water pollution from dissolved salts and runoff of various toxic elements such as boron and mercury.

82. "The Chernobyl Syndrome," *Newsweek* (May 12, 1986). Radiation levels in Poland were reported to be 500 times higher than normal.

83. Flavin, "Ten Years of Fallout."

84. Nuclear Information and Resource Service. 2001 Brochure "Can You Find Your State On This Map? Radioactive waste trains and trucks are headed your way...."

85. In 1997 the Flagstaff City Council made Flagstaff a "Nuclear Free Zone" in response to the announcements of plans to ship waste on the rail line that runs through the city.

86. In 1980 funding for research and development of renewable energy peaked in the United States at $900 million (in 1986 dollars), but since that time appropriations have been cut by 80 percent.

87. For example, energy tax credits that were available from 1978 to 1985 gave a strong financial incentive for the building of wind turbines, small hydropower facilities, geothermal projects, solar collectors, and photovoltaic industries. When the Reagan administration cut out these credits all at once instead of phasing them out gradually, the rug was pulled out from under many underfinanced renewable energy industries. Huge subsidies that are granted to the nuclear, oil, coal, and other conventional power industries should be removed. For example, in 1984 nuclear power supplied less than 5 percent of U.S. energy but received $15 billion in subsidies. Renewables, which produced 9.6 percent of total U.S. energy, received only $1.7 billion. "The Hidden Cost of Energy," *Sierra* (March/April 1986).

88. R&D monies are not the only means through which renewable technologies can be supported. The Public Utility Regulatory Policies Act (PURPA) of 1978 has had far-reaching consequences for renewable energy and could eventually and effectively end the traditional utility monopoly over public power. Among other things, PURPA mandated that utilities interconnect with independent power producers and pay them a fair market value for their electricity. It also exempted independent power producers from state and federal regulations. PURPA created a new spirit of entrepreneurialism in the utility industry. Since 1980, several hundred U.S. companies have entered the power generation business. Federal Energy Regulatory Commission, *Small Power Production and Cogeneration Facilities; Regulations Implementing Section 210 of PURPA of 1978* (Washington, DC: 1980); and Christopher Flavin, *Worldwatch Institute Paper* 61 (1984).

    In 1985 over 6,000 megawatts of renewable energy capacity had been built. By the fall of 1987, private developers had requested regulatory approval for an additional 16,335 megawatts of renewable energy projects. Biomass represented the largest share of this generating capacity followed by wind and small hydropower. Fourteen percent of the nation's electrical generating capacity relied on renewable technologies by 1985. In California where the act was most vigorously enforced, private developers aided by tax credits not only found it economical to build virtually all of the state's new generating capacity, they began to displace existing power plants as well. Cynthia Pollock Shea, *Worldwatch Institute Paper* 81 (1988), p.46.

89. Hydroelectric efficiency is very high—80 percent to 95 percent—and plants produce power 95 percent of the time compared with 55 percent for nuclear and 65 percent for coal. Miller, *Living in the Environment: An Introduction to Environmental Science*, p. 403.

90. Ibid., p. 403.

91. Tim Palmer, "What Price Free Energy?" *Sierra* (July/August 1983).

92. For example, exploiting small hydro sites in water-rich New England would increase its total electrical generating capacity by about 7 percent. John Gever, Robert Kaufmann, David Skole, and Charles Vorosmarty, *Beyond Oil* (Cambridge, MA: Ballinger, 1986).

93. Shea, *Worldwatch Institute Paper*, p. 81.

94. Wisconsin Valley Improvement Company. "Facts About Hydropower." November 2000. Available at *http://www.wvic.com/hydro-facts.htm*.

95. During the 1990s, New Englanders may receive 7 percent of their electricity from Quebec. Lester R. Brown et al., *State of the World 1988* (New York: Norton, 1988).

96. In December of 1995, China began construction on the Three Gorges Dam. With an estimated completion date of 2009 and a price tag of 90 billion yuan, China argues that the dam will help lessen that country's dependence on coal. Critics point to the fact that the dam has displaced over 1 million people and will submerge the Three Gorges area of the Yangtze River, destroying the native ecosystem. The dam will be the largest ever constructed, and many fear that such a project, which is opposed by many industrialized countries, including the United States, might revive interest in massive hydroelectric projects.

97. This discussion is based on James Ridgeway and Fred Pearce, "Watch on the Danube," *Audubon*, 94 (4) (July-August 1992), pp. 46–54.

98. Environmentally the dams were a mixed blessing (or curse). The area is particularly poor and has a heavy reliance on lignite coal that is high in sulfur and titanium and produces an oil that is lethal when burned. Even if an hydroelectric facility was built, however, its electricity would be used to run the nearby petrochemical refinery that produces a horrible chemical smog and related birth defects, cancers, and chronic bronchial infections in the local children.

99. A well-designed passive solar system can provide 50 percent to 100 percent of the space heating of a home or small building with an added construction cost of 5 percent to 10 percent. Miller, *Living in the Environment: An Introduction to Environmental Science.*

100. Sales volume dropped more than 70 percent from the 1984 level, and 28,000 out of the 30,000 people employed in the industry lost their jobs.

101. The Luz method is currently producing 194 megawatts by using long troughs of curved mirrors guided by computers to heat synthetic oil passing through vacuum-sealed tubes to 735 degrees Fahrenheit. The oil in turn heats water to produce steam and run an electric turbine. The company has built five new plants capable of tripling its generating capacity to 600 megawatts, enough to power a city the size of Washington, DC. The new plants' larger size and certain technological improvements will enable the cost of the solar power to decrease to 8 cents per kilowatt hour—the lowest ever achieved by a solar technology. Company officials contend that their power costs would look even lower if governments compared the costs of solar with the environmental effects of air and water pollution and the devastating effects of uranium and coal mining that are inherent in the coal and nuclear power technologies. This is undoubtedly true. As we have seen, the cost of externalities associated with burning coal or oil are estimated to be two to three times the market price for these sources of energy. Building a solar plant is also much quicker than building either a coal or nuclear-fired plant. The solar plant can come on line in 18 months; a coal or nuclear plant takes 5 to 10 years. Many experts feel the Luz project shows that solar power can become a vital supplement to more traditional energy sources, particularly during peak daytime hours in hot, dry climates. "A California Complex Finds Its Place in the Sun," *The Washington Post*, March 20–26, 1989.

102. Growth of 224 percent between 1980 and 1983 allowed production of 8.1 megawatts. Don Best, "Solar Cells: Still a Tough Sell," *Sierra* (May/June, 1988).

103. Ibid.

104. In 1976 the average price for a PV module was $44 per peak watt. Ten years later, costs were down eightfold (in constant 1986 dollars) to $5.25 per peak watt. Ibid., p. 31. Advances such as inexpensive automated methods of manufacturing PV cells of single-crystal silicon could reduce that to $1.50 per peak watt for the PV cell alone and perhaps $3 per peak watt for the complete system exclusive of storage. However even this would not bring the PV industry into a competitive balance with other means of producing electricity. It would produce electricity for 26 cents per kilowatt hour (kwh) while electricity in the late 1980s cost from 5 to 13 cents per kwh depending on location and source of power. The PV industry's dream of reducing costs to .60 cents per kwh, which would bring the cost to the consumer down to 5.2 cents per kwh, would make solar-generated electricity very attractive. Rose, Miller, and Agnew, "Reducing the Problem of Global Warming," *Technology Review* (May/June, 1984).

105. Robert F. Service, "Polymer Cells Achieve New Efficiency," *Science* (August 18, 1995) p. 920.

106. "Turning Down the Heat." Bullfrog Films, Oley, PA. 2000. See bullfrogfilms.com.

107. Ibid.

108. William H. Avery and Walter G. Berl, "Solar Energy from the Tropical Oceans," *Issues in Science and Technology* (Winter 1997), p. 41.

109. Miller, *Living in the Environment*, (8th ed.) p. 465.

110. Shea, *Worldwatch Institute Paper* 81. More than 16,769 turbines have been erected, mainly in the mountain passes of Altamont, Tehachapi, and San Gorgonio. Together these machines have the capacity to produce 1,463 megawatts of power, enough to meet the needs of more than 400,000 households.

111. CNN video "People's Planet" series. "Race to the Sun" aired March 18, 2001.

112. Paul Ehrlich, Anne Ehrlich, and John P. Holdren, *Ecoscience: Population, Resources, Environment* (San Francisco: Freeman, 1977).

113. Shea, *Worldwatch Institute Paper* 81, p. 19. In the United States, industrial utility and commercial applications account for two-thirds of the wood burned for energy. The remainder is used to heat homes.

114. Since 1983, four U.S. utilities have built wood-burning power plants, each able to generate 45 megawatts of electricity. According to a study by the California Energy Commission, wood-fired boilers can be installed for about $1,340 per kilowatt, which is 20 percent less than a coal-fired plant costs. Ibid., pp. 20, 22.

115. The largest market is in California where two dozen 10 to 50 megawatt wood energy projects are on-line as of 1988. Over 500 megawatts of power were under construction throughout the state that

year. In Maine, there are over 250 megawatts of wood energy projects on-line worth over $500 million. Ibid.

116. Dean Mahin, "Wood-Fuel Users Report Cost Savings in Virginia," *Renewable Energy News* (October 1985).

117. In Hawaii, the sugar industry started selling electricity in the late 1970s and in 1985 supplied 58 percent of the power on Kauai and 33 percent on the island of Hawaii. Sugar companies have installed at least 150 megawatts of power based on the burning of bagasse, the sugarcane residue. Researchers at Princeton University estimate that globally some 50,000 megawatts of gas-turbine cogeneration units could be supported with the 1985 level of sugarcane production. The potential for South America alone is 18,000 megawatts. Shea, *Worldwatch Institute Paper* 81, p. 24.

118. Shea, *Worldwatch Institute Paper* 81, p. 26. The United States relied on surplus corn and other grains for 90 percent of the 3 billion liters of ethanol produced in 1987.

119. At 1988 consumption rates, converting 10 percent of U.S. cars to run on ethanol would reduce oil imports by 800,000 barrels per day. This is equal to what the United States imported from Iran, Iraq, and Saudi Arabia per day in 1986.

120. David Pimentel. "Ethanol fuel from corn faulted as 'unsustainable subsidized food burning' in analysis by Cornell." Cornell University News Release, August 2001. Also in September 2001 Encyclopedia of Physical Sciences and Technology. Available at *http://www.news.cornell.edu/releases/Aug01/corn-basedethanol.hrs.html.*

121. Brigid McManamin, "Political Greenmail," *Forbes*, 147 (11) (May 27, 1991), p. 72.

122. David Ivanovich, "EPA Again Delays Plan to Push Ethanol-Gasoline," *The Journal of Commerce*, 395 (27911) (February 9, 1993), p. 7B.

123. Paul Merrion, "Gasohol Stalls Bush Here," *Crain's Chicago Business*, 15 (34) (August 24, 1992), p. 3.

124. The Clinton administration then decided to publish the order and then later put it on hold again. See David Ivanovich, "EPA Again Delays Plans to Push Ethanol-Gasoline," p. 7B.

125. Earl V. Anderson, "Brazil's Fuel Ethanol Program Comes Under Fire," *Chemical News Bureau*, March 20, 1989, pp. 11–12.

126. Earl Anderson, "Brazil's Fuel Ethanol Program Sputters," *Chemical and Engineering News*, January 15, 1990, p.6.

127. "Brazilian Alcohol Bootlegging Fuels Alternative 'Gas' Market," *Platt's Oilgram News*, 69 (156) (August 14, 1991), p. 2.

128. "Turning Down the Heat." Bullfrog Films, Oley, PA. 2000. See bullfrogfilms.com.

129. The price of energy should reflect the cost of replacing the dwindling supplies of depletable resources with renewable resources and alternative fuels. For example, if we know that replacing a $10 barrel of oil with synthetic fuel will cost $30 a barrel, and that the replacement technology will be needed so soon that we must start planning and constructing now, the option exists to either subsidize the synthetic fuel plant to bring it down to the $10 per barrel value, or to gradually raise the price of oil to reflect the value of its replacement, thereby making the replacement technology economically feasible. This would encourage efficient use and allow for an anticipated and gradual adjustment to increased costs of living instead of having to accept a sudden "price shock" at a later date.

130. In 1986 energy use by industry in the United States was actually 17 percent lower than in 1973, despite a 17 percent increase in production. The United States used 23 percent less energy in 1985 than was used in 1973. A new American office building, for example, has about the same lighting levels and temperatures as old ones but uses less than half as much electricity. Even large luxury cars built today get 20 to 25 miles to the gallon, which equals the mileage of much smaller cars built in the 1970s. Christopher Flavin and Alan Durning, "End of the Profligate Age?" *International Wildlife*, 18 (3) (May/June 1988). Since the 1980s energy use has increased but per capita consumption remains lower than in previous years.

131. For example, it is possible to save 40 percent or more of the energy used in existing buildings through retrofitting and 70 percent in new ones. The United States spends 10 percent of its GNP to pay the national fuel bill compared to only 4 percent for Japan. This translates into a national fuel bill which is $200 billion higher than necessary, making the U.S. economy that much less competitive. Ibid., p. 13.

132. Alan B. Durning and Christopher Flavin, "Building on Success: The Age of Energy Efficiency," *Worldwatch Paper* 82 (March 1988).

133. Ibid., p. 12.

134. Ibid., p. 13.

135. Ibid.
136. Commercial buildings—schools, hospitals, stores, and office buildings—use substantially less energy today than they did in 1973. New U.S. office buildings, for example, which used a wasteful 5.7 million kilojoules per square meter of floor space per year in 1973, use 3.0 in 1988. Commercial buildings in Sweden now average less than 1.7. If all commercial buildings in the United States were that efficient, total U.S. energy consumption would drop 9 percent. (These figures are for primary energy consumption. Electricity is counted in terms of energy content rather than the electricity itself.) Ibid., p. 17.
137. Ibid., p. 14. Buildings in these countries use 25 percent less energy per person than they did in 1973, which is more than the equivalent of 3.8 million barrels of oil per day—greater than the output of the rich North Sea discovery. Energy efficiency from U.S. homes and businesses combined is estimated to have increased 27.8 percent between 1973 and 1992, although total consumption still increased more than 22 percent. See "Fuels and Energy," *Air Conditioning, Heating, and Refrigeration News*, 188 (13) (March 29, 1993), p. 46.
138. Since average energy savings in retrofitted buildings run 24 percent, many of the technologies used in new commercial construction are worth installing in existing buildings. The Rocky Mountain Institute has estimated there are potential savings in commercial buildings of 1.8 billion kilowatt hours per year or 73 percent of the buildings' current use. Although these figures seem incredible, they have been corroborated by an expert panel advising the Boston Edison Company. Rocky Mountain Institute, South Texas Project; *Boston Edison Review Panel*, Vol. 2, Appendix 6, (Boston: Boston Edison Company, 1987); and Durning and Flavin, "Building on Success: The Age of Energy Efficiency."
139. According to the Rocky Mountain Institute (RMI), founded by energy expert Amory Lovins, even more savings are technically feasible. RMI calculated that existing homes in Austin, Texas, could save 63 percent of their electricity use by employing specially designed and readily available technologies. These retrofits were estimated to cost between $1,700 and $2,400, an amount that could be repaid through energy savings in about three years. Durning and Flavin, "Building on Success: The Age of Energy Efficiency," p. 14.
140. For example, while average U.S. homes use 160 kilojoules of heating energy per square meter of floor space per degree day, Swedish homes use just 65. New super-efficient homes in Minnesota use only 51 kilojoules; some individual units in Sweden use as low as 18 kilojoules. Ibid., p. 16.
141. Ibid., p. 16. As of the late 1980s there were more than 20,000 superinsulated homes in North America and 5,000 being built each year. However, this is not even 1 percent of new home construction. Superinsulation adds about 5 percent to the cost of new construction, which can be recaptured within five years through energy savings.
142. Analysts at Lawrence Livermore Laboratory of the University of California, Berkeley, calculated that homes in Los Angeles could cut their air conditioning bills in half by changing the controls on the conditioners to substitute ventilation for cooling when possible. Herb Brody, "Energy Wise Buildings," *High Technology* (February 1987).
143. Durning and Flavin, "Building on Success: The Age of Energy Efficiency."
144. Rocky Mountain Institute. "Home Energy Brief: Windows." Available at *http://www.rmi.org/images/other/E-HEB-Windows.pdf.*
145. The most energy-efficient new appliances have substantially lower energy requirements than the average appliances in U.S. homes. For example, the average American refrigerator uses 1,500 kilowatt hours of electricity every year. The average new model uses 1,100 and the most efficient model on the market—made by Whirlpool—uses only 750. This represents an energy savings of 32 percent from the average old model to the best available technology. Howard Geller estimates that placing a 750 kilowatt hour Whirlpool refrigerator in every home and apartment in the United States could shut down 12 1,000 megawatt coal-fired electricity plants. Other appliances also offer dramatic energy savings. The best air conditioner and the best water heater on the market use 75 percent less energy than the old average models. A new electric range uses 50 percent less energy than the old average model. New gas furnaces represent an energy savings of 59 percent. The best gas water heaters and gas ranges save 63 percent and 64 percent of energy usage, respectively. Howard S. Geller, "Energy-Efficient Appliances: Performance Issues and Policy Options," *IEEE Technology and Society Magazine* (March 1986).
146. Electric heat pumps that heat in winter and cool in summer are replacing oil and gas. Since two-thirds of the energy needed to produce the electricity to run the heat pumps is lost at the power plant, the savings are not as spectacular as they might seem. However, heat pump clothes dryers are twice as efficient as conventional dryers. Howard Geller of the American Council for an Energy-

Efficient Economy calculates that installing heat pump water heaters in American homes with conventional water heaters would eliminate the need for 15 large (1,000 megawatt) centralized power plants at a fraction of the cost. Howard S. Geller, "Energy-Efficient Residential Appliances: Performance Issues and Policy Options," *IEEE Technology and Society Magazine* (March 1986); and Durning and Flavin, "Building on Success: The Age of Energy Efficiency."

147. Gary Bosma, "A Realistic Approach to High Efficiency Gas, Water and Space Heating," in ACEEE, Proceedings from the 1986 ACEEE Summer Study on Energy Efficiency in Buildings, Vol. 1 (Appliances and Equipment) (Washington, DC: 1986); and, Durning and Flavin, "Building on Success: The Age of Energy Efficiency."

148. Rocky Moutain Institute. "Home Energy Brief: Lighting." Available at *http://www.rmi.org/images/other/E-HEB-Lighting.pdf.*

149. For example, one new screw-in 18-watt fluorescent bulb provides the light of a 75-watt incandescent bulb and lasts 10 times longer. In terms of energy savings this means that during their useful lives, an 18-watt fluorescent keeps 180 kilograms of coal in the ground and 130 kilograms of carbon out of the atmosphere.

   Phillips has developed another light bulb called the "SL," which screws into a standard socket, provides excellent color, does not flicker, uses only one-quarter of the electricity of an ordinary 75-watt bulb and lasts 13 times longer. The high-priced SL bulb pays for itself two to three times over in electricity costs and replacement bulb costs.

   Other energy-saving lighting technologies include high-frequency electronic ballasts, which cut energy use by 20 percent to 40 percent, and microelectronic sensors, which automatically turn lights off and on according to the amount of sunlight in the room and people walking in and out. Substituting cool fluorescent bulbs for hot incandescent ones also lowers cooling bills. The California Energy Commission calculated that every 100-watt savings on lighting meant an additional 38-watt savings on air conditioning. Durning and Flavin, "Building on Success: The Age of Energy Efficiency," pp. 21, 22.

150. Ibid.

151. Miller, *Living in the Environment,* 1994, 450

152. Durning and Flavin, "Building on Success: The Age of Energy Efficiency," pp. 21, 22.

153. The world's 400 million cars currently spew 547 million tons of carbon emissions into the atmosphere each year, which is 10 percent of the total from fossil fuels. If current trends continue, carbon emissions from cars would nearly double by the year 2010. However, if the number of cars was kept at no more than 500 million by 2010, through mass transit and greater use of bicycles and walking, and if all these cars were getting at least 50 mpg, carbon emissions would fall to 247 million tons per year, half of what they are today. Lester R. Brown, Christopher Flavin, and Sandra Postel, "Outlining a Global Action Plan," *State of the World 1989* (New York: Norton, 1989).

154. "Turning Down the Heat," Bullfrog Films, Oley, PA. 2000. See bullfrogfilms.com.

155. See, "Energy Surprises for the 21st Century," by Amory Lovins and Chris Lotspeich originally published in the *Journal of International Affairs,* Fall 1999, 53, no. 1. Available at *http://www.rmi.org/images/other/E-EnergySurprises.pdf*

156. Marc Ross, "Current Major Issues in Industrial Energy Use," prepared for Office of Policy Integration, DOE, October 24, 1986; and Durning and Flavin, "Building on Success: The Age of Energy Efficiency."

157. Durning and Flavin, "Building on Success: The Age of Energy Efficiency," p. 31.

158. "Fuels and Energy," p. 46.

159. A few widely used technologies show great potential for energy savings. In the United States, 70 percent of industrial electricity goes for electromechanical drives, which can be improved in many ways. The use of electronic speed controls can cut power needs up to 50 percent. Sales of these drives have tripled since 1976. Durning and Flavin, "Building on Success: The Age of Energy Efficiency."

160. Ibid.

161. In 1985 13,000 megawatts were produced through cogeneration. More than 47,000 megawatts of planned cogeneration were registered with the Federal Energy Regulatory Commission (FERC) as of October 1, 1987. This is enough power to displace 47 large nuclear plants and has a market value of over $40 billion. Ibid., pp. 34–35.

162. Ibid., p. 36.

163. American Petroleum Institute, *Basic Petroleum Databook,* 5 (Washington, DC: 1985); and Durning and Flavin, "Building on Success: The Age of Energy Efficiency," p. 43.

164. This is due in part to Americans' love of freedom of travel, and their subsidized desire for suburban sprawl with single-family housing connected only by publicly funded roads instead of mass transit.

8

Toxic and Hazardous Materials and Waste Management

Waste management has been plagued by an "out of sight out of mind" public mentality. We are slowly burying ourselves in our own garbage, as landfills have been the preferred method of waste disposal. Overall, the "ecological footprint" we are leaving is massive due to our consumption patterns and the ensuing waste. To supply all 6 billion plus humans with the resources and land needed to absorb the wastes Americans use and create today, we would need three Earths.[1] Progress, however, is being made.

As indicated in Chapter 1, one of the most interesting examples of the environmental policy paradox may be found in the area of waste management. For several decades we have understood and could have anticipated most of our solid waste problems. In 1992, it was estimated that the United States could run out of landfill space in only 12.5 years.[2] Since then, however, the trends of disposal for municipal solid waste, as well as hazardous wastes, have reflected a steady movement toward more sustainable methods of controlling waste disposal, namely the wide spread use of recycling and composting. In 1996, 28 percent of the solid waste stream was recycled, compared to just 14 percent in 1992.[3] Though slow to react to the need for policy reform, policy makers have begun to increase their attention to the problem of waste disposal. That is not to say that our problems will shortly be overcome. Although it would appear that the growth spurt that occurred in the late 1980s and early 1990s of recycling and other waste mitigation programs is over, it is important to note that the issue of waste stream mitigation has not faded from the public agenda. However, the incremental nature of the policy process; the incentives operating on policy makers to adopt short-term, low-cost policy options; and the lack of, until the late 1980s, any publicly perceived crisis, have all historically operated to produce waste policies that tend not to be viable in the long run.

Toxic wastes and waste management are discussed throughout this book because they are found throughout the environment in our air, water, and soil. In this section we read about solid and hazardous waste management problems. We begin by summarizing the nature of our waste and the relationship between industrial development and waste generation. Due to their different composition and methods of disposal, the discussion is divided into two subsections, one on solid waste and one on hazardous waste.

SOLID WASTE

What Is Solid Waste?

In natural systems, waste products are broken down by decomposer organisms and converted to a form for use by other organisms within the ecosystem. Urbanization, agricultural specialization, and industrialization have produced inorganic by-products that have disrupted these natural systems. Today when an apple is produced on a farm and shipped to the city, organic material in the apple core is usually thrown in a trashcan and eventually hauled to a landfill, thus taken out of the organic production cycle. Back on the farm, fertilizers are necessary to replace nutrients that have been depleted from the soil, some of which now lie—useless—in a landfill. Likewise, when waste was scattered across the surface of the land (as agricultural waste, human or animal waste once were) it all became a part of natural ecological cycles. The concentration of wastes and the removal of wastes from the ecosystems in which they would naturally biodegrade have resulted in massive quantities of refuse, usually referred to as solid waste.

There is no precise definition of solid waste. The term is often applied to liquids as opposed to solids and to things that are not necessarily waste.[4] Here we limit our discussion to municipal waste, agricultural waste, and mining waste, paying particular attention to municipal waste and means of disposal of these wastes.

The difficulty in defining waste is reflected in the fragmented laws that are meant to deal with it. Of the nine major federal laws regulating some aspect of waste, some focus on where the waste is discharged (land, air, or water); where it comes from (for example, a nuclear power plant); how it is disposed of; or the focus is on some characteristic of the waste, for example, if the waste is toxic or radioactive.[5]

Scope of the Problem

In the United States, per capita production of solid waste is estimated to be around 44 tons every year. Of this waste, consumers in the United States throw away enough aluminum to rebuild the country's entire commercial airline fleet every three months, about 2.5 million nonreturnable plastic bottles each *hour*, and enough tires to encircle the earth almost three times each year.[6]

Most solid waste comes from mining (including oil and gas production), agriculture, and industry. It is estimated that of the 11 billion tons of solid waste produced in the United States each year, 75 percent is from mining operations. Most of the wastes generated from this activity are dumped on the ground near where they are generated. In 1994, it was estimated that the abandoned and unrestored metal and coal surface mines in the United States cover an area the size of Indiana. Likewise, agricultural waste, which amounts to around 1.5 billion tons annually, is left in the fields—where it may accumulate or run off the land to pollute rivers and streams.[7]

Municipal waste amounts to approximately 327 million tons a year in the United States.[8] Although smaller in volume than agricultural or mining waste, municipal waste presents greater political and managerial problems, often having serious environmental impacts on land and water resources.

Although solid waste management problems are not unique to the United States, the country is rather singular in terms of the volume of municipal waste generated. The EPA states the United States generated 229.9 million tons of municipal solid waste (MSW)[9] in 1999 (see Table 8–1). On a per capita basis, the United States generates more than twice as much municipal waste as most of the more developed countries in the world.[10] Americans continue to use more and more materials every year, and the population using these materials continues to rise as well. Given a world of limited resources (and space to put all our waste), and the developing status of many other of the world's nations, there is cause for concern in waste management. Though it is discouraging to see more and more waste produced, a positive trend is the increase in recycling. America's recycling rate jumped almost 72 percent from 1990 to 1999.

In 1990 67 percent of municipal solid waste was landfilled, 17 percent was recycled, and 16 percent was destroyed through incineration.[11] By 1999 these numbers improved to 57.4 percent of the solid waste stream being landfilled, whereas 27.8 percent was recycled, and 14.8 percent incinerated.[12] Meanwhile, the number of landfills in operation dropped from 8,000 in 1988 to 3,091 in 1996, to 2216 in 1999, though the average landfill size has increased.[13] The decline in quantity is expected to continue as Resource Conservation and Recovery Act (RCRA) standards are tightened and landfills are closed rather than upgraded. A study undertaken in 1986 found that 75 percent of surveyed states had insufficient solid waste landfill capacity.[14] For example, in New Jersey, over 100 landfills that were handling as much as 90 percent of the state's waste in the late 1970s had been closed by 1987.[15] It was estimated in 1987 that 33 dumps being used by the city of Chicago would be full by the mid-1990s as would the dumps then in use by the city of Los Angeles.[16] Some New England towns that ran out of local dump space operate trucks on a 24-hour basis to carry waste to dump sites in Pennsylvania and Ohio. Towns on Long Island in New York ship their trash as far west as Michigan.[17]

TABLE 8–1   America's Waste

Year	MSW (in millions of tons per year)	Per Capita MSW (in pounds per person per day)	Recycling Rate
1960	88.1	2.68	6.4
1970	121.1	3.25	6.6
1980	151.6	3.66	9.6
1990	205.2	4.5	16.2
1999	229.9	4.62	27.8

Running out of space is only one of the problems associated with solid waste disposal. New York City's Fresh Kills landfill on Staten Island, a monstrosity as tall as 225 feet in some areas, leaks an estimated 1 million gallons a day of toxic fluids into nearby streams.[18] Fresh Kills covers 3,000 acres and contains 150 million cubic yards of trash. Although plans to close the landfill began in 1992, it did not receive the last planned official barge of trash until March 22, 2001.[19]

The cost of closing the landfill is estimated at around $1 billion and is expected to take at least five years to complete. This includes sealing the trash mounds and installing pollution mitigation equipment to cope with the millions of gallons of leachete produced annually.[20] Currently two of the four trash mounds have been permanently capped, and one is in the process of being forever sealed.[21] Such precautions are necessary. Improper disposal of solid waste can lead to a wide range of diseases including typhoid, dysentery, cholera, and infectious hepatitis, not to mention damage to ecosystems and other species.[22] Moreover, New York plans on turning the landfill into a public park and memorial to the World Trade Center and its victims. Development will be pushed back a number of years however, as the city was forced to bring debris from the September 11, 2001 terrorist attacks to Fresh Kills.[23]

Disposal Methods

Adverse health effects, if any, depend on the methods used to dispose of solid waste. Disposal methods for municipal solid waste include open dumping, which is often accompanied by open burning, ocean dumping, and sanitary landfills. While open dumps and open burning are prohibited, and ocean dumping is limited by the Marine Protection, Research and Sanctuaries Act, all of these disposal methods are used by local governments throughout the United States. In theory, sanitary landfills provide a safe and effective means of disposal. Unfortunately, the theory of sanitary landfill operation oftentimes does not match the practice.

A sanitary landfill should be lined with some type of impervious barrier including clay, granite, or some other natural material or some manufactured source, such as plastic. The sides of the landfill should slope, and polluted water that percolates through the landfill should be channeled off and disposed of properly. As waste is added to the landfill, it should be covered with 6 inches of fresh soil at the end of every day to prevent odor and the transmittal of disease by rats, flies, or other rodents and vermin.

As noted in the example of the Fresh Kills landfill in New York City, many landfills do not, for a variety of reasons, meet this ideal. The primary problem is that landfills are often not constructed with satisfactory drainage capacity and the 6-inch daily cover of fresh soil may or may not adequately prevent exposure of the trash to the elements. In 1994, federal regulations went into effect which imposed strict management requirements that included, among other things, upgraded liners be installed on existing landfills. That same year, it was estimated that 85 percent of landfills in the United States had no liners at all, allowing potentially toxic leachete to seep into the soil, possibly causing groundwater contamination.[24]

In the early 1990s, the fastest growing method of municipal waste disposal was the incineration of waste in conjunction with the sanitary landfill disposal of the resultant ash and noncombustible materials. This is the preferred method of disposal in several European countries and it has the advantage of producing electricity as a by-product. In Denmark and Sweden in 1994, municipalities were using 50 percent of their waste to produce energy by burning the waste to produce steam.[25] The United States is still far behind other countries in the use of solid waste to generate energy. (The EPA estimates that about 15 percent of municipal solid waste in the United States is incinerated.)[26]

Most coastal cities have discontinued the dumping of municipal wastewater sludge in the ocean as a means of disposal. Wastewater sludge, what is left after the treatment of sewage, was still dumped into the ocean at a few major coastal cities including New York, Los Angeles, and Boston until a 1989 federal law ordered it stopped by 1991.[27]

Regulations

Although Congress passed the Solid Waste Disposal Act in 1965, this legislation is only advisory.[28] Solid waste disposal has traditionally been the responsibility of the state and, more importantly, the local government. In its findings when considering the Solid Waste Disposal Act, Congress stated "that while the collection and disposal of solid waste should continue to be primarily a function of state, regional, and local agencies" federal action was required through financial and technical assistance.[29]

The Resource Recovery Act of 1970 maintained a largely hands-off federal approach to local solid waste management by providing financial assistance for the construction of solid waste disposal facilities and funds for additional research.[30] It was not until passage of the Resource Conservation and Recovery Act of 1976 (RCRA) that the federal government got involved to any significant degree in the management of solid waste. Although most of the RCRA deals with the disposal of hazardous waste, it also created, for the first time, significant federal regulations for the management of municipal waste.

The RCRA required states to develop solid waste management plans, which, among other things, would stipulate the closing of all open dumps and either the recycling of wastes or the disposal of waste within sanitary landfills.[31] In 1993, 17 years after passage of the RCRA, open dumps were still common in rural areas and many municipalities are either not practicing or inadequately practicing sanitary landfill methods.

As we have seen, some municipalities export their solid wastes into neighboring states. In the 1970s several states and localities, in an attempt to prevent the importation of waste into their areas, passed restrictions aimed at other states that prohibited the flow of waste to local disposal sites. In 1978 the U.S. Supreme Court found that such restrictions violated the commerce clause of the Constitution by restricting interstate commerce.[32]

Solutions

Solid waste management provides a good example of the environmental policy paradox in operation. The problem and its solutions have been well known to policy makers for decades. However, the best long-term solutions to municipal waste problems are expensive whereas short-term solutions seem to be cheap.

Municipal solid waste management in many areas is reaching the crisis stage. Policymakers in some areas are being forced to take what they consider drastic measures that they might not otherwise be willing to consider. California, New York, New Jersey, and Connecticut have all implemented plans designed to recycle 25 percent of their solid waste and to incinerate much of the rest to produce energy.[33] California targeted 50 percent recycling by the year 2000, an optimistic goal not met. Other localities have responded by requiring the separation of trash into recyclables and nonrecyclables, passing bottle bills (a universal deposit on returnable containers), and imposing litter or refuse taxes.

Waste reduction efforts do not have to be slow or impossible. For example, Germany holds manufacturers accountable for most of the packaging waste their products generate. The packaging recycling rate was 12 percent in 1992, the year the law was passed. In 1997 that figure soared to 86 percent.[34] If businesses have to find and recycle their packaging they will. In addition, they will invent new ways to use less packaging in the first place. So long as American policy makers and industry interest groups believe this would cripple the American economy, increase unemployment, and cost politicians votes, such a law will not be passed in the United States, despite the fact that such measures have been effective elsewhere.

It should be noted however that industry will often reuse and recycle when not forced to, because it can make environmental as well as economic sense. Toyota in 1991, for example, switched to reusable shipping containers, each with a life expectancy of 20 years, dramatically reducing long-term costs associated with constantly purchasing new materials and then paying to dispose of them.[35]

Recycling, next to simply consuming less and generating less waste in the first place, holds the most promise for the long-term reduction of solid waste. A great deal of the solid waste generated in the United States could be recycled. 38 percent of municipal solid waste (MSW) is paper and 12 percent yard trimmings, virtually all of which could be recycled.[36] Packaging and containers, much of which are plastic, accounted for about a third of MSW in 1999. While only 17 percent of solid waste was being recycled or reused in the United States in 1993,[37] this figure jumped to a state average of 30 percent in 2000, with more communities expected to establish curbside recycling programs in future years. Today about half of all Americans have access to curbside recycling programs. The mostly rural residents that do not have curbside recycling often live near one of 2,600 drop-off recycling stations.[38] Also encouraging are the trends in composting of yard trimmings and recycling paper products. Yard waste recycling tripled from 1990 to 1999 and currently 41.9 percent of the 87.5 million tons of paper and paperboard are recovered annually.[39] Although the United State is making strides in the area of recycling, many communities in Japan and in parts of Europe recycle in excess of 50 percent of their solid waste. In 1998, two-thirds of the states in America recycled at least 22 percent of their waste stream, with only three states (Alaska, Montana and Wyoming) under the 10 percent level.[40] The major drawback to recycling is its cost and the requirement that individuals participate in the recycling process to attain maximum efficiency. It should be noted, however, that as technology begins to affect waste disposal alternatives, costs will decrease, hopefully attracting a broader consumer base.

Besides the efforts of federal, state, and local governments, private corporations have been making strides toward a reduction in their waste streams. The value of residual materials left over from the production process are beginning to be realized. Anheuser-Busch is one such company that has excelled in its waste management efforts. The company produces an estimated 1.6 million tons of waste per year from its 12 breweries. Since 1996, only about 40,000 tons of that amount, just 2.5 percent, have been disposed of in a landfill.[41] Most of the wastes generated may be used as energy for Anheuser-Busch's production processes. Such accomplishments should stand as models for companies who wish to limit their waste stream, while maximizing their resource use (that is, energy produced from virgin residuals).

A fairly new approach for encouraging citizens to curb their waste disposal streams involves directly linking the amount of waste disposed of in landfills to the amount of money charged for the disposal service. Unit pricing, or pay-as-you-throw, schemes are designed to change people's behavior toward waste disposal through negative reinforcement. About 3,400 communities have employed some form of unit pricing programs. Four states require some type of variable rate scheme for garbage collection. In a study conducted in 1997, researchers found a direct correlation between the economic cost of disposal and the amount of waste landfilled; simply put, as charges climb, a greater amount of waste is diverted from the landfill.[42] Most often these diversions help establish the impetus for local recycling and composting (for yard clippings) programs. The objective of unit pricing programs is a reduction in waste from its sources through the use of economic incentives.

Although there is a greater percentage of waste being diverted to the recycling bin, the tax structure in the United States in a number of ways continues to favor the use of virgin materials over recycled resources. For example, favoritism is shown through accelerated depreciation, depletion allowances, and special deductions for mineral exploration. As well, the U.S. rail freight rates discriminate against recycled materials, since railroads often charge a higher rate for recycled goods as opposed to virgin goods. Therefore many businesses find it profitable to avoid recycling.[43] As the number of landfills decreases, however, costs associated with traditional waste disposal increase. In the late 1980s, tipping fees (the charge associated with landfill disposal) were generally around $10 per ton of waste. In 1997 the national average was triple that price, leading us to ask how much longer before the cost of landfills surpasses that of recycling.[44] Twenty-three states have instituted some type of disposal restrictions on yard clippings. Other items that have been banned outright from landfills include vehicle batteries (41 states), tires (35 states), and motor oil (24 states).[45] Restrictions such as these encourage environmentally friendly diversions in the waste stream.

In addition to restrictions, states may also institute incentives to encourage behavior that does not contribute to the waste stream. As of 1997, ten states had responded to the solid waste problem in part by the passage of "bottle bills" (California, Connecticut, Delaware, Iowa, Maine, Massachusetts, Michigan, New York, Oregon and Vermont).[46] In addition some states, such as California and Florida, have passed nontraditional incentive programs.[47] The first state to pass such a law was Oregon, which in 1971 began requiring a minimum 5-cent deposit on beer and soft drink containers. Bottle laws have significantly reduced roadside litter in Oregon and the other states in which they have been enacted. In addition, these laws have had some significant side benefits, including an increase in employment and a reduction of injuries suffered by children from broken glass in parks. However, these laws encounter strong opposition from industry groups that manufacture beverage containers, as well as supermarkets, and labor unions.

The success or failure of bottle bills in various states is indicative of the decentralization of environmental administration and problems that result therefrom. When local bottling or labor interests are influential in a state or locality, they may be successful in preventing implementation of waste management methods that they perceive to be against their interests, as bottling companies and labor unions were for many years in California.

A related problem is that a solid waste disposal site is a so-called LULU, or "locally unwanted land use." LULUs include power plants, airports, prisons, landfills, and low-income housing, to name a few. LULUs are often located in poor or economically disadvantaged areas. This should not be surprising, for it is in these areas where the inhabitants lack the political influence to prevent the siting of a LULU in their neighborhoods. The siting of a LULU in a poor neighborhood can often mean that such areas become even more disadvantaged.[48]

A sanitary landfill need not, however, be a LULU. The technology exists for the creation of landfills in conjunction with incineration and other disposal methods, making landfills an acceptable neighbor with no unsightly mountains of garbage or nasty smells.[49] However, the controls necessary to make a LULU an acceptable neighbor, and recycle or otherwise process our solid waste, can be expensive. Thus solid waste management is a good example of a policy problem that has short-term, low-cost solutions that are inferior and long-term solutions that are superior yet require relatively high short-term expenditures. As we have seen, the incentives operating in the policy-making process in such situations motivate politicians to select the low-cost, short-term solution. Here it is the opening up or overloading a dump, or transporting waste into an adjacent state.

Fortunately, or unfortunately depending on your perspective, solid waste management has reached crisis proportions in many regions, and consequently, policy makers no longer have the luxury of making the low-cost, short-term decision. The low-cost decision has already been made in previous decades and now the bills must be paid.

Our dominant social paradigm plays an important role in the management of solid waste. The United States has become a throwaway society. Between 30 and 40 percent of all municipal waste in the United States consists of packaging materials; close to half of the cost of many consumer items is taken up in packaging.[50] We have become accustomed to the convenience of individual packaging, of disposable razors, bottles, and other consumer items. Only a generation ago, it was common for people to carry their own containers to the supermarket, to recycle milk and soft drink bottles, and to compost vegetable waste. The accepted convenience of a disposable society will be hard to break. Clearly, however, given the limitations on space for additional landfills, the break will be made. As we have seen, changes have already occurred in some communities; for example, curbside recycling programs have more than tripled since 1990.[51]

At the federal level, the EPA set 30 percent as the municipal solid waste recycling goal for 2000.[52] In order to accomplish this, the recycling rate for paper had to increase from the 1993 levels of 34 percent to at least 42 percent by 2000; aluminum had to increase from 35.4 percent in 1993 to 46 percent in 2000; and yard clippings must be recycled at a rate of 48 percent, as opposed to the 1993 level of 19.8 percent.[53]

Clearly progress has been made. In 1999 yard trimmings were recovered at a 45 percent rate, paper at 41.9 percent, and about a fourth of the glass and a third of steel were recycled that year. Unfortunately, only 5.6 percent of the 24.2 million tons of plastic were recycled in 1999, leaving much room for improvement there. In addition, the 1999 overall recycling rate (27.8 percent) was up over 71 percent from 1990 levels.[54] It appears, therefore, that Americans will come very close to, but not quite meet EPA's recycling goal of recovering 30 percent of municipal waste.

At the local level, the city of Los Angeles is planning to expand its program from its weekly pickup at 720,000 households to over 1 million households and to include yard trimmings, newspapers, corrugated cardboard, plastics, glass, food containers, steel, and aluminum cans.[55] The number of curbside recycling programs outnumbers the number of landfills in the Great Lakes and Mid-Atlantic states. Not surprisingly, such programs have been least accepted in the more spacious Rocky Mountain and Midwestern states.[56] In some states, at least, such measures will become the norm in the not too distant future.

HAZARDOUS WASTES

Toxic pollution affects you whether you know it or not. In the United States 8 out of 10 Americans, over 200 million people, live near a toxic waste dump or a source of toxic waste. Nearly half of all Americans live in counties containing toxic waste sites that have been identified by the Environmental Protection Agency as a priority site for cleanup.[57] Toxic pollutants are found throughout the earth's environment. Even polar bears living in the Arctic wilderness have been found to contain a wide variety of toxic chemicals including DDT and TCBs.[58] Although estimates vary, the U.S. General Accounting Office found there may be as many as 442,482 toxic waste sites that are potential Superfund sites that may need corrective action.[59] Officials of the EPA have been quoted as calling the toxic waste problem "the most grave error in judgment we as a nation have ever made ... one of the most serious problems the nation has ever faced."[60] Although it is not tied to any particular future regulatory action, the EPA in November 2001 made a $22 million grant to establish five new Hazardous Substance Research Centers at universities across the United States.

Nature of the Problem

There are numerous sources of toxic pollutants. Toxic wastes are a by-product of energy development, agriculture, and most industrial activity.

We do not know exactly how much toxic waste is produced in the United States or where that waste is disposed of with any great degree of certainty. As a study by the U.S. Office of Technology Assessment concluded, "There are major uncertainties on how much hazardous waste has been generated, the types and capacities of existing waste management facilities, the number of uncontrolled waste sites and their hazard levels, and on the health and environmental effects of hazardous waste releases."[61]

Perhaps of even greater concern, however, are radioactive wastes. Commercial low-level waste is the term used for nuclear reactors that can deliver lethal doses of radiation in seconds.[62]

Rather than measuring volume, it is more informative to look at the amount of radioactivity, or curies. An uncontaminated area will register 5 to 20 disintegrations per *minute*; one curie is 37 billion disintegrations per *second*. In 1992 commercial disposal sites received over 1 million curies, 86 percent of which came from utilities.[63] These figures do not reflect the total amount of waste generated, only the amount shipped to licensed dumps. They also do not include radioactive wastes from weapons production; wastes from large reactor facilities that were decommissioned (at least four); wastes that have been deregulated and disposed of as hazardous only; or contaminated soils, described by the Nuclear Regulatory Commission's Nuclear Information and Resource Service as existing in "very large volumes."[64] Total annual radioactivity of disposed low-level waste (LLW) (commercial and DOE disposal sites) peaked in 1992 at over 2 million curies. The cumulative radioactivity of LLW disposed of at these sites has stayed fairly steady in the 1990s at around 19 million curies.[65]

In addition to low-level wastes, there are commercial high-level wastes. One metric ton of light-water reactor irradiated fuel is estimated to contain over 177 million curies at discharge; irradiated fuel from nuclear plants is estimated to reach over 40,000 metric tons by the year 2003, or 6.8 trillion curies.

While exact figures of hazardous waste generation are not known, some estimate that only 6 percent of the hazardous waste generated in the United States is handled in a safe manner.[66] The EPA reports that of the estimated 2.26 billion pounds of toxic chemicals released into the environment in 1994, only 13 percent was disposed of on land. Emissions into the air accounted for 69 percent of toxic releases; underground injection accounted for 15 percent.[67] Environmentalists challenge the use of injection wells and the validity of the models on which they are based, saying the models *assume* wastes will behave predictably, though they have never been tested.[68]

Nine billion gallons of liquid hazardous waste are injected into the ground annually. For some corporations, including major producers like BP Amoco, Monsanto and DuPont, it is their primary or only method of disposal. Some, on the other hand, like Dow Chemical, banned the practice back in the 1970s and have since relied on incineration, recycling, and waste reduction. Though the EPA has had an Underground Injection Program since 1974, and Safe Drinking Water Act amendments in 1996 tightened regulations, it may take civil action lawsuits to make the practice too expensive to make economic sense.[69]

There is no question the many chemical substances that have been developed since World War II have contributed to the improvement of our quality of life. Chemicals have improved the control of disease, agricultural productivity, and production of goods and services in ways that we have come to take for granted. However, we do not know what price we have paid, or will pay in the future, for these benefits. The human effects of toxic contaminants are numerous and severe. Cancer, nervous system damage, kidney, liver, chromosomal, and lung damage as well as genetic mutations are some of the human impacts that may result from exposure to toxic pollutants. Perhaps even more frightening than this list of possible dangers is the fact that we know so little about the human impacts of toxins.

Over 7 million chemicals are known of which around 80,000 are in common use, with thousands more being discovered every year. Many of these chemicals are potentially hazardous. Globally, the production of chemicals has skyrocketed from 7 million tons a year in 1950, to 63 million tons in 1970, to 250 million tons in 1985 and 400 million tons at the turn of the century. There is toxicity data for only 14 percent of the 2,700 most produced chemicals in the world.[70] As The National Academy of Sciences reported, "of tens of thousands of commercially important chemicals, only a few have been subjected to extensive toxicity testing, and most have scarcely been tested at all."[71]

In addition to a lack of knowledge, other problems are associated with the regulation of toxic substances. First, there are frequently latency effects on humans where the damage may not show up until decades after exposure to a toxic substance. Second, toxic substances can accumulate in plants and animals at higher dosage than in the surrounding environment and thus build up over time. This accumulation can be in your internal organs. Third, smaller dosages of toxic substances produce harmful effects on humans and plants and other animals than do conventional pollutants. Finally, many toxic substances resist biological breakdown.

The major regulatory problem with respect to toxic or hazardous waste disposal is finding the proper means, and policing those means, of the handling, storage, and disposal of hazardous waste.

Disposal Methods

It is estimated that between 80 and 90 percent of the hazardous waste produced each year is disposed of illegally or improperly. Roughly 64 percent of all hazardous and toxic waste in the United States is injected into deep wells, 22 percent is discharged to streams and sewers, and roughly 14 percent is split evenly between incineration and recycling programs.[72] In addition to underground injection and land disposal, hazardous waste may be disposed of in the oceans, through microbiotic breakdown, or the transport of waste—usually from more developed to less developed countries. Each of these options carry with them associated problems.

In theory, underground injection of hazardous waste provides a relatively cheap and safe method of disposal. A hole is drilled an average of 4,000 feet below the surface of the earth and an inner pipe, known as an injection tube, encased in steel and cement to prevent leaks into groundwater aquifers, is inserted. The waste is then pumped into the hole and, optimally, kept separate from freshwater aquifers. In fact, due to incorrect estimations of the interface between drinking water and hazardous injection sites, as well as leaks and spills and improperly functioning injection equipment, there have been numerous incidences of hazardous waste polluting drinking water.[73] According to the public interest law firm, the Legal Environmental Assistance Foundation (LEAF), at least 25 states have documented evidence of problems caused by underground injection of hazardous waste. As B. Suzi Ruhl, the President and founder of LEAF stated,

> [I]t's a giant problem, but it's a stepchild within both the environmental movement and the regulatory system. I've been distraught over how little attention this has re-

ceived. We can't show dead bodies right now. It's a classic out of sight, out of mind technology. I feel that underground injection is posing the greatest threat to our groundwater because of inadequate regulations. They are just postponing our day of reckoning with the hazardous waste problem.[74]

The ocean dumping of hazardous waste is another serious dilemma—one suffering from the common pool property management problems that plague the oceans generally. An estimated 8 million tons of toxic waste are dumped annually into the coastal waters off the United States. Timothy Kao and Joseph Bishop, of the Catholic University Department of Civil Engineering and Oceanography, stated in a study of toxic pollutants in the ocean that "while major oil spills are highly visible and forced their attention on the public conscience, the dumping of toxic waste, on the other hand, is an idiocy and potentially more serious problem."[75] Many of these pollutants are nonbiodegradable and as Kao and Bishop note,

> [W]hat is worse is that the toxic pollutant moves up in concentrates in the marine food chain. At the base of the marine food chain is phytoplankton, which may act as a primary concentrator of a pollutant. These are ingested by zooplankton, which in turn are fed on by crustaceans and fish. Contaminantly, the pollutant gets progressively more concentrated until it reaches lethal level for landbase species including humans.[76]

The incineration of hazardous waste may be the most promising long-term solution to the hazardous waste disposal problem. As the U.S. Office of Technology Assessment reported in 1983, "All land disposal methods will eventually fail."[77] Liners deteriorate, the ground shifts, it is only a question of when they will fail. Many toxic substances when heated to temperatures above of 2,400E F are broken down. EPA tests of a mobile incinerator in Times Beach, Missouri, found that by heating soil polluted with dioxin to temperatures of up to 4,000° F, 99.99 percent of the dioxin was destroyed.[78]

The major obstacles to incineration of hazardous waste are political. As we see later, the public has generally opposed having disposal sites in their neighborhoods, and in the United States as well as abroad there has been vigorous opposition to building new incineration sites.[79]

As an alternative, incineration may be done on seagoing vessels. Various European countries have been incinerating at sea since 1969. The first officially sanctioned ocean incineration of hazardous waste in the United States occurred between October 1974 and January 1975 in the Gulf of Mexico. Intermittently since then, the EPA has tried to promote the incineration of hazardous waste at sea with varying success. The agency believed that much of the opposition to incineration on shore would not present itself if incineration was at sea. That has not been the case. Residents of coastal zone areas as well as environmental activists have been strongly opposed to the incineration of hazardous waste at sea.

In 1983 the EPA came close to issuing permits to the Chemical Waste Management Company to incinerate 80 million gallons of organic compounds in the Gulf of Mexico. In the face of public opposition the agency withheld the necessary permits. At the time, a spokesperson for the Office of Technology Assessment said, "It's not at all clear if we will be incinerating anything at sea, at least in the near future. There's so much political uproar even over research burns."[80]

Two years later when the EPA announced plans to issue permits for experimental burnings of chemicals in the Atlantic Ocean, environmentalists were again in an uproar. As Eric Draper, the coordinator of the National Campaign Against Toxic Hazards, stated at the time, "[I]t's a stupid decision. At this point, we are fighting for toxic source reduction. It's not the time to start panacea solutions to toxic waste by taking it out in the middle of the ocean and burning it."[81]

One of the problems with incineration at sea is the possibility of leaks or spillage in the transportation of waste from land to the seas. As Peter Carson, director of the Mid-Atlantic Cleanwater Action Project stated, "[P]eople make mistakes, and when you make a mistake out in the ocean, nobody is going to see it."[82]

One approach that some manufacturers and many of the more developed nations have taken for the disposal of hazardous waste has been exporting that waste to other countries. With the current cost of disposal in landfills estimated at $145 to $615 a drum for hazardous solids, and incineration costs that can range from $200 to $400 a drum,[83] many U.S. hazardous waste generators try to avoid waste disposal in the United States. In part, this has been done by corporations establishing manufacturing plants in areas that have environmental protection requirements less restrictive than the United States. For example, among major producers of chemicals in the United States, the Dow Company has 59 manufacturing plants abroad, DuPont has 52, 3M has 41, and the Monsanto Corporation has 20.[84] In 1997, DuPont and Monsanto both made the top ten list for toxic emissions (DuPont with a whopping 86 million tons and Monsanto with 37 million tons of toxic releases).[85]

Attempts to export hazardous waste have, in many cases, created a backlash among the people in the importing countries. For example, in September 1988 in reaction to an Italian government order to let a toxic waste carrier dock in the Italian port of Manfredonia, the city council resigned en masse. The citizens of Manfredonia rioted for three days, setting fire to the town hall door and blocking entrances to the city.[86] In 1989 five ships carrying Italian hazardous waste circled the globe for months in search of a place to dispose of their cargo. In case after case where a hazardous waste disposal destination was identified and the local population informed of the importing agreements, such agreements to accept waste have fallen through. For example, 15,000 tons of toxic ash from Philadelphia municipal incinerators circled the globe for two years in the late 1980s trying to find a disposal site and being rejected by country after country.[87] Ultimately the ship returned to the United States where the ash was landfilled.

Those exporting hazardous waste have been able to find some willing recipients among the less developed countries, however. It is not difficult to understand the willingness of the leadership in some countries to accept the hazardous waste of the more developed nations. The tiny nation of Guinea-Bissau, which had a gross national product of $160 million in 1984, was offered $40 a ton by a Swiss firm to bury drums of hazardous waste. The deal did not go through. However, the $600 million that Guinea-Bissau would have made over a five-year period was an attractive inducement for the poor nation.

Many less developed nations lack the technology or the sophistication necessary to handle the proper disposal of hazardous waste. Furthermore, many more developed countries have few if any restrictions on the exportation of hazardous waste.

In the United States hazardous waste exporters are required to give notice to the EPA prior to exporting waste and to receive the consent of the receiving country. Poor enforcement, due largely to inadequate staffing at the EPA, and loopholes in the law have hampered the effectiveness of the statute. Hundreds of tons of hazardous waste have been exported from the United States without proper notifications of intent to export filed with the EPA.[88]

Most less developed countries are opposed to transboundary shipments of hazardous wastes.[89] However, formal agreements and pronouncements are clearly inadequate to stem the tide of hazardous waste export. For example, Mexico and the United States have signed agreements governing the exportation of hazardous waste as well as the generation of hazardous waste by U.S. companies within Mexico. Nevertheless, Mexico has serious hazardous waste problems both from U.S. firms within its borders and from importation of waste from the United States. In 1986 three Americans and one Mexican were arrested in connection with the dumping of over 100,000 gallons of toxic waste in Mexico into "a few holes in the ground."[90] In 1993 the North American Free Trade Agreement (NAFTA) was approved by the United States. Although there have been various "side agreements"[91] dealing with environmental and pollution control measures, it is unclear what impact NAFTA will have on environmental quality in the United States or Mexico.

The disposal of hazardous waste is a particularly difficult problem for the more developed countries of Western Europe. Many Western European nations are generating two to four times the amount of waste they have the capacity to dispose of within their own countries. And, as with hazardous waste everywhere, a major problem is overcoming local opposition to the construction of hazardous waste disposal facilities. Great Britain, which still relies on land disposal for the bulk of its hazardous waste, has become a major European importer of hazardous waste. Hazardous waste traveling into the United Kingdom increased from 5,000 tons in 1983 to an excess of 350,000 tons in the early 1990s. The UK may be asking for problems both in the short and long term. Three-fourths of the local government authorities that have responsibility for hazardous waste control in the United Kingdom have no formal plan to deal with the waste.[92]

In the mid-1990s, it was reported that from 1950 to 1963 the United Kingdom dumped approximately 18,000 metric tons of nuclear waste into the waters off the coasts of the Netherlands and France. Both areas still host large fishing industries, and fisherman have rejected suggestions aimed at limiting fishing in those areas, regardless of the threat to health.[93] In 1996, a starker reminder of the dangers beneath the North Atlantic began to surface. Incendiary bombs that had been deposited in the ocean, intentionally or otherwise, began to wash up on the shores of Scotland. These bombs, though artifacts of World War II, are still quite dangerous and have caused injury to a few persons who have handled them. More than 4,500 of these bombs washed ashore in the autumn of 1996, just a fraction of the estimated 1.5 million tons of conventional and chemical weapons thought to have been dropped in the waters surrounding Britain, including a German ship containing 17,000 tons of bombs filled with nerve gas. Scientists argue that an accurate assessment of what lies beneath the ocean must be completed in order to avoid future catastrophes.[94]

One possible solution for the management of hazardous and toxic waste is using microbes and enzymes to detoxify, deactivate, or otherwise degrade or break down complex chemicals. This method is particularly promising for pesticides and solvents; however, not all substances break down. Where appropriate this treatment may cost significantly less than other disposal alternatives and is much more environmentally acceptable.[95]

Federal Regulations

Toxic substances are regulated in the United States under a variety of federal acts. Chemicals used commercially are regulated under the Toxic Substances Control Act, the Federal Insecticide, Fungicide and Rodenticide Act, and the Food, Drug, and Cosmetics Act. The Toxics Release Inventory also plays a role in the use and reporting of chemicals in the United States. These acts require that the manufacturers of chemicals conduct their own product safety tests and submit the results to the federal government. The regulatory agency involved then makes a decision on a case-by-case basis as to whether or not to ban the chemical, regulate its use, or leave it unregulated. The tests are also used to determine safe levels of exposure to chemical residues in drinking water, air, food, or the workplace. A major problem with these and other toxic substance control acts is the cost and number of substances that need to be tested. It is estimated that for each chemical, a good test can take from two to four years and cost from $40,000 to $1 million. As a result, critics have charged, only one percent of all commercial chemicals have been carefully tested.[96]

To regulate toxins that find their way into the environment through manufacturing and other industrial processes, Congress has passed the Clean Air Act, the Clean Water Act, the Occupational Safety and Health Act, and the Safe Drinking Water Act. Federal regulators undertake risk assessment to determine safe levels of exposure to regulated toxins under these laws and require that pollutants released into the air, water, or working environment do not exceed those standards. As we discuss in both the chapters on air pollution (Chapter 5) and water pollution (Chapter 6), many pollutants have not been evaluated to determine the "safe" level of exposure. And, as we discussed in Chapter 3, risk analysis is full of uncertainty. The two federal statutes that are most important in regulating the disposal of hazardous waste are the Resource Conservation and Recovery Act (RCRA) and the Comprehensive Environmental Response Compensation and Liability Act (also known as Superfund). The RCRA requires that anyone storing, treating, or disposing of hazardous waste do so under permit from the EPA. Permits are granted only to those firms that can demonstrate they have the financial capacity, the necessary insurance, and the expertise to know how to operate a landfill or disposal facility. The RCRA applies to any producer of hazardous waste generating at least 220 pounds of waste a month, an amount that fills a 55-gallon drum about halfway. The act provides the EPA with the authority to impose fines and hold individuals criminally liable for the improper disposal of waste. Because of their extreme toxicity, certain substances may not be disposed of in landfills or through underground injection.[97]

The RCRA established a fund jointly financed by the federal government and industry to finance the cleanup of hazardous waste sites that have been identified and placed on a hazardous waste site "priority list" by the EPA. The EPA may either cleanup the site on its own using Superfund monies, require that the generator of the waste clean up the site, or sue those responsible for the waste and use the proceeds to clean the site.

Those liable for cleanup cost include waste generators, waste handlers, waste site owners, or any middle person who arranged for disposal of the hazardous waste at the site. Furthermore, generators and handlers of toxic waste are liable for cleanup costs regardless of when the waste was generated or disposed of, even if the disposal was done in compliance with laws in effect at the time. The owners of hazardous waste sites are liable even if they had no knowledge that hazardous waste was being disposed there. In one case, for example, the Monsanto Chemical Corporation agreed to contribute $13 million to the cleaning up of a site where it had dumped acids more than 50 years previously.[98] State and local governments that have operated or are operating waste disposal sites, or allowed others to operate on the sites with governmental approval, are also liable under the act.[99]

Initially budgeted with $1.6 billion in 1980 for use through 1985, $8.5 billion was added to the Superfund in 1986 for use through 1991. Additional appropriations of $5.1 billion were made for fiscal years 1992 to 1994. Another $1.5 billion was again added in 1997.[100] It is estimated, though, that the National Priority List (NPL) of Superfund sites as of 1992 will require $16.4 billion alone to remedy. This is in addition to the $235 billion to $389 billion the Departments of Defense, Energy, and Interior will need to spend to clean up their sites.[101] To help offset cleanup costs, a "potentially responsible party" program was instituted in 1986 wherein the EPA seeks reimbursement for cleanups from potentially liable parties.[102]

The Hazardous Substance Superfund Trust Fund, which was built using Superfund's taxing authority allowed by its original legislation and extended through December 1995, provided much of the funds needed for remediation expenses when liable parties could not be found. Excise taxes were collected from chemical and petroleum corporations. As of September 2000 the fund contained $4.7 billion in assets, though only about $1.4 billion was actually available for distribution.[103] As of this writing, Congress has not reauthorized the Superfund tax, though the fund still receives money from the government's general revenue (that is, an amount is appropriated for the fund annually). Congress will not likely reauthorize the tax that generated about $1.5 billion annually through the end of 1995 without major overhauls to Superfund. Major corporate interests want to make it much harder for businesses to be held financially liable for cleanup costs and want to make it easier for parties to defend themselves from Superfund liability, especially when the law is applied retroactively.

The fund remains alive though. President Clinton included around $2.2 billion for the fund for fiscal year 1999, though Congress only appropriated $1.5 billion, and $1.4 billion in 2000.[104] That figure fell to $1.27 billion in 2001, and President Bush proposes keeping the Superfund appropriation at that level for 2002.[105]

In terms of the number of sites, the EPA initially estimated there would be 400 NPL sites. A 1996 GAO report raises that estimate to between 1,400 and 2,300 possible NPL projects for the future. It has been estimated that using current remediation technologies, the cumulative cost from 1990 through 2020 will reach as estimated $750 billion. In addition to this, the GAO estimates that around $31 billion will be required to cover the cost of monitoring remediated sites over the long term (30 or more years). As of November 2001 there are 1226 final sites on the NPL, 253 deleted sites, and 72 proposed sites.[106] Although remedial action has begun on most of them, cleanup has only been completed on 64 sites since the program began.[107] This slow progress may be correlated with the fact that the time required for listing sites has steadily lengthened. In 1996, it took EPA about 9.4 years to list non-federal Superfund sites in the NPL; this is up from 8.3 years in 1995, and 5.8 years in the period from 1986 to 1990. Cleanup times jumped from 3.9 years in that period to 10.6 years for those completed in 1996, and to 11.5 years for those completed in 1997.

The original goal of the 1986 Superfund Amendments and Reauthorization Act (SARA) was four years for non-federal sites, 2.5 years for federal sites prior to October 1986. The goal was to cut the time down to 1.5 years after October 1986. EPA officials have argued that a backlog of sites predating Superfund, and ever-increasing evaluation standards are responsible for the time lag. Additionally, since becoming listed can cost responsible parties $20 million on average, there is a strong incentive to infinitely litigate the situation, and spread the blame across as many parties as possible.

In some cases cleaning consisted of removing the waste from an unapproved site to an EPA-approved waste disposal facility. For example, in Greenville, Mississippi, 226 drums of toxic chemicals were moved to an approved landfill in Alabama, leading some to question the true extent of Superfund's "success."[108]

Both the RCRA and Superfund are plagued with budgetary, staffing, and enforcement problems. Close to 80 percent of the disposal sites licensed by RCRA are reportedly in violation of the law. The EPA has had to relax RCRA requirements because so few firms handling hazardous waste have been able to meet their requirements.[109] In the case of the Superfund, Congress was quick to pass legislation dealing with a visible environmental problem, but has been slow to appropriate funds necessary to deal with the problem—a good example of the environmental policy paradox. Policy makers were able to take credit for dealing with a problem that had come to the attention of the public but have not followed through with the resources necessary to complete the job.

As noted above the Superfund Trust Fund tax was discontinued in 1994 pending the reauthorization of the Superfund acts. Efforts put forth during the 104th Congress to pass reauthorization legislation fell flat, however. At the opening of the 105th Congress in 1996, Superfund reauthorization was made a priority within the Senate. Senate Bill 8, which was more or less a rehash of a 1995 bill squelched in the 105th Congress, sought to reform the liability structure of Superfund, which many have thought to be unfairly enforced. Generally, these reforms included provisions that would limit the retroactive liability of owners and operators of co-disposal sites, as well as make exempt those business with less than 30 employees or general revenues under $3 million annually. The Senate bill would have also provided $60 million in aid for the redevelopment of blighted industrial areas (known as brownfields).

The Senate bill garnered little bipartisan support because of its failure to abide by a "polluter pays" principle. The Senate bill, which would have reinstated Superfund taxes on the petroleum and chemical industry for five years, remains unresolved at the time of this writing. It is estimated that the legislature's delay in reauthorizing Superfund has cost the government $2 billion in site cleanup costs.[110] As the 105th Congress came to a close, agreement had still not been reached on the provisions of the authorization. With the bill's failure also goes the appropriation of $8.5 billion (total) for the Superfund for fiscal years 1998 through 2002. Although Congressional leaders vow progress during the opening months of the 106th Congress, the partisan conflicts that have thus far prevented reauthorization are not likely disappear overnight. In 1999 and 2000 alone, six Superfund reauthorizations and fourteen brownfield bills have been proposed. Though debate and demands have occurred regularly, Superfund and brownfield related law and funding have changed very little through 2000.

Regulatory Problems

The formal requirements of any regulatory system tell only part of the story. Perhaps more important, and more interesting for what it teaches us about environmental policy, are the regulatory problems that have been encountered in implementing the RCRA.

Major regulatory problems involved in implementing the RCRA include public objections to toxic waste disposal facilities, insurance and liability concerns, the cost of disposal and related effects, and the lack of incentives in the legislation to reduce the generation of toxic substances.

Perhaps the greatest regulatory problem concerning toxic waste, a problem that makes everything the RCRA is attempting to do more difficult, is the position that industries and state regulators have taken toward the disposal of toxic waste in the past. The combination of an "out of sight out of mind" attitude as well as a misunderstanding of the cleansing capacity of the earth and the ability of toxic substances to move underground led, until the late 1960s and early 1970s, to very poor control over the disposal of toxic substances. Companies in the past have allowed waste to accumulate on their property in open lagoons or in drums that often leak with little concern or control over the long-term consequences of their actions. Furthermore, many state regulatory bodies have been lax in their regulatory efforts. For example, in California at the Stringfellow toxic dump site in Riverside County, a geologist hired by the state spent less than one hour investigating the site to determine whether or not the granite bedrock was impermeable and would be a safe repository for toxic waste. Stringfellow was a repository for toxic waste for 32 years and now threatens major sources of drinking water in the Los Angeles basin. It will cost an estimated $600 million to clean up Stringfellow.[111]

A major problem in the implementation of the RCRA and Superfund is the cost of cleaning waste disposal sites. The cost of cleaning up an average Superfund site is $20 million. Some think such a cost estimate is conservative. Appropriations for Superfund had been a fraction of this amount. As we have seen under Superfund and the RCRA, the generators and transporters of hazardous waste as well as the owners of landfills have primary responsibility for disposing of waste properly and cleaning up improperly disposed waste. For a generator of toxic waste, this can be a significant sum. These costs have had two effects, one positive and one negative. On the one hand, the hazardous waste disposal business is booming as many legitimate operators are finding there is money to be made in the handling of hazardous waste. On the other hand, the incidence of "midnight dumping," or the illegal disposal of hazardous waste, has increased significantly.

The RCRA has a system for tracking hazardous waste, but as stated in a *Forbes* article, "[E]nvironmental protection agencies on both the state and federal level have set up elaborate tracking procedures to assure that hazardous wastes are disposed of properly, but circumventing them is easy. You just falsify the manifest."[112] A hazardous waste generator who ignores the EPA requirements by failing to notify the EPA of its existence and shipping the waste offsite without a manifest or disposing of its waste on its own premises without a permit is, according to an article in *Chemical and Engineering News*, "not likely to be found out. Neither is a transporter who forges a manifest stating that waste arrived at its proper destination when it didn't."[113]

A related problem has been the arrival of organized crime into the hazardous waste disposal business. Organized crime is already heavily involved, particularly on the East Coast, in the garbage collection and disposal business. According to a former teamster official, organized crime on the East Coast has utilized their control of the trash collection business to dispose of toxic waste illegally either by blending clean garbage with toxic waste and shipping it to landfills or by bribing dock operators to look the other way.[114] Waste is illegally disposed of by abandoning drums on deserted roads, opening tanker spigots and allowing the toxic liquids to flow onto highways, mixing toxic substances with fuel oil, burying tanker trucks, or pouring liquids into mine shafts, sewer systems or along rivers and streams. All of these things happen with alarming regularity. For example, thousands of gallons of heating oil laced with dangerous chemicals were sold to Manhattan apartment owners before it was discovered the concoction was toxic. In this example the violators, connected to organized crime, profited from disposing of the hazardous waste and again selling it in heating oil.[115]

When polled large percentages of Americans feel that not enough has been done to clean up toxic waste sites. When asked if they would be willing to pay higher state and local taxes to fund cleanup programs, roughly two-thirds say they would.[116] Public support for cleaning up toxic and hazardous waste and public support for building a hazardous waste disposal facility, however, are two different things. A toxic waste disposal facility is a LULU of the greatest magnitude (or a lulu of a LULU, if you will). As the number of new Superfund sites suggests, many new hazardous waste facilities, including treatment facilities, landfills, and incinerators, would be needed in the near future.[117] However, largely because of the public opposition, few new major hazardous waste facilities have been built in the United States in recent years. When asked at what distance they would be comfortable having a variety of new industrial installations constructed from their homes, a hazardous waste disposal site was seen as the least desirable new neighbor.[118]

Given the nature of the policy-making process and the resources necessary for influencing public policy, where would you anticipate hazardous waste sites to be placed? Several studies have found that hazardous waste sites are most likely to be found in poor neighborhoods and neighborhoods with a large percentage of racial minorities. A U.S. General Accounting Office study of hazardous waste landfills in the Southeast found that three out of four landfills were in areas that were predominantly black and poor. A United Church of Christ Commission on Racial Justice study found that, in the words of the commission executive director Benjamin Chavis, "[T]he results of our research conclusively show that race has been the most discriminating factor of all those tested in the location of commercial hazardous waste facilities in the U.S."[119] In Houston, Texas, all of the city's five landfills and six of the city's eight municipal incinerators are located in predominantly black neighborhoods. The director of research for the Church of Christ racial justice study commented, "[T]he unwritten law governing corporate decision making about toxics seems to have been to do what you can get away with. It means that those communities which are poor, less informed, less organized, and less politically influential become more likely targets for abuse from polluters." Ecologist Barry Commoner put it another way. "[T]here is a functional link between racism, poverty and powerlessness, and the chemical industry's assault on the environment."[120] This trend has been called "environmental racism."

Despite a growing movement toward halting the spread of environmental racism, the siting of incineration and other hazardous waste disposal units still plague minority neighborhoods. A 1997 report studying the siting of such facilities in Los Angeles county found a high correlation between the presence of hazardous waste treatment, storage, and disposal facilities and race and economic status as suggested by environmental justice (EJ) proponents.[121] The EPA established the Office of Environmental Justice in 1992, which would appear to indicate awareness and concern about unequal treatment of populations based on income and race. The EPA now has a number of environmental justice programs and advisory committees, and each region has an EJ Coordinator. EJ has also become one of EPA's seven guiding principles.

Specifically, the EPA has, for example, created a Potential Risk Indexing System that tracks pollutant levels in geographic areas and combines that with demographic information to alert the public and officials of current or potential environmental injustices. One that slipped through the cracks recently was a cement plant in New Jersey. It did not get missed by a federal judge in April 2001, however, who stopped the opening of the plant because the surrounding area is already heavily polluted and 90 percent of the population is black or Hispanic. Ironically, the Bush administration's EPA chief, Christie Whitman, was governor of New Jersey at the time the plant was approved and she actually attended the dedication of the facility.[122]

The EJ programs have been generally successful, though. For example, DuPont was fined $1.89 million in April 1998 for omitting protective eye wear instructions on pesticides used primarily by migrant (minority) farm workers. EJ efforts have also led to other crackdowns, such as the one on a Chicago area exterminator who had been spraying outlawed and dangerous chemicals at homes mostly in low-income, African-American neighborhoods. Without EJ programs at the EPA this criminal may not have been identified, and he may have continued to cause damages that had already cost Superfund over $12 million.[123] Still, the debate rages on as to whether environmental injustice even exists. NYU has compiled an extensive list of studies that found conflicting conclusions, though the majority find there *are* income and racial disparities when it comes to environmental issues in general and hazardous waste sitings specifically.[124]

Two related problems concerning the implementation of hazardous waste regulations are bankruptcy and the inability of hazardous waste generators and handlers to secure liability insurance. Amendments to the RCRA in 1984 required that all hazardous waste facility operators comply with certain financial liability standards by the end of 1985.[125] Failure to meet the standards meant the facilities would be required to close. When the deadline arrived, 48 land disposal facilities were unable to meet their financial liability requirements because they were unable to find insurance.[126] Superfund holds liable those transporting, storing, or producing hazardous waste, even if they were following government regulations in force at the time of their activity—that is, even if they were not doing anything wrong at the time of disposal and unanticipated problems develop later. This is referred to as strict liability. Estimating future liability for cleanup cost under such circumstances can be very difficult. Consequently, many insurance companies have pulled out of the pollution liability insurance market.[127] Even when insurance is available, the cost may be so great as to make insurance coverage impossible to afford for all but the largest operators. Yearly premiums on hazardous waste liability insurance policies can run as high as amount of coverage provided for the year.[128]

Faced with what can often be huge cleanup expenses, many companies chose bankruptcy as a way to avoid liability. In 1977 a solvent recovery firm in Massachusetts declared bankruptcy, leaving the state with about a million gallons of toxic waste to dispose of.[129] This problem was corrected, for the most part, in 1986 when the U.S. Supreme Court ruled that companies could not use the U.S. bankruptcy courts to abandon hazardous waste cleanup obligations mandated by federal or state laws.[130]

Major generators of hazardous wastes, such as oil companies, are self-insured and have the resources necessary to satisfy their cleanup obligations. However, in many cases, particularly for the thousands of smaller hazardous facility operators and waste generators, the combination of costly or unavailable insurance and the reality that a major cleanup could cost more than their total net assets, Supreme Court decisions notwithstanding, presents a major problem for long-term enforcement of Superfund in the future.

Another enforcement problem encountered in the regulation of hazardous waste disposal has been motivating some industries to take regulations seriously. Some polluters have taken the position that fines for failure to comply with hazardous waste rules and regulations are just another cost of doing business. In the 1980s the EPA established a Criminal Enforcement Division for prosecuting violators—company officials—with criminal charges. Thus EPA inspectors began carrying a gun in 1984. As an official of the EPA Criminal Enforcement Division was quoted as saying, "[A]dministrative fines are seen by some people as part of the cost of doing business, but going to jail and being a felon is not."[131] The president of Culligan Water Service in Los Angeles, the chairman of the board of Magnum Resources and Energy Company, as well as various chief executive officers, have been sentenced to short jail terms.[132] The policy seems to have had a positive result. To quote a Los Angeles pollution official, "[W]e want to make the message as loud as we can: penalties can result in CEOs spending time in the slammer. We're looking eyeball to eyeball with chairmen of the board and presidents of major companies. It's staggering to think that at this moment, three presidents or CEOs are in jail because of this."[133] However, as an article in *Fortune* magazine stated, "[M]ost corporate felons go to minimum security prisons, where they can play all the tennis or miniature golf they like as long as they do menial work and go to bed by eleven."[134]

HAZARDOUS WASTE CASE STUDY: GE, EPA, PCBS AND THE HUDSON RIVER

1.5 billion pounds of Polychlorinated Biphenyls (PCBs) were produced in the United States prior to 1977 for use as insulation or in the production of dyes, plastics, and rubber.[135] Much of that was dumped into the Hudson River in New York by many industries and municipalities, especially General Electric (GE), which had the proper permits to do so. When news got out of the toxicity and persistence of PCBs, that all came to an end with the 1976 Toxic Substances Control Act (TSCA).

Decades later, these dangerous chemicals remain at the bottom of the Hudson. Many PCBs have been buried by time and sediment and, if undisturbed, may not pose a threat to the ecosystem or humans. GE continues to claim that we should just let nature continue to bury the chemicals, and no harm will come. They even conclude that PCBs are not even carcinogenic and do not cause other serious human health threats.[136]

Nonetheless, EPA Administrator Whitman, on August 1, 2001, decided to proceed with a plan to dredge the Upper Hudson River to remediate PCB deposits. The plan is to dig up 2.65 million cubic yards of river bottom and haul it to specially licensed landfills over the next five years at a cost of $460 million. The EPA disagrees with General Electric in that PCBs *can* cause cancer and other illnesses such as a weakened immune system, low birth weights, and learning disabilities.

EPA has discovered that parts of the Hudson and the fish within it pose a threat that is beyond acceptable limits as set forth in Superfund legislation. They conducted a study that determined eating an average amount of fish from the Upper Hudson would cause three extra cancers for every 100,000 people. For those who eat *a lot* of Upper Hudson River fish, that cancer risk jumps to 1 in 1,000. Superfund considers between 1 in 10,000 and 1 in 1 million extra cases of cancers to be the allowable limit.

The EPA also evaluated noncancer health effects. If a substance has a Hazard Index (HI) above one, there may be cause for concern. The HI for average Hudson fish eaters is 10, and for heavy fish eaters it is 116, that is, 10 to 116 times higher than EPA would like.

However, risks from being exposed to PCBs in the river through skin contact with contaminated sediments and river water, incidental ingestion of sediments, or inhalation of PCBs in air are generally within or below levels of concern. That is, the EPA considers the Hudson safe for swimming and even as a treated source of drinking water.[137] GE would add the only danger is to those who eat giant quantities of fish every week for at least 40 years.

So far, GE has spent in excess of $200 million on Hudson River research and restoration, and it has consistently followed local, state, and federal government regulations. PCB levels are actually down 90 percent from 1977 levels, the year PCBs were outlawed.[138]

Thus we have an environmental policy paradox. The government gave GE and many others permits to spew PCBs into the Hudson. GE has voluntarily spent millions on clean-up efforts. It is possible that dredging the Hudson will only stir up dangerous toxins that have naturally become latent, and cause more problems than it cures? Is it fair to apply a law retroactively to GE and make them pay for a "crime" that was legal when it was committed?

What happens if some freak occurrence disturbs the river sediment and spreads the PCBs uncontrollably, causing serious environmental damage as well as human deaths and sickness? What if even at present levels we discover the PCBs are even more toxic, especially in combination with some other as yet to be determined chemical? These are all important questions with variable answers. However this case ends up, it is possible that just as many people will get hurt as helped, and the losers will be vocal, perhaps causing changes in environmental policy that may be for the better or worse.

The Policy Paradox in Hazardous Waste Management

The EPA estimates that U.S. industries are capable of reducing their hazardous waste output 15 to 30 percent by the year 2010. Many environmentalists and the U.S. Office of Technology Assessment think these estimates are conservative. An Office of Technology Assessment study in 1986 estimated that companies generating hazardous waste could reduce their waste flows by close to 50 percent within a five-year period.[139] In fact, many waste reduction techniques are easily adaptable and would save industry money—yet they are not utilized. Hazardous waste source reduction techniques include pollution prevention, low- and nonwaste technology, source waste reduction, and waste minimization.[140] According to the OTA, the cost of remediating a polluted site is 10 to 100 times as expensive as funding preventative measures early on. If reducing waste at the source could save waste generators money, and would avoid many of the waste disposal problems discussed in this chapter, why isn't there more source waste reduction?

Hazardous waste regulations in the United States are based on two assumptions: (1) Hazardous waste generation is an inevitable by-product of industrial production, and (2) the focus in hazardous waste management should be on the disposal of waste once generated.[141] Both the RCRA and Superfund focus on the management of hazardous waste after it has been produced. And in fact, according to one analyst, through policies developed for the RCRA, "[The EPA has] created disincentives for waste reduction. For example, EPA has kept the cost associated with land filling low, thereby not reflecting long-term cleanup cost ... the true cost of disposal."[142]

If a waste generator has the choice between using a relatively low-cost landfill as opposed to higher cost alternatives such as incineration or modifying production methods, then naturally the low-cost option will be selected. Politically it is easier for state and federal regulators to pursue lower cost hazardous waste management practices, since the opposition from affected industries is less; hence we should not be surprised there has been little pressure on industry to adopt more expensive methods of hazardous waste disposal. This is a good example of the operation of informal incentives in the policy-making process. Landfill disposal of hazardous waste involves short-term relatively low costs and long-term high or unknown cost. Policy makers, when confronted with the choice between one policy that has low short-term costs and high long-term costs, and a competing policy that has a high short-term cost and low or unknown long-term costs, are likely to choose the former policy. Politically, given the concern about rising taxes today, it is the choice that elected officials prefer. The true costs of hazardous wastes utilizing land disposal are eventually paid. They may be paid by future generations in terms of the unavailability of water or increased rates of cancer. But they are paid in some way. Although the public and politicians may benefit today by having less expensive goods and services, since the true cost of their production or delivery is not included in the market price, the public will eventually pay. As two hazardous waste policy analysts wrote in the *Los Angeles Times*,

> [E]verytime government makes it cheaper for industry to casually discard hazardous waste—as the U.S. Environmental Protection Agency recently did by allowing the burial of liquid hazardous waste in landfills—the true cost of disposing that waste is shifted to the general public in the form of massive cleanup expenses, lost resources and spiraling rates of cancer, birth defects and disease.[143]

The longer we wait, or the longer we pursue inadequate disposal methods for our hazardous waste, the more it is going to cost society. However, these costs are easy for policy makers to ignore, since they are deferred and shifted to future generations.

The strict liability provisions of Superfund, specifically liability for the generator of hazardous waste regardless of who handles it or where it goes after it is passed on, is another interesting example of a policy paradox. On the surface, this would appear to be hard-line legislation to deal with a tough problem. In practice, what it has meant is that many hazardous waste generators who might otherwise recycle their hazardous waste by selling it or giving it to others have an incentive to hang on to it because they are, of course, liable for any damage caused by the waste. And this is liability that is easy to ascertain given the tracking and permit requirements of the RCRA.[144]

Even if environmental laws were perfectly written, there are implementation problems. As with many environmental regulations, the EPA has found full enforcement of Superfund and the RCRA virtually impossible. The EPA has had difficulty implementing many environmental regulations according to the timetables and deadlines established by federal statutes.[145] In the case of the RCRA and Superfund, not only have regulations been slow in coming from the EPA, but also regulated industries are often not in compliance with those regulations in effect. For example, a study of leak detection systems, required under the RCRA to detect chemical leakage from hazardous waste disposal sites, found that close to 60 percent of the disposal facilities regulated under the RCRA lacked leak detection systems.[146] Moreover, not all disposal facilities are scrutinized. Perhaps thousands of these facilities have not come to the attention of the EPA.

As in other areas of environmental regulation, economics, politics, and risk analysis play an important role in hazardous waste regulation. Beginning during the Reagan administration, the Office of Management and Budget (OMB) has been given responsibility for weighing the cost and benefits of new federal regulations. Former president Ronald Reagan's first EPA administrator, Anne Gorsuch Burford, eliminated the Enforcement Division of the EPA by reassigning enforcement lawyers to other divisions. The agency also promoted voluntary compliance by industry and sought to limit the role of the federal government.[147]

Furthermore, at various times during the Reagan administration, the OMB put pressure on the EPA to revise hazardous waste exposure requirements in a manner that would allow exposure levels greater than EPA officials thought were necessary to protect human health.[148] Ironically, lax enforcement of hazardous waste regulations was not what industry wanted. As an editorial in *Chemical Week* stated, "[A]n ineffective environmental protection agency is not what the chemical industry needs. What it needs and what it expects from the Reagan administration is an agency that will discharge intelligently its responsibility to the American people.... [A] management attitude that turns off hundreds of confident and dedicated professionals—and EPA has them—is not good."[149]

What can you do if you are worried about exposure to toxic waste? You can have your water supplies tested by state and local officials or, better yet, an independent testing laboratory. For a free directory of independent laboratories, write to the American Council of Independent Laboratories, 1629 K Street N.W. Suite 400, Washington, DC 20006-1633, or visit their website at *http://www.acil.org/public/labreferral/index.html* (or call 202-887-5872). If you suspect serious water quality problems may already be impacting the health of your community, you might attempt to conduct an epidemiological study. Activists in San Jose, California, Willow Springs, Louisiana, and Lowell, Massachusetts, as well as other areas, have conducted such studies on their own and the results have prompted local officials to require the removal of toxic and hazardous waste.[150] The Johns Hopkins University Press has published a guide for citizens to conduct such surveys of their communities titled *The Health Detective's Handbook*. This book explains proper study design, means of community organization, types of data analysis, and provides a sample questionnaire. As in other areas of environmental regulation, citizen suit provisions are available that allow you to force industries that are not complying with federal regulations into compliance.[151] There are also a number of Internet resources available.[152]

An interesting case study of self-help in dealing with water contaminated by toxic pollutants occurred in Southern California in the late 1980s. Two small water companies, the Hemlock Mutual Water Company with 240 customers and the Richwood Mutual Water Company with 217, both located in the San Gabriel Valley, found their groundwater wells were polluted by industrial solvents. The Hemlock Water Company, ignoring heavy pressure from the EPA and its contractor in the area, the CH2M Company, decided to reject federal help. Over a three-day weekend, the president of Hemlock Water, with the assistance of an electrical contractor and a plumber, put in a filtration system costing $40,000. Neighboring Richwood Mutual Water Company decided to follow the consultant's and EPA's advice to accept federal assistance. Three years after the Hemlock system was in operation, Richwood's $1.5 million purification system, with operating costs of $100,000 a year, was still not functioning.[153]

SUMMARY

We began this chapter by summarizing the nature of our waste and exploring the relationship between industrial development and waste generation. The management of solid waste provides one of the most dramatic examples of the paradox of environmental policy. Although for several decades we have understood and could have anticipated most of our solid waste problems, as we have seen, more than half of the cities in the United States will exhaust their landfill capacity and are without acceptable new sites.[154]

In the next chapter we discuss land-use problems. Specifically, we look at local land-use planning and how money and politics operate to determine how our neighborhoods look. Then we examine three things that threaten U.S. and global agricultural production: farmland conversion, desertification, and soil erosion. Finally, we discuss federal land management issues including harvesting trees on federal lands, multiple-use management, wilderness designation and protection, and endangered species.

NOTES

1. Worldwatch Institute. *State of the World: 1999* (New York: WW Norton and Company), p. 46.
2. Jim Glen, "The State of Garbage," *BioCycle* (April 1992), p. 48.
3. Nora Goldstein, "The State of Garbage," *BioCycle* (April 1997), p. 63
4. Conservation Foundation, *State of the Environment: A View Towards the Nineties* (Washington, DC: Conservation Foundation, 1987), p. 106.
5. Ibid., p. 411. The 11 major federal laws are the Clean Water Act, the Marine Protection Research and Sanctuaries Act, the Safe Drinking Water Act, the Clean Air Act, the Resource Conservation and Recovery Act, the Comprehensive Environmental Response, Compensation, and Liability Act, the Surface Mining Control and Reclamation Act, the Nuclear Waste Policy Act, Low Level Radioactive Waste Policy Act, the Uranium Mill Tailings Radiation Control Act, and the Toxic Substances Control Act.
6. G. Tyler Miller, *Living in the Environment* (8th ed.) (Belmont, CA: Wadsworth, 1994), pp. 512–13.
7. Ibid., p. 513.
8. Nora Goldstein, "The State of Garbage," p. 62.
9. The U.S. EPA defines municipal solid waste as, "MSW—otherwise known as trash or garbage—consists of everyday items such as product packaging, grass clippings, furniture, clothing, bottles, food scraps, newspapers, appliances, paint, and batteries. Not included are materials that also may be disposed in landfills, but are not generally considered MSW, such as construction and demolition debris, municipal wastewater treatment sludges, and non-hazardous industrial wastes."
10. Council on Environmental Quality, *Environmental Quality: The Sixteenth Annual Report of the Council of Environmental Quality* (Washington, DC: U.S. Government Documents, 1985), p. 421. Per capita municipal waste generation in the United States was reported as 703 kilograms. Figures for a few other countries were as follows: Canada, 526; Austria, 208; France, 289; Federal Republic of Germany, 338; Norway, 415; Spain, 215; Sweden, 301; Switzerland, 337; United Kingdom, 282; Japan, 334; and Australia, 681. See also Miller, *Living in the Environment*, p. 513.
11. Jim Glen, "The State of Garbage," p. 46.
12. U.S. EPA. Office of Solid Waste. "Municipal Solid Waste in the United States: 1999 Facts and Figures: Executive Summary." Available at *http://www.epa.gov/epaoswer/non-hw/muncpl/pubs/excsum99.pdf.*
13. Ibid, and EPA's "Municipal Solid Waste in the United States: 1999 Facts and Figures: Executive Summary."
14. Conservation Foundation, p. 111.
15. Joseph F. Sullivan, "States Are Making Recycling a Must," *New York Times*, January 11, 1987, p. 9.
16. "Tons and Tons of Trash and No Place to Put It," *U.S. News and World Report* (December 14, 1987), p. 58.
17. Ibid. In response, however, newer landfills opening up have greater capacities—buying some states additional time.

18. Paul Hawken, "Resource Waste," *Mother Jones* (March-April 1997), p. 44.
19. New York City Press Office. March 22, 2001. Press Release 091-01. "Mayor Giuliani, Governor Pataki, and Borough President Molinari Commemorate Arrival of Last Garbage Barge at Fresh Kills Landfill, Staten Island."
20. Vivian Toy, "Sealing Mount Garbage: Closing Staten Island's Fresh Kills Dump Is an Operation of Staggering Complexity," *New York Times*, December 21, 1997, p. 46.
21. New York City Press Release 091-01.
22. Other diseases include myiasis, onchocerciasis, Ozyard's, filariasis, leishmaniasis, African sleeping sickness, yaws, tularemia, bartonellosis, catarrhal sandfly fever, conjunctivitis, salmonellosis, poliomyelitis, entamoebiasis, fish, beef, and pork tapeworms, roundworms (whipworms), hookworms, and many others. See Brian J. L. Berry et al., *Land Use, Urban Reform and Environmental Quality* (Chicago: University of Chicago, 1974), p. 194.
23. Newsday.com. December 7, 2001. "Designs for dump redo include memorials to WTC victims." Available at *http://www.newsday.com/news/local/wire/ny-bc-ny-dumpdesigns1207dec07.story*.
24. G. Tyler Miller, Jr, *Living in the Environment*, p. 527.
25. Ibid., p. 525.
26. U.S. EPA, Office of Solid Waste. "Municipal Solid Waste in the United States: 1999 Facts and Figures: Executive Summary." Available at *http://www.epa.gov/epaoswer/non-hw/muncpl/pubs/excsum99.pdf*.
27. These are 1990 figures—the most recent available as of this writing. Telephone interview with EPA representative, November 1993. See also Conservation Foundation, *State of the Environment*, p. 115.
28. Public Law No. 89–272, *Title Two* (1965).
29. Ibid., Section 202 (a) (2,6).
30. Public Law No. 91–604 (1970).
31. 42 U.S.C.A. Sections 6943 (a) (2).
32. *City of Philadelphia v. New Jersey*, 437 U.S. 617 (1978).
33. Sullivan, "States Are Making Recycling a Must."
34. Worldwatch Institute, *State of the World: 1999*. (New York: WW Norton and Company), p. 53.
35. Worldwatch Institute, *State of the World: 1999*. p. 54.
36. G. Tyler Miller, Jr., *Living in the Environment*, p. 513.
37. Telephone interview with EPA representative, November 1993.
38. Natural Resources Defense Council (NRDC) Website. "Cities&Green Living: Recycling: In Brief: Fact Sheet: Recycling Overview." Available at *http://www.nrdc.org/cities/recycling/fover.asp*.
39. U.S. EPA, Office of Solid Waste. "Municipal Solid Waste in the United States: 1999 Facts and Figures: Executive Summary." Available at *http://www.epa.gov/epaoswer/non-hw/muncpl/pubs/excsum99.pdf*.
40. Jim Glenn, "Ten Years Make a World of Difference," *BioCycle*, April 1998, p. 4.
41. Jim Glenn, "Year End Review of Recycling and Composting," *BioCycle,* December 1997, p. 50.
42. Marie L. Miranda and Joseph E. Aldy, "Unit Pricing of Residential Municipal Solid Waste: Lessons from Nine Case Study Communities," *Journal of Environmental Management*, January 1998, p. 92.
43. Johnathan Turk, *Environmental Studies* (2nd ed.) (Philadelphia: Saunders, 1985), p. 300.
44. Glenn, "Ten Years Make a World of Difference," p. 4.
45. Goldstein, "The State of Garbage," p. 74.
46. U.S. EPA, Office of Solid Waste, "Municipal Solid Waste Factbook." Available at *http://www.epa.gov/epaoswer/non-hw/muncpl/factbook*.
47. Such programs typically provide economic incentives to recycle.
48. Frank J. Popper, "The Environmentalist and the LULU," *Environment*, 28 (March 1985), p. 6.
49. Bill Paul, "New Environmental Controls Improved Outlooks for Dumps," *Wall Street Journal*, October 2, 1987, p. 17.
50. Miller, *Living in the Environment*, p. 513.
51. Nora Goldstein, "The State of Garbage," p. 63.
52. Glenn, "Year End Review of Recycling and Composting," p. 52.
53. American City and County, "EPA Predicts Drop in Waste Production," February 1995, p. 6.
54. U.S. EPA, Office of Solid Waste. "Municipal Solid Waste in the United States: 1999 Facts and Figures: Executive Summary." Available at *http://www.epa.gov/epaoswer/non-hw/muncpl/pubs/excsum99.pdf*.
55. Telephone interview with the City of Los Angeles Recycling Office, November 1993.

56. Jim Glen, "The State of Garbage," p. 46.
57. John E. Anderson, "The Toxic Danger," *American Demographics*, 9 (January 1987), p. 45; and "Toxic Territories," *American Demographics*, 8 (September 1986), p. 67.
58. "Urban Toxic Pollutants Found in Polar Bears," *The Columbus Dispatch*, May 21, 1986, p. 2.
59. Miller, *Living in the Environment*, p. 563.
60. Louis Regenstein, "The Poisoning of America: How Deadly Chemicals Are Destroying Our Country," *USA Today* (magazine), (September 1983), p. 18.
61. U.S. Office of Technology Assessment, "Technologies and Management Strategies for Hazardous Waste Control," (Washington, DC: U.S. Government Printing Office, 1983), p. 13.
62. This discussion is based on data from the EPA and the Nuclear Information and Resource Service, November 1993.
63. Ronald Fuchs and Samuel D. McDonald, "1992 State-by-State Assessment of Low-Level Wastes Received at Commercial Disposal Sites." Department of Energy Publication DOE/LLW-181, September 1993.
64. Telephone interview and written communication with the Nuclear Regulatory Commission, Nuclear Information and Resource Service, November 1993.
65. Florida Center for Public Management. National Air and Radiation Indicators Project. "Safe Waste Management: Waste and Materials Management: Indicators: Volume and Radioactivity of Low-Level Waste" Available at *http://www.pepps.fsu.edu/NARIP/general/waste/saf-wast/llw.pdf*.
66. Miller, *Living in the Environment*, p. 563.
67. Telephone interview with EPA representative, November 1993. See also Council on Environmental Quality, *The Twenty-Fifth Report of the Council on Environmental Quality*, 1995, p. 371
68. Ken Sternberg, "HazWaste Well Accepted—for Now," *Chemical Week*, 146 (20) (May 23, 1990), p. 6.
69. Environmental News Service. "60% of America's Liquid Toxic Waste Injected Underground" July 7, 1999. Available at *http://ens.lycos.com/ens/jul99/1999L-07-07-03.html*.
70. "Hazardous Chemicals," United Nations Environment Program, UNEP Environment Brief Number 4 (no date), p. 2; and Greenpeace Website. "Born Into the Chemical Crisis" Available at *http://www.greenpeace.org/~toxics/html/content/eu.html*.
71. Keith Schneider, "The Data Gap: What We Don't Know About Chemicals," *The Amicus Journal* (Winter 1985), p. 15.
72. Miller, *Living in the Environment*, p. 559.
73. For a discussion of problems associated with the underground injection of hazardous waste, see Michael Brown, "The Lower Depths," *The Amicus Journal* (Winter 1986), p. 14. See also Miller, *Living in the Environment*, p. 558.
74. Ibid., p. 18.
75. Timothy Kao and Joseph Bishop, "Coastal Ocean Toxic Waste Pollution: Where Are We and Where Do We Go?," *USA Today* (magazine), 114 (July 1985), p. 21.
76. Ibid.
77. G. Tyler Miller, Jr., *Living in the Environment* (5th ed.) (Belmont, CA: Wadsworth, 1988), p. 507.
78. Miller, "Living in the Environment," (8th ed.), p. 558.
79. Laurie A. Rich, "Burning of Toxics Faces Rising Protest Worldwide," *Chemical Week*, 136 (May 22, 1986), p. 18.
80. Pamela S. Zurer, "In an Incineration of Hazardous Waste at Sea: Going Nowhere Fast," *Chemical and Engineering News*, 63 (December 9, 1985), p. 24.
81. Maura Dolan, "EPA to Permit Burning of Toxic Waste at Sea as Test," *Los Angeles Times*, November 27, 1985, Pt. 1, p. 1.
82. Ibid.
83. Telephone interview with an EPA representative, November 1993; and Eli Kirschner, "An Anxious Industry Sees New Limits to Its Options," pp. 23–24.
84. "Beyond Our Borders: How U.S. Multinationals Handle Hazardous Waste Abroad," *Conservation Exchange* (National Wildlife Federation), 6 (3) (Fall 1988), p. 1.
85. Sarah Anderson and John Cavanagh, "The Top 10 List: A Four-Star Feast, But who Gets the Check?" *The Nation*, (Dec 8, 1997), p. 8.
86. Tyler Marshall, "Western Europe Has Its Fill of Toxic Waste," *Los Angeles Times*, Pt. 1, p. 1.
87. Dermota O. Sullivan, "Program Targets Issue of Hazardous Waste Exports," *Chemical and Engineering News* (September 26, 1988), p. 24.
88. "Waste Exports Open Door for Crisis," *Conservation Exchange* (National Wildlife Federation), 6 (3) (Fall 1988), p. 7.

89. "Report of the Ad Hoc Working Group on the Work of Its Third Session—Transboundary Movements of Hazardous Waste," United Nations Environment Program, November 16, 1988.

90. "Deadly Gunk from El Norte," *Time* (May 5,1986), p. 27.

91. These are agreements that have been negotiated between the United States and Mexico which are not part of the formal NAFTA accords.

92. Carol Cirulli, "Toxic Boomerang," *The Amicus Journal* (Winter 1989), p. 9; and Marshall, "Western Europe," p. 10.

93. Bernard Thomas, "The World's a Waste Dump," *World Press Review*, (Feb 1996), p. 35.

94. Rob Edwards, "The World's a Waste Dump," *World Press Review*, (Feb 1996), p. 35.

95. Judy R. Berlfein, "A Natural Response to Toxic Waste," *Los Angeles Times*, July 11, 1988, Pt. 2, p. 4; "Enzymes: Alternative for Waste Detoxification," *The Journal of Commerce*, 361 (August 30, 1984), p. 228; and "Bugs Have Big Future in Cleanup of Waste," *European Chemical News*, 44 (June 3, 1985), p. 14.

96. Carl Pope, "An Immodest Proposal," *Sierra* (September-October 1985), p. 43.

97. Gordon F. Bloom, "The Hidden Liability of Hazardous Waste Cleanup," *Technology Review*, 89 (February-March, 1986), p. 58.

98. Ibid., p. 61.

99. The Superfund Amendments and Reauthorization Act, 100 Stat. 1613, P.L. 99–499, 1986. Upheld by the U.S. Supreme Court in *Pennsylvania v. Union Gas*, 1989 LEXIS 2970 (June 15, 1989).

100. Congressional Research Service and the Committee for the National Institute for the Environment. "Superfund Fact Book." Available at *http://www.cnie.org/nle/waste-1a.html*.

101. Congressional Research Service and the Committee for the National Institute for the Environment. "Superfund Fact Book." Available at *http://www.cnie.org/nle/waste-1b.html*.

102. Seventy percent of which was since 1989. Telephone interview with an EPA representative, November 1993.

103. U.S. EPA "Superfund (Section IV) Fiscal Year 2000 Annual Report." Available at *http://www.epa.gov/ocfo/finstatement/2000ar/ar00_sec4.pdf*.

104. This is an excellent source to understand basic political and financial Superfund issues. Congressional Research Service and the National Council for Science and the Environment. Issue Brief 10011: Superfund Reauthorization Issues in the 106th Congress. October 30, 2000. Available at *http://www.cnie.org/nle/waste-28.html#_1_8*.

105. U.S. EPA, "Overview of the 2002 Budget." Available at *http://www.epa.gov/ocfo/budget/2002/2002bib.pdf*.

106. U.S. EPA, Superfund Website, NPL Site Information as of November 16, 2001 at *http://www.epa.gov/superfund/sites/npl/info.htm*.

107. Elliott P. Laws, Foreword, *Hazardous Waste: Impacts on Human and Ecological Health*. Barry Johnson, Charles Xintaras, and John Andrews, Jr. (eds.). (Princeton, Princeton Scientific Publishing, 1997), p. xii.

108. Magnuson, "A Problem That Cannot Be Buried," p. 78.

109. Bloom, "The Hidden Liability of Hazardous Waste Cleanup," p. 60.

110. Gina Robicheaux, "Superfund Remediation Effort Succumbs with 105th Congress; Recycling is Set for Next Year," *FDCH News Service* (November 3, 1998).

111. Kim Murphy, "State Held Liable for Stringfellow Toxic Dump Site," *Los Angeles Times*, June 3, 1989, Pt. 1, p. 1.

112. James Cook, "Risky Business," *Forbes*, 134 (December 2, 1985), p. 112.

113. Janice Long, "Illegal Hazardous Waste Disposal Probed," *Chemical and Engineering News* (April 22, 1985), p. 22.

114. "Witness Says Crime Figures Rule Disposal of Toxic Waste," *New York Times*, September 20, 1984, p. B10.

115. J. Miller and M. Miller, "The Midnight Dumpers," *USA Today*, (magazine) (March 1985), pp. 60–64.

116. Magnuson, "A Problem That Cannot Be Buried," p. 77.

117. Robert Cameron Mitchell and Richard T. Carson, "Citing of Hazardous Facilities: Property Rights, Protest, and the Citing of Hazardous Waste Facilities," *American Economic Review*, 76 (May 1986), p. 285.

118. Frank J. Popper, "The Environmentalist and the Lulu," *Environment*, 27 (March 1985). The other installations measured were for a nuclear power plant, coal-fired power plant, a large factory, and a ten-story office building.

119. Timothy Aeppel, "Civil Rights Group Links Race with Citing of Toxic Waste Dumps," *The Christian Science Monitor*, 16 (April 1987), p. 5. See also Dick Russell, "Environmental Racism," *The Amicus Journal* (Spring 1989), p. 22.
120. Russell, "Environmental Racism," p. 25.
121. J. Tom Boer, Manuel Pastor Jr., James L. Sadd, and Lori D. Snyder, "Is there Environmental Racism? The demographics of hazardous wastes in LA county." *Social Science Quarterly* (Dec. 1997), p. 809.
122. Environmental News Service. "Environmental Injustice—Court Halts Operation of Cement Plant Dedicated by EPA Head Christie Whitman." April 24, 2001. Available at *http://www.mapcruzin.com/news/rtk042401a.htm.*
123. U.S. EPA, Office of Environmental Justice. "1998 Environmental Justice Biennial Report: Working Towards Collaborative Problem-Solving." Issued June 1999. Available at *http://es.epa.gov/oeca/main/ej/98biennial.pdf.*
124. NYU Center for Environmental and Land Use Law, Program on Land Use Law, U.S. Environmental Justice Website. "Discriminatory Siting: Table of Environmental Disparity Studies." Available at *http://www.nyu.edu/pages/elc/ej/studies.html.*
125. 42 U.C.S. Section 6925.
126. Bruce J. Parker, "The Insurance Crisis and Environmental Protection," *Environment*, 28 (April 1986), p. 14.
127. "Some Technical, But Meaningful Facts About Pollution Liability Insurance," *Journal of American Insurance*, 62 (Spring 1986), p. 11; See also U.S. General Accounting Office, *Hazardous Waste Insurance Availability* (Washington, DC: U.S. Government Printing Office, 1988).
128. Linda M. Watkins, "Chemical Firms Battle Insurers on Policy," *The Wall Street Journal*, August 28, 1986, p. 6. Liability insurance is available even though it is costly. In a phone call to the EPA Superfund hotline on June 21, 1989, the author was supplied with the names of eight companies willing to write hazardous waste liability policies.
129. Eleanor Smith, "Angry Housewives," *Omni*, 9 (December 1986), p. 22.
130. For a discussion, see "Bankrupt Firms Liable for Toxic Cleanup," *Oilgram News*, 64 (19) (January 28, 1986), p. 2.
131. "Don't Pass Go, Go Directly to Jail," *Fortune*, 114 (December 8, 1986), p. 9.
132. See, for example, Eleanor Smith, "Midnight Dumping," *Omni*, 6 (March 1984), p. 21; and Steve Taravella, "L.A. Jail's Company Officers for Breaking Pollution Laws," *Business Insurance*, 18 (April 2, 1984), p. 2.
133. Travella, "L.A. Jail's Company Officers for Breaking Pollution Laws," p. 3.
134. "Don't Pass Go, Go Directly to Jail," p. 10.
135. U.S. EPA. Office of Pollution Prevention and Toxics. "PCB Homepage" at *http://www.epa.gov/opptintr/pcb/.*
136. GE's Hudson River Website. Available at *http://www.hudsonvoice.com/auxiliary/faqs/faqs.html.*
137. U.S. EPA. EPA's Hudson River Website. *www.epa.gov/hudson.*
138. GE's Hudson River Website. *http://www.hudsonvoice.com/river_recovery/natural_processes/river_natural_processes.html.*
139. Robert E. Taylor, "EPA Offers Aid for Firms to Cut Hazardous Waste," *Wall Street Journal*, October 31, 1986, p. 48.
140. Larry Martin, "The Case for Stopping Waste with Their Source," *Environment*, 28 (April 1986), p. 35.
141. Roberta G. Gordon, "Legal Incentives for Reduction, Reuse, and Recycling: A New Approach to Hazardous Waste Management," *Yale Law Journal*, 95 (March 1986), p. 810.
142. Ibid., p. 813.
143. James Louis and Katherine Durso-Hughes, "Hazardous Waste: The Public Will Pay," *Los Angeles Times*, March 17, 1982, Pt. 2, p. 7.
144. Ibid., p. 813.
145. Bradford W. Wyche, "The Regulation of Toxic Pollutants Under the Clean Water Act: EPA's Ten Year Rule Making Nears Completion," *Natural Resources Lawyer*, 15 (1983), p. 511.
146. "Many Waste Sites Lack Leak Detection Systems," *Chemical and Engineering News*, 63 (May 13, 1985), p. 16.
147. Robert Cahn, "EPA Under Reagan," *Audubon* (January 1982), p. 16.
148. These efforts were not always successful. See, for example, "EPA Worse Case Guideline Assessing Hazards," *Wall Street Journal*, August 26, 1986, p. 6.

149. Cahn, "EPA Under Reagan," p. 14.
150. John Carey and Susan Katz, "How to Track Down Toxins," *Newsweek* (May 6, 1985), p. 81.
151. See Toxic Substances Control Act, Section 20, 15 U.S.C., Section 2619; The Safe Drinking Water Act, Section 1449, 42 U.S.C., Section 300J-8; and The Resource Conservation and Recovery Act, Section 7002, 42 U.S.C., Section 6972.
152. For example, the Environmental Defense Fund (www.edf.org) and the Natural Resources Defense Council (www.nrdc.org) are two organizations that work toward preventing environmental degradation through legal action.
153. Michael Ward, "Tiny Suppliers' Water Cleanup Is Faster, Cheaper Without EPA Aid," *Los Angeles Times*, June 5, 1989, Pt. 1, p. 3.
154. Miller, *Living in the Environment* (5th ed.) pp. 491–495.

9

Land Management Issues

In this chapter we explore federal land-use problems—broadly defined. First, we examine soil erosion, farmland conversion, and desertification, which all threaten long-term, sustainable food production. Finally, we discuss federal land management issues, including multiple-use, recreation, fee demonstration project areas, commercial recreation permits and concessions, fire, wilderness, loss of endangered species, and ecosystem management.

LOCAL LAND USE PLANNING

In the United States, freedom to do as one pleases with one's property is considered sacrosanct—a very important part of our dominant social paradigm (DSP). Consequently, planning or land use-control is contrary to our dominant social paradigm. In fact, in many communities, land-use planning by government is virtually non-existent. It was not until 1914 that New York became the first state to pass local zoning (land-use planning) enabling legislation. This was not a moment too soon, as in 1870 a quarter of Americans lived in cities. By 1920 half the population was living in urban areas. By 1921 there were 10 million cars congesting unplanned streets and industries polluting unplanned neighborhoods.

Still, government land planning was not acceptable to many, including the courts, which found it to be an infringement upon private property rights, an illegal means of interfering in the economy, and a to limit individual freedoms. The courts found land-use planning to be an unconstitutional "taking." Not until the late 1920s and the Supreme Court's *Village of Euclid* v. *Ambler Realty Co.* decision was unrestrained land usage and laissez-faire land planning ended.[1]

Nonetheless, traditions and social norms die hard, and most major metropolitan areas in the United States have grown without careful land-use planning. Since World War II, cities such as Los Angeles, Chicago, and New York and their suburbs have grown many miles in every direction. This growth has been fueled by subsidized mortgages, which for the first time allowed the middle class to enjoy home ownership, and a freeway system that permitted workers to commute from the suburbs to jobs in the city.

Most of you are familiar with metropolitan traffic problems. In some cities, freeway traffic is bumper to bumper during most of the day. Traffic congestion can cause psychological and physiological stress, and can be expensive. From 1993 to 1995 alone, the average American commuting time jumped 30 percent. It is estimated that such intense traffic due to sprawl and growth in the Phoenix metro area has created an air pollution and stress related illness that costs Phoenicians an extra $500 million in health care costs. This may not be surprising considering an acre and a half of desert in the Phoenix metropolitan area are developed every hour of every day, making the Phoenix metro area ever more spread out.[2] Currently, Paris, Rome, and Manhattan could all fit within the city limits of Phoenix.[3]

Even ignoring damage to our minds and bodies, traffic congestion makes automobiles more expensive to operate. It is estimated that traffic jams add an additional $800 a year to the cost of operating an automobile.[4] It is further estimated that the drivers and citizens of Los Angeles lose $8 billion annually due to traffic congestion, while New York and Chicago lose $7 billion and $3 billion, respectively.[5] Anyone familiar with the transformation of the San Jose or Orange County areas in California or Long Island in New York has to wonder what forces dictate land-use patterns. As we see later, a combination of our DSP and the informal incentives in the political process are what influence land-use decisions in the United States. Therefore, chances are we may not end up with the metropolitan areas we desire, but given the reality of the policy-making process, they are often the only kind of development the system will produce.

Typically, local governments develop "comprehensive plans" designed to provide a blueprint for land use and development in future years. Comprehensive plans are among the most important functions of local government. Zoning and subdivision regulations are designed to carry out the plans. Usually comprehensive plans are revised every five or ten years. More important than these revisions, however, is the issuance of variances, or exceptions to the zoning guidelines that are laid out in plans. In some states, jurisdiction over large projects that have an areawide impact, such as the location of a power plant or prison, have been "kicked upstairs" to state or regional boards. Florida, for example, has state and regional boards that review "developments of regional impact." In Maryland, power plant location is a responsibility of state government.[6] This assertion of state control over large projects has been referred to as the "quiet revolution" in land-use planning.[7] Nevertheless, most planning is still done at the local level.

Local government authority for land-use planning was affirmed by the U.S. Supreme Court in 1926.[8] The Court found that zoning ordinances were presumed to be valid as long as they were reasonably related to public health, safety, morals, or the general welfare of citizens.

Guy Benveniste has identified four basic types of planning: trivial, utopian, imperative, and intentional.[9] The trivial plan is little more than a statement of what will take place. It projects the future but makes no attempt to influences that future. The utopian plan shares with the trivial plan the characteristic that it will have no impact on the status quo but for a different reason. The utopian plan describes the future that no one really expects will occur—hence no one takes it seriously.

The "ideal type" of planning is referred to as imperative planning. Imperative planning is what most people think of when they think of land-use planning. Under imperative types of land-use planning, development plans are mandatory, made well in advance and enforced. However, as Richard Foster and Lawson Veasey point out, "ideally the plan is a guide, implemented by the law and applied to specific situations by rational people operating in a nonpolitical environment. . . . [T]his ideal type of imperative planning conforms with the reality only occasionally. . . . [L]ocal land use decisions are both intense and political in nature."[10]

Finally, intentional planning is planning in which the means of implementation for the plan are unavailable or insufficient and hence the realization of the plan is dependent on factors external to the planning process. For example, planning may be dependent on the agreements of private parties, or individual action.

Planning is an inherently political process. The political nature of planning and zoning was described by Richard Babcock in his book *The Zoning Game* as "part of the political technique through which the use of private land is regulated. When zoning is thought of as part of the governmental process, it is obvious it can have no inherent principles separate from the goals which each person chooses to subscribe to the political process as a whole."[11] The politics of zoning is best demonstrated in the issuance of a variance or a request for land use that is inconsistent with the overall plan. For example, to put a convenience store in a residential neighborhood or a subdivision on previously designated agricultural land requires a variance permit that involves a special process. As Neil Carn describes it, "[W]hen such a request is made, it is likely to be approved only if a proper strategy can be found that fulfills the legal, technical, and political concerns of the zoning officials."[12] In most cases the technical and legal considerations are easy to meet—particularly if the political concerns of zoning officials are also met.

The decisions made in planning are reinforced through zoning ordinances that establish zoning districts, which both identify current usage and establish future uses. Urban planning is carried out with four major types of urban designations: residential, commercial, industrial, and special-use areas. Within these four categories are a number of subcategories. For example, within a commercial zone, there may be large or small commercial areas, industrial heavy or light. Within the residential category may be single-family homes, multiple-family dwellings, or a combination of both. Typically, the intent behind comprehensive land-use planning is to segregate those activities that have negative side effects and to preserve the quality of life by maintaining open space, or the residential character of a neighborhood, or by determining the sustainability of land for particular uses. Despite attempts to segregate land use by activities and characteristics, some mixing is unavoidable and can, at times, be desirable. For example, due to traffic problems, the community of Fort Collins, Colorado, no longer rigidly separates industrial and residential areas. By allowing the clustering of residences with new industry, traffic problems can be minimized.[13]

Some communities prefer mixed zoning, at least to some extent. For example, being able to walk to the store or bike to work, which is only possible when land is zoned in such a way as to place those types of developments, residential and commercial, close together, may be highly desirable. The states of Oregon and Washington have been successful at limiting sprawl and the decay of urban centers through zoning laws. Detroit has reinvigorated its urban core by attracting businesses back from the suburbs through "urban renaissance zones" that provide major tax breaks to businesses if they build in formerly dilapidated urban areas. Using a slightly different approach, Boulder, Colorado, implemented an extra sales tax to buy a greenbelt around the city that will be forever preserved.[14] Many states and localities are allowing private conservation easements that allow citizens or businesses to "zone" their land as permanent wilderness.

Ultimately, most specific zoning decisions are made by planning commissions, or zoning boards that are elected or appointed and usually have no formal training in planning or government. Often times, the planning commission or zoning board is the same body that governs a city or county, and sometimes board or commission decisions are subject to the approval of the city council or county board of supervisors. Still, these politicians may have no knowledge of planning and zoning techniques or what the outcomes may be. Consequently, the same forces that influence decision making in local legislative bodies, such as the desire for reelection, the need for campaign contributions, and the disproportionate influence of economic interest groups, influence the planning and zoning process.

The stakes in zoning can be very high. From the perspective of a developer, it can mean increased wealth or the opportunity to stay in business; from the perspective of those attempting to prevent development, it can mean the loss of the neighborhood, and open space, or an agricultural preserve. As one student of land-use planning wrote, variance decisions "bring out all the chumminess, informality, and deal making qualities of local government."[15]

To summarize, land-use decisions are made by politicians dependent on campaign contributions or the support of local business owners for reelection. Inevitably, those contributions come disproportionately from people who propose to develop the land over which the elected officials have jurisdiction. Hence we should not be surprised at the rate at which agricultural land is being converted to urban use or at the lack of green open space in most metropolitan areas.[16] This is particularly true in a political environment that assumes individuals should have an unrestrictive right to do as they please with their private property. Given the nature of the land-use decision-making system and the incentives operating on political actors, it would be surprising indeed if metropolitan areas in the United States had developed any other way.

The past does not bind us to the future. Local politicians are responsive to political pressures. The business-as-usual relationship between local policy makers and land developers is upset when citizens become organized and vocal. Land-use and zoning decisions provide the entry point for many citizens into environmental politics. The potential that a new subdivision will be put in one's neighborhood, or that old Victorian house on the corner will be torn down to be replaced by a gas station, provides an impetus for many individuals to become involved in the policy-making process who would otherwise be uninvolved in environmental politics. By watching for notices and attending public planning hearings, writing letters to the editor, and joining with others who are concerned, people can have an impact on how their community develops. If we don't watch out for and protect our interests, someone else will define those interests for us.

Soil Erosion

Although less visible than the new shopping center down the street, soil erosion and the loss of agricultural productivity is no less a threat to many communities and, ultimately, to all of us. Every year, slowly but surely, the United States loses potential future agricultural productivity. Agricultural productivity is dependent on the quality and quantity of soil and the availability of water—all of which are in short supply. Many problems facing farmers today are similar regardless of where they occur. Soil erosion presents a threat to future agricultural productivity worldwide. About six pounds of soil in the United States are lost per pound of food eaten. The average person eats about 2,000 pounds of food per year, which means approximately 1.68 billion tons of soil are lost in the United States annually, just through typical eating habits.[17] Globally, the Chinese lose their soil to erosion at a rate three times faster than that in the United States.

Soil erosion is the movement of soil, either by wind or water, off farmlands and into lakes, rivers, streams, or the oceans. Soil erosion is a good example of an environmental problem that develops slowly and seemingly has little impact. It lacks the "crisis" qualities that are sometimes necessary to motivate policy makers to act. Consequently, due to the dynamics of the policy process, it is difficult to mobilize policy makers or the public to take corrective action to prevent soil erosion. Nevertheless, further loss of valuable cropland will surely lead to crisis. As Will Rogers once said, "They're making people everyday, but they ain't makin' any more dirt."

In the United States, close to 6 billion tons of topsoil are lost each year. Historically, about one-third of the topsoil, originally on U.S. croplands, has been lost.[18] It is estimated that the total loss of U.S. topsoil to erosion in the next 50 years will amount to between 25 and 62 million acres.[19] Internationally, topsoil losses amount to some 25.4 billion tons per year. This represents approximately 7 percent loss of topsoil from cropland every 10 years. In some parts of the United States, soil has been measured eroding 17 times faster than it forms, and 90 percent of all U.S. cropland is losing soil at an unsustainable rate.[20]

Some people point to huge increases in agricultural productivity since World War II as evidence that additional corrective measures are not necessary to prevent soil erosion. For instance, U.S. exports of soybeans, wheat, and corn nearly tripled from 1965 to 1985. However, the increased use of fertilizer and the farming of marginal cropland have masked the impacts of soil erosion. Between 1950 and 1992 there was a tenfold increase in the use of fertilizer worldwide and a near tripling of the amount of land put into production.[21] Though some of that production is necessary to sustain human life and growing populations, much is "wasted" on luxuries. About 85 percent of American topsoil loss is associated with raising livestock. Switching from an animal-based to a vegan diet would reduce demands on topsoil by 95 percent.[22]

In the United States, the Soil Conservation Service within the Department of Agriculture has primary authority over soil erosion. Although the service provides technical assistance and produces useful data, they have no authority to require agricultural practices that prevent erosion. Internationally, the United Nations provides expertise; however, the advice is often ignored.

U.S. lawmakers did take a major step toward preventing erosion on previously undeveloped farmland in 1985. In the passage of the 1985 farm bill, a "sodbuster" provision denied federal farm benefits for crops grown on newly plowed grasslands vulnerable to erosion. Although this was a positive measure, the long-term projections are for continued and even accelerated soil erosion. What land is not blown or washed away, furthermore, is being converted to nonagricultural uses at an alarming rate. Farmland conversion, although a national and international problem, most often must be dealt with on the local level—through planning and zoning procedures.

Farmland Conversion

Farmland conversion is a worldwide problem. Often times the best farmland is adjacent to a metropolitan area. As that area grows, the land becomes covered with homes, roads, and other improvements that take it out of agricultural production. Between 1987 and 1996, an average of 3.4 million acres of agricultural land was converted to nonagricultural uses in the United States annually.[23]

Our dominant social paradigm plays an important role in agricultural land conversion. The primacy of markets and individual enterprise in the management of private property can be an insurmountable barrier to attempts to regulate the conversion of agricultural lands. The efficient thing to do with land is to develop and to increase its value.

Some economists argue that when the value of agricultural land is high enough, buildings and pavement will be moved and the land put back into production. This is unlikely from a practical standpoint and perhaps impossible from an ecological standpoint, since the land would no longer be suitable for farming. As Paul and Anne Ehrlich explain,

> [A]fter all, shopping malls and high rise buildings are considered more valuable than today than cornfields. If the value of corn should rise enough to change all that in ten or a hundred years ... presumably ... an economical way would be invented by scientists to peel cities off the land. Sadly, however, if that were possible, the bared land would not be prime farmland but wasteland, since the process of first disturbing and then covering it would destroy the physical and biological characteristics that make the soil productive.[24]

In the United States, government efforts to limit the conversion of agricultural land to urban use have met with limited success. Most measures, such as the Williamson Act in California, provide property tax relief for farmers that agree to keep their land in agricultural production. These have turned out to be temporary measures postponing conversion until the agricultural land adjacent to urban areas is at a premium. As such, they sometimes work as little more than tax breaks for farmers—or, in the case of California, the major corporations that dominate California agriculture. Soil quality also has a major impact on agricultural production and when quality deteriorates to the extent that the land is no longer good for farming, no one wins.

Desertification

Desertification, the process of turning productive land into wasteland, is occurring at an alarming pace. In semi-arid areas, such as the American Southwest, grasses and other vegetation secure the soil and retain moisture. If the plants die, through overgrazing, trampling, or harvesting for fuel, the moisture retention capacity of the ground is lost and the land is slowly converted to desert. In the United States, desertification is impacting an estimated 225 million acres, primarily in the Southwest. Like soil erosion, desertification does not have a simple solution. In addition, the slow and gradual nature of desertification does not lend itself to crisis management.

Although a serious problem in the United States, desertification is even more troublesome internationally—particularly in the less developed world where productive farmland and the capacity to develop sustainable agriculture are disappearing swiftly. International desertification problems are discussed further in Chapter 10.

Farmers are understandably reluctant to support any measures, regardless of how environmentally sound, that threaten their livelihood. With investments in equipment and machinery subject to substantial debt, farmers, for practical purposes, may believe they have no other alternative but to increase their productivity through the use of fertilizer and pesticides, as well as the use of marginal lands for planting.[25]

The conditions just described threaten our future ability to produce food for those parts of the world that have become dependent on our agricultural production, and may, ultimately, challenge our ability to feed ourselves. One group studying domestic agricultural production found that eventually food prices will go up and that Americans will have to change their eating habits to demand less, per capita, of the land. That will probably include eating less meat, growing more food in backyard gardens, and turning to locally grown produce.[26]

Although opinions vary on the severity of the domestic farm/food problem, there is strong evidence that a significant shift to organic farming would increase farm income and reduce soil erosion and nutrient depletion while meeting domestic food needs and reducing oil imports.[27] For a variety of political and institutional reasons, even when the scientific community is in substantial agreement on what needs to be done, we are often unable to pursue those policy ends. Therefore, regardless of the potential benefits of organic farming, and the obvious problems associated with soil erosion, desertification, and other problems, the incentives operating on policy makers in the policy-making process, including the localized strength of agricultural interests, make it very unlikely that any significant changes will be made in the foreseeable future in U.S. farm policy. That is the paradox.

FEDERAL LAND MANAGEMENT

The management of federal land holdings in the United States is of major importance to the economies of the western states. Federal lands make up approximately one-third of the continental United States (some 700 million acres) and contain roughly one-fourth of the nation's coal, four-fifths of our shale oil deposits, and half of U.S. uranium, oil, and gas deposits. Eighty percent of western public lands are permitted to ranchers at relatively low rates for grazing what amounts to only 2 percent of cattle produced in the United States.[28] This is, in effect, a subsidy to western interests. The major federal land management agencies are the Bureau of Land

Management (BLM), U.S. Forest Service (USFS), National Park Service (NPS), and the U.S. Fish and Wildlife Service (FWS).[29] Later, we examine land use management problems that confront these agencies together and independently.

The land management policies of federal agencies reflect the bargaining, compromise, and power struggles that are characteristic of pluralistic democratic systems. Land management policies and goals in the federal bureaucracy reflect the changes over time of constituencies in the political environment of a particular agency. The land management issues we examine here include multiple-use, recreation, fee demonstration project areas, commercial recreation permits and concessions, fire, wilderness, loss of endangered species, and ecosystem management.

Multiple Use

Multiple use, as the term suggests, means various activities can be carried out simultaneously on federal lands. It has been a policy of some federal land management efforts since the turn of the century. You may recall that Gifford Pinchot was an early proponent of the idea of multiple use on federal lands during the conservation movement. In 1960 multiple use was given explicit legislative sanction. The USFS Multiple Use Sustained Yield Act of 1960, the Classification and Multiple Use Act of 1964, and the Federal Land Management and Policy Act of 1976 (FLMPA) provide the statutory basis for multiple-use land management in the BLM and USFS.[30] Multiple use, defined in FLMPA, is the management of the public lands and their various resources in ways that best meet the present and future needs of the American people.[31] This act expanded the use and importance of nontraditional programs on federal lands including recreation, scientific and historical values (cultural resources), wildlife and natural scenic beauty in both nonrenewable and renewable resource areas.

Under multiple-use management, permitting a variety of activities such as logging, mining, and grazing along with recreation and wilderness preservation are all goals of federal land management agencies. The difficulties in reconciling these competing uses have led some to question whether or not multiple-use management is possible or desirable. As Marion Clawson wrote, "Multiple uses applied to national forest, other public forest, and private forests are more a slogan than a blueprint for actual management."[32]

Critics of multiple-use management argue that the discretion allowed administrators to choose among a number of competing uses for the land results in management that reflects the historical institutional bias of the USFS and the BLM. Plans that take a more holistic approach toward land-use management are now preferred over a single discipline management plan because they allow for an increase in public involvement and help to manage whole systems. Greater public interest often creates a slower process; however, the result is usually a higher acceptance rate among the participants and interested public.[33]

Recreation

Recreation on many federal lands has increased significantly over the last twenty years. For example, the Colorado Plateau area (western Colorado, northwest New Mexico, northern Arizona, and central and southern Utah) experienced a 94 percent increase in visitation between 1981–1994.[34] Some of the most popular NPS areas on the Colorado Plateau include Zion, Grand Canyon, Bryce Canyon and Lake Powell. This trend is expected to continue both in the Southwest and on all federal lands. Increased recreational uses have led federal land management agencies, especially in the western United States, to discuss limiting visitation. Clearly, at some point, the growth of one interest (recreation) will infringe upon multiple use principles and specifically another interest, such as the maintenance of wilderness.

The BLM and USFS provide dispersed recreation for visitors who prefer less crowded areas and more solitude than is typically available in a National Park. The popularity of BLM and USFS land as recreational destinations has, in some places, necessitated the creation of a permit system (like that used in the National Park System for many years) to limit recreational visits. Based on the need to limit people and for a return of more revenue to manage site-specific problems, recreation fee demonstration project areas have been created on BLM and Forest Service lands as a tool to manage recreational uses of federal lands.

Fee Demonstration Project

Congress authorized the Recreational Fee Demonstration Program in 1996.[35] The intention of the recreation fee demonstration program was to allow federal land management agencies to recover some of the costs of managing recreation. The program allows the managing agency to retain all of the project revenues and to use at least 80 percent of the fees at the sites where they were collected.

The fees were intended for maintenance projects and for public service enhancements at the project sites. Each agency has approached the collection and management of fees differently, based primarily on the way an agency historically collected fees or disseminated information to the public. Each federal land management agency nominated a different number of project sites. (The experiences of each agency are assessed in this endnote.)[36]

Commercial Recreation Permits and Concessions

Another management tool and source of revenue on federal lands is the issuing of recreation permits for commercial use and licensing of concessions. Recreation permits and concessions licenses are issued by an agency when a private company, individual or organization is operating on public lands to produce a profit. Concession permits are negotiated by the federal land managing agency to provide facilities and services for the public. They are especially popular in NPS areas that provide lodging and food services.

Commercial recreation permits are issued for hunting, hiking, mountain biking, river running, and backpacking activities. For most land management agencies, the cost of administering these permits is more than the generated fees. For example, in Grand Canyon National Park, commercial river permits return only a minimal fee for a trip down the Colorado River. The money collected often falls short of the amount needed for the NPS to monitor concession impacts.[37]

Fire Management

There are two fire management practices that have caused some controversy in federal land management: prescribed burn (which is a human ignited fire used for management purposes) and prescribed natural fires sometimes thought of as a "let it burn" policy (when a naturally ignited fire, or more rarely a human ignited fire, is allowed to burn under certain conditions).

The NPS often uses the controversial forest management practice of the "let it burn" policy, as it is consistent with their mission of managing forests in a natural state. For example, in the summer of 1988 a series of lightning-caused fires led to extensive destruction that burned close to one-half of Yellowstone National Park's 2.2 million acres. NPS employees were determined to let fires burn themselves out in accordance with the NPS policy.[38] However there was a problem with allowing these fires to burn.[39] One hundred years of fire suppression had created in Yellowstone an unnatural and hazardous depth of forest fuel.[40]

To reduce the possibility of catastrophic wildfires, land management agencies use prescribed burning to reduce unnatural forest fuel accumulation. Once prescribed burning occurs, naturally ignited fires should be allowed to occur within the constraints of a prescribed burn plan.[41]

Opponents to prescribed burning believe that the NPS should restore areas to natural conditions by using mechanical manipulation to reduce accumulated fuels before conducting a prescribed burn.[42] Restoring the forest structure and function prior to implementing prescribed fires is very costly and may not be practical across large land areas. However, due to the heightened awareness of fire, the use of prescribed burning to restore wilderness areas has been the most widely accepted forest restoration method.

The NPS, (as well as the BLM and FWS), have identified fire as having a natural role in the wilderness ecosystem, except where it threatens human life or property.[43] The use of fire helps to retain ecological processes that have been altered from their natural condition by human intervention. Ironically, wilderness areas, due to past fire suppression, may already be in an unnatural state and hence impossible to manage in a "hands off" wilderness manner.

Fire is just one of the many controversial issues facing public land managers today, though it is a hot topic (no pun intended). Prescribing burns or allowing natural fires to take their course could threaten the public safety as well as private property. Current fire policies also could reduce air quality and recreational or grazing opportunities. However, they may also be integral in efforts to prevent highly destructive crown fires and to restore ecosystems as much as possible to their pre-European settlement state.[44] That is, such policies may be critical for ecosystem management or maintaining the biodiversity needed to sustain a variety of wildlife.

WILDERNESS

History

The first "preservation" of federal lands came in 1872 with the creation of Yellowstone National Park. The early National Park experience provided many conveniences such as hotels and provided a plethora of amenities for visitors. The NPS philosophy of providing facilities for tourists is still evident today.

The early wilderness use philosophy of the Forest Service differed from that of the Park Service. The USFS wanted to preserve large roadless areas and to protect them from future development. The first USFS wilderness reserve was designated in 1924.

Prior to the passage of the Wilderness Act in 1964, federal land management agencies had little guidance on managing wild areas. The USFS and BLM did manage administrative primitive areas, in a similar manner to congressional wilderness designations except that primitive areas allow multiple uses to occur. The Forest Service designated many wilderness reserves primarily to protect them from being removed from its jurisdiction and added to the National Park System.[45] For example, the USFS prevented the expansion of Yosemite National Park onto its lands by designating over 2.2 million acres as administrative primitive areas, which exceeded the total acreage of Yosemite National Park. BLM areas within close proximity to Grand Canyon National Park were studied to evaluate whether they qualified for NPS status. This created pressure on the BLM to designate wilderness and primitive areas to avoid a transfer of lands to the Park Service.[46]

The Wilderness Act created a National Wilderness Preservation System and directed the Secretary of the Interior and the Secretary of Agriculture to review lands and within ten years make recommendations to Congress regarding their suitability for wilderness designation.[47]

The designation of wilderness areas has been one of the most controversial federal land-use issues in the second half of the twentieth century. As Paul Culhane put it, "[W]ilderness issues evoke more passion among public land interest groups than any other issue."[48]

To designate a wilderness area, it had to contain certain values. The Wilderness Act of 1964 section 2(c) provides that an area may be designated as wilderness if it has the following attributes:

> [It is] an area of undeveloped land retaining its primeval character and influence, without permanent improvements or human habitation, which is protected and managed so as to preserve its natural conditions and which generally appears to have been affected primarily by the forces of nature, with the impact of man's works substantially unnoticeable; has outstanding opportunities for solitude or primitive and unconfined type of recreation; and may also contain ecological, geological, or other features of scientific, educational, scenic, or historic value, and must be comprised of 5,000 acres or be of sufficient size to make practicable its preservation.[49]

Even though the Wilderness Act recommends an area of 5,000 acres the two smallest wilderness areas are less than the recommended acreage. The FWS, Oregon Islands National Wildlife Refuge is comprised of 575 acres to protect sea birds and mammals and the FWS Pelican Island National Wildlife Refuge is comprised of 4,760 acres to preserve a refuge for water birds. The largest wilderness is Wrangell-St. Elias National Park in Alaska comprised of 8.7 million acres.

Shortly after the Wilderness Act became law, the USFS adopted the position that wilderness status should only be granted to lands that were "pure wilderness," defined in part as those lands that were not within the sight or sounds of roads or any other development.[50] Such a designation would have severely limited the number of wilderness areas. Congress was not persuaded by this logic and in 1978 passed the

Endangered American Wilderness Act, which established wilderness in many areas that the Forest Service had found as not worthy of wilderness protection.

Since September 3, 1964, when the Wilderness Act was signed into law, over 105 million acres have been designated as wilderness areas. During the Carter Presidency (1976–1980), the wilderness preservation system in the continental United States grew by some 12.4 million acres and 56 million acres were set aside in 1980 by presidential executive order. The Alaskan Fish and Wildlife Service refuges in Alaska doubled in size to 87 million acres. During President Clinton's administration, another 8.5 million acres of wilderness was designated in Utah and California by executive order.[51]

Land can be considered wilderness and treated as such without specific federal government legislation or protection. Local governments and citizens themselves can ban together to create open spaces or designate areas as wild and protect them.

For example, local governments and individuals in California have taken the initiative to band together outside and across political boundaries to protect open spaces for aesthetic and recreational purposes in addition to protecting various forms of wildlife. The Midpeninsula Regional Open Space District is 45,000 acres of foothill and bayland preserves between the San Francisco Bay and the Santa Cruz Mountains. The District was created by local conservationists who were successful in placing a voter initiative on the ballot in 1972. Annexation has increased the size and scope of the district with subsequent voter initiatives.[52] Local businesses and environmental groups work with cities and counties to manage the open space, which is operated primarily through a voter approved fund in the form of a property tax of 1.7 cents per $100 of assessed property value.

Furthermore, local governments can use concurrency laws or development impact fees to ensure land remains wild or to purchase more open spaces to keep up with the growth and sprawl of human populations. The latter can raise money by charging developers for new developments, where the fees go to a fund used to purchase open space or build parks, for example. The former simply restricts development so it does not encroach on existing wilderness, which may be more valuable to a community than growth.[53]

Proposed Wilderness and Wilderness Study Areas

After the passage of the Wilderness Act of 1964, the USFS and BLM wilderness designation process has been completed largely through congressional action on a state-by-state basis. Both the BLM and USFS were required to inventory lands that were suitable for wilderness designation.

The USFS started a wilderness inventory of areas that would qualify as wilderness study areas by conducting two reviews of roadless areas. The first RARE (Roadless Area Review and Evaluation) study, referred to as RARE-1, involved 55.9 million acres. RARE-1 recommended that 12 million acres should be redesignated as wilderness. Conservationists criticized RARE-1 as being a "rocks and ice" plan, designating only those areas that were inaccessible for timber or mining purposes.

In 1977 the Forest Service began RARE-2, the second inventory of USFS lands to determine areas that should be designated as wilderness. RARE-2, completed in 1978, recommended that Congress designate 15.4 million acres immediately as wilderness, and that 10.6 million acres of potential wilderness be given further study. Unlike the first roadless area review, RARE-2 allowed the USFS to release land for multiple use activities in areas that were determined "not suitable" for wilderness designation. It recommended that 36 million acres be released for timber harvesting and for other multiple-use purposes.[54]

The BLM, under the Federal Land Policy and Management Act of 1976, was required to inventory all roadless areas over 5,000 acres in size to determine if they qualified for wilderness study areas. The BLM's biggest concern with the wilderness designation was how to manage areas over the long term to preserve their wilderness character. The BLM wilderness study area review, using guidelines similar to the USFS, developed a three-step process including an inventory, study, and a report to Congress on a state-by-state basis.

The BLM wilderness review was completed in November 1980 and only included information for the 48 contiguous states. The review determined that out of 150 million acres, only 24 million acres warranted *further* consideration as wilderness study areas.[55]

Once a wilderness study area is established, regulations require the area to be managed as a designated wilderness area. Often this does not occur because the surrounding local populations and agency management supports multiple use and do not want areas to be "locked up."

The Wilderness Act of 1964 had provisions that allowed the establishment of new mining claims in designated wilderness areas until December 31, 1983. Claims made on, or prior to, that date could be mined provided the development was "substantially unnoticeable."[56] For any wilderness areas established after January 1, 1984, no new mineral claims were accepted. Existing claims have to be validated through an assessment.

Traditionally, the Secretary of the Interior has allowed few mining exploration and developments within wilderness areas. This policy of restraint changed after James Watt was confirmed as secretary of the interior in 1980. Secretary Watt was the first to approve large-scale mineral developments, beginning with development within California's Death Valley National Monument. Public and Congressional outcry forestalled further mineral development in wilderness areas, but there are still remain mining claims that have not been developed. These claims promise to become issues at some point in the future.[57]

Another sometimes-controversial issue involves grazing in wilderness areas. Cattle and sheep are grazed in both USFS and BLM wilderness areas. As Section 4 (d) (4) (2) of the Wilderness Act states, "The grazing of livestock, where established prior to the effective date of this Act, shall be permitted to continue subject to such reasonable regulations as are deemed necessary."

The guidelines that both the USFS and BLM use in managing wilderness state, "There shall be no curtailments of grazing in a wilderness area simply because an area is, or has been designated as wilderness, and shall not be used as an excuse by administrators to slowly phase out grazing."[58] Wilderness livestock grazing adjustments follow the same guidelines that pertain to all rangelands to protect them from resource degradation. And, like other federal lands, grazing in wilderness areas is not always well managed.[59]

There may be changes in some aspects of federal land management soon, however. The BLM is currently faced with a dilemma. Should it sell grazing permits to environmental groups? This brings up a number of questions, such as, should markets determine public land use more than administrative decisions made within the context of the current planning system? In this case this means: Should ranchers be exposed to competition for public lands? Does society agree grazing is the best use of that land, and if not, should environmentalists be allowed to pay the public to let the land rest or to try to restore it to a more natural condition? Robert Nelson, a public policy professor and long-time analyst in the Department of the Interior, has concluded "The BLM grazing program cannot be justified by any ordinary economic standard." In terms of market value and grazing subsidies, he adds, "it would cost perhaps $100 million to $150 million to buy out all the grazing rights (Forest Service as well as BLM) in the entire U.S. wilderness system."[60] This begs the question, should our government subsidize ranchers at a cost higher than this *every* year? What are we forgoing by allowing our lands (and tax dollars) to be utilized in such a manner?

National Park Service Management

The NPS, consistent with its mandate to preserve and protect its lands, pursues a hands-off policy toward land management, attempting to let ecological systems develop naturally. However, Park Service policy has been criticized for ignoring past human intervention and natural disturbance regimes. Often the NPS does not take into consideration that parks are not closed ecosystems. Park ecosystems are a part of much larger system over which the NPS does not have control.

A significant management problem the NPS encounters is encroachment. In 1980 the NPS released a report that listed 4,325 specific threats to 320 park units.[61] Over 50 percent of these reported threats were from activities occurring outside of the park boundaries. Threats included dam construction, sewage and chemical runoff, oil, gas, mining, and power plant developments. All of these impact the ability of the NPS to manage its lands in a manner that will prevent degradation. However, if more attempts were made to work with outside agencies and landowners, it is possible that some of these activities could have been mitigated. In addition, the NPS has faced budget cutbacks and increased numbers of visitors leading to overcrowding, noise, and air pollution.[62] Overcrowding has forced the NPS to hire additional law enforcement rangers (sometimes called danger rangers). Wilderness enthusiasts question if these rangers, who are equipped with shotguns and handguns, are a necessary precaution in the wilderness.

Compared to other resource agencies the NPS has enjoyed very little controversy. Most NPS directors have come from within the ranks of the service, and share the philosophy of the NPS to preserve and protect parklands even in those areas within the parks that have been kept out of wilderness designation. For example, the NPS director for the last four years of the Reagan administration, William Mott, was an outspoken proponent of park acquisition and endangered species protection. Though environmentalists greeted his appointment with enthusiasm, Mott's ideas frequently met with a cool reception higher up in the Reagan administration.[63] In 1986, Mott circulated a memorandum in the NPS that was written by William E. Horn in the Office of Assistant Interior Secretary for Fish, Wildlife and Parks. The memo proposed a radical change in park management and indicated that a park be judged in good condition (the highest ranking) if 80 percent of its resource space was undamaged. "For example, the aesthetics of Yosemite Valley are obviously essential to the park, whereas the health of the mule deer herd is not."[64] This suggested policy was not implemented.

Proposed wilderness areas may or may not protect land in the same manner as designated wilderness areas depending, as always, on contemporary political considerations. However, Congress intended that proposed and designated wilderness be considered more or less equally with limited motorized access and mechanical equipment usage. Because Congress must approve wilderness designation, politics play a key role in designation. With the exception of well-publicized national wilderness battles, wilderness disputes are fought on a state-by-state basis. The main actors are resource users, such as timber and mining companies, along with environmental groups organized at the state or local level.

In the future, there promises to be conflict over appropriate management policies to protect the wilderness. The issue of water rights in and from wilderness areas plays a role in wilderness politics. Mining will continue to present wilderness conflicts. The demands for wilderness as recreation areas cannot be accommodated if fragile wilderness ecosystems are to be protected. Managers must also consider protecting or restoring wilderness just for ecosystem health, or even for the protection of a specific (non-human) species.

Endangered Species

Endangered species, the ultimate loss of plants and animals, is a federal land management problem and an important global environmental problem. We first examine the global aspects of species loss, and then look at efforts that have been made to protect species on federal lands in the United States.

It is estimated there are somewhere between 5 million and 30 million plant and animal species on the earth. An average of one species becomes extinct every day. And if we consider all kingdoms of life (bacteria, fungi, mold as well as plants and animals), as many as 137 species disappear *daily*.[65]

Species preservation is very important for the future health and development of humankind. Approximately 40 percent of prescription and nonprescription drugs used by humans have active ingredients that have been extracted from plants and animals. Drugs manufactured from plants have helped to cure typhoid fever, psittacosis, and Rocky Mountain spotted fever.[66] Natural products made from plants have been attributed to increasing life expectancy by 10.3 years.[67]

Of the estimated millions of species, only 1.7 million species have been identified, and less than 1 percent of those identified plant species have been thoroughly studied to determine their possible usefulness to humans. Plants that provide 90 percent of the world's food supply today were developed from previously wild plants growing primarily in the tropics. We have no idea what contributions existing species may make to food, medicine, other necessities or luxuries.[68] Although certain well-known and loved species such as the bald eagle or gray whale are protected for cultural, political, or other reasons, many other lesser known plant and animal species are not so fortunate.

Given ecosystem interdependence and our inability to predict the impact that tinkering with natural systems will have on those systems in the long run, the elimination of species may be permanently damaging the natural balance of the world in a way we do not understand or perhaps will not understand until it is too late. G. Tyler Miller contends that, "The millions of species inhabiting in the earth depend on one another for a number of services. Because of this complex, little understood web of interdependence, the most important contributions of wild species may be their roles in maintaining the health and integrity of the world ecosystems."[69]

Species endangerment primarily results from hunting and habitat destruction. Extinction rates of mammal and bird species have increased along with an increase in the sophistication of hunting techniques. From the period 8000 B.C. to A.D. 1600, approximately one species was lost every 1,000 years. Yet from the period 1600 to 1900, one species was lost every four years, while from 1900 into the mid-1990s, one mammal and bird species was lost every year.[70]

Due to habitat competition and trade, western settlers hunted the buffalo, grizzly bear, Kit fox, red fox, wolf, panther and other species that competed with cattle and sheep grazing. The buffalo herds went from 60 million previous to Euro-American settlers, to 500 in 1868.[71] The grizzly bear was abundant in the early 1800's with populations roaming from Ontario, Canada to Mexico estimated to be at 100,000.[72] In 1992, in the same area, bear populations were estimated at 1,000 with only two areas in the lower forty-eight states including Yellowstone and the northern Continental Divide having reliable bear populations.[73] Severe fragmentation of bear and plant habitats has occurred as a result of modern developments such as roads.

Habitat destruction and extinction of plant species is most closely related to the various activities that we discuss throughout this book including deforestation, desertification, and air and water pollution. By 1975 the estimated annual extinction rate for all species was 100 a year. In the 10-year period between 1975 and 1985, this rate increased tenfold to 1,000 a year and it was estimated that it would increase tenfold again in the five-year period between 1985 and 1990 to 10,000, doubling again by the year 2000 for an estimated annual extinction rate of all species in the year 2000 of 20,000 species per year.[74] Even if these estimates were high, an average extinction rate of 1,000 species a year by the end of the century would still equal the greatest mass extinctions in world history.

Internationally, species endangerment provides a classic example of the problem associated with common pool resource management. For example, ocean fish and mammals in international waters that are not owned by anyone may be harvested by everyone. Several species of whales have been hunted to the brink of extinction, and many commercial fish have been overfished to the point of commercial extinction, meaning it is no longer profitable to harvest them.

The most significant treaty protecting endangered species at the international level is the Convention of International Trade in Endangered Species and Wild Fauna and Flora. This treaty was passed in 1975, by the International Union for the Conservation of Nature and Wildlife Resources and is administered by the United Nations Environment Program. The treaty has been signed by 87 countries and prohibits the hunting or capturing of 700 species.[75] This and other international treaties to which the United States is a signatory have been incorporated into the 1973 U.S. Endangered Species Act as part of U.S. federal law.[76] Nevertheless, although international treaties have helped reduce pressures on some species, enforcement is uneven among the nations.

Wildlife biologists that study international species management have argued that at least 10 percent of a global land area in selected regions should be set aside for ecosystem preservation, thereby preserving plant and animal species habitats that would ensure their protection. There are over 3,500 protected areas throughout the world, but with 1.6 million square miles (or 4.3 million square kilometers), this area represents less than 3 percent of the earth's land.[77]

The United States took the lead in the protection of endangered species with the passage of the Endangered Species Act of 1973.[78] The U.S. Supreme Court lauded the ESA as "the most comprehensive legislation for the preservation of endangered species ever enacted by any nation."[79]

Federal intervention in the protection of endangered species in the United States began around the turn of the century.[80] However, federal legislation prior to the Endangered Species Act of 1973 usually contained qualifying language or lacked necessary sanctions to carry out its provisions. Nonetheless, the act itself was a strong statement and a big step toward species preservation, and although it has been weakened somewhat, the act's passage is an example of nonincremental policy making in Washington, D.C.

The Endangered Species Act authorizes the National Marine Fishery Service, an agency within the Department of Commerce, to identify endangered and threatened marine species. The U.S. Fish and Wildlife Service, within the Department of Interior, is authorized to identify and list other animal and plant species that are endangered or threatened in the United States and abroad. For a species to be endangered there must be so few individuals surviving that the existence of the species is threatened. For a species to be threatened it may still be abundant but declining in numbers such that if existing trends continue, they will be endangered in the future.

In 1998, 1,082 species were identified and included in the endangered and threatened species list in the United States alone.[81] Significantly, and in contrast to administrative procedures in most environmental policy areas in the United States, the determination of endangerment or threatened status is based on biological grounds alone without economic considerations. The 1982 re-authorization of the Endangered Species Act passed both the House and the Senate without opposition and was accepted by both industry and environmentalists.[82] In the early 1990s, however, the Endangered Species Act came under criticism. Some interests criticized the act for unnecessarily interfering with land development and resource utilization (for example, timber harvesting). Many environmentalists, as well as U.S. Fish and Wildlife biologists, feel the act is too narrow and rather than focusing on particular species should be designed to protect ecosystems.

Pursuant to the Endangered Species Act, once a species is listed as endangered, no one may buy or sell the species even if it was acquired lawfully. The act further forbids killing, harming, and the harassing of endangered species with few exceptions.[83] One of the more controversial aspects of the Endangered Species Act has been the impact the act has had on federal land use and development. Perhaps the most controversial case involved the Tellico Dam on the Little Tennessee River in Tennessee. After construction of the dam had begun, the snail darter, a 3-inch-long minnow, was placed on the endangered species list. It was found that completion of the dam would result in the destruction of the only known breeding habitat of the snail darter. In 1975, although the dam was 90 percent complete and in excess of $100 million had been spent on the $137 million project, construction was halted pursuant to court order. In 1979 Congress passed special legislation that exempted the Tellico Dam from the act. And in 1978, partially in response to the Tellico situation, Congress amended the Endangered Species Act and established a seven-person review committee called the Endangered Species Committee that was empowered to grant exemptions from the requirements of the act.[84]

The snail darter case and subsequent congressional reaction illustrates conflict between environmental values and economic values. Congressional intent was clearly focused on protecting endangered and threatened species; however, policy makers did not anticipate the consequences of an absolute ban on federal activity. Environmentalists at the time were concerned a congressional backlash might lead to a wholesale weakening of the Endangered Species Act, and were relieved at the compromise that resulted in establishment of the Endangered Species Committee. Fortunately for the snail darter, additional populations were found in several remote tributaries of the Little Tennessee River in 1981, and in 1983 the fish was downgraded by the Fish and Wildlife Service from an endangered to a threatened species.[85]

In his dissent in the snail darter case, U.S. Supreme Court Justice Powell wrote, "The Court today holds that Section 7 of the Endangered Species Act requires a federal court, for the purposes of protecting an endangered species or its habitat, to enjoin permanently the operation of any federal project, whether completed or substantially completed. This decision cast a long shadow over the operation of even the most important project. . . ."[86]

The Endangered Species Act has delayed or halted construction of a number of projects that either were using federal funding or required federal approval. These include the Columbia Dam on the Dock River in Tennessee, which threatened mussels and snails; a hydropower facility in Wyoming that threatened to impact a stopover area for migrating whooping cranes; oil and gas leases in Alaska for fear of damage to whales; the Dickey-Lincoln water project in Maine that threatened to inundate the only known habitat of the Furbish lousewort, a variety of snapdragon; and other projects all over the United States.[87]

Other federal laws, such as the Fishery Conservation and Management Act, which attempts to prevent over harvesting of fish, and specific laws to protect wild horses, burros, bald eagles, and golden eagles, contribute to the protection of endangered species in the United States. The National Wildlife Refuge System has primary responsibility, mostly through the management of wetlands, for endangered species protection in the United States. Wildlife refuges are the responsibility of the U.S. Fish and Wildlife Service. Most of the species in the United States that are on the endangered list have habitats within the national wildlife refuge system.

There has been some controversy over Fish and Wildlife Service management of the national wildlife system. Unlike the USFS or the BLM, Congress has not yet established clear guidelines such as multiple use for the National Wildlife Refuge System. Consequently, many wildlife refuges allow hunting, trapping, timber cutting, farming, grazing, and mineral development as well as recreational activity.[88] The Reagan and Bush administrations encouraged resource development in National Wildlife Refuges just as it did on all federal lands. The Fish and Wildlife Service has been operating, since 1962, under a "compatible use" doctrine. Implementation of the compatible use doctrine has been challenged by environmentalists' lawsuits, the Clinton administration, and proposed legislation in Congress. Although, to date, the suits have been settled out of court, the Fish and Wildlife Service is now required to identify all potential compatible uses and eliminate all incompatible uses on refuges. The service also operates under a "dominant use" doctrine wherein wildlife is viewed by the service as the primary concern of refuge management, and wildlife-oriented public use is seen as a secondary concern. Studies of secondary uses by the GAO in 1989 and the Fish and Wildlife Service in 1990 have led to review of not only blatant threats to wildlife, such as grazing, but more subtle ones such as recreation.[89]

The National Wildlife Refuge System has experienced both water and air quality problems. In 1983 a Fish and Wildlife Service survey found that 86 percent of federal refuges had water quality problems and 67 percent had air quality problems including visibility problems.[90]

The state of Hawaii deserves special mention in any discussion of endangered or threatened species. Ninety-nine percent of the known animal species, and 95 percent of flowering plants in the Hawaiian Islands, are found nowhere else in the world. Extensive deforestation and urbanization have caused tremendous loss of species in Hawaii. Nearly half the birds classified as endangered in the United States and half of the 300 extinctions of plants and animals in the United States since 1950 are attributable to the loss of native Hawaiian plant and animal species.[91] With the rapid increase in endangered plant and animal species, agencies are looking more holistically at natural systems and have developed a new way to manage, often referred to as ecosystem management.

Ecosystem Management

Ecosystems occur at spatial and temporal scales with small systems found within larger systems and short-term processes occurring within long-term processes.[92] Management of ecosystems should look at the entire range of species rather than at a single species.[93] At first, many agency employees viewed ecosystem management as synonymous with multiple use management. However, ecosystem management is founded on fundamentally different ideas of management, and is not synonymous with, and may not be compatible with, multiple-use management.[94]

Currently, there is no one accepted definition for ecosystem management, however there are common principles. One common principle is that humans are an integral part of the ecosystem. Ecosystem management is looking at past and present human involvement as part of the whole instead of as a separate entity.[95]

Many ecosystems have evolved with the advent of people using fire as a source of heat and food preparation.[96] This has had profound impacts on the evolution of ecosystems.[97] Since people have helped shape the ecosystems, Western science and traditional people's knowledge should be taken into consideration prior to restoring elements of the ecosystem that might not have existed fifty years ago.[98]

Humans depend on ecosystems but also create stress on them, which usually stems from short-term economic motives.[99] Ecosystems have thresholds, or levels of degradation, below which they cannot fall without losing vital attributes or functions.[100] Ecosystem sustainability requires a balance among ecological, economic, and social factors and must be present for an ecosystem to function over long periods of time. Generally, the absence or presence of biodiversity measures the ecological balance. The economic factors are mea-sured by productivity while the social factors are measured by physical or aesthetic values.

To accomplish a sustainable ecosystem, a base line reference point (or condition) must be chosen. A reference point should consider past conditions, projected future conditions, and changes in stochastic (natural) events and climatic conditions.[101] Enough information may not be available to determine a specific reference point, but it is clear that traditional approaches to conservation programs need refinement.[102]

Ecosystem management plans are becoming more widely used in the USFS and BLM administered lands. One large-scale ecosystem management plan on BLM and USFS areas covers 41,787,000 acres in Oregon, Washington, Idaho, and Montana.[103] This plan was part of President Clinton's 1993 ecosystem management plan for the Pacific Northwest. It considers public expectations, management capabilities, biological and ecological capabilities, science processes, and scientific literature.[104] The 1996 Upper Columbia River Basin scientific summary mentioned three options for the Interior Columbia River Basin. The preferred public option is to reduce risks to ecological integrity and species viability by aggressively restoring ecosystem health. This will restore the area by replicating natural disturbance processes including insects, disease and fire in intervals of 5–10 years.[105]

Because the ecosystem management plan for the Interior Columbia Basin is on such a large scale, it will provide a model for the USFS and BLM for future ecosystem management plans. A smaller BLM ecosystem management project is occurring in northern Arizona.[106] The implementation of ecosystem management plans, such as the Interior Columbia Basin and the northern Arizona ecosystem restoration project, clearly show that the agencies are trying to manage for ecological, economic and social factors.

Although ecosystem management holds much promise for balanced management in the future it should be noted that there are going to be implementation problems. There is little agreement on how to define an ecosystem and determine its boundaries. Also, related to the definition problem, one must determine how to measure the health of an ecosystem.

Some have argued that ecosystem management should be used in place of other federal land management guidelines—notably the Endangered Species Act. This is problematic. Protecting a single species or determining if it is threatened or healthy is a much more straightforward process than managing an ecosystem—given the disagreement on terms and definitions just noted. Still, political and scientific barriers aside, we learn more everyday about the intricacies and delicate balances within ecosystems that are crucial to all life. While ecosystem health is vital to the well-being of all species, notably our own, it is something that can be ignored in land-use planning.

SUMMARY

In this chapter we looked at land-use problems—broadly defined. First we examined soil erosion, which threaten U.S. and global agricultural production. We have discussed the federal land management issues including multiple use, recreation, fee demonstration projects, commercial recreation permits and concessions, fire, wilderness, loss of endangered species, and ecosystem management.

Species loss at a global level is, as we have indicated, a good example of an international common pool problem and the environmental policy paradox. In the chapter that follows, the obstacles to efficient, or even effective, international environmental management are explored in greater detail.

NOTES

1. Chused, Richard. "Symposium on the seventy-fifth anniversary of *Village of Euclid v Amber Realty Co.*: Euclid's historical imagery," *Case Western Reserve Law Review*. Summer 2001. 51 Case W. Res. 597.
2. "Subdivide and Conquer: A Modern Western." Video produced by Red Oak Films and First Light Films; produced and directed by Jeff Gersh and Chelsea Congdon. Distributed by Bullfrog Films, Oley, PA, 1999.
3. "Cadillac Desert: An American Nile." Video produced by KTEH/San Jose and Trans Pacific Television; director, writer and producer Jon Else. Distributed by Home Vision Cinema: Public Media Incorporated, Chicago, IL, 1997.
4. Richard Wolkomir, "A High Tact Attack on Traffic Jams Helps Motorists Go with the Flow," *Smithsonian* (April 1986), p. 44.
5. Ginny Finch, Federal Highway Administration. "Congestion Pricing: Reducing Traffic Jams Through Economics." Available at *http://www.tfhrc.gov/pubrds/fall96/p96au4.htm.*
6. Carol M. Rose, "New Models for Local Land Use Decisions," *Northwestern University Law Review*, 79 (5&6) (1984–85), p. 1156.
7. U.S. Council on Environmental Quality, *The Quiet Revolustion in Land Use Control* (Washington, DC: U.S. Government Printing Office, 1971).
8. *Village of Euclid v. Ambler Realty Co.*, 272 U.S. 365 (1926).
9. Guy Benveniste, *The Politics of Expertise* (Berkeley: Glendessary Press, 1972), pp. 106–116.
10. Richard H. Foster and R. Lawson Veasey, "Shootout at Blackrock: The Politics of Land Use Planning," *Natural Resource and Environmental Administration* (American Society for Public Administration), 5(6) (Spring 1982), p. 2.
11. Richard F. Babcock, *The Zoning Game: Municipal Practices in Policies* (Madison: University of Wisconsin Press, 1966), pp. 124–125.
12. Neil G. Carne, "Is Highest and Best Use a Justification for Zoning?" *The Appraisal Journal*, 52 (April 1984), p. 180.
13. Wolkomir, "A High Tact Attack on Traffic Jams Helps Motorists Go With the Flow," p. 45.
14. "Subdivide and Conquer: A Modern Western." Video produced by Red Oak Films and First Light Films; produced and directed by Jeff Gersh and Chelsea Congdon. Distributed by Bullfrog Films, Oley, PA, 1999.
15. Rose, "New Models for Local Land Use Decisions," p. 1171.
16. For discussion of greeenbelts and open space, see Judith Kunofsky and Larry Orman, "Greenbelts and the Well Planned City," *Sierra* (November-December 1985), p. 42.
17. Ecology Action Website. "Worldwide Loss of Soil and a Possible Solution." *http://www.growbiointensive.org/biointensive/soil.html.*
18. G. Tyler Miller, Jr., *Living in the Environment* (8th ed.) (Belmont, CA: Wadsworth, 1994), p. 324.
19. R. Neil Sampson, "Saving Agricultural Land," with Nannem Blackburn, (ed.), *Pieces of the Global Puzzle: International Approaches to Environmental Concerns* (Golden, CO: Fulcrum, 1986), p. 67.
20. The U.S. Global Change Research Information Office. "Soil and Sediment Erosion." Available at *http://www.gcrio.org/geo/soil.html.*
21. Miller, *Living in the Environment*, (8th ed.) p. 328.
22. "Vegetarian Guide: Reasons for Vegetarianism." Available at *http://michaelbluejay.com/veg/index.html.*
23. Bureau of Statistics, Treasury Department, *Statistical Abstract of the United States* (Washington, DC: GPO, 1997), p. 665–669.
24. Paul and Anne Ehrlich, "Space Age Cargo Cult," in Kent Gilbreath, (ed.), *Business and the Environment: Toward Common Ground* (Washington, DC: Conservation Foundation, 1984), p. 177.

25. The United States is one of the few nations to have actively addressed this problem, however. The 1977 Rural Development Act called for a thorough study of land use and soil loss. In hilly areas around the Washington, Oregon, and Idaho borders, wheat, barley, peas, and lentils are dryfarmed where runoff from snowmelt results in annual soil losses of 50 to 100 tons per acre. Similarly, even the flat, Midwestern lands of Iowa and Missouri lose 9.9 to 10.9 tons of cropland soil per acre per year. Even by the late 1970s, these two and another three agricultural regions in the nation had lost more than 250 thousand tons of soil. See U.S. Department of Agriculture, Soil Conservation Service. 1977. "Some serious erosion areas in the United States." Available at *http://www.ciesin.org/docs/002-220/002-220.html*.

26. Maryla Webb and Judith Jacobsen, *U.S. Carrying Capacity: An Introduction* (Washington, DC: Carrying Capacity, 1982), p. 33.

27. Miller, *Living in the Environment*, p. 259.

28. Rennicke, "Sacred Cows?" *Backpacker*, 20 (5) (August 1992), pp. 47–58.

29. Lands controlled by the Department of Defense are not included in this analysis.

30. See, for example, Multiple Use Sustainable Yield Act of 1960, 16th Space U.S.C. Section 528–531 (1974); and Federal Land Policy and Management Act, 43 U.S.C. Section 1710–1784 (Supp. 1984).

31. Federal Land Management and Policy Act of 1976, Section 103.

32. Marian Clawson, "The Concept of Multiple Use Forestry," *Environmental Law*, 8(2) (1978), p. 281.

33. Some have called for newer techniques and strategies. Mark Brunson, for example, writes about managing public lands within Limits of Acceptable Change (LACs). He argues managing public land or nature is about managing conflicting goals, such as recreation, biodiversity, wilderness, grazing, and so forth. To get anything done in a pluralist democracy within an incremental policy-making framework, all goals must be compromised somewhat.

    This is why we need limits of acceptable change (LACs). A dominant goal or combination of goals must be selected and LACs set, which constrain all other goals. These subsidiary goals must then be established and defined, with clear indicators devised and closely monitored. Managers must then optimize all these goals within the LACs set forth based on the primary objective, which could be to optimize multiple uses so long as no single use harms another use beyond an acceptable limit (LAC).

    All this implies land management must be mutually beneficial to various constituencies, and it must provide give-and-take both for nature and humans, and for both short- and long-term interests. Brunson argues this could best be achieved within a participatory democratic framework that views and manages land on a continuum, as opposed to one heavily biased in favor of ranching interests, or any one narrow set of interests. See Mark Brunson, "Managing Naturalness as a Continuum: Setting Limits of Acceptable Change." In Paul Gobster (ed.), *Restoring Nature* (Washington, DC: Island Press. 2000). For more on the current status of land management in the National Forests, see S. Anderson, S. Newman, A. Oakes, M. Plane, and T. Welch, "The state of the law: The National Forest Management Act: Law of the forest in the year 2000." *Journal of Land, Resources, & Environmental Law*. 2001. 21 J. Land Resources & Envtl. L. 151.

34. The Grand Canyon Trust, *Charting the Colorado Plateau: An Economic and Demographic Exploration* (Flagstaff, AZ: Grand Canyon Trust, 1996), p. 21.

35. The recreation fee demonstration program was within section 315 of the Omnibus Consolidated Rescission Act of 1996 (P.L. 104–134). It was later amended under Public Law 104–108 and Public Law 105-18, (National Park Service, U.S. Fish and Wildlife Service, Bureau of Land Management, U.S. Department of the Interior, Recreational Fee Demonstration Program Progress Report to Congress (1998). [online] Available *http://www.iso.doi.gov/nrl/RECFEE.HTM*. It is widely believed that the program will be extended beyond 1999.

36. The BLM initially had eighteen fee demonstration project areas collecting a total of $3.7 million in 1997. Prior to the implementation of new fees, the BLM sought public comment on the fee demonstration project sites. The NPS, as of late, 1997 had ninety-seven fee demonstration sites, collecting a total of $122.2 million ($20.6 million which, was spent on the collection of fees). Grand Canyon National Park, one of the first parks to be nominated, quickly instituted their fees. The USFS has 40 fee demo projects in 1997, collecting a total of $8.7 million. The FWS had 61 fee demonstration projects in 1997, collecting $2.9 million. Fish and Wildlife entrance fees allow visitors entry into the refuge while user fees were collected for hunting permits, boat launches, guided tours, and canoe trails.

    A number of problems have arisen during the fee demonstration project program. A person who purchases an annual Golden Eagle passport is allowed entry into most BLM, NPS, USFS, or FWS areas that charge an entrance fee. This approach has helped with the sales of the Golden Eagle passports, however, specific sites may lose revenue. Another problem is the fee program may unduly impact low income families as they are less able to afford an entrance or user fee. The USFS is experimenting with allowing low-income families passes into one recreation fee demonstration area and the NPS allows one free day a year. See U.S. Department of the Interior, Recreational Fee Demonstration Program Progress Report to Congress (1998). [online] Available *http:// www.iso.doi.gov/nrl/RECFEE.HTM.*

37. On the Colorado River, 19,000 people embark on commercial river trips per year with only $190,000 returned to the NPS. Many times restoration of beaches and trail maintenance cost more than the returned commercial fees.
38. Susan Schauer, "Let-it-Burn Policy Assailed in Hearings," *Arizona Daily Sun* (February 6, 1989), p. 2.
39. R.H. Wakimoto, "National Fire Management Policy: The Interagency Review Team Report," *Journal of Forestry*, v.88(1990), p. 24.
40. Fire suppression along with livestock grazing, logging, and climate changes have all been attributed to a change in the historical fire regime. *See* Wallace W. Covington, Peter Z. Fule, Margaret M. Moore, Stephen M. Moore, Stephen C. Hart, Thomas E. Kolb, Joy N. Mast, Stephen S. Sackett, and Michael R. Wagner, "Restoring Ecosystem Health in Ponderosa Pine Forests of the Southwest," *Journal of Forestry* 95(1), 1997, p. 13.
41. D.J. Parson, D.M. Graber, J.K. Agee, and J.W. Van-Wagendonk, "Natural Fire Management in National Parks," *Environmental Management* 10(1), p. 21–24.
42. Ibid., p. 480.
43. U.S. Department of Agriculture, U.S. Forest Service, "Manual 2300- Recreation, Wilderness and Related Resource Management," (1990), p. 16.
44. For more on fire policies and ecological restoration in general, see Paul Gobster (ed), *Restoring Nature* (Washington, DC: Island Press. 2000); Higgs, Eric (1995). *Conservation Biology*, v11, n2, pp. 338–348. "What is Good Ecological Restoration?" Fulé, P. Z. and W. W. Covington. 1999. "Fire regime changes" in La Michilia Biosphere Reserve, Durango Mexico. *Conservation Biology* 13(3):640–652.
45. Craig W. Allin, "Wilderness Preservation as a Bureaucratic Tool," in Foss, *Federal Lands Policy*, p. 132.
46. Bureau of Land Management and National Park Service, U.S. Department of the Interior, U.S. Forest Service, U.S. Department of Agriculture, "Adjacent Lands Study," (1981), p. 2.
47. John C. Hendee, George Stankey, and Robert C. Lucas, *Wilderness Management* (Golden, CO, Fulcrum Publishing, 1990), p. 160. Over half of the designated wilderness areas, are located in Alaska and less than 5 percent of wilderness is located in the Eastern United States. The Wilderness Act of 1964, because of multiple-use interests, was a difficult bill to pass through Congress.

    Howard Zahniser, the executive director of the Wilderness Society prepared the first draft of the wilderness bill, with assistance from the National Parks Association, National Wildlife Federations, and the Wildlife Management Institute in 1955. After eight years, eighteen hearings, and sixty-six versions of the proposed bill, the Wilderness Act was passed in 1964.
48. Paul J. Culhane, "Sagebrush Rebels in Office," in Norman J. Vig and Michael E. Kraft (eds.), *Environmental Policy in the 1980s* (Washington, DC: Congressional Quarterly, 1984), pp. 293–318.
49. The Wilderness Act, *Public Law* 88–571: 78-stat.-890.
50. Douglas W. Scott, "Securing the Wilderness," *Sierra* (May/June 1984), p. 42.
51. The Grand Staircase Escalante National Monument established 1.7 million acres in southern Utah. In the face of known opposition, President Clinton made the monument proclamation on September 18, 1996 under the 1906 Antiquities Act, which authorizes presidential discretion in declaring National Monuments. The management of this monument was delegated to the BLM, which was unprecedented, because most monuments are managed by the NPS.

    The BLM monument stunned many environmental organizations. They are hopeful that BLM will protect the area from facility development that would usually occur in a National Monument managed by the NPS. However, there is concern that the monument will be impacted by the extraction of its rich coal resources, especially since the BLM has less stringent wilderness mining regulations than the NPS.

    For example, four months after the designation of the monument, Conoco purchased oil leases on state lands within the monument in addition to what they already had on federal lands. Therefore, the State of Utah and BLM granted Conoco permission to drill on state lands using heavy equipment (Southern Utah Wilderness Alliance [1998]. Clinton Administration Okays Drilling in Year-old National Monument. [online] Available *http://www.suwa.org/gsenm/conoco.html#head.*)

The BLM was bound by regulations, since it was on state lands, to grant Conoco permission to allow machinery to cross public lands to drill on state lands. Prior to the drilling, the BLM and SUWA tried to acquire the mineral rights on federal and state lands, but they could not purchase the lands for reasonable market prices.

Conoco holds 140,000 acres of pre-existing oil leases of federal and state land within the monument, which threaten 1.3 million acres. The BLM is required to prepare an environmental assessment or an environmental impact statement on the potential development of oil leases within the monument.

52. Website of the Midpeninsula Regional Open Space District. Available at *www.openspace.org.*
53. See, for example, Strachan, Adam. "Concurrency laws: Water as a land-use regulation," *Journal of Land, Resources, & Environmental Law.* 2001. 21 J. Land Resources & Envtl. L. 435. Also see Peter Lacy (2001). "Our sedimentation boxes runneth over: Public lands soil law as the missing link in holistic natural resource protection," *Environmental Law.* Spring 2001. 31 Envtl. L. 433. For more innovations see G. Heal, G. Daily, P. Ehrlich, J. Salzman, C. Boggs, J. Hellmann, J. Hughes, C. Kremen, and T. Ricketts, "Protecting natural capital through Ecosystem Service Districts," *Stanford Environmental Law Journal.* May 2001. 20 Stan. Envtl. L.J. 333.
54. Hoyt Gimlin (ed.), *Earth's Threatened Resources* (Washington, DC: Congressional Quarterly, 1986), pp. 65–68.
55. For example, the BLM wilderness inventory on the Arizona Strip District studied 2.7 million acres of potential wilderness and actually designated only 268,020 acres. Shortly after the inventory, wilderness areas were designated on the Arizona Strip under the Arizona Wilderness Act of 1984 (Public Law 98-406) and later more wilderness areas were added under the Arizona Desert Wilderness Act of 1990.
56. The Wilderness Act, 16 U.S.C. Section 1131 (c) (1982).
57. Mining and wilderness are potentially a divisive issue for the BLM. In defense of the BLM, mining activity is halted in wilderness areas until an examination of the validity of the claim is conducted and a plan of operations is approved. The BLM has also prohibited recreational mining in certain areas. The BLM, in accordance with a 1992 amendment to the Mining Law of 1872, must charge claimants a $100 annual fee; claimants must also show that assessment work was conducted. As a result of these requirements, many marginal mining claims have been vacated. See Olen Paul Matthews, Amy Haak, and Kathryn Toffenetti, "Mining and Wilderness: Incompatible Uses or Justifiable Compromise," *Environment*, 27 (April 1985), p. 12.
58. U.S. House Committee Report 96-617 (1979).
59. Although it has improved on BLM lands, in 1979 the BLM found that 135 million of its 170 million acres of western rangelands were in fair condition or worse. By 1992, when the BLM completed its wilderness review, 38 percent of all of its rangelands were rated to be in good to excellent condition. The percentage of lands rated in poor condition was cut by more than half, down to 13 percent, when compared with 1936. Telephone interview with BLM representative, November 1993.
60. Nelson, Robert H. "Should Grazing Permits Be Saleable to Environmental Groups?" Speech to The College of Law, Arizona State University, Tempe, AZ, November 14, 1997. Available at *http://www.puaf.umd.edu/faculty/papers/nelson/arizstat.pdf.* This speech is generally insightful in regards to bureaucracy and environmental policy. Also see Nelson's University of Maryland website for similar papers and generally at *http://www.puaf.umd.edu/faculty/papers/nelson/Nelson%20 papers%20title%20page.html.*
61. National Park Service, U.S. Department of the Interior, *State of the Parks—1980, A Report to Congress* (1980).
62. Maura Doland, "National Parks Beset by Mounting Pressures," *Los Angeles Times*, May 25,1986, p. 1.
63. Nancy Shute, "Howling at the Moon," *The Amicus Journal*, (Winter 1987), p. 39.
64. Ibid., p. 43.
65. Rainforest Action Network. "Species Extinction: Rainforest Fact Sheet." Available at *http://www.ran.org/info center/factsheets/03b.html.*
66. Michael Frome, *Battle for the Wilderness* (New York: Praeger Publishers, 1974), p. 55.
67. Ibid.
68. G. Tyler Miller, Jr., *Living in the Environment* (5th ed.) (Belmont, CA: Wadsworth, 1988), pp. 292–293.
69. Ibid., p. 293.
70. Ibid., p. 295.

71. Frome, "Battle for the Wilderness," p. 67.
72. R. Edward Grumbine, *Ghost Bears: Exploring the Biodiversity Crisis* (Washington, DC: Island Press, 1992), p. 67.
73. Ibid.
74. Ibid. These estimates were developed from Edward O. Wilson, *Biophilia* (Cambridge, MA: Harvard University Press, 1984); and Norman Myers, *A Wealth of Wild Species: Store House for Human Welfare* (Boulder, CO: Westview Press, 1983).
75. See also "Promise and Peril: A New Look at the Endangered Species Act of 1973," *St. Louis University Law Journal*, 27 (November 1983), p. 959.
76. Ibid.
77. Miller, *Living in the Environment*, p. 306.
78. 16 U.S. Section 1531–1543 (1981). The Endangered Species Act was amended in 1976, 1978, 1979, 1982, and 1987.
79. *TVA v. Hill*, 437 U.S. 153, 180 (1978).
80. In 1900 Congress passed the Lacey Act, ch. 553, 31 Stat., which banned interstate traffic in illegally killed wildlife and was designed primarily to protect birds that were being killed for their plumes.
81. U.S. Fish and Wildlife Service Division of Endangered Species (May 31, 1997). "Endangered Species General Statistics" [online].
82. "House, Senate Passed Endangered Species Bills," *Congressional Quarterly*, 40 (1982), p. 1403.
83. Exceptions include Alaskan natives who are not subject to the prohibitions of the act if a species is taken for subsistence purposes or, at the discretion of the secretary of interior, those who have entered into contracts involving endangered species prior to the notice of the species protection appearance in the federal register may be exempted by the secretary of the interior if the act would cause a person to suffer undue economic hardship. See Endangered Species Act, 16 U.S.C. Sections 1539 (1987).
84. The Tellico Dam Case. *Tennessee Valley Authority v. Hill*, 4378 U.S. 153 (1978).
85. Miller, *Living in the Environment*, p. 305.
86. *TVA v. Hill*, 437 U.S. 153, 195 (1978).
87. See George Cameron Coggins and Irma S. Russell, "Beyond Shooting Snail Darters in Forth Barrels: Endangered Species and Land Use America," *The Georgetown Law Journal*, 70 (August 1982), pp. 1433–1434.
88. Miller, *Living in the Environment*, p. 304.
89. Telephone interview with U.S. Fish and Wildlife Service, November 1993.
90. Miller, *Living in the Environment*, p. 305.
91. Ibid., p. 296.
92. Forest Service, United States Department of Agriculture, *An Ecological Basis for Ecosystem Management*, Rocky Mountain Forest and Range Experimental Station, GTR RM-246,(1994).
93. Southwest Forest Alliance, *The Southwest Forest Alliance, Forests Forever!* (Flagstaff, AZ: Southwest Forest Alliance, 1996), p. 29.
94. Kristina A. Vogt, John C. Gordon, John P. Wargo, and Daniel J. Vogt, *Ecosystems — Balancing Science with Management,* (New York: Springer-Verlag, 1997), p.97.
95. Ibid, p. 105.
96. Charles E. Kay, "Aboriginal Overkill and Native Burning: Implications for Modern Ecosystem Management," *Western Journal of Applied Forestry*, 10(4), 1995.
97. In the Sierran ecosystem in California, people have managed the area in a non-random fashion using burning and horticultural techniques, which is supported by ethnographic records, paleoecological findings, fire scar studies, and ecological field studies. M. Kat Anderson and Michael J. Moratto, *Sierra Nevada Ecosystem Project: Final Report to Congress on Assessments and Scientific Management Options* (Davis: University of California, Center for Water and Wildland Resources, 1996, p. 188).
98. Dennis Martinez, "A First People Firsthand Knowledge," *Sierra* (November/December, 1996), p. 71.
99. Forest Service, United States Department of Agriculture, *An Ecological Basis for Ecosystem Management* (1994), p. 2.
100. Vogt, Gordon, Wargo, and Vogt, *Ecosystems Balancing Science with Management*, p. 106.
101. Forest Service, United States Department of Agriculture, *An Ecological Basis for Ecosystem Management*, p. 7.
102. Hal Sawasser, "Conserving Biological Diversity: A perspective on Scope and Approaches," *Forest Ecology and Management*, 35 (1990), p. 89.

103. Forest Service, U.S. Department of the Interior, and the Bureau of Land Management, U.S. Department of the Interior, *Upper Columbia River Basin Draft Environmental Impact Statement* (Interior Columbia Basin Ecosystem Management project), p. 5.

104. Forest Service, Pacific Northwest Research Station, U.S. Department of Agriculture, *A Framework for Ecosystem Management in the Interior Columbia River Basin*, Pacific Northwest Research Station, PNW-GTR- 374 (Portland, Oregon), p. 57.

105. Ibid.

106. The Mt. Trumbull ecosystem management plan is recreating a reference condition to a scene that would have been viewed by the first European visitor if settlers had not manipulated the landscape. Manipulations occurred through livestock grazing, logging, and over 100 years of fire suppression. (Covington, Fule, Moore, Hart, Kolb, Mast, Sackett, and Wagner), "Restoring Ecosystem Health in Ponderosa Pine Forests of the Southwest.")

For Mt. Trumbull, during the presettlement period of 1870, there were 15 trees per acre compared to 1996 tree densities of 254 trees per acre (Mt. Trumbull Ecosystem Restoration Project, Report for the Bureau of Land Management, Arizona Strip District, Prepared by: Northern Arizona University, College of Ecosystem Science and Management, 1996 p. 12). The ecosystem management plan is to restore 4,800 acres to allow natural processes to reinstate important ecological process (Mt. Trumbull Ecosystem Restoration Project, Report for the Bureau of Land Management, Arizona Strip District, Prepared by: Northern Arizona University, College of Ecosystem Science and Management, 1997, p.1). Research before and after restoration of the ecosystem includes: vegetation changes, small and large mammal response to restoration, birds and arthropod changes.

International Environmental Issues

The international environmental crisis is more pervasive and, in some ways, more difficult to manage than any of the other environmental problems we have studied in this book. International pollution transcends ideological and political boundaries. Furthermore, our technical ability to manipulate and exploit the global environment may have surpassed our ability to manage the negative impacts of those actions. Damage that has been done to the environment, particularly stratospheric ozone depletion and the buildup of global warming gasses—and damage that can be anticipated if current trends continue—threaten worldwide disaster.[1] As Mostafa K. Tolba, the executive director of the United Nations Environment Program said, "[U]nless all nations (mount) a massive and sustained effort into safeguarding their shared living resources, we will face a catastrophe on a scale rivaled only by nuclear war."[2]

In this chapter we examine the international environmental problems that impact all others—overpopulation, food production and, relatedly, desertification. In addition we summarize four global common pool pollution problems: destruction of the ozone layer due to the production of chlorofluorocarbons (CFCs); the warming of the earth's environment due to the release of gasses, or the greenhouse effect; and, briefly, deforestation and ocean pollution. Finally, we examine some of the unique problems facing the less developed countries of the world and the relationship of international environmental issues to global security.

The leadership of all political parties in the Western democracies agrees the world has serious food and population problems. Some argue that population problems are not environmental problems in the same way as, for example, air pollution. However, all environmental problems—including overpopulation—are related. The press of an expanding population impacts forests, soil erosion, energy needs, and many other environmental problems.

POPULATION AND FOOD PRODUCTION

The carrying capacity of an environment, that is, the population an ecosystem can sustain over a long-term period, is only sustainable if a balance is achieved between renewable resources and the population dependent on them. When the population of one species, rabbits for example, grows to the point where the renewability of its food source is put in jeopardy, the species is threatened with extinction as food runs out. This die-off in turn impacts other species. Using the example of rabbits, when the rabbit population grows, so do the populations of the rabbits' natural predators—perhaps mountain lions. As the grass, which is the rabbits' food supply, is destroyed, the rabbits die and so do the lions that became dependent on an abundant rabbit population. This explosion–die-off sequence is common in nature.

Humankind has overshot the earth's historical carrying capacity. Through reliance on fossil fuels—stored energy—we have been able to develop intensified agriculture, concentrated housing, and labor saving that has resulted in a population far in excess of what we thought sustainable two centuries ago. We are facing a crisis situation. As a U.S. National Academy of Sciences and Royal Society of London study reported, "If current predictions of population growth prove accurate and patterns of human activity on the planet remain unchanged, science and technology may not be able to prevent either irreversible degradation of the environment or continued poverty for much of the world."[3]

The food and population problem is not new. Throughout recorded history world food supply and demand have never been in close balance.[4] However, never before in the world's history have we seen population rates increase as dramatically as they have in the nineteenth and twentieth centuries.

Today, at the turn of the century, the world population is about 6 billion.[5] This is an increase from 4.5 million in 1980. In 1980 it was estimated the population of the developed countries would increase by 12 percent between 1980 and the year 2000 and the population of the less-developed countries would grow 50 percent during the same period.[6] Population growth during this period was actually somewhat less than predicted. Studies conducted by the United Nations show a slight decrease in the rate of growth of the world's population. From 1975 to 1990, world population grew at an annual rate of 1.72 percent annually; from 1990 to 1995, that figure decreased to 1.48 percent annually, with an average of 81 million people being born each year. This is down from 87 million, which was the average annual addition to the population between 1985 and 1990. Eighty percent of the population (around 4.59 billion) lives in less developed countries. The annual growth rate in this region is 1.8 percent, compared to 0.4 percent in other, more developed regions.[7] It is interesting to note that in 1950 roughly one-third of the world's population resided in more developed countries.

The world population in 1996 is actually 29 million persons below the United Nations 1994 estimate of what the world population would be. This decline may be attributed to a number of factors including high mortality rates caused by military conflict (civil wars in Rwanda, Liberia, and Burundi) and the increased spread of disease (namely AIDS). The life expectancy for eastern Africa between 1990 and 1995 is estimated at 46.7 years; this is 3.9 years lower than projected in the 1994 UN Revision.[8]

In addition to studying incidents of mortality, an examination of fertility rates can also determine if a given country is headed toward a stable, declining, or growing population. A fertility rate of 2.1 births per woman is considered the replacement level fertility rate and results in a stable population size.[9] In 1996, the average global figure for Africa between 1990 and 1995 was 5.7 children per woman, lower than the 1996 projected estimate of 5.8 children taken in 1994.[10]

Population growth has accelerated at a pace unknown in all of human history up until the present time. There were 2.56 billion people in the world in 1950 and 6.08 billion in 2000, a 138 percent increase over 50 just years. To put this in perspective, there were only about 791 million humans in 1750, and that figure did not increase 138 percent until about 170 years later.[11] Before that it took around four million years for the human population to hit 1 billion.

Moreover, 99 percent of the approximately 83 million people being added to the planet every year are born in less-developed countries. At this rate, by 2025 only three more developed nations will remain in the 15 largest nations of the world. An important question, beyond how many humans can the Earth sustain, is what will happen when the "have nots" far outnumber the "haves"? As of 1999, data on Gross National Income per capita, adjusted for purchasing power show Americans have almost $32,000 to spend, whereas it is less than $7,000 in Russia and Brazil, and about $3,500 in China, and less than $1,000 in Ethiopia and Nigeria.[12]

From an environmental perspective it would take several earths to obtain all the natural resources and sinks from disposal of waste needed for 6 billion to live an American lifestyle. It seems only two unattractive alternatives present themselves. One, cut the global population significantly; or two, start massive redistribution where the developed nations significantly reduce their consumptive patterns. Still, some argue that population can grow forever without any dire consequences. In light of this argument, it is important to try to calculate the planet's carrying capacity.

Fertility rates and the projections of world population become an important concern when we consider the carrying capacity of the world. The earth's carrying capacity, meaning that human population the world can sustain over a long term, is extremely difficult to measure globally. However, a 1982 United Nations study examined the population-sustaining capacity in 117 developing countries and concluded that by the year 2000, 65 of the countries studied, with the combined population of 1.1 billion people, would be unable to provide their inhabitants with even minimum levels of nutrition. Lester Brown observed, "[In these 65 countries] population would overshoot the numbers who could be sustained by 440 million, implying a heavy dependence on imported food, widespread starvation, or more likely, both."[13]

In 1995 about 75 percent of the world's population lived in developing nations where they had access to only 20 percent of the world's resources. Per capita land for agriculture that year was as low as .17 hectares and even this little land could only be farmed to deliver .5 to 2.5 tons per hectare versus 4.5 tons per hectare in the developed world.[14]

Worldwide food production has declined in per capita terms each year since 1984. From 1951 to 1984 the production of grain, for example, increased at a rate of 3 percent a year. When measured against population growth, this represents a 6 percent decline in corn, wheat, and rice production. At the turn of the century there exists only a two month stockpile of grain.[15] In the two areas with the greatest population growth—Africa and Latin America—food production has declined significantly over the last few decades. In Africa, per capita production has declined 27 percent since 1967. In Latin America, food production has declined roughly 10 percent since 1981. Latin America was a net exporter of grain up until the early 1970s. Africa, while not a grain exporter, did supply most of its needs up to the 1970s.[16] These decreasing food yields are due primarily to the environmental problems discussed throughout this book: deforestation, dwindling water supplies, and soil erosion.

What *exactly* is the world's carrying capacity? Average estimates vary from as low as 7.7 billion to as high as 12 billion, and some have argued there are no practical limits. William Ophuls, after studying the issue and citing numerous scholars, argued a realistic limit is one person for each acre of arable land. Ophuls concludes that the maximum population the world could sustain would appear to be 8 billion people—there being at most 8 billion acres of potentially arable land. Studies by Alan S. Feinstein, a researcher with the World Hunger Program at Brown University, and by researchers at the Center for Conservation Biology have reduced the sustainable population of vegetarians to 7 billion.[17] These numbers assume we would all be vegetarians, thereby saving the energy loss by converting plant proteins to animal proteins for human consumption.[18] About one-third of the world's grain is fed to animals for the production of meat, milk, and eggs.

The United Nations has estimated world population will be about 9.3 billion by the year 2050. If fertility levels were reduced worldwide to a replacement rate by the year 2000, demographers estimate the world's population would eventually stabilize at 8.5 billion.[19] This has not occurred. The world population in 2000 was growing at 1.2 percent annually. Six nations account for half that growth, and all of them are less developed.[20] As the figures have demonstrated, we are very far from replacement fertility rates in virtually the entire less developed world. At current fertility levels, the population could theoretically climb to 296 billion people in the span of 150 years.[21]

What do all these figures mean? For some analysts, not very much. For example, Julian Simon, the late economics professor at the University of Maryland, argued that greater numbers of people will mean an enhanced quality of life for everyone. Using aggregate population and economic figures, Simon found that, "[T]he bigger the population of the country, the greater the number of scientists and the larger the amount of scientific knowledge produced. . . . This argues that faster population growth—which causes faster growing industries—leads to faster growth of productivity."[22] Simon's ideas, although provocative, are very much in the minority. Noted biologists Paul and Anne Ehrlich, in a critique of Simon's work, found little or no causal relationship between the variables examined and the conclusions of Simon's research. After examining an article Simon wrote arguing that market forces and other resources would operate to provide an abundance of whatever materials are needed by humans, the Ehrlichs conclude, "Simon's weird ideas are not, by any means, restricted to physics. He treats us to mathematical amusements as well. . . . [O]ne might be tempted simply to write off Simon's views as being unworthy of consideration by any educated person."[23] The problem is, the

Ehrlichs point out, Simon's work was and is taken seriously by many and is commonly reproduced in publications of wide circulation.

The Ehrlichs have used the example of Easter Island, once a lush, 64 square mile subtropical Pacific island, about 2,000 miles west of Chile, to show that more people do not necessarily mean better solutions to sustainability. About 1,500 years ago, Polynesians colonialized the island and sent it's population soaring to as high as 20,000 inhabitants. Forests were razed at an unsustainable rate to provide building materials and agricultural lands. This led to soil erosion and degradation, and eventually to famine. Even then the inhabitants didn't think to reduce fertility rates, turning instead to cannibalism as a technique for controlling population. To quote the Ehrlichs, "having more people today is not the solution for generating more geniuses. Creating environments in which the inherent talents of people now disadvantaged—by race or gender discrimination, poverty, or malnutrition—can be fully expressed, is."[24]

A great deal depends on what numbers one examines and how they are interpreted. For example, Simon measures pollution in one study by plotting life expectancy over time and concludes that increased life expectancy is evidence of decreased pollution. Some might argue there are better ways of measuring pollution, since many other factors enter in to confound the pollution/life expectancy relationship.

Few scholars that study ecology agree with Simon and the other optimists. A combination of environmental stresses, including a rising population and decreasing agricultural productivity, suggest, to most observers, that the world is in for a rocky future unless mitigation measures are taken soon.[25] Absent some change or unforeseen developments, we are headed, in this or the next generation, toward widespread starvation that will make the famine in northern Africa in the early 1980s seem mild by comparison. Furthermore, the United States is not likely to be in a position to provide much food assistance far beyond the year 2000.[26] Though the United States donated 6 million metric tons of food to foreign nations in 2001, ecological and population problems may make impossible the goal set at the 1996 World Food Summit to cut the number of hungry people in the world in half by 2015.[27]

Food and population presents perhaps the greatest environmental policy paradox of all. We have a fairly good idea of the steps that need to be taken to mitigate widespread starvation and disruption. We have been slow to take these steps. This is due in part to something called the "demographic trap" or the "demographic transition."

In 1945 demographer Frank Notestein outlined a theory of demographic change known as the demographic transition. Notestein essentially classifies societies as being in one of three stages. During the first stage, both birth and death rates are very high and population grows very slowly, if it all. This first stage characterizes premodern societies. In the second stage, health measures improve living conditions causing death rates to decline while birthrates remain high and population grows rapidly. In the third stage, birthrates level off to a replacement rate as families, enjoying economic security and lower infant mortality rates, are smaller. In the third stage, births roughly equal deaths.[28] Most of the industrialized world has undergone the transition from the second to the third stage as is reflected by the fact that fertility rates are at or below that necessary for replacement. Unfortunately, much of the less developed world may never get out of the second stage. Lester

Brown refers to this as the demographic trap. Once incomes begin to rise and birthrates begin declining,

> [T]he process feeds on itself and countries can quickly move to the equilibrium of the demographic transition's third stage. . . . Once a population expands to the point where their demands begin to exceed the sustainable yield of local forest, grasslands, croplands, or water supplies, they begin directly or indirectly to consume the resource base itself . . . not only have they failed to complete the demographic transition, but the deteriorating relationship between people and ecological support systems that is lowering living standards may prevent them from ever doing so.[29]

Leaders of the less developed countries may not notice they are headed for the demographic trap. The relatively slow pace of desertification, soil erosion, and deforestation mitigated by imported food, borrowed money, and the development of marginal farmland, can mask the slide of a country into perpetual poverty and eventual starvation.

The DSP of many less developed nations also contributes to the slide into the demographic trap. We discussed the impact of religion on environmental management in Part One. Here it is worth noting that two major religions in the less-developed world, Roman Catholicism and Islam, promote fertility and, directly or indirectly, large families.

The leaders of many less-developed countries are understandably reluctant to limit their population growth rates or to undertake other measures proposed by the more developed countries.

Moreover, assistance from more developed countries to less-developed countries has typically placed emphasis on nonrenewable development, like road building, mineral extraction, and large-scale hydropower projects, instead of sustainable development, such as agriculture or renewable forestry.[30] Assistance has also taken the form of food transfers to the starving.

The policy of shipping reserves of food to those that have showed little inclination to control their population growth may only be prolonging the inevitable. Such policies keep more people alive to be even hungrier when the next shortage occurs. Clearly, food alone is not enough unless it is accompanied by the means for people to become self-sufficient. Unfortunately, because of the demographic trap, the capital necessary (in terms of natural resources) for self-sufficiency may be exhausted before self-sufficiency is achieved. Alofchie and Commines wrote in *The Futurist*, "[I]f the resources in human energy allotted to food aid programs could be channeled towards improving the countries' own systems of economic management, transportation, storage and distribution, this would undoubtedly do more to alleviate hunger on a long-term basis than any quantity of external food assistance."[31] Humanity will survive the population explosion. After a crash, as in the rabbit example, most systems reach a steady state. Preparing for a sustainable global population today could prevent a human population crash. As Paul and Anne Ehrlich put it, "[N]ature may end the population explosion for us—in very unpleasant ways—well before 10 billion is reached. . . . We should not delude ourselves: the population explosion will come to an end before very long."[32]

Perhaps the greatest environmental policy paradox, therefore, is in the area of food and population policy. The consequences of a future of unrestricted growth are clear. Yet, again quoting the Ehrlichs, who studied population biology for over 40 years, "[O]ne of the toughest things for a population biologist to reconcile is the contrast between his or her recognition that civilization is in imminent serious jeopardy and the modest level of concern that population issues generate among the public and even among elected officials."[33] Sustainable agriculture, instead of transfers of food, is what is needed over the long term.

What can we do as individuals to address the world food situation? You and I can contribute to the world food balance in a small way by eating nonprocessed food such as whole oats, rice, or wheat, and low-processed foods such as bread and tortillas. Also, since it is much more efficient to eat grain proteins directly rather than getting protein in the form of animals, becoming vegetarian would contribute to the available food supply. When grain is fed to beef, only about 10 percent of the calories in the grain are delivered to people eating the beef. If vegetarianism is a bit more than you are willing to sacrifice, eat less beef and more chicken or fish grown through aquaculture. Both chicken and fish grown for harvest are much more efficient converters of grain to animal proteins than beef, hogs, or sheep.[34]

DESERTIFICATION AND FOOD PRODUCTION

Closely related to food and population problems are the food production problems caused by desertification. Desertification, the process of turning productive land into wasteland, is occurring at an alarming pace—particularly in countries in the less developed world. In semiarid areas, grasses and other vegetation secure the soil and retain moisture. When plants die, through overgrazing, trampling, or harvesting for fuel, the moisture retention capacity of the ground is lost and the land is slowly converted to desert.

All continents are suffering from some desertification. Areas with high or very high desertification potential include most of the southern part of South America, southern Africa, most of central Asia, the west and southwestern United States, parts of the Canadian midwest, and nearly all of Australia.[35] The greatest impacts have been felt in Africa. The Sahara Desert expanded 100 kilometers eastward between 1958 and 1975.[36] In the North African countries where desertification has been particularly severe, per capita food production declined 40 percent between 1950 and 1980.[37] In 1997, the United Nations Environmental Program estimated that nearly one-fourth of the earth's total land area is threatened by desertification; as a result, about 1 billion people in 100 countries are at risk of losing their livelihoods to desertification.[38] It is estimated that the current rate of desertification is about 20,000 square miles of land, with another 70,000 square miles at serious risk.[39] Currently 250 million people are directly impacted by desertification, and all of us indirectly as we annually lose $42 billion in foregone income.[40]

Although natural phenomena, such as drought, may contribute to desertification, it is widely accepted that human activities are generally responsible for the majority of degradation. Forests are cleared to make way for agricultural or grazing purposes. As these forests are destroyed, so to is a key tool in the prevention of soil erosion. Overcultivation and overgrazing of these converted lands may work to hasten the process of desertification, while poorly designed irrigation systems, where water cannot drain at a proper rate, lead to massive mineral depositions as the water evaporates. These mineral deposits, which mostly are comprised of salts, rob the soil of its fertility. It is estimated that the amount of land destroyed through salinization (500,000 hectares annually) is about equal to the amount of land subject to new irrigation.[41]

Although the causes of desertification involve many social, cultural, and political factors, many researchers point to economic conditions that encourage excessive exploitation of the natural environment. Excessive foreign debts may be a leading factor for less-developed countries to push for greater short-term returns from their lands, without much concern for future productive capability.

The cost of restoring lands that have been rendered useless through desertification will require massive resources from the global community. Lester Brown estimates that if we take into consideration the cost of converting the land unsuitable for cultivation (about 128 million hectares) into grass or woodlands, the annual cost would be about $16 billion. Add to that the preservation of topsoil in already threatened land regions (an additional 100 million hectares) and the cost jumps to $24 billion annually.[42] Brown points out that, while this cost is large, it is less than the U.S. government has paid in some years to support crop prices. Considering our estimated population growth and food production problems, it might be wise to consider this investment.

Desertification is a difficult problem. The slow and gradual nature of desertification does not lend itself to crisis management, and in many countries the activities that lead to desertification—overgrazing and harvesting fuel for example—are seen as essential to maintain life. Desertification is part of a cycle in the struggle for existence in these countries. As it continues, nations fall further and further into the demographic trap.

GLOBAL POLLUTION

As discomforting as the long-term population and food problems the world faces may be, global pollution problems are no less severe. Like overpopulation and desertification, we understand much about the causes and solutions to global pollution problems. Yet paradoxically, because of the nature of global pollution and the international institutions and incentive systems operating on international actors, it is quite possible that timely solutions to global environmental problems, including overpopulation, will not be found.

Many global pollution issues have been discussed in previous chapters. Here we review and summarize some of the major global pollution problems that are clearly common pool in nature and hence whose solutions will require international cooperation.

Although there are many international environmental problems that may require international solutions, four, the ozone layer, the greenhouse, deforestation, and ocean pollution, have been the focus of the most attention by the public and policy makers.

The Ozone Layer

As we saw in Chapter 5, ozone in the stratosphere protects us from the sun's ultraviolet radiation. Without this protection, the earth would be uninhabitable. CFCs have been used since 1955 in aerosol spray cans, refrigeration units, industrial solvents, and in plastic foams for insulation, packing, furniture, and the plastic foam used in the manufacture of some coffee cups and fast-food containers.[43] CFCs in aerosol cans have been banned in the United States, Canada, and most Scandinavian countries since 1978. Still CFC production has increased globally since the late 1970s. International agreements have been reached that seek to stem, somewhat, the increase in global CFC production in the future. It is believed that without substantial decreases in the production of CFCs and other ozone depleting chemicals, the ozone layer could suffer a depletion of between 5 and 9 percent in the next century, causing an increase in ultraviolet exposure on the magnitude of 10 to 18 percent.[44] (Reread Chapter 5 if you don't remember the international environmental paradox problems associated with CFC production.)

For every single percentage decrease in ozone in the stratosphere, skin cancers increase by an estimated 5 to 10 percent. The increase in ultraviolet light can have a negative impact on the ocean food chain by destroying microorganisms on the ocean surface, causing crops on land to suffer decreased yields and can cause genetic damage and inhibit immune system functioning in humans and other animals.[45] It is estimated that from 1969 to the 1980s, ozone losses have averaged between 2 and 3 percent over North America and Europe and as high as 5 and 6 percent over parts of the Southern Hemisphere.[46] In the 1990s average annual ozone loss was between two and four percent at mid-latitudes. Ozone loss is expected to peak during the next decade, with losses of 12 to 13 percent over North America and Europe in the winter and spring, and six to seven percent in summer and fall. The southern mid-latitudes are expected to lose about 11 percent annually year round.[47] Each spring since 1997 there has been an ozone layer hole above Antarctica measuring about 8.2 million square miles, larger than the United States and Canada combined.[48]

CFC production causes global pollution problems that necessitate international cooperation if they are to be addressed before catastrophic damage is done to the atmosphere. Fortunately, as we saw in Chapter 5, some steps have been taken in the international political arena to deal with the CFC problem. The most notable among these efforts have taken place in conjunction with the Montreal Protocol on Substances that Deplete the Ozone Layer, originally signed in 1987. Great effort has been put into noticeably reducing the international manufacture of CFCs and other ozone causing particles, in developed, as well as less developed countries. Since 1987 the Protocol has been strengthened several times with little objection from member nations. At the 1999 Beijing Adjustments, the 11th meeting of signatories since the original 1987 Montreal Protocol, major strides were made. First, $440 million was added to the Multilateral Fund to help developing nations phase out CFCs 50 percent by 2005 and completely by 2010. HCFCs, the less damaging cousin of CFCs, were agreed to be phased out as well. Production will freeze in 2004 for developed countries and in 2016 for less-developed nations, with the goal of total production phase-out by 2020 and 2040, respectively.[49]

Currently, the greatest barrier to preventing the production of ozone depleting materials concerns the economic gains that may be realized through smuggling operations. It is estimated that about 20,000 tons of CFCs are traded illegally each year.[50] Because of the two-tiered system of the Protocol (outlawing the use of CFCs in developed nations, while still allowing less-developed nations to purchase and produce CFCs on a limited basis) smugglers are able to find loopholes to ply their trade (selling newly produced CFCs as recycled CFCs, for example). The economic benefits are substantial. It has been reported that for a while, only cocaine had a higher street-value in Miami than CFCs.[51] The good new is, it has been estimated that if ozone depleting chemicals were no longer released into the atmosphere, natural processes would repair the ozone layer within 50 years.[52]

The successes of combating ozone depletion have not been replicated in efforts to combat other types of environmental degradation. One reason for this lies in a wide consensus on the risks posed by decreased protection from ultra-violet radiation. No one wants to develop skin cancer. For other issues, such as global warming, the perceived risk tends to be more diffused and less personalized. As such, consensus is hard to come by, creating a context for non-cooperation at the international level. In the case of greenhouse gases, limited and cautious measures have been taken to deal with production; however, given the world's dependence on fossil fuels, future prospects for international cooperation in time to avert serious environmental problems seem uncertain.

The Greenhouse

For over 100 years we have understood the possibility of atmospheric warming due to human carbon dioxide emissions. According to many scientists, the greenhouse effect has seriously been altered by humankind's impact on the composition of the atmosphere. As a 1995 report on global climate change states, based on the warming recorded over the past century, and especially in recent decades, "the balance of evidence suggests that there is a discernible human influence on global climate."[53] Perhaps not coincidentally, the 1990s were the hottest decade of the millennium, and 1998 was the hottest year ever recorded.[54] It is estimated that global levels of carbon dioxide in the atmosphere will reach 550 ppm sometime between 2040 and 2100 (they are currently at 360 ppm, 28 percent higher than at the start of the Industrial Revolution); however *most* analysts feel those levels will be reached closer to the middle of the twenty-first century.[55] Carbon dioxide levels of 550 ppm could raise average atmospheric temperatures anywhere from 3.6 to 6.3 degrees F.[56] These increased temperatures would cause the expansion of seawater and the melting of ice in both polar regions, resulting in a rise in sea level, predicted by climatologists to be up to 1.5 meters (about 5 feet) by the year 2050.[57] The result will be worldwide coastal flooding, including the inundation of significant portions of the coastal United States in what are now heavily populated areas. Bangladesh would lose most of its land, while some island nations may disappear altogether. At the poles, we are already starting to see some indication of the impacts of global warming. As Bill McKibben tells us

> One researcher watched as emperor penguins tried to cope with the early breakup of ice: their chicks had to jump into the water two weeks ahead of schedule, probably guaranteeing an early death. They (like us) evolved on the old earth.[58]

Noticeable changes are occurring right in our backyard, as well. In 1996, a group of scientists studying climate changes in the Pacific Northwest reported that the region was warming at four times the global rate. Richard Gammon, an oceanographer argues "that the Northwest is warming up fast is not a theory. It's a known fact, based on simple temperature readings."[59]

All over the world, food production will become erratic. The impact on agriculture would be particularly severe in the United States, since most food is grown in the middle or higher latitudes of the Northern Hemisphere where the greatest impact from the greenhouse effect will be felt. As climatic zones shift northward, animals, and particularly plants, will have a difficult time adapting to the change. This will lead to a significant loss in species variety and loss of genetic diversity.

Despite this overwhelming evidence, critics still persist. The National Center for Public Policy Research released an article in April 2001 concluding, "There is no way ... that a significant increase in atmospheric carbon dioxide will necessarily lead to any global warming." In fact, they continue, "Indeed, far from being a poisonous gas that will wreak havoc on the planet's ecosystem, carbon dioxide is arguably the Earth's best friend in that trees, wheat, peanuts, flowers, cotton and numerous other plants significantly benefit from increased levels of atmospheric carbon dioxide."[60]

Nonetheless, steps have been taken toward restraining the increase in the greenhouse effect, by focusing primarily on carbon dioxide emissions reductions. In 1988, the United Nations Environmental Program and World Meteorological Organization created the International Panel on Climate Change (IPCC) in an attempt to assess the bodies of scientific research that were steadily being built and recommend realistic response strategies for the management of global climate change. It is through the IPCC that most of our information concerning global climate change is gathered and analyzed.

The IPCC's second assessment of global climate change, released in 1995, was followed two years later with the first international conference devoted entirely to confronting the problem of global warming, and promulgating policies designed to reduce human influence on the greenhouse effect. Held in Kyoto, Japan, in late 1997, the conference resulted in an agreement signed by 160 countries, that pledges to dramatically reduce carbon dioxide emissions by 2010. The conference, while significant as a symbolic representation of an international commitment to global climate change, has drawn criticism from environmental groups for its short-term emphasis and lack of overall enforcement provisions. Critics fear that by setting the reduction goal as early as 2010 will result in a crash reduction of carbon dioxide emissions that is unsustainable over the long term. The Montreal Protocol, by comparison, has scheduled phase-outs of CFCs over a longer period of time, allowing for the research and development of CFC alternatives.

It should be noted that the Kyoto Protocol is a timely first step to limiting the production of greenhouse gases. However, much work remains to be done, and its symbolic value and potential are high. However, in another highly symbolic event, President George W. Bush, sympathizing with critics who believe the Treaty may harm the economy, pulled the United States completely out of the Kyoto Protocol in 2001.

Indeed there will be some costs associated with reducing greenhouse gas emissions. Some estimates find reducing carbon dioxide emissions just below 1990 levels could cost as much as three percent of GDP. On the other hand, studies also show that given currently available energy efficient technologies and the increased use of renewable energies, a 50 percent reduction could occur with little or no long-term costs.[61] In either case there will be political costs. Some industries and individuals will inevitably lose money and jobs, or we will all live with the costs of increased global warming and having to make even more drastic cuts in the future.

Deforestation

Deforestation of rain forests largely for agricultural development is related to the greenhouse effect in several important respects. Although not an international common pool problem per se, deforestation has serious impacts on common pool air resources.

Deforestation is occurring in many parts of the world and is particularly intense in less developed countries. Reforestation is the primary means of effectively reducing carbon dioxide in the atmosphere. Worldwide rates of deforestation are about 10 times the rate of reforestation. According to the Food and Agriculture Organization of the United Nations (FAO), forests covered about 3,454 million hectares worldwide in 1995, a little more than half of which were located in developing countries. Between 1990 and 1995 the world's forest had a net loss of an estimated 56.3 million hectares. Forest loss was not, however, as great as predicted by past FAO reports, and the rate of deforestation has decreased overall.[62] Regardless, the World Wildlife Fund has estimated that close to half of the world's original tropical rain forests have been destroyed or degraded.[63]

Currently, about 86,000 hectares of rainforest are lost daily, an area equivalent to the size of New York City; with this loss of habitat, approximately 137 species become extinct daily. Though they cover less than seven percent of the earth's land surface, they are home to over 50 percent of all earthly life forms. Brazil alone cuts down about 5.4 million acres of rainforest annually, primarily for agricultural purposes.

Though such unsustainable practices are the result of locals clearing land for their own crops, cattle, and homes, large-scale destruction via international interests are a much more significant problem. Still, the problem is complex. Meat wholesalers may pay Brazilians $148 to clear-cut or burn a hectare of forest to graze cattle on for a year or so until the land has been robbed of its nutrients. This provides Americans with very cheap hamburgers, and quick, easy cash for poor Brazilians. Some argue that if markets were properly setup, locals could sustainably harvest the rainforest for fruit, nuts, latex, and some lumber for as much as $6,800 per year *indefinitely*.[64] However, these markets do not yet exist, and organizations such as the World Bank have made loans to developing countries so they could become more "developed" that need to be paid back with interest *now*, and not after lucrative fruit and nut trades are established.

Most deforestation occurs in the less-developed areas, notably Brazil, Indonesia, and Zaire, because they rely on the forests for energy, increased agricultural production, and immediate cash supplies. Consequently, the prospects for a dramatic end to deforestation are not encouraging.[65] Deforestation also has a dramatic effect on termite populations, increasing the number of termites by anywhere from three to ten times their pre-deforestation population. Termites give off methane gas. Scientists believe termites may be the cause of up to half the methane gas that enters the atmosphere.[66] Increases in atmospheric methane, an important greenhouse gas, have been measured at between 1 and 2 percent each year, due in part, some scientists fear, to deforestation and the related increase in the termite population.[67]

Related to desertification, deforestation often occurs when already available agricultural land has been eroded and rendered infertile. Less-developed societies often have little choice other than to cut down forests in order to replace crop lands or to provide fuel for cooking and materials for building. The rate of deforestation is hastened as less-developed nations struggle to keep up in the global economy. According to the FAO, the development of subsistence farming practices in Africa and tropical Asia, combined with economic development programs in Latin America and Asia are leading to a considerable decrease of forest cover in these regions. Demographic growth is expected to force certain parts of the world such as sub-Saharan Africa and Latin America to transform forest into farmland. It is important to note, however, that there is no guarantee that such a conversion will ultimately benefit the populations in question.[68]

Efforts to combat deforestation have been largely futile in the face of a growing global economy. Industrialized and developing nations alike depend too much on resources gained from forest ecosystems (especially rain forests) for their development. This is a paradoxical arrangement considering that nations could greatly secure the long-term availability of the forest resource through protective management. Unfortunately, the economics involved in the situation preclude this sort of valuation for natural systems. In the logic of economics, if it is more profitable to harvest a grove of old growth redwoods for timber, and then put the proceeds from the sale of that timber in the bank to draw interest, and the interest grows faster than the value of the forest as timber, then the trees must go. Economists are beginning to look at ways in which a value may be placed on environmental resources that will reflect their true utility. Preliminary estimates hover around the $20 trillion per year mark, nearly equal to the gross global product.[69]

Ocean Pollution

Pollution that occurs on the high seas is the fourth example of an international common pool environmental management problem we review here. (Ocean pollution is covered in greater detail in Chapter 6.) The effects of international ocean pollution are clear and solutions are not difficult to understand, but many of the causes of ocean pollution will require international cooperation and action. Given the common pool nature of the problem, and the fact that problems are taking place in international waters, it is likely ocean pollution will be with us for some time to come.

Ocean pollution is a problem worldwide. Coastal areas on all continents suffer from sewage and industrial pollution entering the oceans via river systems.[70] This pollution threatens the health and welfare of the over 3.5 billion people who live at or near coastal areas, as well as coastal ecosystems (for example, marshes, estuaries, and wetlands).[71]

The sources of ocean pollution include wastewater from municipal treatment plants, municipal sludge, agricultural runoff, ocean dumping, and one of the most important international pollution problems, oil pollution.[72]

Oil from the cleaning, unloading, and loading of oil tankers, and accidents and blowouts of oil tankers contribute significant amounts of oil pollution to the ocean. Annually millions of tons of crude and refined oil are discharged, intentionally or accidentally, into the world's oceans from various sources, killing hundreds of thousands of marine birds and mammals. It is estimated that the United States is responsible for a third of all pollution that is dumped into the ocean.[73] The inability of government to deal with international ocean pollution—when the causes and solutions are so clear—is an example of the environmental policy paradox.

The international environmental problems discussed so far in this chapter often involve conflicting interests of one or a group of countries against another group or the rest of the world. Often the interests and concerns of the more developed world, primarily Western democracies, are at odds with the interests and concerns of less developed countries. These conflicts and their implications for a healthy global ecosystem, as well as a stable global political system, are the subject of the rest of this chapter. In Chapter 11 we examine political and institutional relationships that impact environmental management globally and discuss institutions that may need to be created to deal with international environmental problems.

LESS-DEVELOPED COUNTRIES: NORTH VS. SOUTH

Less-developed countries of the world, the poorer nations concentrated in the Southern Hemisphere, play a vital role in global environmental management. As many of these countries rush headlong into industrialization, they encounter serious environmental problems. The less-developed nations burn forests for agricultural land or immediate timber profits, yet tropical forests reduce carbon dioxide concentrations in the earth's atmosphere. Deforestation of tropical rain forests, primarily in Africa, southern Asia, and South America, promises to speed global warming and the greenhouse effect worldwide. As we have seen, these forests, which contain one-half of the world's species of plants and animals, are being destroyed at an incredibly rapid rate. Forests are cleared for fuel, to open grazing land, and to allow cultivation and settlement. Even the most stable less-developed countries, firmly committed to environmental protection, experience difficulties controlling environmental degradation due to deforestation.[74] Already close to half of the world's original tropical rain forests have been destroyed or degraded.[75] This is a major global environmental problem that threatens both long-term sustainable agricultural productivity in less developed countries and air quality in the more developed world.

Yet it is difficult to fault less developed countries for the destruction of their tropical rain forests. Often deforestation is vital to survival. In many less-developed countries, in excess of 40 percent of the population lack incomes sufficient to provide the necessities for sustaining life. It is not unusual, in some countries, for half of the workday to be taken up by the collection of fuel wood to provide energy. To expect countries with populations struggling to meet basic living requirements to forgo deforestation so more developed nations can continue to burn fossil fuels strikes many as bizarre.

Even when it is not a question of survival, economic incentive systems provided by international markets make deforestation very attractive to less-developed countries and their political leaders. For example, the market for beef has induced South American ranchers to clear vast areas of rain forest (an estimated 55 square feet of forest must be cleared to produce a quarter pound of beef) to supply international markets.[76]

There is no small amount of irony in the fact that many less-developed countries find themselves saddled with environmental problems that are a direct outgrowth of interaction with the more developed world. The African colonizers, like colonizers throughout the world, had policies that undermined the delicate balance between humans and nature and set in motion the disruption and decimation of social, political, economic, cultural, and environmental systems in the lands they colonized.[77]

The colonizing nations of Europe used their advanced technology to exploit their colonies' resources. This exploitation has not ended. Even though colonial systems are less prevalent today, America's toxic waste, as we saw in Chapter 8, finds its way into many less-developed countries. Also, pesticides and other goods banned in the United States are used in agriculture in less developed countries, often without regard to precautions necessary to protect worker health. That food often finds its way back into U.S. markets.

Although done in the name of self-determination and with the best intentions, the activities of developed countries in the less developed world have, paradoxically, often had negative impacts on the environment. The model of development set for the less-developed world has proven to be detrimental to the ecosystems of those nations, and ultimately the global environment. Much of the money borrowed from the World Bank and other international lenders goes to development projects that are not ecologically sound.[78] Instead of supporting sustainable development, such as agriculture or renewable forestry, the emphasis has been on road building, mineral extraction, large-scale hydropower, and agricultural exports.[79] The idea is that if capital is more freely flowing across borders and into less developed nations, and large infrastructure investments are made, some of that capital must remain in and help the less developed nations. Such an ideal should not always be expected to be met.

For example, World Bank and African Development Bank financing paid for a huge dam on the Awash River in Ethiopia. The Awash Dam resulted in the displacement of thousands of people, many of whom became the Ethiopian famine victims of the early 1980s. In the lead paragraph of an article discussing the Ethiopian famine, the author wrote, "[L]ittle did the world know it was helping to rescue victims of earlier aid efforts."[80] Yet the need to improve living conditions through development spurs countries to act for short-term developmental gains without regard for the long-term environmental costs. Only in the late 1980s, largely in response to the demands of environmental organizations, did some international lending institutions begin to take environmental degradation into consideration when making loans. There is no evidence, however, that these institutions have any inclination to move away from large-scale intensive development projects and toward ecologically sustainable development.

The foregoing discussion of the environmental problems facing the less developed world, and the relationship between the environmental problems of the less developed nations and the more developed nations suggests a potential for conflict in the future. Many feel that is what the future holds.

International Conflict

The pollution, population, and other environmental problems facing the less developed world threaten the survival of everyone. As Richard Tobin wrote,

> The population, development, and environmental problems of the Third World dwarf those of the developed world and are not amenable to immediate resolution, but immediate action is imperative. To meet their daily needs for food and fuel, millions of peo-

ple are steadily destroying their biological and environmental support systems at un-precedented rates.... Whether this situation will change depends on the ability of Third World residents, not only to reap the benefits of sustained economic growth, but also to meet the demands of current populations while using their natural resources in a way that accommodates the needs of future generations. Unless the developing nations are able to do so soon, their future will determine ours as well.[81]

It may not seem like an environmental issue, but there is a growing consensus among environmental and international relations analysts that environmental degradation and resource scarcity will have an impact on global security and world peace in the future. If it comes to the point where less developed nations have no natural resources left, or all the capital has gone, and environmental problems lead to political instability, these people will not fade away quietly, they will come knocking loudly on the doors of the developed nations.

At the United Nations Conference on the Human Environment in 1972 (known as the Stockholm Conference), a major disagreement arose between less- and more developed nations over the impact environmental controls would have on future economic growth and development. Similar to the concerns of unions and representatives of the urban poor in the United States who were, and to a lesser extent remain, skeptical of environmental regulations for fear they slow economic development, the leadership of many less developed countries fear the road to prosperity, or out of poverty, may necessarily involve increased industrial pollution.

When the leaders of less developed countries reflect on the history of industrial development in the United States, they find it is replete with resource exploitation. The destruction of eastern forests, pollution of urban air and water, and the continued use of renewable resources at rates that are in excess of natural rates of return all suggest the United States is prescribing an austerity medicine for other nations after our own prosperity has been assured, medicine we have been reluctant to take ourselves or to take in sufficiently high doses. The developed world continues to consume resources at a much more rapid rate than the less-developed world, and the less developed world's *population* is expanding at a much higher rate (see endnote, for example).[82]

Since the Stockholm Conference, most less-developed countries have accepted that the environment needs to be protected. Only nine nations had environmental ministries in 1972. Twenty-five years later 115 had established some kind of environmental protection organization. Although often poorly staffed or ineffective, this is, at least, evidence of global recognition of the need for environmental protection.

Nevertheless, conflict between rich and poor nations will be a big part of international environmental administration in the future. The finite resources the more developed nations have that are used to fuel economic expansion and a comfortable lifestyle will not be available for a repeat performance for future, or even present, generations in the less-developed world.

In fact, citizens of more developed countries can count on lifestyle changes that reflect resource scarcity. In the last 30 years, for example, Americans have had to accept that they may never own a single-family detached home, a second home, or an array of high-powered recreational vehicles. Though these are certainly not necessities, they have been common among the middle class in America a generation ago, but less so today. The day may not be long off when automobile travel, beef consumption, the pleasure of a household pet, or a room heated to 72 degrees F in the winter will be luxuries only a few can afford. Bill McKibben puts it like this:

> The numbers are so daunting that they're almost unimaginable. Say, just for argument's sake, that we decided to cut world fossil-fuel use by 60 percent—the amount that the UN panel says would stabilize world climate. And then say that we shared the remaining fossil fuel equally. Each human being would get to produce 1.69 metric tons of carbon dioxide annually—which would allow you to drive an average American car nine miles a day. By the time the population increased to 8.5 billion, in about 2025, you'd be down to six miles a day. If you carpooled, you'd have about three pounds of CO2 left in your daily ration—enough to run a highly efficient refrigerator. Forget your computer, your TV, your stereo,your stove, your dishwasher, your water heater, your microwave, your water pump, your clock. Forget your light bulbs, compact fluorescent or not.[83]

As resource scarcity begets other lifestyle changes for middle-class Americans, we can anticipate that pressure will be put on politicians to find political solutions to domestic scarcity problems. This may lead to conflict and the exploitation of the poor by the rich. As Daniel Henning and William Mangun put it, "[T]he less developed countries face the additional threat of technological and resource exploitation by the developed countries themselves experiencing resource scarcity as they attempt to maintain high consumption levels."[84]

Several well-written and widely received books and reports have examined the relationship between international environmental problems and global peace and security.[85] One, *Our Common Future* (the Brundtland commission report to the United Nations), reported,

> The deepening and widening environmental crisis presents a threat to national security—and even survival—that may be greater than well-armed ill-disposed neighbors and unfriendly alliances.... Environmental stress is both a cause and an effect of political tension and military conflict. Nations have often fought to assert or resist control over raw materials, energy supplies ... and other key environmental resources. Such conflicts are likely to increase as these resources become scarcer and the competition for them increases.[86]

In light of the consequences of ignoring global environmental problems and watching as the less-developed world slides deeper and deeper into irreversible capital resource loss, it would seem, as Robert Paehlke put it, "[R]eal security ... requires a transfer of funds from military expenditure to sustainable development."[87] The funds are there. The fiscal year 2003 U.S. military budget request is nearly $400 billion, which is more than six times greater than the world's second largest military spender, Russia. Indeed, this amount is more than that of the remainder of the world's top 25 military spenders combined. Total global military spending in 2000 was about $812 billion.[88]

Terrorists and "rogue nations" are not the only security threats. Even the infamous Zapatista rebellion in Chiapas, Mexico was caused in part by the poor and marginalized being pushed into environments where they could not feed themselves due to poor land and dense populations. In addition, water scarcity continues to exacerbate tensions in Gaza between Israel and Palestine. Finally, in South Africa resource scarcity and population growth have led to an exodus off the rural, wasted lands to urban areas where squatters, poor environmental conditions and a sudden influx of people into already crowded urban areas has led to serious ethnic violence.[89]

Meanwhile, the United Nations Population Fund (UNFPA), which has taken the lead in efforts to stabilize the global population, had revenues of $366.1 million in 2000, up from $287.7 million in 1999, due largely to cost sharing programs like the Netherlands $41 million contribution in 2000 for contraceptives.[90] If military spending remained at the same percentage of the world's GNP that it was just prior to 1960, $225 billion could be made available on an annual basis.[91] Unfortunately, international policy formation, like domestic policy formation, often requires a crisis situation before policy makers act, despite evidence linking environmental, social, and ultimately security and defense issues. Indeed, most environmental policy analysts and other environmental specialists agree we are in a crisis situation. Yet for political and institutional reasons little happens—another environmental policy paradox.

SUMMARY

The picture this chapter paints is not pleasant, though not entirely without hope. Most of the less-developed world finds itself with growing populations, a deteriorating resource base, and an unhealthy environment. Furthermore, the continuing scarcity of world resources, the future necessity of sacrifice, and less material abundance (or the prospect, for many countries, of never becoming more developed and enjoying the privileges the more developed world takes for granted) have turned environmental problems into national security problems.

Solving the international environmental problems discussed in this chapter— overpopulation and its related effects, ozone depletion, global warming, deforestation, and ocean pollution—as well as the other environmental problems we have discussed throughout the book, will require money and organization. The World Resources Institute has estimated it will take $20 billion to $50 billion a year to save the environment in the developing world.[92] In contrast, the budget for the United Nations Environment Program was less than $60 *million* a year in 2000.[93] Yet, as we have seen with our summary of defense expenditures, the money is there. What is lacking is the will or the incentives and the institutional framework.[94] In the next chapter we examine international environmental management and the prerequisites to successful global pollution control.

NOTES

1. Bill McKibben, "A Special Moment in History: The Future of Population," *The Atlantic Monthly*, (May 1998), p. 55.
2. Larry B. Stammer, "Saving the Earth: Who Sacrifices?" *Los Angeles Times*, March 13,1989, Pt. 1, p. 16.
3. Royal Society of London and the U.S. National Academy of Sciences, *Population Growth, Resource Consumption, and a Sustainable World* (London and Washington, DC: Royal Society of London and the U.S. National Academy of Sciences, 1992). Cited in Lester R. Brown, "A New Era Unfolds," in Lester R. Brown et al. (eds.), *State of the World* (New York: Norton, 1993), p. 3.
4. S. Wortman and R. Cummings, Jr., *To Feed This World: The Challenge and the Strategy* (Baltimore: Johns Hopkins University Press, 1979), p. 83.
5. *UN Chronicle,* "Population 2050: 9.4 billion" (Fall 1997) p. 72.

6. Jonathan Turk, *Introduction to Environmental Studies* (2nd ed.) (Philadelphia: Saunders, 1985), p. 90.
7. *U.N. Chronicle,* p. 72.
8. Ibid.
9. Ibid.
10. Ibid. Fertility is now estimated to have declined in Bangladesh from 6.2 children per woman from 1980 to 1985 to 3.4 from 1990 to 1995, in India from 4.5 to 3.4, in Pakistan from 6.5 to 5.5, in Turkey from 4.1 to 2.7, in Myanmar from 4.9 to 3.6, in Syria from 7.4 to 4.7, in Kenya from 7.5 to 5.4, and in Cote d'Ivoire from 7.4 to 5.7.
11. U.S. Census Bureau, International Database and U.N. "World Population Prospects." Available at *www.geohive.com.*
12. Population Reference Bureau. 2001 World Population Data Sheet. Available at *http://www.prb. org/Content/NavigationMenu/Other_reports/2000-2002/2001_World_Population_Data_Sheet.htm.*
13. Lester Brown (ed.), *State of the World,* 1977, manuscript, pp. 2–8.
14. Rao, U. R. "Space Remote Sensing for Achieving Food and Environmental Security." Delivered to International Symposium on Spectral Sensing Research, Melbourne, Australia, November 27, 1995. Available at *http://ltpwww.gsfc.nasa.gov/ISSSR-95/spacerem.htm.*
15. McKibben, "A Special Moment in History: The Future of Population," (May 1998), p. 55.
16. Lester R. Brown, "Reexamining the World Food Prospect," in Lester R. Brown et al., *State of the World: 1989* (New York: Norton, 1989), pp. 43, 55.
17. Paul R. Ehrlich and Anne H. Erhlich, "Ehrlichs' fables," *Technology Review* (Jan. 1997), p. 38.
18. William Ophuls, *Ecology and the Politics of Scarcity* (San Francisco: Freeman, 1977), p. 55.
19. Turk, *Introduction to Environmental Studies,* p. 90.
20. Population Division of the U.N. "World Population Prospects: Highlights Draft" from February 28, 2001. Available at *http://www.un.org/esa/population/publications/wpp2000/wpp2000h.pdf.*
21. McKibben, "A Special Moment in History: The Future of Population," (May 1998), p. 55.
22. Julian L. Simon, "The Case for More People," in Kent Gilbreath (ed.), *Business and the Environment: Toward Common Ground* (2nd ed.) (Washington, DC: Conservation Foundation, 1984), p. 169.
23. Paul and Anne Ehrlich, "Space Age Cargo Cult," in Gilbreath, *Business and the Environment,* p. 174.
24. Paul and Anne Ehrlich, "Ehrlichs' fables," p. 38.
25. Although total food outputs are high, world capital food production is not increasing at the same rates as it has in the past. Production rose 15 percent from 1950 to 1960, 7 percent in the decade from 1960 to 1970, and then only 4 percent from 1970 to 1980. "Supply Side Ideas Challenge Old Population Theory," in Gilbreath, *Business and the Environment,* p. 184.
26. Maryla Webb and Judith Jacobson, *U.S. Carrying Capacity: An Introduction* (Washington, DC: Carrying Capacity, 1982), p. 33.
27. USDA Foreign Agricultural Service. "Food Aid Programs Fact Sheet" Available at *http://www. fas.usda.gov/food-aid.html.*
28. For summary, see Lester R. Brown, "Analyzing the Demographic Trap," *State of the World 1977* (New York: Norton, 1987).
29. Ibid.
30. Borrelli, "Debt or Equity?" p. 48.
31. M. Alofchie and S. Commines, "Famines and Africa," *The Futurist* (April 1985), pp. 71–72.
32. Paul R. Ehrlich and Anne H. Ehrlich, "The Population Explosion," *The Amicus Journal* (Winter 1990), pp. 24–25.
33. Ibid., p. 22.
34. Fish harvested from the sea by trawlers require large amounts of energy. Hence, even though fish caught in the sea are very efficient converters of protein, the energy required to harvest makes this a resource-intensive food. See Albert Sasson, "Aquaculture: Realities, Difficulties and Outlook," in Jacques G. Richardson (ed.), *Managing the Ocean: Resources, Research, Law* (Mount Airy, MD: Lomond, 1985), pp. 61–72.
35. Edward A. Keller, *Environmental Geology* (4th ed.) (Columbus, OH: Merrill, 1985), p. 454.
36. Turk, *Introduction to Environmental Studies,* p. 184.
37. Ibid.
38. *UN Chronicle,* "Land Degredation" (Summer 1997), p. 27.
39. Giselle V. Steele, "Drowning in Sand," *E* (Jan-Feb 1997), p. 15.
40. United Nations Convention to Combat Desertification (UNCCD). "Fact Sheets on the Convention to Combat Desertification." Available at *http://www.unccd.int/publicinfo/factsheets/menu.php.*

41. *UN Chronicle,* "Land Degradation," p. 27.
42. Lester R. Brown, "Solving the Food/Population Equation," *UNESCO Courier* (Jan 1995), p. 42.
43. Another threat to the ozone layer may be presented by U.S. space shuttle flights. Experts from the former Soviet Union have claimed that every time the U.S. craft flies, it destroys massive amounts of atmospheric ozone. Calculations by Valeri Burdkov, one of the former Soviet Union's leading geophysicists and Vyacheslav Filin, deputy chief designer at the S.P. Korolyev Design Bureau, have shown that in "one flight, the space shuttle destroys up to 10 million of the three billion tons of atmospheric ozone. Three hundred launches is enough to do away altogether with the thin ozone layer which is already holed." The solid fuel used in the Titan rockets burns to produce hydrogen chloride, one molecule of which is said to destroy 100,000 molecules of ozone. The rocket emits 187 tons of chlorine and chlorine compounds as well as ozone-depleting nitrogen compounds (7 tons), aluminum oxides (177 tons), and 378 tons of carbon oxidizers. However, NASA maintains the shuttle is ecologically sound. See Nick Nuttall, "Russians say US Shuttle Is Damaging Ozone Layer," *The Times* (London), December 20, 1989, p. 5.
44. James Close and Greg Playford, "Ozone: The Pollution paradox," *New York State Conservationist* (June 1997), p. 23.
45. Union of Concerned Scientists. "Frequently Asked Questions About Ozone Depletion and the Ozone Hole." Available at *http://www.ucsusa.org/environment/ozone.faq.html.*
46. See Thomas H. Maugh II, "Ozone Depletion Far Worse Than Expected," *Los Angeles Times,* March 16, 1988, Pt. 1, p. 1; and "Ozone Depletion Worsens, NRDC Leads Drive for Total CFC Phase Out," *Newsline* (Natural Resources Defense Council), 6 (2) (May/June 1988), p. 1.
47. Singapore Ministry of the Environment. "Frequently Asked Questions on Ozone, Ozone Depleting Substances, and Persistent Organic Pollutants." Available at *http://www.env.gov.sg/faq/faq2.htm.*
48. Union of Concerned Scientists. "Frequently Asked Questions About Ozone Depletion and the Ozone Hole." Available at *http://www.ucsusa.org/environment/ozone.faq.html.*
49. About.com's Environment Section. "Ozone Depletion: International Cooperation." Available at *http://environment.about.com/library/weekly/blozone4.htm.*
50. "Phew, The Ozone Layer May be Saved," *The Economist* (Sept. 13, 1997), p. 48
51. Ibid.
52. About.com's Environment Section. "Ozone Depletion: International Cooperation." Available at *http://environment.about.com/library/weekly/blozone4.htm.*
53. Intergovernmental Panel on Climate Change, AIPCC Second Assessment: synthesis of scientific technical information relevant to interpreting article 2 of the UN Framework Convention on Climate Change 1995 (Geneva: UNEP, 1995) as quoted by Paul and Anne Ehrlich, "Ehlichs' fables," p. 36.
54. United Nations Environment Program. "UNEP 2000 Annual Report: Overview of UNEP's Activities." Available at *http://www.unep.org/Evaluation/Reports/2000/Overview/over.asp.*
55. Jeremy Rifkin, "The Doomsday Prognosis," *The Guardian,* August 21, 1988, p. 19; and Miller, *Living in the Environment,* p. 441.
56. McKibben, "A Special Moment in History: The Future of Population," p. 55.
57. Rifkin, "The Doomsday Prognosis," p. 19.
58. Bill McKibben, "A Special Moment in History: The Future of Population," p. 57.
59. Ibid.
60. The National Center for Public Policy Research. *National Policy Analysis #334.* April 2001. "Carbon Dioxide is Good for the Environment." Available at *http://www.nationalcenter.org/NPA334.html.*
61. World Resources Institute. "World Resources: A Guide to the Global Environment, 1996–1997". Available at *http://www.wri.org/wri/wr-96-97/.*
62. France Bequette, "Forests: a breathing space for the planet," UNESCO Courier (July-August 1997), p. 82. Note: The decline in forest area in developing countries was 65.1 million hectares. This was partly offset by an increase of 8.8 million hectares in the industrialized countries.
63. Daniel H. Henning and William R. Mangun, *Managing the Environmental Crisis* (Durham, NC: Duke University Press, 1989), p. 281.
64. Rainforest Action Network. "Rates of Rainforest Destruction and Species Loss." Available at *http://www.ecuadorexplorer.com/html/body_rf_destuction.html.*
65. Bequette, "Forests: A Breathing Space for the Planet," p. 81.
66. Tom Morris, *Principles of Planetary Biology.* Biosynthesis chapter. Available at *http://www.planetarybiology.com/biosynthesis/biosynth13.htm.*
67. David M. Schwartz, "The Termite Connection," *International Wildlife* (July/August 1987), p. 38.
68. Bequette, "Forests: A Breathing Space for the Planet," p. 83.

69. Paul and Anne Ehrlich, "Ehrlichs' fables," p. 36.
70. Anastasia Toufexis, "The Dirty Seas," *Time*, (August 1, 1988), p. 47.
71. *UN Chronicle,* "Stronger Measures to Protect the Ozone Layer" (Spring 1996), p. 73.
72. Conservation Foundation, *State of the Environment* (Washington, DC: Conservation Foundation, 1987), pp. 115, 415.
73. G. Tyler Miller, Jr. *Living in the Environment* (8th ed.), (Belmont, CA: Wadsworth, 1994), p. 605. (In 1985, 3.6 million tons of crude and refined oil were discharged into the world's oceans.)
74. For example, the Central American nation of Costa Rica, perhaps the most democratic and stable government of Latin America, has a rate of deforestation that is inconsistent with its expressed commitment to conservation. Experts predicted that despite its commitments, logging will proceed and the country will have virtually depleted its hardwood stocks by 1995. See Borrelli, "Debt or Equity?" p. 47.
75. Henning and Mangun, *Managing the Environmental Crisis*, p. 281.
76. Arnold J. Heidenheimer, Hugh Heclo, and Carolyn Teich Adams, *Comparative Public Policy* (New York: St. Martin's Press, 1990), p. 331.
77. Christine H. Russell, "Squandering Eden," *The Amicus Journal* (Fall 1988), p.50.
78. Borrelli, "Debt or Equity?" p. 48.
79. Ibid.
80. Patricia Adams, "All in the Name of Aid," *Sierra* (January/February 1987), p. 45.
81. Richard J. Tobin, "Environment, Population and Development in the Third World," in Norman J. Vig and Michael E. Kraft (eds.), *Environmental Policy in the 1990s* (Washington, DC: Congressional Quarterly Press, 1990), p.298.
82. The consumptive differences between those living in developed nations vs. those living in developing nations is staggering. Consider these facts:
   • An American uses seventy times as much energy as a Bangladeshi, fifty times as much as a Malagasi, twenty times as much as a Costa Rican.
   • Since we live longer, the effect of each of us is further multiplied. In a year an American uses three hundred times as much energy as a Malian; over a lifetime he will use 500,000 times as much.
   • Even if all such effects as the clearing of forests and the burning of grasslands are factored in and attributed to poor people, those who live in the poor world are typically responsible for the annual release of a tenth of a ton of carbon each, whereas the average is 3.5 tons for residents of the "consumer" nations of Western Europe, North America, and Japan. The richest tenth of Americans the people most likely to be reading this book annually emit eleven tons of carbon apiece.
   • During the next decade India and China will each add to the planet about ten times as many people as the United States will but the stress on the natural world caused by new Americans may exceed that from new Indians and Chinese combined. The 57.5 million Northerners added to our population during this decade will add more greenhouse gases to the atmosphere than the roughly 900 million added Southerners. Bill McKibben, "A Special Moment in History: The Future of Population," p. 58.
83. Ibid.
84. Henning and Mangun, *Managing the Environmental Crisis*, p. 299.
85. See, for example, International Union for Conservation of Nature and Natural Resources, *World Conservation Strategy* (Gland, Switzerland: International Union for Conservation of Nature and Natural Resources, 1980); Independent Commission on Disarmament and Security Issues, *Common Security: A Blueprint for Survival* (New York: Simon & Schuster, 1982); and Willy Brandt, *World Armament and World Hunger* (London: Victor Gollanez, 1986).
86. World Commission on Environment and Development, *Our Common Future* (New York: Oxford University Press, 1987), pp. 6–7, 290. Cited in Robert Paehlke, "Environmental Values and Democracy: The Challenge of the Next Century," in Norman J. Vig and Michael E. Kraft (eds.), *Environmental Policy in the 1990s* (Washington, DC: Congressional Quarterly Press, 1990), pp. 349–367.
87. Paehlke, "Environmental Values and Democracy: The Challenge of the Next Century," pp. 359–360.
88. Center for Defense Information. "World Military Expenditures: US vs World." Available at *http://www.cdi.org/issues/wme/*.
89. Peace and Conflict Studies Program, University of Toronto, "The Project on Environment, Population, and Security." Available at *http://www.library.utoronto.ca/pcs/eps.htm*. Also, for more on environmental security issues, see the Environmental Security Database at *http://www.library*.

utoronto.ca/pcs/database/libintro.htm. The Pacific Institute is also a valuable resource, and particularly relevant is its "Environment and Terrorism Report" at *http://www.pacinst.org/environment_ and_terrorism.htm.*

90. United Nations Population Fund (UNFPA), "2000 Report." Available at *http://www.unfpa.org/ about/report/2000/index.htm.*
91. Paehlke, "Environmental Values and Democracy: The Challange of the Next Century," p. 360.
92. *UN Chronicle*, "Ministers Call for Stronger, Revitalized UNEP" (Summer 1997), p. 49.
93. Environment News Service. February 1, 1999. "UNEP Chief Asks $60 Million Annual Budget." Available at *http://ens.lycos.com/ens/feb99/1999L-02-01-07.html.*
94. To learn more about international environmental issues, foreign policy, and how environmental policy paradoxes are currently being viewed and solved, a useful source is *Foreign Policy In Focus: The World in Numbers* at *www.foreignpolicy-infocus.org/papers/win_body.html.*

International Environmental Management

Because of the nature of current global environmental problems and the international institutions and incentive systems operating on international actors, it is quite possible that timely solutions to many of the problems discussed in the previous chapter and throughout this book will not be found. In this chapter we discuss the nature of international environmental cooperation—specifically the elements necessary for any satisfactory international solution to global pollution problems—and the prerequisites and prospects for responsible international environmental administration. In addition, we compare the environmental records of communist and capitalist countries and examine the conditions necessary for the creation of international organizations and conventions that will have the authority necessary to deal with those problems. As Norman Vig and Michael Kraft have written, "Governments are ill equipped to resolve many long-term and severe problems in the global environment; hence, institutional reforms and new methods of decision making will be critical to success in such cases."[1] We examine obstacles to the creation of such new methods of decision making.

Environmentalism is becoming a dominant political force in nations all over the globe. In many countries environmental concern has manifested itself in the development of "green movements" and "green" political parties. Beginning in the late 1970s, first in West Germany, new environmentally oriented political parties emerged to challenge the ecological management policies of established parties. Spokespersons for green parties argued that established political parties could not deal with the world's problems, because opposition "to this dominant world view cannot possibly be articulated through any of the major parties, for they and their ideologies are part of the problem."[2] Although the ideology of green parties varies from country to country, they usually include beliefs in "ecological wisdom, grass-roots democracy, personal and social responsibility, nonviolence, decentralization, community based economics, postpatriarchal values, respect for diversity, global responsibility, and future focus."[3] These general beliefs manifest themselves in a variety of policy proposals including nonnuclear defense, feminism, local control, recycling, mass transit, self-reliance, renewable energy, and requiring that one's work be personally satisfying.[4] Green parties have been formed all over the world including Brazil, Costa Rica, Japan, Canada, and the United States. The 1996 and 2000 elections also saw activity from the American Green Party, rallying around well-known consumer advocate Ralph Nader, and candidates from green parties have been elected to national parliaments in Switzerland (first in 1979); Belgium (1981); Finland, Portugal, and West Germany (1983); Luxembourg (1984); Austria (1986); Italy (1987); Sweden (1988); and the Netherlands (1989).[5] In Germany the Greens, for the first time, in 1998, became part of the government when the Social Democratic Party in Germany won the election and brought the Green party into the governing coalition.

The environmental policies of other nations, Communist or capitalist, are remarkably similar both in terms of their objectives and their implementation problems. To varying degrees, environmental management in the industrialized countries is decentralized. Even in countries where central authorities were responsible for overseeing environmental management, such as the former Soviet Union, bargaining and negotiation between authorities in different ministries at various levels was the norm.[6]

In industrial democracies, approaches to environmental enforcement vary from the standards and enforcement approach of the United States (with standards set, usually nationwide, enforced by fines or punishment) to a consultation, negotiation approach characteristic of Great Britain (where pollution requirements not governed by the European Community are negotiated in partnership with businesses and industry).[7] Most industrial democracies fall somewhere in between these extremes, using a combination of bargaining and standardized regulations.[8]

As you may have noticed in earlier chapters, I have been rather critical of the policy-making process in the United States and the environmental policies that system has produced. Due to the formal and informal incentives operating on policy makers, I am not optimistic about future environmental policies the system, in the United States as well as internationally, will produce. Although I have tried to suggest throughout the book ways in which you can have an impact on environmental policy formation, you might conclude at this point that the policy-making system in the United States and democracy itself is fundamentally flawed. Indeed, some of the best known observers of the environmental policy-making process and of environmental problems have concluded that existing governmental arrangements will fail and should be replaced by oligarchic governments staffed by environmental experts with the power to enforce sound environmental policy.[9] I don't agree. To paraphrase Winston Churchill, democracy is the worst form of government—except for all the others.

Even though the trend in the world is clearly away from communism and toward democratic capitalism, it is not unusual for commentators to blame capitalism and the private enterprise system for the woes of the environment. Because of this fact I think it is important we look at alternative political systems and see what kind of a job they have done in protecting the environment.

ALTERNATIVE POLITICAL SYSTEMS

The main doctrines of political systems focus on the scope of political freedom accorded to the individual, including personal freedom to interact, organize, and dissent. Important differences exist between the doctrines of democratic and communist systems. How societies based on these doctrines actually work is equally diverse.

Industrialization brings the same environmental problems to developed and developing nations—Communist or capitalist. Neither societies with high degrees of political freedom nor those with little political freedom have fared demonstrably better at ecologically sound management.

In practice, many nations combine free market and collective socialist activities within one "mixed economy," combining predominantly private initiative and property with public responsibility for social welfare. So although most nations do not engage exclusively in one economic system or another, those states advocating public ownership of the means of production with a centrally planned economy are here termed collective ownership systems and include socialist as well as communist states; states that protect private ownership and competition of the free market economy are called capitalist. The system of government within which an economy operates is an important factor, but only one among many that affect a country's economic activity and the resultant pollution.

Market-Based Economies

Capitalist nations, where private ownership of industry is the rule, are driven by the profit motive in a free-market economy. Under communist governments theoretically the economy is planned, but in the comparatively unregulated operation of the free-market economy, supply and demand by consumers drives production. The incentive is to make money by selling a manufactured goods at a profit. Industrialists in general and capitalists in particular traditionally have been unconcerned or unable to internalize the environmental costs of their goods. Internalizing environmental costs, or eliminating externalities, means reduced profits or decreased output.[10]

Capitalism, in Western industrial societies, means that ownership and control of the means of production, for example factories and equipment, are, with some exceptions, generally held by individuals, not by the government.

According to its critics, one problem with democratic capitalism is that corporation managers wield far-reaching power over stockholders and employees and make decisions that affect the public without any clearly defined responsibility to the people. In addition, they wield power over politicians and public policy by virtue of their ability to make campaign contributions in greater amounts than groups representing environmental organizations. As corporations continue to grow, they take on the unhealthy characteristics of big bureaucracy, which is the same problem that large-scale socialized enterprise faces. As Denis Healey, a

British socialist stated, "Industrial power in every large, developed economy now rests with a managerial class which is responsible to no one. The form of ownership is irrelevant. State control over nationalized industries is as difficult as share-holder control over private firms."[11]

The environmental problems and societal responses within a democracy have been detailed throughout this book. How much better have communist systems fared? Is capitalism the culprit?

Collective Ownership Systems

Central planning in the communist command economy determines how, for what purposes, and in what relative proportions available capital resources and labor are to be allocated. In practice this has meant the state not only controls what is produced but how it is produced, and with what materials. With public ownership, production is said to be limited only by scarce resources and incomplete knowledge, not by social institutions, such as the private profit motive.[12]

Under communist systems, the state owns the means of production and sets an overall goal of what is to be produced and how available resources of labor, land, and capital are to be employed. The freedom of the consumer, worker, and producer (what to produce, where to work, live, travel) is replaced by the orders of the state. Since the communist state possesses widespread power, it can work to turn the plan into reality. It is the collective control and planning function of communist systems that have led some to conclude those systems provide the means necessary for effective environmental management. In theory perhaps these people are correct. A centralized economic system could internalize pollution externalities, develop renewable resources, and in other ways establish sustainable economic and agricultural activities. In practice, however, the environmental policies and records of the two largest collective systems, China and the former Soviet Union, illustrate some of the problems collectivist societies have had in dealing with environmental problems.

Eastern Europe and the Former Soviet Union

A summary of environmental problems in what was the Soviet Union and Eastern Europe and the conditions that lead to these problems, illustrate the utility of alternative political systems (in this case, communist systems) for providing wise environmental management.

Since Stalin, communist leaders have placed a high priority on transforming their nations into industrial powers. This rapid modernization was accomplished with only minimal attention to pollution controls and with industrial processes that inefficiently consumed copious amounts of polluting fossil fuels.[13] For example, in the former Soviet Union the leadership took the view

> that nature is simply a source of raw materials which can be exploited to permit nearly unlimited growth for man's benefit. The environmental damage that results from such exploitation is either ignored or seen as a temporary problem that can be overcome without affecting development. This is the primary reason for many of the Soviet Union's severe pollution problems.[14]

In general, the former Soviet Union did not suffer from a shortage of environmental laws. What was lacking was enforcement. (Does that sound familiar?)

The environmental record of the communist systems in the former Soviet Union and communist Eastern Europe was very poor. When faced with trade-offs between economic growth and pollution control, the former almost always won out over the latter.

The political reforms that swept across Eastern Europe in 1989 and 1990 opened up those societies and brought to international public attention some of the worst pollution problems imaginable. In fact, people living in, what were then, communist controlled states used the occurance of environmental degradation to rise up against Moscow. From 1985 to the eventual collapse of the Soviet Union, environmental movements in Poland, Hungary, Armenia, and Estonia helped hasten the downfall of the Soviet Union. However, the environmental revolutions in these countries have now ended. These concerns have been replaced, in large part, by the economic hardships the region is now facing as it attempts to transition from a command to a market economy. Unemployment and skyrocketing inflation have led to greater ethnic conflict and political instability. At this writing, there doesn't appear to be much of a chance that the former Soviet Union, namely the Russian Republic, will be able to quickly fix their economic and political systems. As such, environmental concerns are considered a low priority. It may behoove the rest of the world to actively assist Russia rebuild its economy so that effort may be directed toward environmental protection. Until that time, the region will continue to sink deeper into environmental despair.

The environmental problems faced by former communist states are multifaceted. Scientists believe that up to 10 percent of the deaths in Eastern Europe are due to pollution. Before it became a part of a united Germany, air pollution in East Germany was 13 times as high as air pollution in West Germany. In a number of East European cities, the air was so polluted that cars turned on their headlights in the middle of the day to improve visibility and avoid running into each other. Doing laundry can be difficult under such conditions. As a housewife in the former Czechoslovakia put it, "You cannot hang your clothes outside. If you do, they will be filthy before they are dry."[15]

And it is not only a problem of air pollution. In Poland, 65 percent of the rivers were so polluted that factories did not use the water for industrial purposes for fear the water would damage their pipes. The water quality situation was similar throughout Eastern Europe.[16]

Today things have improved somewhat but in most instances there is much to be done before levels of pollution control match those in Western Europe.

Eastern European pollution problems are aggravated by the geography of the region. The countries lie in a narrow corridor without a large landmass to spread the pollution, like in the United States and China. The most notorious of these areas may be found on where the borders of the Czech Republic, Germany and Poland converge. Known as the "Black Triangle," this region is shielded by the Giant Mountains of North Bohemia and Southern Silesia from the easterly wind, which, if given a clear path, would help alleviate the concentration of pollution produced by coal-burning electrical plants and other heavy industry located in the area. Towns in this area, Chomutov in the Czech Republic, for example, may expect the maximum admissible concentration levels of sulfur dioxide for the region to be exceeded 117 days of the year.[17] According to a UN study, "The industrial regions of Central Europe are so choked by pollution that the health of children is impaired and the lives of adults shortened."[18]

Why did these countries fail to prevent resource depletion and pollution? In theory, collective systems would protect the environment, since "state ownership of the means of production would remove the motives for pollution because there was no reason for the state to contaminate itself and reduce its own wealth."[19] In practice, factory managers were pressured to meet production goals and had little incentive to prevent pollution. Managers were often paid bonuses for increasing production and faced few if any penalties for depleting resources or polluting the environment. In many communist countries there were systems of fines for pollution, but these were poorly enforced.[20]

China

In the People's Republic of China, traditional Chinese values have emphasized the necessity of harmony between humans and nature.[21] This is in contrast to Judeo-Christian Western belief systems that have emphasized the conquest of humans over nature. Yet the Chinese respect for nature must exist only in the abstract. As with other communist countries, economic pressures have created priorities of their own, and pollution of the Chinese environment is the result.

As in the former Soviet Union, a factory manager's performance in China is judged either by the amount they are able to increase productivity or by their political consciousness. "Since pollution control equipment would have meant the non-productive divergence of labor, capital and material, no manager would have undertaken to install such devices unless mandated by party policy."[22] Since none of the frequent shifts in economic policy that occurred from 1949 to 1979 contained any industrial pollution control policy, no pollution control equipment was installed in China during this period. The result is that the Chinese now are forced not only to deal with the physical effects of years of industrial pollution, but they must also overcome the reluctance of officials and factory managers to take the consequences of pollution seriously.[23]

Since the adoption of the "Forestry Act" and the "Law on Environmental Protection" in China in 1979, there has been a new attitude and approach toward environmental problems in China. Articles, conferences, and other activities sanctioned by the government suggest there is now serious concern about threats to the environment.[24]

The Chinese face a number of obstacles in attempting to deal with pollution problems. First, China is a large country, both geographically and in numbers of citizens. And, as in the West, compliance with requirements that existing factories correct their pollution problems is expensive and does not contribute to a primary domestic goal—increasing productivity.

Yet another problem stems from the government's land-use policies. Part of the industrial pollution problem is the location of factories—there is very little of what we would call zoning in China. Furthermore, peasants have been encouraged to plow up pastureland and forests, and to terrace mountains to plant grain. Serious erosion problems exist where the land has been cleared.[25] Since 1979, the goals of reducing industrial pollution, better land use, and the protection of national relics and historical sites have forced the Chinese to choose among government policies and have met with mixed results. The Chinese have taken a positive approach toward cleaning up their environment. In addition to the aforementioned laws, the Chinese have moved to adopt a formal legal system better suited to enforcing environmental policies. As Bruce Ottley and Charles Valauskas have written, "[T]hese new policies, however, have been formulated at the same time that the Chinese have embarked on a program of 'four modernizations' with its emphasis on rapid economic growth."[26]

Critics, however, claim that China may be merely creating the illusion of environmental protection.[27] Because the bulk of international regulations are without strict compliance mechanisms, China is able to take the high road as leader of developing nations with respect to environmental protection, without having to significantly reduce pollution.

Without adequate support or enforcement, it should not be surprising that China's actual accomplishments are few and far between. Like other communist nations, China lacks the technology and financial ability to introduce sophisticated pollution control devices in its factories. Damage from burning coal is a particularly difficult problem. This energy, necessary for continued industrial expansion, produces extensive air pollution. The northern part of the country is blanketed with high levels of both sulfur dioxide and suspended particulate matter; the southern half is feeling the effects of acidification, damaging soils and buildings.[28]

Product and profit orientation, regardless of the system, drives nations in ways not conducive to sound long-term ecological management. Collectivist societies with public ownership of agriculture and industry in a centrally planned society have not fared better in their management and prevention of pollution.[29] As "state capitalists," socialist states and capitalist private managers have a similar concern for profits.[30]

The environmental problems of planned economies, such as those in the former Soviet Union and today in China, can be traced to the fact that they are state monopolies. A monopoly and the resulting concentration of economic and political power in a capitalist democracy can be opposed by the political power of the state. But "When the monopolist is the state itself, who will protect the citizen against the state?"[31] The environmental problem of a state monopoly has been exacerbated by the changes that have occurred over the years in communist countries. Industrial policy has concentrated on maximum production capacity with little concern for environmental consequences.

It is becoming increasingly obvious in advanced economies that perpetual growth is causing enormous environmental problems. Great rivers in industrialized countries worldwide, regardless of political system, have been rendered unfit for human consumption. In Russia, the Volga River is polluted by publicly owned factories; in the United States the Mississippi is just as polluted by waste and refuse from privately owned plants. It makes little difference to the environment if the polluter is a privately or publicly owned enterprise. Both systems have equally materialistic production and consumption values, pay little heed to environmental degradation, and ignore externalities. "In our own day, the experience of communist economic change teaches again that the principal issue is not whether the government owns the means of production, but who owns the government."[32]

INTERNATIONAL ENVIRONMENTAL MANAGEMENT

Lynton K. Caldwell, a recognized expert on international environmental management who has been studying environmental policy for over 30 years wrote,

> [P]lanetary environmental developments occurring beyond America's borders are now perceived, or anticipated, to be beyond national control. The concept of national sovereignty is of declining significance in a world that increasingly faces environmental problems affecting people everywhere. The fates of the first, second, and third worlds are interlinked through the biosphere.[33]

In 1972 representatives from 113 nations met in Stockholm for a Conference on the Human Environment. At the time only nine countries had internal administrative organizations set up to deal with environmental problems. Since then, numerous treaties, programs, organizations, and international regimes have been created to deal with environmental problems. The United Nations Environment Program, created at the Stockholm conference to provide environmental education and training, is one of the more visible organizations. Yet global environmental problems are worse now than they were in 1972. What happened?

Common Pool Resources

Common pool property problems are very much a part of global environmental management. Air is an example of a common pool resource. Individual manufacturers polluting the air have no incentive to limit their polluting activities assuming there are no restrictions. The cost of air pollution in this instance is not borne by the polluter but rather by everyone. Each individual polluter has no incentive to protect the common pool resource of clean air, and, in fact, the individual has every incentive to continue polluting.

As we have seen, two major international common pool resource problems that are associated with air pollution are depletion of the stratospheric ozone layer through the release of chlorofluorocarbons (CFCs) and the warming of the earth's atmosphere from the accumulation of greenhouse gasses.[34] These long-term problems with pressing *immediate* economic and health needs, in addition to the common pool nature of the problems and the lack of certainty as to long-term effects even in the face of certainty of *some* negative effects, make global warming and ozone depletion issues that will not go away any time soon. All of these uncertainties allow those that benefit from fossil fuel consumption and CFC production, or those who fear the negative political fallout from limiting that consumption, to argue against taking corrective actions.

Given the common pool nature of global pollution problems and the incentives, or lack thereof, operating on governments to restrict production of CFCs and greenhouse-producing gasses, it would seem that some type of international government organization (IGO) is necessary for dealing with these problems. By way of analogy, the farmers in Garret Hardin's common pasture are nations. Unless these nations are willing to give up low-lying coastal areas and live with disruptions in agricultural production as well as significantly increased skin cancer rates, the community of nations that makes up the global commons will have to restrict access to global common pool air resources. This means an IGO, either in existence or created for the purpose, will be necessary.[35] As we have seen, the common pool nature of international environmental problems makes cooperation—which may involve sacrifice—difficult. For example, the 1992 Rio Conference did result in carbon emission reporting agreements (154 countries, including the United States, signed a climate treaty requiring reporting), but the conference failed to agree on goals and timetables for restricting carbon emissions, largely because of the opposition of the United States.

A threshold issue for international environmental management must be, therefore, under what conditions and constraints can a successful IGO be created.

Creation of an IGO

An international government organization is an international or multinational organization established "with the objective of structuring communication and cooperation between member states on a continuing basis."[36] The Rhine River Commission, created in 1815 to regulate traffic on the Rhine, was the first modern IGO.[37] Although estimates vary, the number of IGOs is in excess of 600.[38]

An IGO is created when there is the perception of an existing or pending crisis by two or more governmental actors. This first step is relatively easy to make. Conferences have been held on the environment generally (Stockholm, 1972); on food (Rome, 1974); population (Bucharest, 1974, and Mexico City, 1984); desertification (Nairobi, 1977); and biological diversity (Rio de Janeiro, 1992) among others. Global conferences on the atmosphere were held in 1987 (the Montreal Protocol), 1989 (in London), and 1997 (in Kyoto). Once a group of nations decides to cooperate on a problem by forming an IGO, participants must decide on the appropriate procedures and decision-making rules the IGO will follow. Participants must also agree on the means of detecting compliance with any agreements and enforcement of agreements. Enforcement is a particularly difficult task if, as in the case of the production of greenhouse gasses, there is strong disagreement over the nature of, and responsibility for, the problem.

The problem with an IGO approach to managing international environmental problems is that the creation of an IGO, as well as the agreement on appropriate procedures and enforcement mechanisms, requires the mutual consent of all parties involved. However, as Marvin Soroos has pointed out, "[P]roblems are in the eyes of the beholder, for to refer to any actual or potential condition as being problematical presumes a certain interpretation."[39]

Decisions within IGOs are either by consensus or through some decision-making rule such as the will of the majority or plurality. Obviously, decisions reached by consensus are preferred, since problems of compliance are likely to be minimized—all the participants agree on the policy. Unfortunately, with ozone and greenhouse gasses in international environmental common pool management, consensus decision making is unlikely. As *Los Angeles Times* environmental writer Larry Stammer wrote, "Will China deny citizens the chance to own a refrigerator? Will Brazil go deeper in debt by cutting back logging on its lush rain forest? . . . In short, will the nations of the world—rich and poor alike—make huge sacrifices in an effort to spare the global environment from further destruction?"[40] The answer depends on the perception of a crisis situation that needs to be addressed and perceptions of national self-interest.

The sacrifices some countries will need to make will be great. This suggests there will be compliance problems. Noncompliance with agreed upon environmental controls is an example of a common pool free-rider problem. A nation that continues to produce CFCs or greenhouse gasses reaps the benefits of less atmospheric pollution globally at no cost to itself. The free-rider problem necessitates some means of enforcement.

The first problem of enforcement is to identify violators. This raises certain sovereignty questions and questions of whether or not access will be available to check on compliance. The International Atomic Energy Commission (IAEA) has a great deal of experience in this regard. Founded in 1957, the Vienna-based IAEA is an international organization comprised of more than 100 nations. The IAEA is credited with being the major international actor responsible for preventing the proliferation of nuclear weapons. Nevertheless, the activities of the IAEA are limited by national sovereignty questions. As Leonard Spector wrote, "[I]f a country does not openly display its nuclear capacities or break IAEA rules, it may approach and actually cross the nuclear weapons threshold with virtual impunity."[41]

Once identification problems have been solved, then the question becomes one of enforcement. An IGO and member nations may decide to use negative or positive sanctions. Negative sanctions would include economic sanctions such as boycotts or embargoes, which are rarely effective as the experience of Rhodesia and South Africa have shown, or military negative sanctions up to and including going to war. Positive sanctions could include cash transfers, debt relief, or the delivery of expertise or other positive inducements to persuade noncomplying nations to agree with policies that have been established by the IGO.

Equity considerations would seem to require that positive sanctions be used for enforcement of IGO air pollution regulations. By far, the greatest percentage of buildup of ozone in the stratosphere and of greenhouse gasses has been due to the activities of the more developed countries. An estimated 90 percent of the world's CFCs are produced and consumed in the industrialized countries.[42]

In a sense, the atmosphere has been used, much the way water is drawn from a nonrecharging well, to assist in the economic development of the more developed countries since the beginning of the Industrial Revolution. Because there is no effective means of "cleansing" the atmospheric environment so we might start with a fresh slate of a valuable stock of global resources, our protective air cover, which has been depleted by one group of nations, is no longer available for the use of the rest.

Is it equitable for the United States and Western Europe, which together produce 4 times as many CFCs as Asia and 20 times as many CFCs as Latin America, to call for a ban on production? The more developed world already has in place the refrigeration units, automobiles, and other consumer goods for which the world has paid with its protective ozone layer. Is it fair, for example, to tell China, which built 12 CFC plants during the 1980s to provide refrigerators for its population (fewer than 10 percent of whom owned refrigerators in 1989), that it must now close those plants?[43] India has similar concerns, and both China and India let it be known at the 1989 London CFC conference that it would be difficult for them to agree to limit

CFC production without financial and technological assistance.[44] As Joan Martin Brown, the United Nations Environment Program liaison to the United States put it, "The Third World says you're telling us not to do what you did to achieve your high standard of living. What are you going to do for us? Do you want to rent the trees from us? You know you can rent them for $1 billion a year in hard currency and we won't cut them down."[45]

Fortunately, the world may not need to rely on perceptions of equity. It is in the self-interest of the more developed countries to begin *now* with transfer payments and technological assistance to less developed countries to stem CFC production and the growth of greenhouse gasses. The cost to the more developed countries of mitigating damages due to global warming and increased solar irradiation will be much greater in the future and for decades to come than will the short-term cost of protecting the earth's atmosphere. The question is, will the leadership of the more developed countries see it as being in their best interest to begin transfers now rather than waiting for a crisis? Given the incentives operating on politicians to think in short-term cycles and the propensity of politicians as well as people generally to discount the future, the answer would appear to be no.

Each step in the process of environmental common pool management through an IGO requires the perception on the part of the actors involved that there is a crisis that needs to be addressed. Furthermore, the perception of crisis must be greater at each stage of the process. The overriding question for international pollution management becomes, then, whether the crisis situation necessary to facilitate IGO organization and action will be so bad that by the time action is taken much of the damage to the environment will have been done.

As Soroos pointed out, perceptions of problems differ. In less developed countries, illiteracy, poverty, as well as other internal factors, may limit domestic perceptions of, or pressure to respond to, any crisis. This further increases the level of damage (or perception of crisis) necessary for the leaders of those countries to act. For example, Brazil, Indonesia, and Congo, countries suffering from illiteracy as well as a host of other internal problems, are also suffering deforestation problems. The more developed world has an interest in protecting the forests in these countries. By the time the leaders of these and other less developed countries move deforestation to the top of their political agendas, significant global environmental damage may have already been done.

International environmental problems require a multinational effort. Perhaps the human race, due to a variety of factions, will be more inclined to undertake that effort in the future. As Maurice Strong put it, "[P]eople have learned to enlarge the circles of their allegiance and their loyalty, as well as the institutions through which they are governed, from the family to the tribe to the village to the town to the city to the nation state. We are now called upon to make the next and final step, at least on this planet, to the global level."[46]

By the time appropriate perceptions of crisis are reached to facilitate the necessary intergovernmental cooperation and action, much damage will have been done and the cost of mitigating that damage will be much higher than would have otherwise been the case.

Although it would be less costly for developed nations to recognize the hazard now—and not wait for a crisis situation—and to begin transfers of technology and other resources to assist in the transfer to a CFC- and fossil-fuel-free global commons, the incentives operating on international policy makers make this un-likely—another paradox of environmental policy.

ECONOMIC GLOBALIZATION AND THE SECOND INDUSTRIAL REVOLUTION

Maintaining biodiversity among the earth's species is a central reason we need more international cooperation in the realm of environmental protection. Further-more, the cause of species loss, like many global environmental problems, can not be traced to any single nation-state. The world we live in today entails a progressive march toward the development of a global economy. What happens in Tokyo today impacts markets in London tomorrow. Multinational corporations have expanded their operations to include every corner of the globe, with few restrictions on how they go about defining new, undiscovered markets. It is very similar to what oc-cured at the beginning of the twentieth century as the Industrial Revolution was tak-ing place. Industrialists such as J.P. Morgan and John D. Rockefeller were able to make billions of dollars during this time largely due to the lack of regulation on how they did business. These "robber barons," as they are often referred to were fo-cused on obtaining maximum return with minimum resources and little or no regard to the equity or fairness of the market. Practices such as price fixing and monopo-lization (that is, the domination of a market by only one corporate entity) were com-mon; that is, until the government stepped in and began to regulate industry to provide correction in areas where the market produced unsavory results.[47] Govern-ment regulation led to greater equity in the market, and greater economic opportu-nity in society.

What we are facing at the dawn of the twenty-first century is remarkably sim-ilar to the rise of the Industrial Revolution at the dawn of the twentieth century. New technologies are allowing for the global expansion of the economic system, but with little direction or regulation to inhibit new "robber barons" from pursuing a similar course of exploitation and wealth and power concentration. This time, how-ever, we are not talking only about the exploitation of human resources. Certainly the Industrial Revolution had no concern for natural resource depletion; there ap-peared to be plenty of iron ore, forest timbers and coal to keep industry going. In what could be called the Second Industrial Revolution, this is no longer the case. As technology and population have increased, our demands for natural resources on a per capita basis have increased significantly. In addition we have become much more efficient developers of natural resources. We drill deeper for petroleum, airlift timber from remote forests, and mine the most geographically and geologically challenging areas on the planet. We do this because our society has built a depen-dency on natural, largely nonrenewable resources.

Great advances in transportation and communications technology have led to the creation of multinational corporations. Often these corporations have no real corporate "home" other than a nominal headquarters. These operations shift to where they find inexpensive labor, or production inputs (including natural re-sources) or sympathetic (or easy to influence) governments (with lax environmental laws). The allegiance of such a corporate entity is to a difficult-to-identify (and impossible-to-hold responsible) stockholder. Environmental concerns (as well, often, social, cultural or any other noneconomic human concern) become secondary to expanding market share and increasing profits.

The dangers posed by these types of corporations are many, especially from an environmental standpoint. As we have discussed in this chapter, environmental protection agreements among sovereign nations are often weak and without adequate enforcement measures. In a globalized economy, multinational corporations are able to mine resources in countries, such as Brazil, that do not have adequate environmental protection themselves, ship these resources to countries, such as China, with low cost labor (often including child labor) for production, and then ship the finished product to richer countries, such as the United States, for sale. Usually such multinational business practices are poorly regulated.

The situation we have just described will have a great impact on the continued stability of our environment. We are rapidly approaching a point at which our natural resources will become so scarce that the economic price of harvesting them will exceed the benefits. There is no strong international government that will impose regulations on multinational business practices in the name of environmental protection. In this second Industrial Revolution it is up to the different nations to promulgate regulations amongst themselves to solve the problems of economic disparity and environmental degradation. Nearly 200 agreements have been thus far negotiated, though the successes of these are few and far between in the face of accelerating environmental destruction. But a dialogue on international environmental protection is progressing; it is showing up on the agendas of a greater number of nations, rich and poor alike.

The next section will discuss a few of the more prominent attempts to protect the environment at a number of levels, including protection of the oceans, the protection of the atmosphere, the safe disposal of hazardous wastes, and the protection of endangered and threatened species. These actions comprise the core of international efforts toward tackling the problem of environmental protection across national boundaries. We will conclude with a brief discussion of the successes and failures of these policies as a whole, and suggestions of where we might refine our pursuit of adequate international provisions for environmental protection.

INTERNATIONAL REGULATORY EFFORTS

Controlling Oceanic Pollution

Concern for the earth's oceans and seas may be seen as early as the mid-1920s. The United States was the first country to take a stand toward controlling the indiscriminate dumping of wastes in oceanic waters in 1926, arguing for a total ban on the discharge of oil. An international conference that took place that year opted instead for less-comprehensive, zone-based restrictions. Such zone-based approaches were repeated throughout the mid-twentieth century in a multitude of international agreements governing the pollution of the oceans. However, the deficiencies in such fragmented policies led to the Convention on the Prevention of Marine Pollution by Dumping of Wastes and Other Matters (known as the London Dumping Convention of 1972). In contrast to earlier agreements on oceanic dumping, the London Convention was comprehensive, limiting not only regular discharges of wastes, but also outlawing the dumping of radioactive wastes in the earth's oceans. Recent studies have shown that since the convention's passage, radioactivity levels have decreased substantially.[48]

In November 1994, the United Nations put into place the most comprehensive set of international regulations governing the protection of the seas we have ever known: the United Nations Convention on the Law of the Sea (UNCLOS). Described by Lakshman Guruswamy, "UNCLOS deals with conservation and the management of living resources, pollution prevention, reduction and control, vessel pollution, and environmental management."[49] Of the many significant elements found in UNCLOS, perhaps the most telling of the commitment to controlling oceanic pollution is that it's regulations are binding on all countries, whether they be signatories or not. It is not surprising, then, to consider former U.S. Secretary of State, Warren Christopher's words as he pointed out in a letter of submittal to the President that UNCLOS "[i]s the strongest comprehensive environmental treaty now in existence or likely to emerge for quite some time," and can be considered the foundation of a "Constitution for the Oceans."[50]

With it's strong emphasis on compliance, regardless of full consensus among nations, UNCLOS is designed to overcome the problems that have been associated with the enforcement of international agreements. Because it originated from the United Nations, its authority may be considered to be more clearly established among member nations. Regardless, the provisions included within the convention (there are 320, with 59 dedicated specifically to environmental protection) are intended to place a firm hand of control upon the use of our seas and oceans as waste sinks.

Atmospheric Conventions

There are essentially two issues concerning international action in the arena of atmospheric protection. The first is concerned with the depletion of the ozone layer, resulting from the emission of chemicals that actively breakdown ozone particles (for example, CFCs and halons). The second issue approaches the problem of greenhouse gas emissions that contribute to the problem of global warming. Although both issues address environmental problems associated with potentially harmful chemical emissions, each has been received differently by the international community with widely varying degrees of success. We will look at the primary international attempts toward resolving these two issues.

The problem of ozone-depleting chemicals was addressed in 1987 by the Montreal Protocol. This protocol, whose signatories now include 163 countries, sought to control consumption of certain ozone-depleting chemicals, including CFCs, halon gas (used in fire extinguisher systems), and some types of organic solvents, with the eventual goal of reducing the overall production and usage of chemicals harmful to the ozone layer. As you read in Chapter 5, the ozone layer protects the earth's surface from harmful ultraviolet radiation. It is estimated that for every one percent decrease in the ozone layer, an additional two percent increase in ultraviolet radiation is realized. This increased exposure to radiation roughly equates to a 4 to 6 percent increase in skin cancer rates.[51]

Approaches preceding the adoption of the Montreal Protocol included the 1995 Vienna Convention, which established the foundation for cooperative research efforts. Also, it was realized that precautionary measures should be taken to limit the potential risk that the depletion of the ozone layer might cause. What distinguishes the strides made at the Vienna Convention is that scientific uncertainty still loomed over the linking of manmade chemicals and the depletion of the ozone layer. This connection was not truly accepted until 1988, three years after this first step was taken in Vienna.[52]

The articles within the Montreal Protocol, initially, were somewhat weak in their recommended reductions of certain ozone-depleting chemicals. As we entered the 1990s, however, more chemicals were included in the protocol, while phase-out time lines became shorter. Also, because industrialized countries were in a position that would allow an easier shift toward safer alternatives, a fund was set up to support developing countries with financial aid and technological development in an effort to wean them off of ozone-depleting agents as quickly as possible. Since 1987, the United States has contributed over a billion dollars to this fund.[53]

As a result of the Montreal Protocol, there has been a slight decline in the emissions of ozone-depleting agents. 1993 figures show an average decrease of 45 percent among participating countries.[54] Because of the resilience of certain agents, depletion is expected to continue until the mid-twenty-first century at which time the ozone layer will begin to recover its mass.

Efforts to control the release of greenhouse gasses, however, have not fared as well as those directed toward protecting the ozone layer. Unlike the Montreal Protocol, the United Nations Framework Convention on Climate Control (UNFCCC), which sprang from the Rio de Janeiro Conference held in late 1992, did not attack the problem of global warming as comprehensively as the Montreal Protocol attacked ozone-depleting agents. The intial articles focused generally on the need to address issues of precaution, equity, cooperation and sustainability of development, but did not specify particular measures to tangibly address these issues. The primary objective of the Framework is "the stabilization of atmospheric gas concentrations at levels that will prevent human activities from interfering with global climate systems. . . ." However, this objective was not accompanied by target emissions or strict deadlines. The reason for this lack of direction may be directly related to opposition from industrialized countries who saw strict limitations to greenhouse gas emissions as threatening to their economic interests.

Subsequent meetings of signatories have attempted to define a more particular course of action. In 1996, the UNFCCC endorsed a 1995 report from the Intergovernmental Panel on Climate Change (IPCC) that linked greenhouse gas emissions to global climate change, and called for binding goals and significant reductions in greenhouse gas emissions. Specific measures were to be decided upon during the 1997 meeting of UNFCCC in Kyoto, Japan.

The most significant aspect of the talks in Kyoto was an agreement to reduce carbon dioxide emissions to 5 percent below 1990 levels by the year 2010. This agreement has been criticized by many observers as akin to a crash course in limiting climate change.[55] Citing the excessive costs involved in such a short-term effort, as well as the perceived need for a long-term plan of action, the Kyoto Protocol is seen as a nearly impossible goal. Compounding the problem is the absence of adequate enforcements and incentives to encourage compliance. Supporters of the Kyoto plan point to the use of tradable emissions credits (recall our discussion of emissions trading schemes in Chapter 5) as evidence that the goals established are not beyond reach. As a result of many obsolete industries closing their doors, the emissions allowed by Russian Federation and Eastern European countries are expected to fall well below their quota. This will provide available credits to more industrialized countries who, for the most part, will not be able to fall within their quota. In response, critics argue that these credits will be allocated to nations, not businesses. There are many questions concerning the distribution of credits, and how trading will occur.

Many of these questions were expected to be decided at the Conference of Parties of the UNFCCC that was held in Buenos Aires in November of 1998. It was expected that this meeting would hammer out the specificities of the articles within the Kyoto Protocol. Issues that were considered included the need for a long-term plan of action, the need for an effective secretairait to oversee enforcement of goals and timelines, and how uncertainty in science is to be handled.

Hazardous Waste Control at the International Level

Each year, 300 to 500 million tons of hazardous wastes are generated internationally; roughly 10 percent of this is shipped across international boundaries. Approximately 5.2 million tons of hazardous wastes were exported by industrialized states to Eastern Europe and developing countries in the period 1986–1990.[56] There exists only one comprehensive, international convention that seeks to control the transport and subsequent disposal of hazardous wastes across borders. The Basel Convention on the Control of Transboundary Movements of Hazardous Wastes and Their Disposal, promulgated in 1989, recognizes the potential environmental degradation possible when nations attempt to find alternate disposal sites in other nations. Usually the transfer involves a wealthier country buying waste storage space in poorer countries. The overarching intent of the Basel Convention is to promote the local deposition of wastes, preferably as close to the source site itself. In order to accomplish this, the convention imposes restrictions on the import and export of hazardous wastes, requiring that sound environmental management be practiced in cases where transfers do take place.

Protection of Endangered and Threatened Species

There are currently two, strong international movements toward the protection of species. One is designed as a catchall for endangered and threatened species (flora and fauna), while the other is mainly concerned with the practice of whaling on the high seas. The elements of each are described below.

The Convention on International Trade in Endangered Species of Wild Fauna and Flora (CITES) is an international treaty that seeks to protect endangered and threatened species at risk for exploitation due to global commerce. CITES is a broadly defined program designed to apply to both marine and terrestrial flora and fauna. Species are listed in one of three appendices of the treaty, which corresponds to the level of exploitation the species is subject to (one being the most threatened).

Adopted in 1972, CITES is considered to have many problems, particulary in the areas of finance and enforcement.[57] CITES is using political pressure and scientific guidance to encourage countries to manage their wildlife use and trade. Controlling the black marketing of protected specied has proved to be a very difficult task, though provisions, such as an external control system, have been implemented.

Of the many problems with CITES, circumvention by members and non-members is considered the most prevelant.[58] A survey conducted in 1994 showed that less the 20 percent of the parties involved in CITES had promulgated laws to enforce the elements of the treaty.[59] Also, it has been reported that only 45 percent of species transactions are reported to CITES.[60]

Related to CITES emphasis on protecting a number of threatened or endangered species, there exist numerous other efforts aimed at protecting specific species. One of the most prominent is the International Whaling Commission (IWC). The IWC, which was created through passage of the 1946 International Convention for the Regulation of Whaling, governs international whaling activities. Intended as a management tool for managing the severly depleted whale population, the Commission placed a moratorium on commercial whaling in 1986, allowing for limited subsistence whaling by a small number of nations (mostly by native populations whose aboriginal culture depended on the whale). However, the moratorium has not ended all commercial whaling, despite the creation of a whale sanctuary in the waters of the Southern Ocean and Antarctica.[61]

As with many international agreements, their are no sanctions that may be enforced for noncompliance. Countries such as Norway and Japan have continued taking whales under the guise of "scientific research," a loophole within the IWC. In many cases, enforcement is attempted through the use of publicity and the harnessing of public sentiment toward preservation of whale stocks. In the United States, particular pressure has come from Washington state's Makah Indian Tribe for an exemption allowing the annual kill of four California gray whales in accordance with the IWC's aboriginal subsistence clause. This exemption request was strongly opposed by various IWC delegations, environmental groups, members of the U.S. Congress and some Makah tribal elders.[62] (No living members of the Makah tribe has participated in whale hunts.)

TRENDS IN THE INTERNATIONAL REGULATORY PROCESS

As you can see from the regulatory examples presented above, the results of international accords and conventions are perhaps best described as restrained optimism. Agreements such as the Montreal Protocol show that real progress is being made toward reducing emissions of harmful agents into our atmosphere. On the other hand, international efforts toward controlling greenhouse gases, protecting endangered species, and preventing widespread hazardous waste nightmares have been much less successful. Why is this so?

One of the reasons for this mixed bag of results can be attributed to the positive circumstances surrounding the Montreal Protocol with respect to the economic and health interests of the United States and other developed nations. Although uncertainty still existed concerning the linkage between CFCs and ozone depletion, there was firm evidence that a decrease in ozone protection increases the amount of ultraviolet radiation that is allowed to penetrate the Earth's atmosphere. This type of radiation, in turn, was known to be a highly contributing factor in the development of skin cancers. Under the concept of the precautionary principle the prudent course of action was to pursue a reduction in ozone-depleting agents.

The estimated health factors involved in decrease in the ozone layer, however, were not enough to drive the process. From an economic standpoint, the phase out of ozone-depleting materials was not seen as a monumental economic hardship. Alternatives to many ozone-depleting materials have existed for decades, although their effectiveness, on average, was a good deal lower than that of CFCs. Regardless, the point is that a broad phase-out of ozone-depleting chemicals was not seen as an excessive economic hardship to developed countries.

As we have seen, other international environmental problems have recognized the existence of neither immediate health impliactions, nor easy economic opportunities that may be considered necessary for comprehensive international cooperation. Without incentives such as these, the prospects for effective international agreements are grim. We must remain optimistic, however; there is much to be gained from opening a dialogue between nations to address environmental issues that have global impacts.

SUMMARY

One might think that different political systems would produce different environmental outcomes. As we have seen, that is not the case. Differences in government forms do not matter much in pollution control outcomes.[63] Some problems are universal. For example, studies have shown that regardless of the political system, a municipality, or other local authority that is powerful, is likely to hinder rather than help in the implementation of a pollution control program.[64] Even when a plan exists to solve environmental problems, and even when it is well executed, it will frequently not have the desired outcome—regardless of the political system in place.[65]

Furthermore, we have seen that some international environmental problems will require global cooperation and international organizations and the obstacles to creating such organizations are great. It may be that international actions are only taken after serious damage has been done to the environment. On the brighter side, in the 1980s and 1990s there have been a number of international environmental meetings and agreements, and "green parties" have sprung up everywhere. As we have seen these have had mixed success. It seems that under certain conditions, particularly where the economic livelihood of member states is at stake, these institutional agreements succeed. In other cases, notable where the agreement is seen as an economic threat to one or more parties, the agreements have been less successful. Ironically all healthy economic activity is predicated on a healthy functioning ecosystem. Perhaps its just a question of where and when political leaders make the connection. In the concluding chapter we speculate on the future ability of democratic societies to deal with the environmental policy paradox.

NOTES

1. Norman J. Vig and Michael E. Kraft (eds.), *Environmental Policy in the 1990s* (Washington, DC: Congressional Quarterly Press, 1990), p. 4.
2. Petra Kelly, quoted in Jonathon Porritt, *Seeing Green: The Politics of Ecology Explained* (New York: Blackwell, 1985), p. x.
3. Raymond Dominick, "The Roots of the Green Movement in the United States and West Germany," *Environmental Review*, 12 (3) (Fall 1988), p. 4.
4. See Jonathon Porritt, *Seeing Green: The Politics of Ecology Explained* (New York: Blackwell, 1985), Ch. 10.

5. Michael G. Renner, "Europe's Green Tide," *World Watch*, 3 (1) (January/February 1990), p. 25. The ability of a green party to win seats in any national government is a function of the electoral system used in the country. Most European governments have some form of proportional representation wherein parties are given seats in the national legislature that approximate their popularity with the voters. For example, the West German green party, *Die Grunen*, won about 5.6 percent of the national vote in 1983. In the districts where *Die Grunen* ran the strongest, the party only polled approximately 10 percent of the vote. Yet they were rewarded with 27 of the 518 seats in the lower house of the national legislature. In the United States, representatives are elected to Congress and state legislatures on a single-member plurality basis—the person with the most votes represents the district. For an American green party to win a legislative seat, their candidate would have to get 50 percent of the vote in a given district, a difficult task given the propensity of voters in the United States to stick with one of the two established parties. Many European green parties have the advantage that their governments will pay the campaign expenses of minor parties even if they are not successful. In 1980 the West German greens polled only 1.5 percent of the national vote, far below the 5 percent minimum necessary to win seats in the national legislature but enough to receive one million German marks from the federal government. (See Dominick, "The Roots of the Green Movement," p. 21.) Successful minor political parties often find the more established parties adopt the issues that led to the creation of the minor party in the first place. When this happens, the minor party may disappear. We then say that the issue has been coopted by the major party. In the United States, both major political parties have adopted environmentalism—to varying degrees—as part of their national platforms. In other nations, green parties have been coopted or have joined in coalitions with the more dominant parties. Although green parties have played an important role in bringing environmental issues to the attention of the public in many countries, they are not likely to play a major role in governing any of the countries where they have emerged.
6. Joan de Bardelaben, *The Environment and Marxist–Leninism: The Soviet and East German Experience* (Boulder, CO: Westview Press, 1985).
7. Ernst R. Klatt, "The Evolution, Operation and Future of Environmental Management in the European Union," in *Environmental Law and Policy in the European Union and the United States*, ed. Randall Baker (London: Praeger, 1997), pp. 77–96.
8. Arnold J. Heidenheimer, Hugh Heclo, and Carolyn Teich Adams, *Comparative Public Policy* (New York: St. Martin's Press, 1990), pp. 323–325.
9. See, for example, William Ophuls, *Ecology and the Politics of Scarcity* (San Francisco: Freeman, 1977), Ch. 4; and Garrett Hardin, "The Tragedy of the Commons," *Science* 162 (1968), pp. 1243–1248; Robert L. Heilbroner, *An Inquiry into the Human Prospect* (New York: Norton, 1974); and Ted Robert Gurr, "On the Political Consequences of Scarcity and Economic Decline," *International Studies Quarterly*, 29 (1985), pp. 51–75.
10. William Ebenstein and Edwin Fogelman, *Today's Isms: Communism, Fascism, Capitalism, Socialism* (8th ed.) (Upper Saddle River, NJ: Prentice Hall, 1980), p. 152.
11. Denis Healey, *The New Leader* (August 17, 1957), quoted in Ebenstein and Fogelman, *Today's Isms*, p. 239.
12. William Echikson, "Dissident Groups Defy Government to Aid Environment," *Los Angeles Times*, January 17, 1988, p. 2.
13. Hilary F. French, "The Greening of the Soviet Union," *World Watch* (May/June 1989), p. 22.
14. Bruce L. Ottley and Charles C. Valauskas, "China's Developing Environmental Law: Policies, Practices and Legislation," *Boston College International and Comparative Law Review*, 4 (1) (1983), p. 91.
15. All these examples were taken from Mark M. Nelson, "As Shroud of Secrecy Lifts in East Europe, Smog Shroud Emerges," *Wall Street Journal*, CXXII, (42) (March 1, 1990), p. A1.
16. Larry Tye, "Pollution a Nightmare Behind the Iron Curtain," *Arizona Republic*, February 25, 1990, p. C1.
17. Egbert Tellegen, "Environmental conflicts in transforming economies: Central and Eastern Europe," in *Environmental Policy in an International Context*, ed. Peter B. Sloep and Andrew Blowers (London: Arnold, 1996), pp. 69–70.
18. The World Resources Institute, The United Nations Environment Programme and The United Nations Development Programme, *World Resources: 1992–93* (New York: Oxford University Press, 1992), p. 57.
19. Ibid., p. 60.
20. Ibid.
21. Ottley and Valauskas, "China's Developing Environmental Law: Policies, Practices and Legislation," p. 84.

22. Ibid., p. 108.
23. Ibid., pp. 108–109.
24. Ibid., p. 121.
25. Ibid., pp. 125–127.
26. Ibid., p. 130.
27. Elizabeth Economy, "Chinese policy-making and global climate change: two-front diplomacy and the international community," in *The Internationalization of Environmental Protection*, ed. Miranda A. Schreurs and Elizabeth Economy (Cambridge: Cambridge University Press, 1997), pp. 19–41.
28. Don Hinrichsen, "Like First World, Like Third World," *The Amicus Journal*, (Winter 1988), p. 7.
29. William A. Echikson, "Pollution Seeps to the Forefront of Eastern Bloc's Consciousness," *Los Angeles Times*, Jan. 17, 1988, p. 2.
30. Stanley J. Kabala, "Poland: Facing the Hidden Costs of Development," *Environment* 27 (November 1985), p. 39.
31. Ebenstein and Fogelman, *Today's Isms*, p. 235.
32. Ibid., p. 42.
33. Lynton K. Caldwell, "International Environmental Politics: America's Response to Global Imperatives," in Norman J. Vig and Michael E. Kraft (eds.), *Environmental Policy in the 1990s* (Washington, DC: Congressional Quarterly Press, 1990), p. 301.
34. Other gasses are involved, but the discussion here is limited to CFCs, being by far the largest contributor. See Thomas H. Maugh, II, "Ozone Depletion Far Worse Than Expected," *Los Angeles Times*, March 16, 1988, Pt. 1, p. 1; and "Ozone Depletion Worsens, NRDC Leads Drive for Total CFC Phase Out," *Newsline* (Natural Resources Defense Council), 6 (2) (May/June 1988), p. 1; Christopher Flavin, "The Heat Is On," *World Watch*, 1 (6) (November/December 1988), p. 19.
35. The creation of an IGO is not necessary for dealing with all international environmental problems. For example, international agreements for international coordination of responses to nuclear accidents might be arranged on a contractual basis without the creation of an IGO. However, in international common pool situations where there are clear winners and losers, where no individual nation has an incentive to restrict its activities, and hence where some enforcement mechanism may be necessary to ensure compliance with rules designed to protect the commons, an IGO likely is necessary, most analysts have concluded. See Oran R. Young, *International Cooperation: Building Regimes for Natural Resources and the Environment* (Ithaca, NY: Cornell University Press, 1989).
36. Marvin S. Soroos, *Beyond the Sovereignty: The Challenge of Global Policy* (Columbia: University of South Carolina Press, 1986), pp. 81–82.
37. Ibid., p. 83.
38. Harold K. Jacobson, *Networks of Interdependence: International Organizations and the Global Political System*, (2nd ed.) (New York: Knopf, 1984), p. 9.
39. Soroos, *Beyond the Sovereignty: The Challenge of Global Policy*, p. 34.
40. Larry B. Stammer, "Saving the Earth: Who Sacrifices?" *Los Angeles Times*, March 13, 1989, Pt. 1, p. 1.
41. Leonard S. Spector, "Silent Spread," *Foreign Policy*, 58 (Spring 1985), p. 56.
42. Stammer, "Saving the Earth: Who Sacrifices?" p. 16.
43. Larry B. Stammer, "Global Talks on Ozone Described as Successful," *Los Angeles Times*, March 8, 1989, Pt. 1, p. 6.; CFC production in the United States in 1986 was estimated at 1,070 million pounds; for Western Europe 1,100; for Asia and the Pacific, 550; the Eastern bloc 250; and in Latin America, 100.
44. Stammer, "Saving the Earth: Who Sacrifices?" 1989, p. 16.
45. Ibid.
46. Maurice F. Strong, presented to the International Development Conference, Washington, DC, March 19, 1987. Reprinted in Lester R. Brown, Christopher Flavin, and Sandra Postel, "A World at Risk," in Lester R. Brown et al.(eds.), *State of the World: 1989* (New York: Norton, 1989), p. 20.
47. These include huge economic and social disparities between the rich and the poor and repressive child labor practices as well as noncompetitive business practices which the business class itself finds objectional.
48. Rob Edwards, "Leaky Drums Spill Plutonium on Ocean Floor," *New Scientist* (July 22, 1995), p. 5.
49. Lakshman Guruswamy, "The promise of the United Nations Convention on the Law of the Sea (UNCLOS): Justice in trade and environment disputes," *Ecology Law Quarterly* (May 1998), p. 189.

50. Ibid.
51. Lorraine Elliot, *The Politics of the Environment* (New York: New York University Press, 1998), p. 54.
52. Ibid.
53. Ibid.
54. Ibid, p. 60.
55. See, for example, "Implementing the Kyoto Protocol," *Issues in Science and Technology*, (Spring 1998), p. 66
56. Kummer, "United Nations Environment Programme, 1994," Organization for Economic Cooperation and Development, 1997.
57. Ginnette Hemley, "CITES: How useful a tool for wildlife conservation?" *Wildlife Society Bulletin*, (Winter 1995), p. 635.
58. Elliot, *The Global Politics of the Earth*, p. 32.
59. Anon., "CITES: 9th Conference of the Parties," *Environmental Policy and Law* (August–September 1995), p. 89.
60. Valerie Karno, "Protection of endangered gorillas and chimpanzees in international trade: Can CITES help?" *Hastings International and Comparative Law Review*, 14(4), p. 1001.
61. Elliot, *Global Politics of the Earth*, p. 35.
62. Nathan LaBudde, "IWC debates whaling proposals," *Earth Island Journal* (Winter 1997), p. 8.
63. Paul B. Downing and Kenneth Hanf (eds.), "Cross-National Comparisons in Environmental Protection: A Symposium," *Policy Studies Journal* (September 1982), p. 38; see also Paul B. Downing, "Cross-National Comparisons in Environmental Protection: Introduction to the Issues," *Policy Studies Journal* (September 1982), p. 184.
64. See Bruno Dente and Rudy Lewanski, "Administrative Networks and Implementation Effectiveness: Industrial Air Pollution Control Policy in Italy," *Policy Studies Journal*, 11 (1982), p. 129; Robert F. Durant, *When Government Regulates Itself: EPA, TVA, and Pollution Control in the 1970s* (Knoxville: University of Tennessee Press, 1985); and David Vogel, *National Styles of Regulation: Environmental Policy in Great Britain and the United States* (Ithaca, NY: Cornell University Press, 1986).
65. See, for example, Downing, "Cross-National Comparisons in Environmental Protection: Introduction to the Issues," p. 186.

Conclusion

We have examined environmental policy in America within the context of a paradox: Policy makers often seem to know what to do but for a variety of reasons, it doesn't get done. In air pollution, for example, its causes and the long-term environmental consequences of burning fossil fuels are relatively clear. However, political and economic realities seem to guarantee we will continue our dependence on fossil fuels for the foreseeable future. Also, in solid waste management, we have known for many decades the consequences of a policy of ever-expanding landfill operations. Yet it has not been until the 1990s that most municipalities have seriously considered alternatives to landfill disposal of solid waste.

Although the environmental policy paradox concept is useful for understanding problems in environmental policy, it does not apply to all situations equally well. In some areas of environmental policy, the problem is an *uncertainty* of knowledge often coupled with a lack of agreement over values, trade-offs, and the appropriate course of action. Or the scientific community may not be in agreement on the nature of the problem or the appropriate solution.

The paradox of environmental policy is very useful, however, for understanding some aspects of the policy-making process, such as informal incentive systems that operate on policy makers. Such systems, discussed in Part One, promise that long-term solutions to environmental problems with high immediate costs are unlikely to be pursued. In some cases, this is unfortunate. Deferring action on serious environmental problems is very much like accumulating debt. Eventually the debt must be paid off. When it becomes clear the environmental deficit needs to be retired—renewable energy must be developed, the burning of fossil fuels must be cut back, the flow of solid waste must be drastically reduced—the cost of retiring that deficit will be very high.

Students of the environmental policy process often question the ability of democratic political systems to cope with environmental problems. Given what you have learned in this book, do you think an ecological government is possible? If such a government is possible, how can it develop or rule, given the political and institutional obstacles that create the paradox in environmental policy?

Some of the best-known observers of the environmental policy-making process and of environmental problems have concluded that existing governmental arrangements will fail. It has been argued by some of the most respected environmental policy analysts that democratic systems need to be replaced by oligarchic governments staffed by environmental experts with the power to enforce sound environmental policy.[1] It is also not unusual for commentators to blame the private enterprise system for our environmental problems. But as we saw in the last chapter, state-controlled economies are no more likely to protect the environment than are market-based/capitalist economies.

Some have concluded there is a fundamental conflict between democratic systems and the sacrifice, decisiveness, and speed with which environmental policy needs to be developed and implemented if it is to be effective. For example, William Ophuls has argued that some type of oligarchy run by technological elites may be necessary. In contrast, others, such as Dean Mann, have argued that "[T]he environmental program in the United States remains of sufficient vitality that it will continue to mitigate, in halting but meaningful ways, the current and foreseeable threats to ecological systems and the quality of the environment."[2]

I think the truth lies somewhere between these two positions. Basically, the policy-making process in our American democracy will work reasonably well in some cases, but it will not work well at all in others. The system does respond to crisis situations and those controversies that attract a great deal of public attention. The amount of media attention and the nature of the problem itself will determine whether or not the system responds well and in a timely manner to an environmental problem. The attention, in this decade, that is being focused on solid waste and recycling provides an example. Even though many communities have run out of landfill space, there are practical, if not particularly desirable, solutions to our long-term solid waste problems. Other environmental problems, such as global warming and the depletion of the ozone layer, may not lend themselves to satisfactory solutions given the constraints in the policy-making process. Simply put, by the time we reach a crisis situation in the global environment and action is taken both in the United States and internationally, the damage will be severe—and irreversible.

Surrendering democratic power to a central governmental authority with the power to deal with environmental problems in a timely and comprehensive manner has certain attractions, and promises quick solutions to our environmental problems. However, the cost for many, myself included, is too great.

Oligarchic governments established to deal with environmental problems would bring other problems. Who will rule the rulers? Nevertheless, an argument can be made that oligarchic political systems are both necessary and inevitable. The environmental crisis, unless mitigated, could lead to the establishment of a fascist or some other oligarchic system in the United States. The editors of *State of the World* wrote, "[A]s the world enters the twenty-first century, the community of nations either will have rallied and turned back the threatening trends, or environmental deterioration and social disintegration will be feeding on each other."[3]

Extremism that polarizes blocks of people within a society can force the people into choosing between anarchy and repression. Such a polarizing force as terrorism, racism, or a rapidly deteriorating environment that disrupts a society and accepted standards of living could force the choice. And as former U.S. Senator Margaret Chase Smith cautioned, "[M]ake no mistake about it, if that narrow choice has to be made, the American people, even with reluctance and misgiving, will choose repression."[4]

The first decades of the new millennium will be crucial in our battle for the environment. Many of the environmental problems discussed in this book will reach a critical stage during these years. Unfortunately, in some cases, environmental problems that are now manageable, such as global warming, ozone depletion, or overdependence on fossil fuels, will be much worse—given current trends—if action is not taken soon.

What the world will look like in the future is an open question. Throughout this book I have tried to address ways that we, as individuals, can have an impact on the quality of our environment. Over the long term, a shift must be made in our dominant social paradigm. Lester Milbrath's work suggests a paradigm shift may be in process. It remains to be seen if the environmentalists, the "vanguard for a new society" as Milbrath calls them, will become a majority or remain a minority. But, as Milbrath concludes, "In modern society, we have developed a socio-technical-economic system that can dominate and destory nature. Alongside it, we have retained a normative and ethical system based on 2000-year-old religions. The lack of congruence between these two systems threatens the continued existence of our civilization."[5]

On an individual level, you can work to live a less energy-intensive life. Switching to fluorescent light bulbs, walking or cycling instead of driving, insulating your home, shunning disposable products, recycling, conserving water, and eating less meat are all things you can do that will help the environment. There are several books available that provide extensive suggestions on how you can live a less environmentally destructive life.[6]

More than anything else, it takes getting involved. Politically involved—in city council meetings, following events in the Congress and your state legislatures, attending agency hearings, and writing letters to the editor of your local newspaper. The informal incentives that operate in the policy-making process, particularly the importance of special interest money, political action committees, and the natural tendency of politicians to avoid tough decisions, can be derailed if enough people become interested and involved in the policy-making process. It is up to each of us. It is our future.

NOTES

1. See, for example, William Ophuls, *Ecology and the Politics of Scarcity* (San Francisco, CA: Freeman, 1977), Ch. 4; and Garrett Hardin, "The Tragedy of the Commons," *Science*, 162 (1968), pp. 1243–1248.
2. Dean E. Mann, "Democratic Politics and Environmental Policy," in Sheldon Kamieniecki, Robert O'Brien, and Michael Clarke (eds.), *Controversies in Environmental Policy* (Albany: State University of New York Press, 1986), p. 32.
3. Lester R. Brown, Christopher Flavin, and Sandra Postel, "Outlining a Global Action Plan," in Lester R. Brown et al. (eds.), *State of the World: 1989* (New York: Norton, 1989), p. 194.

4. Quoted in William Ebenstein and Edwin Fogelman, *Today's Isms: Communism Fascism, Capitalism, Socialism* (8th ed.) (Upper Saddle River, NJ: Prentice Hall, 1980), p. 131.

5. Lester W. Milbrath, *Environmentalists: Vanguard for a New Society* (Albany: State University of New York Press, 1984), p. 101.

6. See, for example, Ruth Caplan, *Our Earth, Ourselves* (New York: Bantam Books, 1990); John Elkington, Julia Hailes, and Joel Makower, *The Green Consumer* (New York: Penguin Books, 1990); Diane MacEachern, *Save Our Planet: 750 Everyday Ways You Can Help Clean Up the Earth* (New York: Dell, 1990); and Earth Works Group, *50 Simple Things You Can Do to Save the Earth* (Berkeley, CA: Earthworks Press, 1989).

Index